R I T A   A E R O's

W9-CHS-751

WALT DISNEY WORLD®
FOR
ADULTS

...and families, too!

FODOR'S TRAVEL PUBLICATIONS, INC.

NEW YORK • TORONTO • LONDON • SYDNEY • AUCKLAND

Copyright © 1997, 1998 by Rita Aero

Fodor's is a registered trademark of Fodor's Travel Publications, Inc.

All rights reserved under International and Pan-American Copyright Conventions.

Published in the United States by Fodor's Travel Publications, Inc., a subsidiary of Random House, Inc., New York, and simultaneously in Canada by Random House of Canada Limited, Toronto. Distributed by Random House, Inc., New York.

No maps, illustrations, or other portions of this book may be reproduced in any form without written permission from the publishers.

ISBN 0–679–03299–1

SPECIAL SALES: Fodor's Travel Publications are available at special discounts for bulk purchases for sales promotions or premiums. Special editions, including personalized covers, excerpts of existing guides, and corporate imprints, can be created in large quantities for special needs. For more information, contact you local bookseller or write to Special Markets, Fodor's Travel Publications, 201 East 50th Street, New York, NY 10022. Inquiries from Canada should be directed to your local Canadian bookseller or sent to Random House of Canada, Ltd., Marketing Department, 1265 Aerowood Drive, Mississauga, Ontario L4W 1B9. Inquiries from the United Kingdom should be sent to Fodor's Travel Publications, 20 Vauxhall Bridge Rd., London SW1V 2SA.

PRINTED IN THE UNITED STATES OF AMERICA

10 9 8 7 6 5 4 3 2 1

THE WALT DISNEY WORLD FOR ADULTS TEAM

Although there is only one author on the cover, it takes an entire community of people to produce a book like this. I am particularly grateful to my readers who thoughtfully filled out the Reader Survey and sent it in with their impressions, and to those who visited the book's website. Their questions and comments inspired many of the new features that we are so proud to present in this Third Edition. The Walt Disney World for Adults Team members dedicated themselves to the tasks they were assigned, and as always, went far beyond that to to gather special information or invent new ways to make this a better book. I am indebted to each of them.

Production and Design Director: David Villanueva
Senior Editor: Kathleen Clark
Contributing Editor: Stephanie Rick
Research Editors: Jane Cartelli, Bob Richmond
Associate Editors: Robin Clauson, Susan Wolver
Copy Editor: Carolyn Miller
Cover Art: Catherine Venturini

Mapping Team: Harry Driggs, Catherine Venturini
Ratings Consultants: Augie Ray, Rick Namey, Bing Futch, Rich Koster, Carol Koster, Jane Cartelli, Debbie Wills, Michael Koster, Bob Richmond
Electronic & Premium Rights: Immedia Publishing, 420 McKinley St., Ste 111-328, Corona, CA 91719
Legal Counsel: Sheldon Fogelman, Richard Rosenberg

Special Thanks: Bob Mervine, Suzanne White, Stephanie Flasch, Connie Gay, Amy Sadowsky, Kathy Burns, Rob Madden, Connie Bolles, Mace Bailey, Larry Cartelli, Stephen Haight, Don Duffy, Jacki Diener, Elson Haas, Jeff McCullough, Janet Hutchison, Dave Richardson, Janet and Jack Teich, John Sumser, Doug Rapp, Frank Bertolini, Michael Bachand.

CONTENTS

◆ WALT DISNEY WORLD: WHERE THE MAGIC
  IS WAITING FOR YOU TO HAPPEN   5
◆ WHAT'S NEW AT WALT DISNEY WORLD?   5
◆ COOL NEW FEATURES IN THIS EDITION   6
◆ WHAT YOU SHOULD KNOW BEFORE YOU GO   8

PLANNING POWERTOOLS   9
The Best Times to Visit and Smart Ways to Save

◆ ADMISSION TICKETS   9
◆ CROWDS & WEATHER   10
◆ MONTH BY MONTH AT WALT DISNEY WORLD   12
◆ HOLIDAY EVENTS & CELEBRATIONS   15
◆ DISCOUNT TRAVEL TIPS   17
◆ VACATION PACKAGE VALUES   20

ATTRACTIONS   21
Complete Descriptions, with Maps and Touring Plans

◆ WALT DISNEY WORLD AT A GLANCE   22
◆ FUTURE WORLD AT EPCOT   24
◆ WORLD SHOWCASE AT EPCOT   37
◆ DISNEY-MGM STUDIOS   48
◆ MAGIC KINGDOM   58
◆ DISNEY'S BOARDWALK   73
◆ PLEASURE ISLAND   78
◆ DISNEY'S WEST SIDE   85
◆ DISNEY VILLAGE MARKETPLACE   88
◆ TYPHOON LAGOON   94
◆ BLIZZARD BEACH   100
◆ FORT WILDERNESS & RIVER COUNTRY   106
◆ DISCOVERY ISLAND   114
◆ DISNEY'S ANIMAL KINGDOM   121

HOTELS   123
Detailed Reviews and a Comparison of Features and Costs

◆ WALT DISNEY WORLD RESORTS   126
◆ OFF-SITE HOTELS & SUITES   152

RESTAURANTS   157
Reviews, Sample Menus, Prices, and Selection Guides

◆ THEME PARK DINING   160
◆ RESORT DINING   197

CONTENTS

DINING EVENTS   **205**

Dinner Shows, Entertainment Dining, and Character Meals

SPORTS   **213**

Activities and Recreation at Walt Disney World

- YEAR-ROUND SPORTS EVENTS   213
- DISNEY'S WIDE WORLD OF SPORTS   214
- BICYCLING   216
- BOATING & MARINAS   218
- FISHING   223
- FITNESS CENTERS & SPAS   226
- GOLF & MINIATURE GOLF   229
- HORSEBACK RIDING   234
- JOGGING   235
- NATURE WALKS   236
- SWIMMING & BEACHES   238
- TENNIS & VOLLEYBALL   239
- WATERSKIING & PARASAILING   242

FAMILY & FRIENDS   **243**

Great Family Vacations and Travel Strategies for Groups

- HOTELS FOR LARGER FAMILIES & SMALL GROUPS   243
- CELEBRATIONS & GATHERINGS   244
- BABYSITTING & DAY CAMPS   245
- GUIDED TOURS   247
- DISNEY INSTITUTE   248
- WEDDINGS & HONEYMOONS   250
- DISNEY CRUISES   251

TRAVELERS' TOOLKIT   **253**

Getting There, Getting Around, Getting What You Need

- DISNEY VACATION PLANNING DIRECTORY   252
- PACKING TIPS   253
- ORLANDO INTERNATIONAL AIRPORT   254
- LOCAL TRANSPORTATION & PARKING   256
- VISITORS WITH DISABILITIES   258
- SHOPPING & SERVICES   261

- READER SURVEY   269
- THE WALT DISNEY WORLD WIDE WEB   271

VACATION DISCOUNT COUPONS!   **272**

WALT DISNEY WORLD
WHERE THE MAGIC IS WAITING FOR YOU TO HAPPEN

Walt Disney World is unlike any travel destination in the world — if it can even be categorized as simply a "travel destination." The fact is, when you travel to Walt Disney World, you are really journeying more to a state of mind than to the state of Florida. Just about everyone knows what that state of mind is like, because it has become a part of the embedded mythology of our culture. There are now grandparents taking their grandchildren to Walt Disney World, who were themselves taken on a Disney vacation when they were youngsters. In another generation, no one will remember a time when this mecca of magic did not exist.

Walt Disney World differs from other travel destinations in one more important way, and it's the reason we all return again and again: You can never visit the same Walt Disney World twice. It's always different, something's always changed, and your experiences are always filled with new wonder. When you finally arrive, after months of planning and anticipation, it's just like Aladdin tells Jasmine as she steps on the magic carpet: "I will show you the world … *A whole new world.*" And it is. Every time.

This constant change is one of Walt Disney World's most remarkable qualities. It is an imaginary universe that sprang from the mind of one very interesting man, and behind it all is a huge corporation, that continues to expand upon his extraordinary vision. The Walt Disney Company assembles some of the world's most creative minds — the Disney Imagineers — and directs this pool of talent to evolve this imaginary universe, to add details and decorations, events and anthems, and to create new attractions and themed environments. They are told to make all of it magic and fun and so completely real that visitors can enter the experience with their hearts and minds, be caught up in the continuing fantasy woven through it, and forget all about the world they came from. In short, the Imagineers create the ultimate vacation — one that engages all your senses and carries you away on the adventure of a lifetime — for a few short days.

At the most practical level, that's where this guidebook comes in. It will introduce you to all that is new at Walt Disney World, show you some great ways to make your vacation really memorable, and best of all, make sure that it doesn't cost you any more than it has to. When I began this new edition, I stepped on the magic carpet to look around, and said: "Oh no! It's a whole new world! This is going to be a lot more complicated than I thought!" And, believe me, it has been. In fact, so much has changed and been transformed in such a short time that this Third Edition became a "whole new book" with a whole new look. Inside, you'll find features that will streamline vacation planning, such as our new comparison charts of the restaurants and hotels that will help make your selections a breeze and take some of the guesswork out of logistics. And to make your next Disney vacation the best it can possibly be, you'll discover really smart ways to save money, and some of the best touring advice available anywhere. ◆

WHAT'S NEW AT WALT DISNEY WORLD?

If you haven't been to Walt Disney World in a while, you'll want to divide your time between visiting your favorite places and touring some of the exciting new areas. Interesting restaurants have opened everywhere, particularly at the resorts and entertainment complexes. Some of them, like Fulton's Crab

House, Flying Fish Café, 'Ohana, and California Grill, have developed a large, loyal following. New themed resorts have also opened in several price ranges. Particularly impressive and affordable is the moderately priced and exquisitely detailed Disney's Coronado Springs Resort. Disney's BoardWalk Resort features two new premier hotels, and although open for just a little while, this waterfront entertainment complex feels like it has always been part of the scene. It's loaded with charm and is one of my favorite places to play on a weekend night. Coming up fast is Downtown Disney, the soon-to-be entertainment capitol of Walt Disney World, chock-full of celebrity-owned restaurants, nightclubs, and concert halls, and host to a steady stream of world-class performers and television broadcasting events. Disney's Animal Kingdom, a combination theme park and zoo that is five times larger than the Magic Kingdom, is bringing a brand new dimension to the Disney Experience: *reality*. Disney-MGM Studios will have the lion's share (naturally) of sensational new attractions as it approaches its ten-year anniversary in 1999. Meanwhile, Mickey's Toontown Fair is now the newest land in the Magic Kingdom; the thrilling Test Track attraction has forever changed the face of Future World at Epcot; and Disney's Wide World of Sports has opened an international sports complex large enough to host the Olympics. It's all new and waiting for you. ◆

COOL NEW FEATURES IN THIS EDITION

More than any other factor, your Disney vacation experience will be influenced by your traveling companions. Where you stay, where you eat, the way you tour, the attractions you see, the special events you attend, and the memorable moments you take away will all depend on who you are with. Most of our readers travel with family members, in every imaginable combination. Many travel with their parents or older relatives, and many go with children, often teens and pre-teens. We hear from families of just two, usually couples, as well as extended families of twenty or more who are staging reunions at Walt Disney World. The next largest category among readers is friends vacationing together, ranging from twosomes to small groups. The Walt Disney World for Adults Team came up with several features to make Disney vacations with family or friends easier to plan and even more enjoyable.

FAMILY & FRIENDS MEDALLION: This icon, found throughout the book, is intended for large or extended families, groups of friends traveling together, and solo travelers who would like to meet other visitors. It's found on restaurants enjoyed by groups or with communal seating; on hotels with very good setups for large families and groups; and on attractions, activities, and events that are ideal for groups or individuals, where people of all ages come together to share an experience.

ROMANTIC MEDALLION: Every square inch of Walt Disney World can be romantic if you're in the right frame of mind, but the places and activities marked with this medallion are especially wonderful settings for romance.

SMART RATINGS: This simple yet sophisticated attraction rating system can enhance the quality of your theme park tour by helping you to predict which attractions you will enjoy most, and avoid long lines for attractions that hold little interest for you. It can also help you to select attractions to share with traveling companions of any age or temperament. It works great for families and can add to your enjoyment of an attraction by revealing who and how it was intended to entertain. (See page 21.)

INTUITIVE MAPS: To make getting around easy, there are detailed maps of every theme park, entertainment complex, and recreation area — something you cannot find anywhere else, not even at Walt Disney World. They're smart, too: One glance and you'll know where to go.

WEBSITE: We wanted to create a guidebook that would stay up to date longer than any other, so we became the first Disney guidebook with a companion website to make sure the book's information stays fresh and to provide Disney vacation news and entertainment information to our readers. (See page 271.)

DISCOUNTS: At all times, we scouted money-saving tactics that really worked to pass on to you, and we found some great ones. They are highlighted throughout the book so you can't miss them. Also, we are especially pleased to include in this edition some of the best coupons ever put into a Walt Disney World guidebook.* (If you used the last edition, you know what we mean!) Many of them were created exclusively for our readers. (See page 272.) We hope you have a chance to enjoy them — they're good through the end of 1998! ◆

BEHIND THE SCENES: We research much farther ahead than other guidebooks so that the information stays up to date longer. That means that early readers may see listings for attractions that do not yet exist (but will soon). I've made notations in the text when this is the case. Certain restaurant reviews are missing because the restaurants are closing; their replacements are included, instead. Ratings that appear on restaurants that were not open at the time of publication were gathered, in every instance, from the same restaurant in an established location. In the case of new hotels and attractions where ratings appear, we were fortunate in our opportunities to preview them. Here are a few of the many photos taken along the way as this edition came together.

The book's popular website (www.wdw4adults.com) has played an important role in keeping readers up to date. This is what it looks like on the other side of the monitor when you visit. Kathy and David are working on the Reader's Clubhouse, where exclusive hot tips and travel discounts can be found. (See page 271.)

A week before this edition was finished, Disneyland premiered its new Light Magic parade for the press. I dropped by and ran into an old friend! Had to crop him out of the picture, though. His face is under exclusive contract and we're not supposed to be seen together.

Big entertainment is coming to Downtown Disney over the next few years, and I couldn't publish a worthwhile guide without a map of it. Here I am in Arthur's, at the Buena Vista Palace — twenty seven floors above the construction site — sketching the map that appears on page 86.

The search for money-saving strategies took me on a quest for the best deals on Walt Disney World theme park merchandise. Jane, from my Orlando Team, brought me here. The products and prices were great! Even I couldn't resist. This is where you want to shop. (See page 93.)

---

* A Note About the Coupons: The coupons are my way of saying "thank you" to early purchasers, who help us launch the book and establish its continuing presence in bookstores. The book is not affiliated with the companies offering the coupons. Like all coupons, these will expire as they did in the last edition. Most readers are familiar with promotions and deadlines, and most purchase this book for its thoroughness and for the real value it offers in planning memorable and affordable vacations. Nevertheless, the participating companies did agree to an unheard of eighteen month deadline, so the coupons are more likely to be valid during your Walt Disney World vacation..

WHAT YOU SHOULD KNOW BEFORE YOU GO

In answering hundreds of vacation-planning questions, I've noticed that most of them spring from simple misconceptions about how the business-side of Walt Disney World works. The commonsense information below should eliminate much of the confusion, and make many of your vacation decisions easier and smarter.

HOTELS: The Disney Resorts offer three types of accommodations: campsites (full hookups start at about $50 per night), hotel rooms (standard rooms start from about $80 to $300 per night, depending on the resort), and "vacation homes" with cooking facilities (they range from about $190 to $900 per night, depending on the size).

There are five "Resort Areas" inside Walt Disney World. Each is convenient to particular theme parks, and each has specific transportation options. **The less convenient the location and the fewer the transportation options, the lower the price of the hotel.** Disney does not build budget hotels on the monorail or premium hotels in the middle of nowhere. See the hotel map, page 125.

Hotels are most expensive during school holidays and least expensive when most schools are in session. You can save big on accommodations by not vacationing during school holidays. You can save even more by shopping for value-season specials; find out how on pages 17 through 20.

Hotels outside Walt Disney World usually offer lower prices, but not all deliver a better overall value. To match Disney transportation options, you will need to factor in the cost of a rental car. See "Off-Site Hotels & Suites," starting on page 152, for a selection that offers good overall values.

ATTRACTION TICKETS: There are no legitimate deals or significant discounts on theme park tickets. Don't waste time looking; instead, analyze which ticket combination works best for you. Rough out a daily plan. Group non-theme-park activities and recreation into whole days. Go to theme parks on the days they are open late and take afternoons off. Don't buy more days than you need. See "Admissions," page 9, for details.

ORLANDO WEATHER: From May through September, it is extremely hot and there are showers or storms at least once a day. At that time, it is essential to stay in a hotel with convenient transportation so you can take the afternoons off to relax. During the months with the most pleasant weather, hotel rates are lower but park hours are shorter and there are fewer entertainment and fireworks events. See the weather chart, page 11, to help you decide the best times to go.

LONG LINES: There will be crowds and lines whenever you go — park hours are adjusted constantly to create crowds so that it is economically feasible to keep the parks open. Even so, you can control the *quality* of your vacation and how much of it you will spend waiting in lines. Here's how: ❶ Do not wait in lines for more than fifteen minutes except for attractions *you know* you will enjoy. ❷ Take advantage of *any attraction* without a line. ❸ Every morning a different theme park opens early just for Disney resort guests. **Use the Early Entry Mornings to your advantage, regardless of where you are staying.**

This early touring strategy is a must during busy peak seasons: **If you have Park Hopper passes,** go to the Early Entry park, then switch parks after after ninety minutes to avoid the all-day crush of visitors that always follows. **If you do not have Park Hopper passes, or cannot go to the Early Entry park,** then get to any other theme park one half hour before opening time. The other parks often open earlier, too, and crowds are lighter.

DO YOU NEED A CAR? The Disney transportation system is designed ONLY to take visitors from the resorts to the theme parks that charge admissions, and back again. This is how the system pays for itself. **It is NOT designed to carry visitors from resort to resort** (where the better restaurants and dining events are located) and rarely from resorts to recreation areas, such as Disney's BoardWalk or Fort Wilderness. It can take hours worth of bus transfers from distant hubs to reach these destinations. The more you want to do (sightseeing, shopping, dining, dancing, dinner shows, nightclubs, sports), and the fewer your hotel's transportation options, the the more you need a car. (See "Guide to Hotel Features," page 124.) Taxis are fast and plentiful at Walt Disney World and, if used only when traveling to places with **no direct transportation from wherever you are,** they can cost less per day than a rental car, without the hassle of driving or parking. ◆

PLANNING POWERTOOLS

Here you'll find the important facts you need to plan a Walt Disney World vacation that is perfect for you. The pages that follows describe your vacation options as they relate to your first critical decision: **when** to go. You will also find money-saving strategies that can significantly boost your vacation budget.

ADMISSION TICKETS

Walt Disney World theme park admission tickets come in a range of prices to match different vacation touring styles. Once purchased, tickets are always valid until used, even if prices increase (which they tend to do each year, usually in late winter). To lock in prices or avoid lines, tickets can be purchased in advance at any Disney Store, or purchased directly by telephone with a credit card (407 824-4321). Magic Kingdom Club and AAA members receive small discounts (see "Discount Travel Tips," page 17).

ONE-DAY ONE-PARK TICKET: One day's admission to a major theme park, either the Magic Kingdom, Disney-MGM Studios, or Epcot costs about $46 (about $37 for children). Prices for the minor parks are: Typhoon Lagoon, about $28 (about $22 for children); Blizzard Beach, about $28 (about $22 for children); River Country, about $19 (about $15 for children); Discovery Island, about $14 (about $8 for children); and Pleasure Island, about $20 for entry after 7 PM. All prices include tax.

FOUR-DAY VALUE PASS: Four days' admission to a specific theme park each day: Disney-MGM Studios, Magic Kingdom, and Epcot. The fourth day can be used to revisit any single park. Pass-holders cannot park hop, or split their visit between different parks on the same day. The Four-Day Value Pass has no expiration date and costs about $153 (about $122 for children), including tax.

FOUR-DAY PARK-HOPPER PASS: Four days' admission to the Magic Kingdom, Disney-MGM Studios, and Epcot, including the use of Walt Disney World transportation linking the parks. Visitors can visit more than one theme park each day. The Four-Day Park-Hopper Pass has no expiration date. About $172 (about $137 for children), including tax.

ALL-IN-ONE HOPPER PASSES: Five, six, or seven days' admission to the Magic Kingdom, Disney-MGM Studios, Epcot, Typhoon Lagoon, Blizzard Beach, Pleasure Island, River Country, and Discovery Island, including the use of Walt Disney World transportation to hop from park to park. Including tax, a five-day pass is about $235 (about $188 for children); a six-day pass is about $265 (about $212 for children); and a seven-day pass is about $292 (about $234 for children). All-In-One Hopper Passes have no expiration date.

LENGTH OF STAY PASS: Guests staying at a Walt Disney World resort can purchase a Length of Stay Pass that includes admission to the Magic Kingdom, Disney-MGM Studios, Epcot, Typhoon Lagoon, Blizzard Beach, Pleasure Island, River Country, and Discovery Island. The pass must be purchased for the entire length of stay and cannot be saved for future visits. Prices vary according to number of days covered. For example, a three-day Length of Stay Pass is about $155 (about $125 for children), and a five-day Length of Stay Pass is about $230 (about $185 for children), including tax. This can be a fair deal when it is used every day to visit multiple parks.

POWERTOOLS

ANNUAL PASSPORTS: Visitors who plan to visit for more than seven days or who plan to return within the year should consider buying an Annual Passport. The basic Annual Passport, which includes one year of unlimited admission to the Magic Kingdom, Disney-MGM Studios, and Epcot, as well as free parking and the use of Walt Disney World transportation, is about $308. The Premium Annual Passport, which has all the features of the basic one, but also includes unlimited admission to Typhoon Lagoon, Blizzard Beach, Pleasure Island, River Country, and Discovery Island, is about $410. Both prices include tax. Annual Passholders are also eligible for special resort discounts. ◆

CROWDS & WEATHER

As you might expect, crowd size is directly related to school vacations and national holidays. Although park hours are extended during peak-attendance times, the parks can be impossibly crowded, and long lines can waste much of your vacation time. Try to avoid these busy times, especially during the summer, which is very hot and humid. Late fall and spring weather are ideal; winter can bring cold snaps, so pack accordingly (see "Packing," page 253), and before you leave, check with Disney Weather (407 824-4104).

WINTER: From Christmas week until New Year's Day, the crowds at Walt Disney World are overwhelming and the lines intimidating. The three weeks preceding Christmas, however, are an ideal time to visit. The holiday decor and festivities are underway and yet attendance is generally sparse, so you can experience many attractions without long lines. After New Year's Day, attendance drops again and remains low. The temperature may drop, too, and the weather can turn cold, although there is little precipitation. The theme parks close early in the winter, but the light crowds make attractions far more accessible. Attendance builds in February and peaks during Presidents' Day week.

SPRING: From early March until Easter, the crowds become moderate to heavy, as schools across the country stagger their spring vacations. During Spring Break, the parks are crowded, and during Easter week they are packed. Attendance dips slightly in late April as students return to school. During May there are large crowds, but pleasant weather makes the lines tolerable. The days grow steadily warmer, although the nights remain balmy until June.

SUMMER: Summer attendance builds, and by mid-June there are vast crowds and long lines. The weather can be brutally hot as well, climbing into the nineties with very high humidity. Almost-daily afternoon showers tend to clear out the parks a bit, so if you don't mind getting wet, it is a good time to tour. Although the lines can go on forever, the parks stay open late with many entertainment events. The beginning of June and the end of August have slightly lower attendance, but while evenings can be balmy and delightful in June, it is just plain hot in August, day and night.

FALL: In September, the weather is still hot and wet and it remains so until mid-October. Attendance plummets and the parks close early, but lines are short and attractions are again accessible. The beginning of October until the week before Christmas marks some of the most pleasant vacation time at Walt Disney World. Thanksgiving is the best possible holiday for a visit, and although that week is busy, on Thanksgiving Day the crowd is almost always gathered around a dinner table. After Thanksgiving, the weather can turn cold, but the holiday decor, seasonal entertainment, and easy access to the theme park attractions are the right ingredients for an ideal vacation. ◆

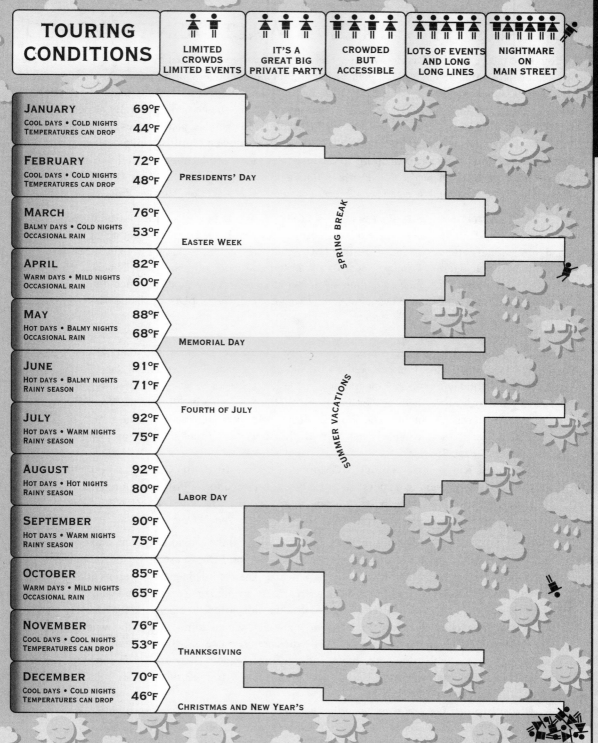

TOURING CONDITIONS		LIMITED CROWDS LIMITED EVENTS	IT'S A GREAT BIG PRIVATE PARTY	CROWDED BUT ACCESSIBLE	LOTS OF EVENTS AND LONG LONG LINES	NIGHTMARE ON MAIN STREET
JANUARY COOL DAYS • COLD NIGHTS TEMPERATURES CAN DROP	69°F 44°F					
FEBRUARY COOL DAYS • COLD NIGHTS TEMPERATURES CAN DROP	72°F 48°F	PRESIDENTS' DAY				
MARCH BALMY DAYS • COLD NIGHTS OCCASIONAL RAIN	76°F 53°F	EASTER WEEK		SPRING BREAK		
APRIL WARM DAYS • MILD NIGHTS OCCASIONAL RAIN	82°F 60°F					
MAY HOT DAYS • BALMY NIGHTS OCCASIONAL RAIN	88°F 68°F	MEMORIAL DAY				
JUNE HOT DAYS • BALMY NIGHTS RAINY SEASON	91°F 71°F			SUMMER VACATIONS		
JULY HOT DAYS • WARM NIGHTS RAINY SEASON	92°F 75°F	FOURTH OF JULY				
AUGUST HOT DAYS • HOT NIGHTS RAINY SEASON	92°F 80°F	LABOR DAY				
SEPTEMBER HOT DAYS • WARM NIGHTS RAINY SEASON	90°F 75°F					
OCTOBER WARM DAYS • MILD NIGHTS OCCASIONAL RAIN	85°F 65°F					
NOVEMBER COOL DAYS • COOL NIGHTS TEMPERATURES CAN DROP	76°F 53°F	THANKSGIVING				
DECEMBER COOL DAYS • COLD NIGHTS TEMPERATURES CAN DROP	70°F 46°F	CHRISTMAS AND NEW YEAR'S				

MONEY $AVING PAGE

POWER

MONTH BY MONTH AT WALT DISNEY WORLD

Throughout the year, Walt Disney World presents a wide variety of annual events, special festivals, and seasonal celebrations that can make your vacation a memorable one. During peak seasons (the summer months and annual holidays), the theme parks stay open late and feature evening parades and fireworks shows. During the slower months, September through May, the theme parks generally close early, about 6 PM, although Epcot remains open until 9 PM daily, and there is plenty of evening entertainment throughout Walt Disney World. **Periodically during these slower months, value-season resort rates are in effect. Hotel prices can drop up to 20 percent or more and budget-priced vacation packages are offered, such as Disney's Fall Fantasy Package.** Like everything at Walt Disney World, value seasons are based on attendance and are subject to change. (See "Vacation Package Values," page 20.)

NEW ATTRACTIONS AND EVENTS: Walt Disney World put on a once-in-a-lifetime celebration for its twenty-fifth year and attracted record crowds all year long. To commemorate the event, several significant new attractions and recreation areas made their debut, including Mickey's Toontown Fair in the Magic Kingdom, Disney's BoardWalk Resort and recreation complex, Disney's Wide World of Sports, and the West Side entertainment center at Downtown Disney. Also debuting is Fantasmic! at Disney-MGM Studios and Disney's Animal Kingdom, the largest Disney theme park ever built.

JANUARY: Special events include New Year's Eve fireworks shows at the major theme parks, and resort-wide New Year's Eve celebrations, including parties at Pleasure Island and Disney's Board-Walk (see "Holiday Events & Celebrations," page 15). Chinese New Year celebrations begin in mid-January and are usually held at Pleasure Island and at the China pavilion in the World Showcase at Epcot. Sporting events include the Walt Disney World Indy 200 car races, the month-long Fitness Festival at Epcot, and the Walt Disney World Marathon, which runs through the major theme parks (see "Sports," page 213).

    The Magic Kingdom and Disney-MGM Studios close early during January and often do not offer fireworks shows or evening parades. Blizzard Beach is closed for refurbishing throughout the month.

SAVE

    Disney's Sunshine Getaway vacation package begins in January at select Walt Disney World resorts. The lowest value-season resort rates begin on New Year's Day.

FEBRUARY: Special celebrations include Valentine's Day at the Magic Kingdom, a Mardi Gras party at Pleasure Island, and a Mardi Gras Carnaval in the World Showcase at Epcot. In mid-February, Epcot hosts the African-American Music Experience. The crowds begin to swell as college students bound for Walt Disney World during Spring Break take advantage of special student promotions such as the Disney Break, which offers a discount admission to one theme park for one day plus free admission that evening to Pleasure Island, and optional discount admissions to the water parks.

    The Magic Kingdom and Disney-MGM Studios are open late only on weekends and during Presidents' Day week, with fireworks shows and evening parades. Blizzard Beach remains closed for refurbishing until mid-February; Discovery Island closes for refurbishing in mid-February and remains closed the rest of the month.

SAVE

    Disney's Sunshine Getaway vacation package continues through the middle of the month. Value-season resort rates continue until a week before Presidents' Day, when peak season begins.

MARCH: Special events include the Bryant Gumbel/Walt Disney World Celebrity–Am Golf Tournament and St. Patrick's Day festivities at Pleasure Island. The Disney Break promotion for students continues throughout the month.

The Magic Kingdom has fireworks shows and evening parades on the weekends. Disney-MGM Studios has fireworks shows on Saturdays. Discovery Island remains closed for refurbishing until the second week in March.

Peak-season resort rates apply throughout March.

APRIL: Special events include Earth Day celebrations at Epcot and Disney Village Marketplace, and the Happy Easter Parade at the Magic Kingdom (see "Holiday Events & Celebrations," page 15). In mid-April, Epcot hosts the "Pops" Concert Series in the tradition of the Boston Pops. In late April, the International Garden and Flower Festival begins at Epcot. The U.S. Men's Clay Court Championships are held at Disney's Wide World of Sports in late April.

All theme parks stay open late one week before and during Easter week. The Magic Kingdom has fireworks shows and evening parades on the weekends. Disney-MGM Studios has fireworks shows on Saturday nights. The Disney Break student promotion continues until mid-April.

Peak-season resort rates continue throughout April at most resorts.

MAY: There are Mother's Day festivities at the Magic Kingdom, Disney Village Marketplace, and other resort locations. On Cinco de Mayo, celebrations are often held at Pleasure Island and at the Mexico pavilion in the World Showcase at Epcot. The International Garden and Flower Festival and the "Pops" Concert Series continue throughout the month at Epcot. Epcot also hosts the Technology Expo in May.

The Magic Kingdom stays open late with fireworks shows on Saturday nights and Memorial Day weekend. Disney-MGM Studios continues to close early until Memorial Day weekend.

Peak-season continues. Value-season may apply at the Swan, Dolphin, Hilton, and Grosvenor.

JUNE: Special events include the Classic Car Show at Disney Village Marketplace and Father's Day festivities at Disney-MGM Studios and other Walt Disney World locations. The All-American College Band and Chorus performs throughout the month at Epcot.

The theme parks are open late, with a full schedule of parades, special events, and fireworks shows.

Peak-season continues. Value-season may apply at the Swan, Dolphin, Hilton, and Grosvenor.

JULY: Special events include extended Fourth of July fireworks shows in all theme parks (see "Holiday Events & Celebrations," page 15). Bastille Day, July 14, is celebrated at Epcot with special festivities. Space Week at Epcot takes place in mid-July in commemoration of the first visit to the moon. The All-American College Band and Chorus continues at Epcot throughout the month.

The theme parks are open late, with a full schedule of parades, special events, and fireworks shows.

Value-season resort rates may apply at all resorts except Disney's budget resorts.

AUGUST: Latin Rhythm Month at Epcot begins in late August. The All-American College Band and Chorus performs at Epcot through mid-August.

All theme parks are open late, with a full schedule of special entertainment events, fireworks shows, and parades until the week preceding Labor Day.

At the end of the month, the Walt Disney World resorts begin offering Disney's Fall Fantasy vacation package. Value-season rates apply at all resorts by the end of August.

SEPTEMBER: Special events include Annual National Inventor's Expo and the World Festival of Kites at Epcot, and the Night of Joy Christian-music program at the Magic Kingdom. Sporting events include the annual Walt Disney World Soccer Classic.

The Magic Kingdom has fireworks shows and evening parades only on Labor Day weekend. After Labor Day weekend, the Magic Kingdom and Disney-MGM Studios close early. Some theme park attractions are closed for refurbishing during the fall.

$AVE

Disney's Fall Fantasy vacation package continues throughout the month. Value-season resort rates apply throughout September.

OCTOBER: Special events include the Boat Show at Disney Village Marketplace, the Pleasure Island Jazz Festival, and the Walt Disney World/Oldsmobile Golf Classic (see "Sports," page 213). Oktoberfest is celebrated at Pleasure Island and at the Germany pavilion in the World Showcase at Epcot. The World Showcase also hosts the International Food and Wine Festival, featuring special cuisines and wines from around the world. Toward the end of the month, Shriek Out! Saturdays at Disney-MGM Studios feature extended hours and live bands. Halloween festivities include Mickey's Not-So-Scary Halloween Party at the Magic Kingdom, along with special hauntings at Pleasure Island and Disney Village Marketplace.

The Magic Kingdom closes early. Disney-MGM Studios stays open late with fireworks shows on Saturdays only. Some theme park attractions are closed for refurbishing during the fall. River Country is closed for refurbishing.

$AVE

Disney's Fall Fantasy vacation package continues throughout the month. Value-season resort rates apply throughout October.

NOVEMBER: Special events include the annual Festival of the Masters art show at Disney Village Marketplace, and the Walt Disney World Teddy Bear and Doll Convention. Resort-wide Christmas events begin after Thanksgiving (see "Holiday Events & Celebrations," page 15).

The Magic Kingdom and Disney-MGM Studios close early; Magic Kingdom fireworks shows and evening parades occur on Saturdays only. Some theme park attractions are closed for refurbishing during the fall. Typhoon Lagoon closes for refurbishing in early November and remains closed the rest of the month.

$AVE

Disney's Fall Fantasy vacation package continues until Thanksgiving week. Selected Walt Disney World resorts begin offering Disney's Magical Holidays vacation packages the week after Thanksgiving. Value-season resort rates apply throughout November.

DECEMBER: Christmas events and New Year's Eve celebrations are featured at the theme parks and at selected resorts. Christmas celebrations, tree-lighting ceremonies, and other holiday festivities occur daily until Christmas Eve. On selected evenings, Mickey's Very Merry Christmas Party is held at the Magic Kingdom, and the Christmas Candlelight Processional is held in the World Showcase at Epcot. (See "Holiday Events & Celebrations," page 15.)

The Magic Kingdom and Disney-MGM Studios close early until mid-December. From the week before Christmas through New Year's Eve, the theme parks are open late, with a full schedule of parades, fireworks shows, and live entertainment. Typhoon Lagoon remains closed for refurbishing until the end of December.

$AVE

Disney's Magical Holidays vacation packages continue until the week of Christmas. Value-season resort rates continue until the week before Christmas, when peak season begins. ◆

HOLIDAY EVENTS & CELEBRATIONS

Any holiday is fair game for the entertainment designers at Walt Disney World, where just about every holiday from around the world is celebrated somewhere, including Chinese New Year, Mardi Gras, and St. Patrick's Day. If you are visiting during a major holiday, you may encounter some of the following:

SPRING BREAK: Walt Disney World is the ultimate destination for Spring Break. *From mid-February to mid-April, college students can take advantage of the special Disney Break promotion, which offers them substantially discounted admission to one theme park for one day plus free admission that evening to Pleasure Island, and optional discount admissions to the water parks.*

EASTER: The Magic Kingdom celebrates with its nationally televised Happy Easter Parade. The parade features Disney characters, singers and dancers, the Easter Bunny, remarkable Easter bonnets, and giant Easter-themed floats. Epcot is specially decorated with *Fantasia* topiary. Disney Village Marketplace and many resorts hold egg hunts and other holiday events, and selected restaurants throughout Walt Disney World offer special Easter dinners.

MOTHER'S DAY AND FATHER'S DAY: Restaurants throughout Walt Disney World offer special Mother's Day meals. On Father's Day, past events have included a classic and hot rod car show, lookalike contests, monster truck exhibitions, and the Father's Day Parade at Disney-MGM Studios.

JULY FOURTH: Flags are raised and bunting draped for Independence Day celebrations at Walt Disney World. Pleasure Island starts the festivities on July 3 with an expanded midnight fireworks show. Marching bands parade through the Magic Kingdom and Epcot, and on the night of the Fourth, the fireworks shows at the Magic Kingdom and Disney-MGM Studios are the longest and most spectacular of the summer. A special patriotic IllumiNations presentation in the World Showcase at Epcot lights up the sky in traditional red, white, and blue.

HALLOWEEN: The Magic Kingdom presents Mickey's Not-So-Scary Halloween Party, which guests are encouraged to attend in costume. This special-admission event includes parade festivities, hayrides, pumpkin-carving demonstrations, and a special fireworks show. Liberty Tree Tavern serves a haunted dinner complete with Disney Characters. Pleasure Island and Disney Village Marketplace feature costume contests, live music, and fortune tellers.

THANKSGIVING: Over the long Thanksgiving weekend, Walt Disney World offers two holidays in one. On Thanksgiving Day, selected full-service restaurants in the theme parks and resorts offer guests traditional Thanksgiving dinners. (Make your reservations early.) Late Thursday night, Disney Cast Members work overtime to transform all of Walt Disney World into a Christmas wonderland. When the parks open on Friday, they feature special holiday entertainment and ceremonies.

CHRISTMAS: It's Christmas from Thanksgiving Day on at Walt Disney World. The theme parks sport overhanging garlands and towering decorated fir trees that come alive in nightly tree-lighting ceremonies. At the Magic Kingdom, Mickey's Very Merry Christmas Parade, complete with colorful floats and holiday music and characters, travels down Main Street on the weekends. On selected evenings, the Magic Kingdom reopens at 8 PM to celebrate Mickey's Very Merry Christmas Party with holiday food, carolers, seasonal shows, the Christmas Party Parade, and an extended fireworks show set to holiday music. A separate admission is charged for the Very Merry Christmas Party.

POWERTOOLS

It's Christmas in New York at Disney-MGM Studios, with carolers and roast-chestnut vendors. On Residential Street, at the Osborne Family's "Spectacle of Light," more than three million twinkling lights adorn two blocks in a dazzling display that includes angels, Christmas trees, and carousels.

The World Showcase at Epcot presents Holidays Around the World. Each pavilion's version of Santa Claus describes Christmas and the holiday traditions unique to that nation. The nightly lighting ceremony of the sixty-five-foot tree includes trumpeters and the Voices of Liberty choir. The Christmas Candlelight Processional, with a 450-member chorus, fifty-piece orchestra, and bell choir, parades from Germany to the America Gardens Theatre. There, the Story of Christmas show is narrated by a celebrity guest. (Special Candlelight Dinner admission tickets are available and include dinner at selected Epcot restaurants, complimentary preferred parking, VIP seating at the Candlelight Processional, and merchandise discounts.) Restaurants in the World Showcase feature traditional holiday menus from each nation. IllumiNations bursts forth with a special Christmas-themed fireworks show.

Disney Village Marketplace has a totally themed Christmas shopping atmosphere. Santa is on hand for those with a wish list, and every night there is a charming ceremony to light the fifty-foot fir tree. Visitors can rent ice skates for a spin on the frozen pond, or take a break from shopping and listen to the strolling carollers. Next door, Pleasure Island is decked out as a mock office to put a new twist on the traditional with its Longest Holiday Office Party, complete with food, prizes, and a chance to win tickets to the "REAL New Year's Eve" party on December 31.

The Contemporary resort hosts the popular Jolly Holidays dinner show (see "Jolly Holidays," page 210). This dining event includes an all-you-care-to-eat holiday dinner, along with singing, dancing, and favorite Disney Characters and holiday figures. The resorts are decked out for Christmas, and host daily events and entertainment. **Disney's Magical Holidays vacation package, which includes accommodations, park admissions, and the Jolly Holidays dinner show, is offered at selected Walt Disney World resorts and is a good value for an unforgettable holiday vacation with family and loved ones. (See "Vacation Package Values," page 20.)**

NEW YEAR'S EVE: On New Year's Eve, the theme parks stay open into the wee hours with park-wide celebrations and midnight fireworks shows. The Magic Kingdom presents a special fireworks show and live music events. The World Showcase at Epcot has a separate party in each pavilion and a special presentation of IllumiNations. Disney-MGM Studios hosts dance parties, live music, and a special fireworks show. Pleasure Island stages a special-admission "REAL New Year's Eve" street party, with buffets, complimentary Champagne, favors, celebrity performers, fortune tellers, jugglers, and a ticker-tape frenzy at midnight. Disney's BoardWalk has a special-admission New Year's Eve party along the Promenade, featuring live music, hors d'oeuvres, complimentary Champagne, and an after-hours Continental breakfast; and ESPN Club hosts an end-of-the-year bash with complimentary Champagne and appetizers. At the Hoop-Dee-Doo Musical Revue dinner show, a country music band creates a down-home New Year's celebration.

Several Walt Disney World resorts, including the Yacht Club, Beach Club, and Wilderness Lodge offer cocktails in their lobby areas. The Grand Floridian, Contemporary, and Grosvenor resorts, among others, stage themed festivities that range from fifties dance parties to elegant balls. Guests at Arthur's 27, at the Buena Vista Palace Resort & Spa, celebrate with an elegant meal, Champagne, and great views of the Walt Disney World fireworks shows.

So parents can celebrate New Year's Eve, many Walt Disney World child care centers will keep children until about 2 AM (see "Babysitting & Day Camps," page 245). ◆

VERTOOLS

DISCOUNT TRAVEL TIPS

Many Walt Disney World visitors join travel clubs to help take the bite out of their vacation budgets. Travel clubs affiliated with Walt Disney World include the American Automobile Association and American Express, as well local convention bureaus and Disney-sponsored clubs. Most travel clubs offer discounts on accommodations, car rentals, and meals, along with complete vacation packages. (See also "Vacation Package Values," page 20.) **If you are looking to save even more money on your vacation, check out the Walt Disney World for Adults Vacation Discount Coupons, on page 272!**

MAGIC KINGDOM CLUB GOLD CARD

The Magic Kingdom Club, operated by the Disney Company, has been around for more than forty years. Club members receive an embossed card that entitles them to benefits and discounts at Walt Disney World in Orlando, Disneyland in California, Disneyland Paris, and Tokyo Disneyland.

WDW HOTEL DISCOUNTS: A 10 to 30 percent discount at selected Disney-owned hotels year-round; a 10 percent discount at the independently owned hotels on Disney property (Swan, Dolphin, and Hotel Plaza resorts); and a wide selection of Walt Disney World vacation packages at discount rates.

ADMISSION DISCOUNTS: A slight discount (about 5 percent) on park admissions; a 10 percent discount on golfing fees during selected seasons; and a 10 percent discount on some dinner shows.

ADDITIONAL BENEFITS: Significant savings on Walt Disney Travel Company vacation packages. (See "Vacation Package Values," page 20.) A 10 percent discount at selected restaurants in the Magic Kingdom, Epcot, and Disney-MGM Studios; a 10 percent discount on merchandise purchased at selected stores at Disney Village Marketplace, Pleasure Island, and at Disney Stores anywhere in the world. Members also receive a 10 percent discount on new AAA memberships, discounts up to 30 percent at National Car Rental, a two-year subscription to *Disney News* magazine, and a trial membership in the Travel America at HalfPrice hotel discount club. Magic Kingdom Club members are also given a toll-free telephone number for reservations and information.

MEMBERSHIP FEE: The fee for a two-year family membership is about $65.

REVIEWERS' COMMENTS: It can be good value on accommodations and vacation packages at the Disney resorts, although in recent years there seem to be fewer "discount" rooms available. You can also save quite a bit on telephone calls to Walt Disney World. The admission ticket discounts are insignificant, and the National Car Rental discount has many restrictions.

CONTACT: Magic Kingdom Club, P.O. Box 3850, Anaheim, CA 92803-3850 (800 413-4763).

DISNEY'S FOOD 'N FUN PLAN

Disney's Food 'N Fun Plan is a prepaid dining debit system that is an add-on option to Disney vacation packages. For the "Food" portion of the plan, guests use their resort ID to charge meals at the Disney-owned restaurants in the resorts and theme parks. The "Fun" portion offers guests unlimited free access to many of the excellent recreational facilities throughout Walt Disney World.

HOW IT WORKS: The Food 'N Fun plan is modified continuously. Currently, it must be purchased for the entire length of the vacation package, for all members in the party. Thus, guests pay in advance for the meals they will eat, and they receive a 10 percent bonus credit on the total amount prepaid. Each time the guest charges a meal, it is deducted from the account total. Guests may spend as much of their account as they like as quickly as they wish. If all of the account is used up before the end of their stay, guests still have unlimited use of the recreational facilities. If any money remains in the account at the end of their stay, guests forfeit the unused balance, and there are no refunds.

PROGRAM FEES AND ALLOWANCES: The Food 'N Fun plan costs about $50 per day per person (about $22 for children). The guest's prepaid account is credited with about $55 for each $50 deposited (about $25 for each $22 paid).

RESTAURANTS: The Food 'N Fun plan can be used for meals, including Character Meals and dinner shows, in the theme parks and at Disney-owned resorts. Snack bars and restaurants at non-Disney-owned hotels are not included. Restaurant reservations are always essential and should be made up to sixty days ahead through Disney Dining Reservations (407 939-3463).

RECREATION: Food 'N Fun plan participants have free access to many recreational activities, including tennis, bicycles, boating, pole fishing, hayrides, pony rides, and horseback riding — but not golf, waterskiing, excursion cruises, fishing excursions, spas, or massage.

REVIEWERS' COMMENTS: The Food 'N Fun plan is essentially a prepaid credit card with a 10 percent kickback. Since all Disney resort guests can charge meals with their resort ID, the plan offers no special convenience. It can, however, be a good value for visitors who are less focused on the theme parks and have the time and inclination to take full advantage of the unlimited recreational activities.

CONTACT: The cost of the Food 'N Fun plan is added to the price of a guest's vacation package. Contact the Walt Disney Travel Company (800 828-0228) for additional information.

ORLANDO MAGICARD

The Orlando Magicard is sponsored by the Orlando/Orange County Convention & Visitors Bureau, Inc. Visitors are given a card that entitles them to discounts on accommodations, car rentals, restaurants, and some Orlando-area attractions.

WDW HOTEL DISCOUNTS: Special discounts (ranging from 10 to 20 percent) on accommodations and vacation packages at Buena Vista Palace Resort & Spa, Grosvenor Resort, Caribe Royale Resort Suites, Homewood Suites, Buena Vista Suites, Holiday Inn SunSpree Resort, and other area hotels. (See "Hotels," page 123, and "Off-Site Hotels & Suites," page 152.)

ADMISSION DISCOUNTS: Discounts on admission to other Orlando-area attractions, including Sea World, Universal Studios, Wet 'N Wild, and Medieval Times Dinner and Tournament.

ADDITIONAL BENEFITS: A 10 to 15 percent discount on Alamo, Avis, and Dollar rental cars, and a toll-free number for discount hotel reservations.

MEMBERSHIP FEE: The Orlando Magicard is free and can be used for groups of up to six persons.

REVIEWERS' COMMENTS: This card can be a real savings for active visitors. Be sure to call and request your card well ahead of your visit. It takes about six to eight weeks for the card to arrive.

CONTACT: Orlando Magicard (800 643-9492 or 407 363-4871).

KISSIMMEE–ST. CLOUD VACATION DISCOUNTS

Walt Disney World reaches across two counties, Orange to the north, and Osceola to the south. Kissimmee is the town that stretches along Highway 192, where the Main Gate to the Magic Kingdom is located. Moderately priced lodging can be found here, as well as numerous outlet malls and gift shops. The Kissimmee–St. Cloud Convention and Visitors Bureau offers a free vacation discount booklet that includes coupons for local attractions and dinner shows, and special rates on area hotels, including Homewood Suites. The booklet has a toll free number for reserving accommodations at discounted rates.
CONTACT: Call Kissimmee–St. Cloud Convention and Visitors Bureau (800 327-9159).

DISNEY-AAA TRAVEL CENTER

Located off State Route 200 at Exit 68 of I-75 near Ocala, this information center is worth a stop for anyone driving to Walt Disney World. **Walk-in visitors can make same-day reservations for Walt Disney World hotel rooms at up to a 50 percent discount; however, this can only be done in person.** Visitors can also make dining reservations, purchase theme park tickets, and pick up Walt Disney World guides. Some AAA services are also available here. Open daily from 9 AM until 6 PM (352 854-0770).

NATIONAL TRAVEL CLUBS

AMERICAN AUTOMOBILE ASSOCIATION: Members receive a small discount on admission tickets (about 5 percent), however, if they purchase their tickets through AAA, they may park in preferred parking areas near the entrances (parking fees apply). **Members are also offered a 10 to 40 percent discount at the Swan and Dolphin resorts, at most Hotel Plaza resorts, and many off-site hotels in the area.** Members can also choose from a range of very reasonably priced Disney vacation packages that include accommodations, park admissions, and other amenities. Members also receive discounts of up to 20 percent on Disney Cruises.
CONTACT: Call your local chapter of the American Automobile Association for information.

AMERICAN EXPRESS: American Express card holders can now use their Membership Rewards Program points to earn Walt Disney World vacation packages and theme park passes. Card holders also receive a 10 percent discount on selected dinner shows, Disney merchandise, and boat rentals, and a 20 percent discount on Disney tours. American Express vacation packages to Walt Disney World include accommodations, park admissions, 250 Disney Dollars, and other amenities.
CONTACT: American Express Vacation Packages (407 827-7200).

ENTERTAINMENT PUBLICATIONS: This vacation coupon book offers 50 percent discounts at Hotel Royal Plaza, Grosvenor Resort, Travelodge, and many off-site hotels in the area, as well as discounts at Pleasure Island, Disney Institute Day Visitor Programs, and occasionally Disney Vacation Club, which offers a 25 percent discount on accommodations. Participants change yearly.
COST: The Entertainment Publications discount book for Orlando or any other city in the United States, good for one year, is about $30.
CONTACT: Entertainment Publications, 2125 Butterfield Rd., Troy, MI 48084 (800 374-4464). ◆

MONEY $AVING PAGE

POWERT

VACATION PACKAGE VALUES

Visitors, especially first-time visitors, may find planning a trip to Walt Disney World easier and more affordable with the purchase of a vacation package, which includes some combination of travel, accommodations, admissions, meals, and car rental. Vacation packages are offered by hotels, airlines, cruise lines, and travel clubs. Some travel clubs, such as American Express, the American Automobile Association, and the Magic Kingdom Club also offer vacation packages in partnership with Walt Disney World (see "Discount Travel Tips," page 17). The vacation packages listed below are are among the most affordable offered by Walt Disney World. Most do not include theme park admissions, and rates vary depending on the hotel you select and the time of year you visit. Many are available only during certain months. The prices shown are based on the starting price at Disney's lowest-priced All-Star Resorts.

DISNEY'S BASIC PLANS: The Walt Disney Travel Company offers vacation packages throughout the year. The package prices shown are based on adult double occupancy for the minimum three-night stay during value season, including taxes. The Basic Plan, which includes one-day admission to River Country, starts at about $125 per person and is Disney's lowest priced vacation package. At the next level, the Magic Plan (which includes theme park admissions) starts at about $320 per adult, $200 per junior, and $170 per child); and the Deluxe Magic Plan (which includes both admissions and meals) starts at about $750 per adult, $540 per junior, and $320 per child. **Magic Kingdom Club Card members may receive a substantial discount on these packages.** (See "Discount Travel Tips," page 17.) To request a catalog, contact the Walt Disney Travel Company (800 828-0228).

DISNEY'S SUNSHINE GETAWAY PACKAGE: Available from January 1 through mid-February, this value-season package includes a minimum three-night stay, daily breakfasts (including Character Breakfasts at a choice of restaurants), and a coupon book with discounts for restaurants, recreational activities, and merchandise in Walt Disney World. *This is the best value low-cost vacation package that Disney offers.* Three-night plans start at about $140 per adult, plus tax (based on adult double occupancy), and about $45 per child or junior. Contact Disney Central Reservations (407 934-7639).

DISNEY'S FALL FANTASY PACKAGE: Available from late August until mid-November, this package includes a minimum three-night stay, daily breakfast (including Character Breakfasts at selected Walt Disney World hotel restaurants), and a coupon book with discounts for restaurants, recreational activities, and merchandise in Walt Disney World. Three-night plans start at about $160 per adult, plus tax (based on adult double occupancy), and about $55 per child or junior. **(Prices are often lowest in late August and September, and although still reasonable, they increase in October and November. Be sure to ask!)** Contact Disney Central Reservations (407 934-7639).

DISNEY'S MAGICAL HOLIDAYS PACKAGE: Available after Thanksgiving until the week of Christmas, this vacation package is one of the most popular among frequent visitors. Features include a minimum three-night stay and choice of one of the following: admission to the Jolly Holidays Dinner Show (see "Dining Events," page 210); admission to Mickey's Very Merry Christmas Party at the Magic Kingdom, along with dinner at a selected restaurant; or the Candlelight Dinner Package in the World Showcase at Epcot, including the Candlelight Processional. Three-night plans start at about $170 per adult, plus tax (based on adult double occupancy), and about $55 per child or junior. Contact Disney Central Reservations (407 934-7639). ◆

ATTRACTIONS

The Attractions section explores all thirteen theme parks and recreation areas inside Walt Disney World. It is filled with mini tours to help you plan your days, and the ratings are designed to help you select attractions that match your interests and get the most enjoyment for the time and money you will spend.

THE RATINGS

On a typical vacation, you will have time to experience only a small part of what Walt Disney World has to offer. What's important is that you make your vacation as rewarding as possible by spending time in lines only for those attractions you will truly enjoy. The rating system shown below can help you achieve this.

★ ★ ★ ★	★ ★ ★	★ ★	★
DON'T MISS IT!	GOOD ENTERTAINMENT	MILDLY AMUSING	OF LIMITED APPEAL

ENJOYED MOST BY:

A ADULTS	T TEENS	C CHILDREN	Y THE YOUNG AT HEART

STARS: *Overall Quality* — The STARS represent the overall quality of the attraction — how well it is presented, how engaging the experience is, and how creatively it is expressed. Any attraction or ride, for any age group or special interest, can have between one and four STARS.

LETTERS: *Emotional Age Groups* — Combinations of the orange LETTERS will appear with the stars, showing who enjoys the attraction most. The LETTERS represent the "emotional ages" of the happiest viewers, *not* their chronological ages. These emotional ages enjoy attractions with the following qualities:

ADULTS	TEENS	CHILDREN	THE YOUNG AT HEART
AESTHETIC	THRILLING	FRIENDLY	CHARMING
CLEVER	FUTURISTIC	SIMPLE	FUNNY
BALANCED	TRENDY	SAFE	SENTIMENTAL
INTRIGUING	SCARY	SILLY	JOYFUL

Your emotional age is determined by your mood, your traveling companions, and your personality (after all, some of us are adults at eleven, while some of us are forever teens around a roller coaster). The Young at Heart can be a parent or grandparent whose enjoyment is enhanced through the experiences of a delighted child, or a dedicated Disney fan, or anyone who carries a childlike sense of wonder.

TOURING STRATEGIES

HALF-DAY TOURS: Most attraction descriptions include three- to six-hour mini tours for mornings, afternoons, or evenings, and for various times of year. You can mix and match and combine mini tours, map out each day of your Walt Disney World vacation, and then predict where you will be so you can secure those all-important restaurant and entertainment reservations in advance.

FOLLOW-THE-RATINGS TOURS: When touring the major theme parks, many readers use a simple and effective strategy, which is based on the attraction ratings: They find all the top-rated attractions that match their interests, mark them on the maps, connect the dots, then off they go! They may wait in line at some attractions, but their overall experience is upbeat, carefree, and satisfying. ◆

WALT DISNEY WORLD AT A GLANCE

Walt Disney World lies south of Orlando on Interstate 4, about a thirty-minute drive from the Orlando International Airport. This sprawling forty-seven-square-mile playground contains thirteen distinct theme parks and recreation areas, nearly thirty resorts, more than 150 miles of road, a dozen lakes with miles of interconnected waterways, and five PGA golf courses — all surrounded by wilderness areas, wetlands, and forests. It's a self-contained, self-sustaining world with its own telephone system, power plant, waste management and recycling center, and transportation system, as well as a computer control center linked with three Disney-owned space satellites that coordinate every aspect of this vacation paradise. There are five main resort areas in Walt Disney World, each with themed resort hotels spanning a range of prices and amenities. (See also "Hotels," page 123; and "Off-Site Hotels & Suites," page 152.)

MAGIC KINGDOM RESORTS AREA: This area embodies the heart and spirit of Walt Disney World, and includes the Magic Kingdom, Fort Wilderness & River Country, Discovery Island, Magnolia Golf Course, and Palm Golf Course. Bay Lake, Seven Seas Lagoon, and the Fort Wilderness Waterways provide marinas and boating. A fourteen-mile monorail system connects several of the resorts in this area with the Magic Kingdom and Epcot. The resorts located here include Disney's Polynesian Resort, Disney's Contemporary Resort, Disney's Grand Floridian Beach Resort, Disney's Fort Wilderness Resort and Campground, Disney's Wilderness Lodge, and Shades of Green.

EPCOT RESORTS AREA: This diverse and eclectic area is coveniently located in the center of Walt Disney World. It incorporates Epcot, Disney-MGM Studios, Disney's BoardWalk, and Fantasia Gardens miniature golf. Water launches or buses provide transportation between the resorts in this area and Epcot, Disney-MGM Studios, and Disney's BoardWalk. The monorail provides transportation between Epcot and the Magic Kingdom. The resorts located here include Disney's Beach Club Resort, Disney's Yacht Club Resort, Disney's Caribbean Beach Resort, Walt Disney World Dolphin, Walt Disney World Swan, Disney's BoardWalk Inn, and Disney's BoardWalk Villas.

DISNEY VILLAGE RESORTS AREA: Downtown Disney, a shopping, restaurant, and evening entertainment district, is located here along with Pleasure Island, Disney Village Marketplace, Disney's West Side, the Disney Institute, and Typhoon Lagoon. The golf courses located here are Osprey Ridge, Eagle Pines, and Lake Buena Vista. Water launches provide transportation between Downtown Disney and the resorts in this area, which all offer marinas and boating. The resorts located here include Disney's Old Key West Resort, Disney's Dixie Landings Resort, Disney's Port Orleans Resort, and The Villas at the Disney Institute.

HOTEL PLAZA AT DISNEY VILLAGE: Sophisticated Hotel Plaza lies within walking distance to Downtown Disney. The Hotel Plaza resorts are on Walt Disney World property, but are privately owned. Hotel shuttle buses provide transportation to the attractions. The resorts located here include Buena Vista Palace Resort & Spa, The Hilton Resort, Grosvenor Resort, Hotel Royal Plaza, Courtyard by Marriott, DoubleTree Guest Suites Resort, and Travelodge Hotel.

ANIMAL KINGDOM RESORTS AREA: This undeveloped area is at the southernmost point of Walt Disney World. The newest Disney projects can be found here, including Blizzard Beach, Disney's Wide World of Sports, and Disney's Animal Kingdom. Buses service the resorts located here, which include Disney's All-Star Resort complex and Disney's Coronado Springs Resort. ◆

ATTRACTIONS

WALT DISNEY WORLD AT A GLANCE

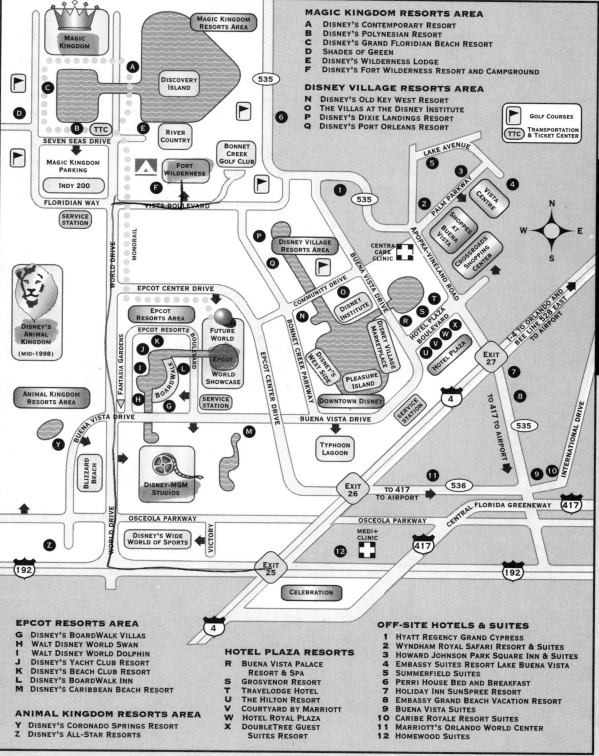

MAGIC KINGDOM RESORTS AREA

A DISNEY'S CONTEMPORARY RESORT
B DISNEY'S POLYNESIAN RESORT
C DISNEY'S GRAND FLORIDIAN BEACH RESORT
D SHADES OF GREEN
E DISNEY'S WILDERNESS LODGE
F DISNEY'S FORT WILDERNESS RESORT AND CAMPGROUND

DISNEY VILLAGE RESORTS AREA

N DISNEY'S OLD KEY WEST RESORT
O THE VILLAS AT THE DISNEY INSTITUTE
P DISNEY'S DIXIE LANDINGS RESORT
Q DISNEY'S PORT ORLEANS RESORT

GOLF COURSES
TTC TRANSPORTATION & TICKET CENTER

ATTRACTIONS

EPCOT RESORTS AREA

G DISNEY'S BOARDWALK VILLAS
H WALT DISNEY WORLD SWAN
I WALT DISNEY WORLD DOLPHIN
J DISNEY'S YACHT CLUB RESORT
K DISNEY'S BEACH CLUB RESORT
L DISNEY'S BOARDWALK INN
M DISNEY'S CARIBBEAN BEACH RESORT

ANIMAL KINGDOM RESORTS AREA

Y DISNEY'S CORONADO SPRINGS RESORT
Z DISNEY'S ALL-STAR RESORTS

HOTEL PLAZA RESORTS

R BUENA VISTA PALACE
RESORT & SPA
S GROSVENOR RESORT
T TRAVELODGE HOTEL
U THE HILTON RESORT
V COURTYARD BY MARRIOTT
W HOTEL ROYAL PLAZA
X DOUBLETREE GUEST
SUITES RESORT

OFF-SITE HOTELS & SUITES

1 HYATT REGENCY GRAND CYPRESS
2 WYNDHAM ROYAL SAFARI RESORT & SUITES
3 HOWARD JOHNSON PARK SQUARE INN & SUITES
4 EMBASSY SUITES RESORT LAKE BUENA VISTA
5 SUMMERFIELD SUITES
6 PERRI HOUSE BED AND BREAKFAST
7 HOLIDAY INN SUNSPREE RESORT
8 EMBASSY GRAND BEACH VACATION RESORT
9 BUENA VISTA SUITES
10 CARIBE ROYALE RESORT SUITES
11 MARRIOTT'S ORLANDO WORLD CENTER
12 HOMEWOOD SUITES

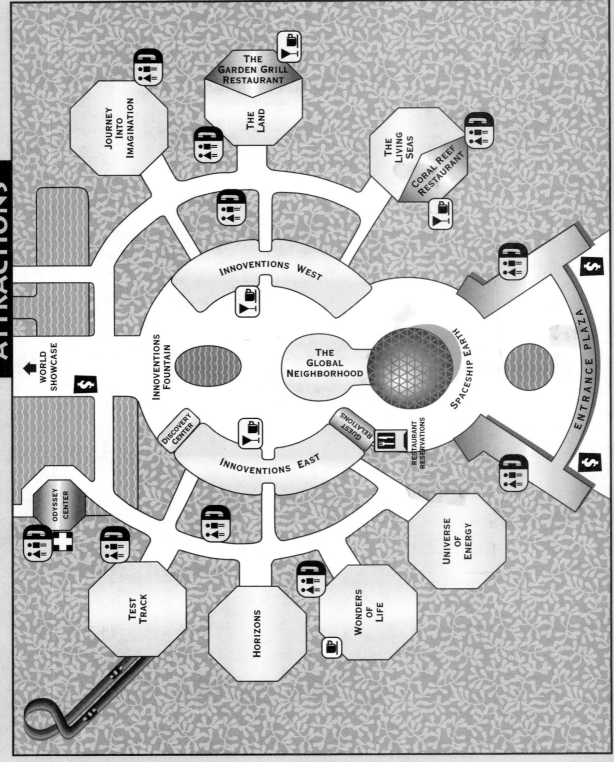

FUTURE WORLD AT EPCOT

Walt Disney's Experimental Prototype Community of Tomorrow, better known as Epcot, is distinguished by Spaceship Earth, the enormous silver geosphere at its entrance. The front half of Epcot is occupied by Future World, where eight themed pavilions present informative attractions on topics such as transportation, energy, communications, agriculture, and health. Many are of considerable interest to adults, and some pavilions are actually ongoing experiments designed to test innovations in energy management, food production, and waste and water recycling. Future World's most recent additions are Ellen's Energy Adventure in the Universe of Energy pavilion, and the Test Track pavilion, where visitors can experience first-hand the harrowing tests that automobiles are put through before they are brought to market.

WHEN TO GO: If you prefer a morning visit, arrive at Epcot's Main Gate about one half hour before the scheduled opening time so you can enjoy some of the popular attractions before the park gets crowded. Spaceship Earth and Innoventions East and West generally open one half hour before the rest of the park officially opens. The Future World pavilions and attractions are most accessible after 4 PM; however, most Future World attractions close about two hours before the World Showcase does, at about 7 PM. Check ahead with Walt Disney World Information (407 824-4321).

HOW TO GET THERE: Future World is located at the main entrance to Epcot. The large Epcot parking lot is free to guests staying at a Walt Disney World resort (other visitors are charged about $6). The parking lot is serviced by trams. Buses travel between Epcot and all Walt Disney World resorts, theme parks, and the Transportation and Ticket Center (TTC). The monorail travels between Epcot and the TTC, the Magic Kingdom, and the following resorts: Contemporary, Polynesian, and Grand Floridian. Epcot can also be entered at the World Showcase through the International Gateway, which is serviced by water launches that stop at the following resorts: Dolphin, Swan, Yacht Club, Beach Club, and BoardWalk. Trams sometimes service the following resorts: Swan, Dolphin, and BoardWalk. The Beach Club and BoardWalk are within walking distance.

ATTRACTIONS

★★★★	★★★	★★	★
DON'T MISS IT!	GOOD ENTERTAINMENT	MILDLY AMUSING	OF LIMITED APPEAL

ENJOYED MOST BY:

A ADULTS	T TEENS	C CHILDREN	Y THE YOUNG AT HEART

EMOTIONAL AGE GROUPS • SEE PAGE 21

EPCOT'S ENTRANCE PLAZA: As visitors enter the sprawling Entrance Plaza and pass by its sleek tripod sculpture fountain, they face the huge multifaceted 180-foot-high silver geosphere that houses Spaceship Earth. The geosphere, clearly visible from any part of Epcot, serves as a point of orientation. The Entrance Plaza is the site of many of Epcot's services, including the Tour Window, Guest Relations, wheelchair rentals, lockers, camera center, ATM, and American Express.

SPACESHIP EARTH ★★★★ T The Disney Imagineers collaborated with world-renowned science fiction writer Ray Bradbury to design this ride, which actually travels inside the Epcot geosphere. Spaceship Earth was updated several years ago with new music, narration, and finale. Visitors journey through the history of communication, from the earliest cave paintings to the printing press, and from the age of radio to the future of satellite communications. The lifelike Audio-Animatronics figures, carefully researched dioramas, and a conceptual visualization of an interconnected earth make Spaceship Earth one of Future World's not-to-be-missed experiences. Spaceship Earth is frequently open about an hour before the rest of Future World. This is a real advantage for visitors who arrive early, since lines can be very long during the day. Duration: 17 minutes.

THE GLOBAL NEIGHBORHOOD ★★ **T Y** Spaceship Earth exits into this exhibit hall sponsored by AT&T. Here, visitors can experiment with the communications technologies of the future or explore interactive television in one of several small living room–like areas. Simulatorlike devices at Ride the AT&T Network allow visitors to experience the sensation of traveling through the fiberoptic system of the AT&T Worldwide Information Network.

INNOVENTIONS EAST ★★ **A** Located in one of a pair of large semicircular buildings facing the Innoventions Fountain at the center of Future World, Innoventions East houses exhibits that change frequently and focus on tomorrow's consumer goods. Here, manufacturers showcase new products and give visitors the chance to try some of them out. Recent exhibits include time-saving appliances and gadgets, virtual reality and other interactive multimedia, computers connected to the Internet, the *Encyclopedia Britannica* on-line, lessons in using a computer to edit home videos, and a tour of an electronically managed "smart" house. **CENTORIUM** sells clothing, books, and videos, and features Disney collectibles upstairs at **THE ART OF DISNEY**. **GUEST RELATIONS** is located in the first entryway to the building, and the **WORLDKEY INFORMATION SERVICE** for making dining reservations is in a nearby alcove. The **ELECTRIC UMBRELLA RESTAURANT** is located here.

EPCOT DISCOVERY CENTER ★ **A** The Discovery Center was originally designed as a place where visitors could gather background and technical information about many of the exhibits at Epcot and throughout Walt Disney World. Recently, its facilities and services have been scaled back. Attendants have access to a databank on specific topics, and this is the place to ask any and all Disney-related questions, such as how many people Walt Disney World employs or how Walt Disney World's land and nature conservation programs work.

RESOURCES FOR TEACHERS ★★ **A** Visiting teachers will find an interesting array of educational materials and resources here designed to enhance their knowledge on a variety of subjects. Printed educational materials and programs, previews of educational software, and access to professional education journals are provided. A computer network allows educators to exchange ideas with other teaching professionals throughout the world.

INNOVENTIONS WEST ★★★ **T** Directly across the central plaza from Innoventions East, a matching structure houses Innoventions West. Here, the focus is on personal entertainment and communications systems of the future. Recent exhibits include virtual reality experiences, interactive television, and a variety of educational and entertainment software and high-tech toys. Sega of America, Inc., showcases its latest game systems here. Other software innovators have demonstrated the concept of virtual-travel-anywhere-anytime museums with a virtual walkthrough of Rome's Basilica of St. Peter's as it was in the fifteenth century, and a virtual walkthrough of Egyptian Queen Nefertiti's tomb. At the AT&T exhibit, visitors can fax postcards to anyone in the world, log on to the World Wiide Web, or communicate with each other in the pavilion using wrist phones. **PASTA PIAZZA RISTORANTE** and **FOUNTAIN VIEW ESPRESSO & BAKERY** are also located here.

UNIVERSE OF ENERGY PAVILION: Housed in a pyramidal building surfaced with mirrors, the Universe of Energy is a traveling theater that is part ride, part film, and total technical marvel. There is always a crowd, however, the attraction accommodates about six hundred people at a time, so lines disappear quickly. During peak hours, longer waits are the norm.

THE ENERGY ADVENTURE ★★★ T C This lengthy attraction takes visitors back in time to the dinosaur era to explore the origin of fossil fuels. In the preshow waiting area, a short film about energy is shown. The film introduces the tour guide who will narrate the journey, most recently, television actress Ellen DeGeneres in *Ellen's Energy Adventure.* Visitors are then seated in what appears to be a large theater, where another film describes the beginning of the universe. At this point, the "theater" breaks apart into six large traveling vehicles that journey through a primeval world populated with impressive Audio-Animatronics dinosaurs, and you-are-there sensory effects achieved with lighting, sound, and smell. The vehicles pass through a fog into an adjacent theater where visitors are shown a final film (with a rather uncertain editorial message) that explores the many sources of energy that are available on earth, which fuels are being used currently, and how long our remaining fossil fuels will last. Duration: 42 minutes, including preshow.

WONDERS OF LIFE PAVILION: Just beyond the Universe of Energy pavilion, where a steel DNA sculpture looms near a gigantic golden dome, is the Wonders of Life pavilion. This pavilion houses the Fitness Fairground exhibition center, the AnaComical Players theater, and three popular attractions: Body Wars, Cranium Command, and the film *The Making of Me.*

BODY WARS ★★★ T Y In this thrill ride, visitors are "miniaturized" and injected into a human body to retrieve a technician investigating the effects of a splinter. Naturally, problems develop, and visitors find themselves hurtling along in the circulatory system in need of rescue as well. The theater is actually a flight simulator that moves, tilts, and rocks dramatically during the show. The seat belts provided are a definite must for this ride, which is not for those prone to motion sickness. Some health restrictions apply. Expect long lines. Duration: 5 minutes.

CRANIUM COMMAND ★★★★ T C Y One of the funnier attractions in Future World, this show opens with a preshow cartoon introducing the Cranium Command, a specialized corps of Brain Pilots trained to run the systems that make up the human body. Those who fail get stuck running the bodies of chickens, as General Knowledge, the loudmouth trainer, continually reminds his cadets. Visitors then enter a multimedia theater, where they follow Buzzy, the youngest Cranium Command cadet, on his first venture into a truly frightful environment: the body and mind of a twelve-year-old boy on a typical school day. The clever humor strikes on an adult level. Cranium Command is hidden in the back of the pavilion, so lines are generally short. The animated preshow helps to make the rest of the show clear. Duration: 25 minutes, including preshow.

THE MAKING OF ME ★★ T C This light and humorous film tells visitors all about the facts of life. Created for a younger audience, *The Making of Me* once aroused considerable controversy because of its open approach to the topic of sex and reproduction, which culminates with superb, though graphic footage of the stages of pregnancy from initial conception through birth. Lines are common at this attraction because of the theater's small size. Duration: 14 minutes.

ANACOMICAL PLAYERS ★★ The actors and comedians in this small open theater in the Fitness Fairground put on an improvisational comedy performance, tagging a member of the audience to appear as a contestant in a game show about health. Duration: 15 minutes.

ATTRACTIONS

ATTRACTIONS

FITNESS FAIRGROUND ★★ **A C** This large, lively exhibition center presents both serious and lighthearted exhibits that focus on lifestyles and personal health. Visitors can try out the latest workout and fitness-monitoring equipment, or use touch-screen computers to get personalized suggestions for improving their health or to learn about the latest medical and health breakthroughs. A gift shop features health-oriented books and products, and the Pure and Simple cafe is a great place to grab a wholesome snack. Fitness Fairground always attracts a crowd.

HORIZONS PAVILION: The large building next to the Wonders of Life pavilion that looks like a giant flying saucer is the Horizons pavilion. Enclosing the domed OmniSphere theater, with one of the largest movie screens in the world, the pavilion is dedicated to an engaging ride and show that explore how we will live and work in the twenty-first century. In the near future, this pavilion will house a new attraction based on space travel and employing thrilling special effects.

HORIZONS ★★★ **T C** Visitors travel aboard four-passenger vehicles to explore past and current speculations about the future. Starting with visions from the past, such as Jules Verne's imaginary flight to the moon, visitors travel through time until they reach the present in the OmniSphere theater. Here, they are treated to dramatic images of new technologies in action. Turning to the future, twenty-first-century lifestyles are presented as visitors travel through convincingly futuristic environments. *This pavilion is scheduled for a complete redesign over the next two years and is often closed. (See "On the Drawing Board," page 34.)* Duration: 15 minutes.

TEST TRACK PAVILION: It's impossible to miss the high-pitched whine of vehicles zipping overhead on a track around this massive circular pavilion. The automobile is the focus at this pavilion, which was completely remodeled in 1997 to showcase Test Track, a wild ride through a new-vehicle testing facility. A huge exhibition area, patterned on an assembly plant, has a variety of interactive demonstrations, the latest GM models, and a boutique with car-motif collectibles and merchandise.

TEST TRACK ★★★★ **A T** Visitors enter a large queuing area filled with exhibits and videos that explain the extensive procedures for testing the quality and safety of a new vehicle before it goes into full-scale production. After a briefing on the harrowing tests ahead, they then board the six-passenger test vehicles that speed up a steep incline, jounce over rough roads, brake and slide on slick surfaces, endure the rigors of extreme heat and cold in environmental chambers, and experience a head-on collision. Crashing through a wall, their vehicle shoots out of the pavilion onto a high-speed track, careens along straightaways and tight turns, and circles the pavilion's exterior at speeds up to 65 m.p.h. on a steeply banked track. This is the fastest, and at nearly one mile, the longest ride at Walt Disney World. The preshow lasts about 30 minutes. Ride duration: 5 minutes.

TEST TRACK EXHIBITS ★★ **A T** Visitors can enter this line-free exhibition area at any time through doors at the side of the pavilion. The area has a driving technology lab where they can try out new onboard navigation and hazard warning systems and test their night-driving and other vehicle-handling skills on arcade-type virtual reality stations. The latest GM vehicles are on display here, and a retail boutique offers a selection of automotive collectibles and merchandise.

JOURNEY INTO IMAGINATION PAVILION: This pavilion is housed in a pair of leaning glass pyramids fronted by unpredictable spurting and leaping fountains. It features the Journey Into Imagination attraction, a ride that explores the creative process; the Magic Eye Theater's special 3-D movie presentation; and The Image Works exhibition center, a hands-on electronic playground.

JOURNEY INTO IMAGINATION ★★★ C Y Visitors are introduced to an eccentric adventurer named Dreamfinder and his purple sidekick Figment, who lead them on a flight of fancy, exploring the realms where imagination and ideas flourish: music, art, theater, literature, science, and technology. Huge, fanciful sets are interspersed with laser effects and bursts of music. The underlying story in the sequences of this popular attraction are not often clear to first-time visitors, who may find it disjointed and sometimes boring. It is best enjoyed as a purely sensory experience, with a heavy cuteness factor. *This attraction is scheduled for a rehab and may be closed at times.* Duration: 14 minutes.

MAGIC EYE THEATER ★★★★ A T C *Honey, I Shrunk the Audience* — This clever attraction is preceded with a short presentation about images and the imaginative process. Visitors are given 3-D glasses and enter a theater where they become the audience that the movie characters address directly. The "Imagination Institute" is presenting the Inventor of the Year Award to Wayne Szalinsky (the lead character from the popular movies *Honey, I Shrunk the Kids* and *Honey, I Blew Up the Kid).* During the show, a variety of mishaps occur and the audience is accidentally reduced to the size of insects, experiencing a rush of harrowing and thrilling mayhem. The 3-D effects are enhanced by exceptional sound, motion, visual, and sensory effects. This attraction is definitely worth seeing, even with a wait; however, arriving early in the day or late in the afternoon may alleviate waiting in long lines. Duration: 25 minutes.

THE IMAGE WORKS ★★ C Y This popular electronic environment is an interactive playground of light, sound, color, and video. Recent hands-on exhibits include neon light tunnels, electronic paint boxes, and lasers with artistic skills. The Image Works appeals primarily to children, who can spend vast amounts of time in the area. However, adults who like simple razzle-dazzle and have time to spare may find this active gallery worth a look, especially if they can elbow their way to the controls of an exhibit. A nearby shop sells a variety of film and a small selection of cameras, lenses, and video tapes.

THE LAND PAVILION: Food and farming — past, present, and future — are explored in The Land, the largest pavilion at Future World. The massive tri-level building, with its glass roof and greenhouses, is a combination science experiment and theme attraction. The Land pavilion houses the Harvest Theater film attraction, the Food Rocks stage show, the Living with The Land boat ride, and the Behind the Seeds Tour. Also in the pavilion are The Green Thumb Emporium (a gift shop selling gardeners' goodies), the Sunshine Season Food Fair food court, and The Garden Grill Restaurant, one of two full-service restaurants in Future World.

LIVING WITH THE LAND ★★★ A Located on the lower level of The Land pavilion, this boat ride is a pleasant, relaxing, and informative journey through the history and future of agriculture. A Cast Member travels with visitors explaining the ecological biomes they pass through, including a tropical rain forest; a hot, harsh desert; and a replica of the American prairie, depicting a small family farm at the turn of the century. As they cruise through The Land's impressive experimental greenhouses, visitors learn about emerging technologies in agriculture. Much of the produce and fish grown in the greenhouses is served in some of the full-service restaurants at Walt Disney World. Duration: 13 minutes.

HARVEST THEATER ★★ A C *Circle of Life* is a new 70mm film presented at the Harvest Theater. Simba, Timon, and Pumbaa, characters from the Disney film *The Lion King,* examine the interrelationship between humans and the land. The movie portrays Timon and Pumbaa

ATTRACTIONS

as land developers creating "Hakuna Matata Lakeside Village," with Simba stepping in to tell his father's tale of the human creatures who often forget that everything is connected in the great Circle of Life. Combined with the animated fable is a series of spectacular images, some beautiful and some nightmarish, depicting environmental scenes from around the world. Some of this footage is taken from *Symbiosis,* the movie that was formerly presented here. Overall, the film provides good entertainment, while presenting this serious topic. Duration: 20 minutes.

FOOD ROCKS ★★ Ⓒ Ⓨ Host Füd Wrapper and a cast of singing and dancing Audio-Animatronics fruits, vegetables, and other foods — including stars such as Pita Gabriel, The Peach Boys, and Chubby Cheddar — present a musical revue based on the basic food groups and nutrition. Variations of familiar lyrics and tunes and the transformation of popular stars into vegetables is really quite humorous. Food Rocks turns a lesson in nutrition into an unexpectedly enjoyable experience. Duration: 13 minutes.

THE LIVING SEAS PAVILION: The rippling façade of this massive pavilion suggests a natural shoreline, complete with crashing waves. In The Living Seas, visitors glimpse life under the oceans in one of the world's largest saltwater aquariums. There is a marine mammal research center here, as well as a living reef and many exhibits on marine topics. The Living Seas Gift Shop features marine-themed gifts, and the Coral Reef Restaurant offers diners a dramatic view of the aquarium as they eat.

CARIBBEAN CORAL REEF RIDE TO SEA BASE ALPHA ★★★ Ⓐ Ⓣ After a short dramatic film on the interrelationship between humans and the ocean, visitors descend in the Hydrolator (a simulated elevator ride) to the "ocean" floor, where they board Seacabs for a trip to Sea Base Alpha, an underwater research facility. Here, visitors can take some time to view the more than two hundred species of sea life in the huge, walk-through aquarium, watch the sleepy manatees and other residents of the Marine Mammal Research Center, and explore the exhibits on aquaculture and ocean ecosystems. A marine biologist is on hand to answer questions. Duration: 20 minutes; visitors may explore Sea Base Alpha as long as they wish.

✳

SPECIAL EVENTS AND LIVE ENTERTAINMENT

Live entertainment is scheduled throughout the day until about 6 PM at various Future World sites. As you enter the park, pick up an entertainment schedule at the guide-map racks just inside the turnstiles. Schedules are also available at most Future World shops and at Guest Relations, located in Innoventions East.

ILLUMINATIONS ★★★ Ⓐ Ⓣ This fireworks, laser, music, and water show occurs over the World Showcase Lagoon nightly between 9 and 10 PM, depending on the time of year. The show is periodically re-created and redesigned. Its most recent transformations have lacked the thematic unity it is capable of conveying, lowering its rating, although it is still a very impressive, must-see spectacle. There are no really good viewing areas in Future World, since the show is oriented to the World Showcase. For a good view, visitors need to arrive at the World Showcase at least one half hour before show time. Some of the best viewing locations close to Future World are along the World Showcase Lagoon from Mexico to China and, on the opposite side of the Lagoon, from the United Kingdom to the bridge promenade in front of France. The show is best viewed from an upwind location, since the fireworks produce a large amount of smoke. Duration: About 15 minutes.

ATTRACTIONS

MONEY
SAVING PAGE

TOUR — THE LAND: *Behind the Seeds Tour* ★ ★ ★ A This walking tour takes up where the Living with The Land boat cruise leaves off. Covering many of the same topics, the tour explores them in greater depth, with an emphasis on the experiments underway in the greenhouses. Visitors glimpse cutting-edge research laboratories, including the Biotechnology Lab, take an informative walk through several experimental greenhouses, and have a chance to ask questions and pick up horticultural tips from the tour guides, all of whom hold degrees in agricultural fields. The daily tours are limited to ten people and depart every half hour between 10 AM and 4:30 PM from the Behind the Seeds Tour podium, near The Green Thumb Emporium on the lower level of the pavilion. Reservations are required and should be made early in the day, since the tour is popular and fills quickly. Only same-day reservations are taken, which must be made in person at the Behind the Seeds Tour podium. The price of the tour is about $6 for adults ($4 for children). Duration: about 1 hour.

TOUR — THE LIVING SEAS: *DiveQuest* ★ ★ ★ A T This tour allows SCUBA-certified (open water) visitors to dive for 30 minutes in the coral reef environment of the aquarium at The Living Seas pavilion. The tour includes a pre-dive overview of The Living Seas pavilion and a presentation on the aquarium's marine life, the dive itself, and a post-dive question-and-answer period. All dive equipment is provided, along with lockers, showers, and changing rooms. DiveQuest, limited to eight people (two dives of four people), departs daily at 4:30 PM and 5:30 PM from the Guest Relations window outside Epcot's Main Gate. Reservations must be made at least one day ahead, and can be made up to one year in advance through Walt Disney World Tours (407 939-8687); the cost is about $150. Duration: 2½ hours.

COOL EVENT — INNOVENTIONS FOUNTAIN ★ ★ A T C On Epcot's opening day, as a gesture of international goodwill, representatives from more than twenty countries each poured a gallon of water from their nation to provide the substance and spirit of this energetic fountain. Located in the center of Innoventions Plaza, the fountain's jets shoot streams of sparkling water up to one hundred feet into the air, dancing in perfect synchronicity to sprightly Disney music in a mesmerizing water ballet. After nightfall, colored lights play on the spirited water ballet, creating a particularly dramatic effect. This delightful show is a good reason to take a break from a day of touring in the hot sun. A good place to view the show is from the patio at the Fountain View Espresso & Bakery. The music and water effects change with each show. Shows start every fifteen minutes.

✳ FULL-SERVICE RESTAURANTS

Save up to 30 percent on dinner! Throughout the year, from 4 until 6 PM, a changing selection of restaurants in the adjacent World Showcase at Epcot offer Early Evening Value Meals that include an appetizer, menu entree, and beverage. You must ask which restaurants offer this when making reservations. You can also arrive at the restaurant after 4 PM without a reservation.

Any visitor can make restaurant reservations up to sixty days in advance. Same-day reservations should be made as early as possible at the WorldKey Information Service at Innoventions East, at the WorldKey Information Service kiosk near the Germany pavilion in the World Showcase, or at the restaurant itself. Smoking is not permitted. See "Restaurants," page 157, for reviews and reservation information.

ATTRACTIONS

THE LAND PAVILION: *The Garden Grill Restaurant* — This pleasant restaurant is furnished with comfortable booths and revolves slowly through The Land's ecosystems: rainforest, desert, and prairie environments. Popular family-style Character Meals are served here, hosted by Farmer Mickey, featuring all-you-care-to-eat traditional American cuisine including chicken, steak, and fish. Beer, wine, and spirits are served. Open for breakfast, lunch, and dinner; reservations necessary.

THE LIVING SEAS PAVILION: *Coral Reef Restaurant* — The giant aquarium in The Living Seas pavilion forms one wall of this atmospheric, dimly lit restaurant. Tables are arranged in tiers so that everyone has a clear view. On arrival, guests receive picture cards to help them identify the marine life they are watching. The menu features fresh seafood. Beer, wine, and spirits are served. Open for lunch and dinner; reservations necessary.

✳

COCKTAIL LOUNGES AND CAFES

A number of refreshment stands in Future World serve snacks and fast food. Those listed below are especially pleasant and make ideal rendezvous spots. Two are located in the World Showcase, but they are directly adjacent to Future World. For before-dinner cocktails, try the lively Rose & Crown Pub in the nearby United Kingdom pavilion in the World Showcase.

INNOVENTIONS EAST: *Electric Umbrella Restaurant* — This counter-service restaurant is open for lunch and dinner. The menu features chicken sandwiches, hamburgers, and salads. Visitors can find seating inside or outside. Coffee, beer, and hot chocolate are available. ☕Ⲩ

INNOVENTIONS WEST: *Pasta Piazza Ristorante* — This counter-service restaurant offers all-day dining, from an early-morning omelette or pastry to an evening meal of pasta, pizza, and salad. There are dining tables indoors and outside on the terrace. Coffee and beer are available. ☕Ⲩ

Fountain View Espresso & Bakery — Open earlier and later than most restaurants in Future World, this is an ideal spot for that early-morning cappuccino and pastry or for a glass of wine or beer in the evening. The outdoor terrace provides a wonderful view of the occasional water and music performances that occur at Innoventions Fountain. ☕Ⲩ

THE LAND PAVILION: *Sunshine Season Food Fair* — Counter-service booths line one side of this large food court offering pasta, barbecued chicken, soup, salad, and some the best ice cream in Future World. Also available are coffee, beer, wine, and frozen alcoholic beverages. This food court is mobbed at peak meal times; the best times to eat are before 11 AM, or between 2 and 5 PM. ☕Ⲩ

UNITED KINGDOM PAVILION IN THE WORLD SHOWCASE: *Rose & Crown Pub* — Several fine British ales are on tap in this busy and beloved hangout for World Showcase veterans. Along with beverages, pub snacks such as Stilton cheese and Scotch eggs are offered. Visitors who order snacks or drinks at the bar can carry them to the adjacent outdoor terrace. ☕Ⲩ

MEXICO PAVILION IN THE WORLD SHOWCASE: *Cantina de San Angel* — This outdoor cafe overlooking the World Showcase Lagoon serves Mexican fast food such as burritos and tostadas, as well as frozen Margaritas, beer, coffee, hot chocolate, and churros. There's a quick shortcut from Future World to the Mexico pavilion, past the Odyssey Center, near Test Track. If you arrive well before IllumiNations begins, the Cantina is also a great viewing spot for the show. ☕Ⲩ

SERVICES

WORLDKEY INFORMATION SERVICE: This interactive information and restaurant-reservation system is headquartered at Innoventions East. Visitors should arrive early in the day to make restaurant reservations for lunch or dinner. There is also a WorldKey Information Service kiosk located near the Germany pavilion in the World Showcase. The system's simple-to-use touch-screen computer terminals offer detailed information about all of Epcot, including schedules for the day's events and shows. By touching the words *Call Attendant,* visitors can speak directly to a Guest Relations representative to make restaurant reservations.

REST ROOMS: Public rest rooms are located outside Epcot's Main Gate; on either side of the Entrance Plaza, near Spaceship Earth; on the far side of Innoventions East; on the far side of Innoventions West; inside Innoventions West, near the Pasta Piazza Ristorante; and outside the Journey Into Imagination pavilion. There are fairly deserted rest rooms in The Land pavilion, next to The Garden Grill Restaurant; and in The Living Seas pavilion, in the entrance hall to the Coral Reef Restaurant.

TELEPHONES: Public telephones are located on both sides of Epcot's Main Gate; on either side of the Entrance Plaza, near Spaceship Earth; on the far side of Innoventions East; on the far side of Innoventions West; in the breezeway through Innoventions West; and outside the Journey Into Imagination pavilion. For quieter, air-conditioned conversations, use the modern telephone booths at The AT&T Global Neighborhood, or slip into the Coral Reef Restaurant or The Garden Grill Restaurant, where phones are in an alcove near the entrance.

MESSAGE CENTER: The Message Center is located at Guest Relations in Innoventions East. The Message Center is on a network also shared by the Magic Kingdom and Disney-MGM Studios. Here, visitors can leave and retrieve messages for one another and exchange messages with companions visiting elsewhere. Anyone can phone in a message by calling (407) 824-4321.

FILM AND TWO-HOUR EXPRESS DEVELOPING: Film is available at most Future World shops. Drop-off points for two-hour express developing are at the Kodak Camera Center at Epcot's Entrance Plaza, and at the Cameras & Film shop in the Journey Into Imagination pavilion. Developed pictures can be picked up in the Kodak Camera Center at the Entrance Plaza or delivered to any WDW resort.

CAMERA RENTAL: Video camcorders, replacement batteries, and 35mm cameras are sold and rented at the Kodak Camera Center at Epcot's Entrance Plaza, and at Cameras & Film in the Journey Into Imagination pavilion. Rented equipment may be returned to a Kodak Camera Center in any major theme park.

MAIL DROPS: There are mail drops at the following locations in Future World: Epcot's Main Gate, the Guest Relations window at Epcot's Entrance Plaza, and near the telephones on the far sides of Innoventions East and Innoventions West. A postage stamp machine is located near the lockers at Epcot's Entrance Plaza.

BANKING: There is an automated teller machine (ATM) just outside Epcot's Main Gate on the left, and one near the Showcase Plaza in the World Showcase. There is an American Express cash machine just outside Epcot's Main Gate, near the Guest Relations window. Personal checks up to about $25 can be cashed at Guest Relations in Innoventions East.

ATTRACTIONS

LOCKERS: There are lockers located near the Kodak Camera Center at Epcot's Entrance Plaza, at the Bus Information Center in front of Epcot, and at the International Gateway in the World Showcase.

PACKAGE PICKUP: Visitors can forward purchases free of charge to the Gift Stop, outside Epcot's Main Gate, or to Showcase Gifts at the International Gateway in the World Showcase, and pick them up as they leave the park. Allow two to three hours between purchase and pickup. Guests staying at a Walt Disney World resort may have packages delivered to their hotel.

FIRST AID: The first-aid office is adjacent to the Odyssey Center. Aspirin and other first-aid needs are dispensed free of charge. Over-the-counter medications are available at the Centorium in Innoventions East and at the Stroller Shop in Epcot's Entrance Plaza. They are not on display and must be requested.

VISITORS WITH DISABILITIES: A complimentary guidebook for visitors with disabilities is available at Guest Relations in Innoventions East. All attractions in Future World have wheelchair access; however, visitors must leave their wheelchairs to board the ride vehicles at Journey Into Imagination, Body Wars, Horizons, Test Track, and Spaceship Earth.

WHEELCHAIR RENTALS: Wheelchairs can be rented outside the Main Gate at Epcot, on the right in the Gift Stop; inside Epcot's Entrance Plaza; and at the International Gateway in the World Showcase. Electric Convenience Vehicles can be rented at Epcot's Entrance Plaza on a first-come, first-served basis. Replacement batteries, if needed, will be brought to your vehicle if you alert a Cast Member.

VISITORS WITH HEARING IMPAIRMENTS: A written text of Epcot's attractions is available at Guest Relations in Innoventions East. Assistive listening devices are also available there for some Epcot attractions. A telecommunications device for the deaf (TDD) is available in The AT&T Global Neighborhood. Hearing aid–compatible and amplified telephones are located throughout Epcot.

VISITORS WITH SIGHT IMPAIRMENTS: Tape players, touring cassettes that describe the park, and guidebooks in Braille are available at Guest Relations in Innoventions East.

FOREIGN LANGUAGE ASSISTANCE: Epcot maps are available in Spanish, French, Portuguese, German, and Japanese. Personal translator units (PTUs) that offer French, Spanish, and German translations of some of the Epcot attractions and presentations are available at Guest Relations in Innoventions East in Future World. The Walt Disney World Foreign Language Center can answer questions, help with travel arrangements, and offer assistance in a number of languages to visitors who call between 8:30 AM and 9 PM (407 824-7900).

✳

ON THE DRAWING BOARD

Walt Disney conceived of Future World as a technology-of-the-future showcase that would continually evolve. As a result, plans are always on the drawing board to revamp or update the pavilions, but until construction actually begins, these plans have a way of changing or becoming delayed. At the time of publication, the Horizons pavilion was next in line for a major concept redesign.

SPACE PAVILION: In the planning stages for some time, this new attraction may replace Horizons. High-tech simulators and thrilling special effects will let visitors experience asteroids, space travel, and life aboard a space station. Horizons may be closed in the near future.

Half-Day Tours at Future World

The morning and evening tours that follow are designed to let visitors sample the best of Future World in four to six hours, including a lunch or dinner in one of the park's restaurants. The Morning Technology Expedition focuses on the popular attractions and is designed to give you exceptional access during peak-attendance times and year-round. The Afternoon and Evening in the Future Tour is less hurried, but also effective year-round. You may not have time to visit every attraction listed on the tours, but you will have a quality experience if you follow these guidelines: ❶ Never pass up an attraction if you can walk right in without a line. ❷ Do not wait in lines longer than fifteen minutes *unless* it is for an attraction you know you will enjoy. ❸ Do not visit Future World during the day on Early Entry days (usually Tuesday and Friday) unless you are entering early to take advantage of that uncrowded ninety minutes. ❹ Don't get too caught up racing to the top attractions — the magical and memorable moments lie in between. Look around... Future World is rich with detail and filled with playfulness hidden in plain sight.

You can create your own custom vacation at Walt Disney World by combining a half-day Future World tour with a half-day tour of any other theme park. For example, combine the Morning Technology Expedition with an evening tour at the Magic Kingdom.

MORNING TECHNOLOGY EXPEDITION

Five to six hours — year-round — including lunch.
Well in advance, reserve a late lunch (1 PM or later) at The Garden Grill or the Coral Reef Restaurant.

⬇ Arrive at Epcot's Entrance Plaza about forty-five minutes before the official opening time, and pick up an entertainment schedule at the guide-map racks just inside the turnstiles. If you need a lunch reservation, go to the WorldKey Information Service at Innoventions East and reserve lunch for 1 PM or later at a Future World restaurant. If reservations are not available or if you prefer a light meal, plan on eating at the Sunshine Season Food Fair in The Land pavilion, the Electric Umbrella Restaurant in Innoventions East, or Pasta Piazza Ristorante in Innoventions West.

⬇ The front part of the park opens at least one-half hour early, so you can ride **SPACESHIP EARTH**. The ride exits into **THE GLOBAL NEIGHBORHOOD**. Try out some of the exhibits, but don't linger since the main park often opens before the announced time.

⬇ When the park opens (usually early), visit, in the order listed below (counterclockwise), as many of the attractions that interest you as possible (you can return later to explore the no-line exhibits):

- ◆ **Test Track** *pavilion* — **TEST TRACK**
- ◆ **Wonders of Life** *pavilion* — **BODY WARS** and/or **CRANIUM COMMAND**
- ◆ **Universe of Energy** *pavilion* — **THE ENERGY ADVENTURE**
- ◆ **The Land** *pavilion* — **LIVING WITH THE LAND** and/or **HARVEST THEATER** (*Circle of Life*)
- ◆ **Journey Into Imagination** *pavilion* — **MAGIC EYE THEATER** (*Honey, I Shrunk the Audience*)

⬇ If you have a lunch reservation, pause your tour to arrive there ten minutes early. If you are lunching at a counter-service restaurant, eat at your leisure — the later the better for avoiding crowds.

ATTRACTIONS

Continue the tour with the following or return to pavilions that interest you for a more in-depth look:

◆ **The Living Seas** *pavilion* — CARIBBEAN CORAL REEF RIDE
◆ INNOVENTIONS EAST AND WEST — exhibits and demonstrations.

AFTERNOON AND EVENING IN THE FUTURE TOUR

Four to six hours — year-round — including dinner.
Well in advance of your tour, reserve a 7:30 PM dinner at The Garden Grill or the Coral Reef Restaurant.
If you do not have reservations on the day of your tour, call Same Day Reservations after 10 AM (939-3463).

Arrive at Epcot's Entrance Plaza at 3:30 PM. Pick up an entertainment schedule at the guide-map racks just inside the turnstiles to check the show times for live performances and IllumiNations.

If you do not have a dinner reservation or if you prefer a light meal, plan to eat at the Sunshine Season Food Fair in The Land pavilion, Pasta Piazza Ristorante in Innoventions West, the Electric Umbrella Restaurant in Innoventions East, or the Cantina San Angel in the Mexico pavilion.

Visit the attractions that interest you in the order listed below (clockwise). Go ahead and linger at the exhibits that interest you.

◆ **Universe of Energy** *pavilion* — THE ENERGY ADVENTURE
◆ **Wonders of Life** *pavilion* — BODY WARS and/or CRANIUM COMMAND
◆ **Test Track** *pavilion* — TEST TRACK and exhibit hall
◆ **Journey Into Imagination** *pavilion* — MAGIC EYE THEATER (*Honey, I Shrunk the Audience*)
◆ **The Land** *pavilion* — LIVING WITH THE LAND and/or HARVEST THEATER (*Circle of Life*)
◆ **The Living Seas** *pavilion* — CARIBBEAN CORAL REEF RIDE
◆ SPACESHIP EARTH (which usually stays open late)
◆ INNOVENTIONS EAST AND WEST — for the exhibits and demonstrations, if you have time.

Plan to arrive about ten minutes early for your 7:30 PM dinner reservation. If you are dining at a counter-service restaurant, arrive no later than an hour before IllumiNations is scheduled.

After dinner, head over to the World Showcase to secure a viewing spot. If you still have time before ILLUMINATIONS begins, you can tour the following pavilions:

◆ **Mexico in the World Showcase** — EL RIO DEL TIEMPO (if there is no line)
◆ **United Kingdom in the World Showcase** — to explore the shops.

About twenty minutes before ILLUMINATIONS is scheduled to begin (usually at 9 PM; at 10 PM June through August), position yourself along the World Showcase promenade. The fireworks can produce large amounts of smoke, so it is best to view the show from a spot upwind of the center of the lagoon. Some better views of IllumiNations can be found at the following locations:

◆ Behind the wheelchair viewing area at the World Showcase Entrance Plaza.
◆ Along the promenade near Mexico or Norway
◆ Along the promenade near Canada or the United Kingdom.

After IllumiNations ends and as the crowds rush out, you may want to linger in the World Showcase to view the uncrowded night-lit pavilions. ◆

WORLD SHOWCASE AT EPCOT

The World Showcase, which covers more than half of Epcot, was designed to be a permanent and ever-expanding world's fair. Currently, eleven international pavilions encircle the forty-acre World Showcase Lagoon. Each pavilion features restaurants and shops, and offers visitors a glimpse of its national culture through its architecture, horticulture, music, dance, cuisine, crafts, and fine arts. Throughout the day, live performances, engaging exhibitions, and atmospheric theatrics are occurring in each of the pavilions.

WHEN TO GO: Although large crowds arrive here between lunch and dinner, the World Showcase rarely feels overcrowded because it is spread out over a very large area. The best time to visit is at opening, usually about 11 AM, and at night when the pavilions are strikingly lit. In the early evening, the World Showcase restaurants fill with diners, and crowds linger on the promenade to wait for the IllumiNations fireworks show held at closing time (generally about 9 or 10 PM). Opening and closing times vary throughout the year, so check ahead with Walt Disney World Information (407 824-4321).

HOW TO GET THERE: Visitors can enter the World Showcase by walking through Epcot's Future World from the Main Gate toward the World Showcase Lagoon. The large Epcot parking lot is free to guests staying at a Walt Disney World resort (other visitors are charged about $6). The parking lot is serviced by trams. Buses travel between Epcot and all WDW resorts, theme parks, and the Transportation and Ticket Center (TTC). The monorail travels between Epcot and the TTC, the Magic Kingdom, and the following resorts: Contemporary, Polynesian, and Grand Floridian. The World Showcase can also be entered directly through the International Gateway, which is serviced by water launches that stop at the following resorts: Dolphin, Swan, Yacht Club, Beach Club, and BoardWalk. Trams sometimes service the following resorts: Swan, Dolphin, and BoardWalk. The Beach Club and BoardWalk are within walking distance.

IN-PARK TRANSPORTATION: The promenade around the World Showcase Lagoon is 1¼ miles long. Watercraft called FriendShips carry passengers back and forth across the lagoon, from Germany or Morocco to the Showcase Plaza near Future World.

ATTRACTIONS

MEXICO: The Mexico pavilion spans both sides of the World Showcase promenade. On the lagoon side, Cantina de San Angel serves Mexican food and beverages. Across the promenade is a massive Mayan pyramid surrounded by tropical foliage. Just inside the entrance, past an exhibition of pre-Columbian art, the pyramid opens onto a night scene in a Mexican village square lined with colonial-style façades. Colorful shops are filled with handicrafts, jewelry, clothing, and souvenirs. At the rear of the pavilion, San Angel Inn Restaurante overlooks an indoor river and a distant view of a smoking volcano. Mariachi bands often perform inside the pavilion or on the promenade.

ATTRACTIONS

ATTRACTIONS

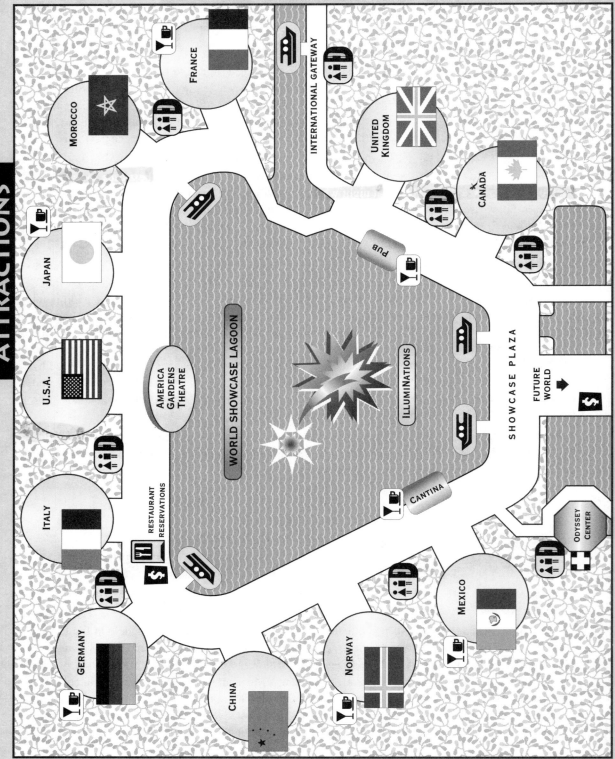

FRANCE

MOROCCO

INTERNATIONAL GATEWAY

UNITED KINGDOM

CANADA

JAPAN

PUB

U.S.A.

AMERICA GARDENS THEATRE

WORLD SHOWCASE LAGOON

ILLUMINATIONS

SHOWCASE PLAZA

FUTURE WORLD

ITALY

RESTAURANT RESERVATIONS

CANTINA

ODYSSEY CENTER

GERMANY

NORWAY

MEXICO

CHINA

EL RIO DEL TIEMPO ★★ A C This charming Mexican travelogue by boat lacks the sophisticated special effects of many Disney attractions, but its simplicity is refreshing. The ride is a pleasant and relaxing interlude after lunch or dinner. Duration: 7 minutes.

NORWAY: As visitors enter this serene Old World pavilion, a medieval church and fourteenth-century fortress give way to the cobblestone courtyards and steep gabled rooftops of a traditional Norwegian town square. Shops inside the fortress offer Norwegian hand-knit woolens, carved wood, and metal and glass handicrafts. At times, a brass band performs in the courtyard.

MAELSTROM ★★★ A T C Special effects and Audio-Animatronics enliven this short, dramatic boat ride that travels through the era of Viking sea exploration and into the present. Visitors in the front of the boat may get splashed. Afterward, a short film showcases the spirit of the people of Norway. *A new and updated film is in production to replace the current one.* Duration: 15 minutes.

CHINA: A colorful half-scale model of the Temple of Heaven is the spectacular centerpiece of this exotic pavilion. Traditional Chinese music accompanies visitors as they stroll through charming Oriental gardens accented with landscaped reflecting pools and filled with roses, mulberry trees, water oaks, and pomegranates. The large shopping gallery offers a multitude of Chinese gifts and goods, including furniture and fine art. The art exhibition at the House of the Whispering Willows gallery is particularly impressive. Chinese acrobatic troupes often perform in front of this pavilion.

WONDERS OF CHINA ★★★ A This vivid, fast-paced Circle-Vision 360 film portrays the people and culture of China as narrated by Li Po, the treasured poet of ancient China. The lyrical movie, projected on a huge circular screen, surrounds viewers and transports them from the vast grasslands of Mongolia to modern-day Shanghai. There is no seating. Duration: 19 minutes.

GERMANY: Fairy-tale Bavarian architecture surrounds the charming town square of the Germany pavilion. A statue of St. George and the dragon dominates the center of the square, which is ringed by a festive Biergarten restaurant and entertainment hall, along with several colorfully stocked shops offering wines, toys, glassware, and timepieces. At the rear of the square, a chiming glockenspiel rings the hour, and a strolling musician plays waltzes and polkas on the accordion. Off to the side of this pavilion is a railroad garden with three model trains running through a German village scene.

ITALY: A scaled-down version of the Venetian Campanile and a faithful replica of the Doge's Palace dominate the piazza of the Italy pavilion. The fountain at the rear of the piazza is a true-to-life replica of the Fontana de Nettuno. Venetian bridges lead to a gondola landing at the edge of the World Showcase Lagoon. Live entertainment, ranging from operatic arias to street theater, is scheduled from time to time in the piazza. At Cucina Italiana, visitors can sample the foods and wines of Italy.

U.S.A.: The American Adventure pavilion is housed in a huge colonial-style red-brick mansion. The colorful gardens surrounding the pavilion are dotted with sycamore and magnolia trees, and a carefully tended rose garden at the side of the pavilion blooms with varieties named after U.S. presidents. At the edge of the World Showcase Lagoon, the America Gardens Theatre is a showcase for live entertainment throughout the day.

VOICES OF LIBERTY ★★★ This a cappella singing group has been performing an appealing mix of patriotic and folk songs in the rotunda of the U.S.A. pavilion since it opened in 1982. There are several short performances throughout the day. The best acoustics will be found underneath the dome, which greatly enhances the sound. Duration: approximately 15 minutes.

ATTRACTIONS

ATTRACTIONS

THE AMERICAN ADVENTURE ★★★★ 🎬 T Ⓒ Disney's brilliant entertainment technology is highlighted in this remarkable Audio-Animatronics attraction. Mark Twain and Benjamin Franklin guide visitors on a patriotic multimedia tour through American history. The Disney penchant for detail shines in every vignette, from Will Rogers' lazily spinning lariat to Theodore Roosevelt's notoriously ruddy complexion. Duration: 29 minutes.

JAPAN: In the lovely gardens of the Japan pavilion, rocks, manicured trees, fish ponds, and wind chimes have been carefully blended to create a mood of serene reflection. A scarlet *torii* gate, symbol of good luck, greets visitors arriving by way of the World Showcase Lagoon, and the pavilion's prominent pagoda is a replica of the eighth-century Horyuji Temple of Nara. Traditional dance and music is performed throughout the day, including a remarkable taiko drumming demonstration.

MOROCCO: This pavilion meticulously re-creates the architectural mystery of North Africa. A replica of the Koutoubia Minaret of Marrakesh greets visitors at the entrance to a flower-filled courtyard, complete with a splashing fountain. The Bab Boujouloud gate leads into the Medina, a bazaar where rugs, jewelry, clothing, leather goods, brassware, and pottery spill out of shops into narrow passageways. Belly dancers and troups of acrobats appear throughout the day.

FRANCE: La Belle Epoque reigns once more in the France pavilion, where the Parisian streets are lined with mansard-roofed buildings, poster-covered kiosks, and sidewalk cafes. Quaint shops offer wine, perfumes, leather goods, jewelry, and crystal. Strolling street musicians sing familiar French ballads, mimes and comics perform on the street, and visitors are sketched by artists at their easels along the waterfront. The Eiffel Tower and the Galerie des Halles are reproduced here, and the French landscape is captured by the sweeping lawn and Lombardy poplars at the side of the pavilion.

IMPRESSIONS DE FRANCE ★★★ 🎬 T This exquisite wide-screen film, shown in the Palais du Cinema, immerses viewers in the rich culture and graceful landscapes of France. The soundtrack highlights France's contributions to the world of classical music. Duration: 18 minutes.

UNITED KINGDOM: In this picturesque pavilion, visitors stroll from a British town square through English gardens and down a street filled with charming shops in small Tudor, Georgian, and Victorian buildings. London plane trees and box hedges line the sidewalks, and visitors can make calls from a classic red phone booth that was once a hallmark of the United Kingdom. Of special interest are a replica of Anne Hathaway's thatched-roof cottage and the hedged herb and perennial gardens behind the Tea Caddy. Periodically, musical performances are held in the gazebo at the rear of the pavilion and an acting troupe involves visitors in humorous street plays.

CANADA: Magnificent towering totem poles frame the Northwest Mercantile trading post at the entrance to the Canada pavilion. The natural beauty of the Canadian Rockies is captured here, complete with a waterfall and a rushing stream. Northwest Mercantile sells Native American and Eskimo crafts and traditional trapper's clothing. The Caledonia Bagpipe Band can be heard by visitors walking under the birch, willow, maple, and plum trees in the pavilion's Victoria Gardens, where more than forty different flowering plants are always in bloom.

O CANADA! ★★★ 🎬 T From the rugged Pacific Coast to the majestic Rockies to the Arctic Ocean, this scenic film sweeps across the countryside of Canada. The Circle-Vision 360 screen surrounds visitors with Canada's natural wonders, along with scenes of its sporting events and urban and rural life. Visitors stand in the center of the theater during the show. Duration: 18 minutes.

SPECIAL EVENTS AND LIVE ENTERTAINMENT

The World Showcase has a festival-oriented atmosphere, with unique and lively entertainment events scheduled daily in each pavilion. The "street entertainment" is one of the most interesting and memorable experiences at the World Showcase. In addition, visiting artisans from the individual nations demonstrate their crafts, and the younger set can participate in "kid zones" at most pavilions. As you enter the park, be sure to pick up an entertainment schedule at the guide-map racks just inside the turnstiles, or at the International Gateway near the France pavilion. Schedules are also available at most World Showcase shops.

AMERICA GARDENS THEATRE ★★ **A** This covered outdoor theater located on the edge of the World Showcase Lagoon and in front of the U.S.A. pavilion showcases concerts highlighting American music and other special performances. On summer weekends and during holidays, guest celebrities may make appearances, ratings vary with the performance. Duration: about 30 minutes.

ILLUMINATIONS ★★★ **A T C** This fireworks, laser, music, and water show bursts into action over the World Showcase Lagoon nightly at 9 or 10 PM, depending on the time of year. The show is redesigned periodically, and recent versions lack emotional cohesiveness, but it's a spectacle nonetheless. Arrive at the World Showcase early for a good viewing position along the promenade. Some of the best viewing locations are the Cantina de San Angel in Mexico; lagoonside at the Rose & Crown Dining Room in the United Kingdom; along the promenade between China, Germany, and Italy; and along the promenade between France, the United Kingdom, and Canada. There are somewhat limited but dramatic views at the gondola landing in front of Italy and on the upper deck in front of the Matsu No Ma Lounge in Japan. Since the fireworks from this show produce a large amount of smoke, try to get a spot that is upwind from the center of the lagoon. Duration: 20 minutes.

SEASONAL EVENTS ★★★ **A** The World Showcase has become the center for many annual festivals and seasonal events. Chinese New Year and Mardi Gras are celebrated with colorful parades. During April and May, the Flower and Garden Festival is featured, with displays, workshops, demonstrations, and garden tours. At the International Food and Wine Festival in October, numerous food and wine booths are set up along the World Showcase promenade, where visitors can sample the tastes of the world. The Teddy Bear and Doll Convention comes in November, while December is devoted to seasonal celebrations, with storytellers from each country describing their holiday traditions. The pavilions are traditionally decorated, as well, and there are festive holiday events and special performances every day leading up to Christmas and New Year's Eve.

TOUR: *Hidden Treasures of the World Showcase* ★★★ **A T** The unique architecture and inventive construction techniques of the international pavilions are explored in these 2$\frac{1}{2}$-hour walking tours. Half of the World Showcase (Mexico, Norway, China, Germany, Italy, and U.S.A.) is toured on Tuesdays at 9:30 AM; the other half (Canada, United Kingdom, France, Morocco, Japan, and U.S.A.) is toured on Saturdays at 9:30 AM. All tours leave from the Tour Garden in Epcot's Entrance Plaza. A five-hour tour is also offered, which visits all eleven pavilions and includes lunch (usually at Restaurant Marrakesh in Morocco). It departs at 9:30 AM on Wednesdays from the Guest Relations window outside Epcot's Main Gate. Advance reservations are required for all tours and can be made through Walt Disney World Tours (407 939-8687). The price for the 2$\frac{1}{2}$-hour tours is about $35. The price for the five-hour comprehensive tour and lunch is about $65 (including lunch). Tour days may change, and prices do not include theme park admission.

ATTRACTIONS

ATTRACTIONS

TOUR: *Gardens of the World* ★ ★ **A** This walking tour explores the unique landscaping found throughout the World Showcase. Many of the plants and care techniques were imported from the nations represented. The tour covers the entire World Showcase and departs at 9:30 AM from the Tour Garden in Epcot's Entrance Plaza. Tours usually run on Tuesdays and Thursdays. Advance reservations are recommended; call Walt Disney World Tours (407 939-8687). If space is available, visitors without reservations can sign up in person at the Tour Garden on the morning of the tour. The price is about $35 (excluding theme park admission). Tour days may change. Duration: 3 hours.

$AVE FULL-SERVICE RESTAURANTS

Save up to 30 percent on dinner! Throughout the year, from 4 until 6 PM, a changing selection of restaurants in the World Showcase offer Early Evening Value Meals that include an appetizer, menu entree, and beverage. You must ask which restaurants offer this when making reservations.

Any visitor can make restaurant reservations up to sixty days in advance (except for Bistro de Paris, where reservations can be made up to fourteen days in advance). Same-day reservations can be made at the WorldKey Information Service kiosk near the Germany pavilion; at the WorldKey Information Service at Innoventions East in Future World; or at the restaurant itself. Smoking is not permitted. See "Restaurants," page 157, for reviews and reservation information.

MEXICO: *San Angel Inn Restaurante* — This restaurant, located at the edge of an indoor river, serves Mexican specialties under a cleverly simulated evening sky. The atmosphere, complete with a pyramid and smoking volcano in the distance, is both romantic and entertaining. Beer (Dos Equis), wine, and spirits are served. Open for lunch and dinner; reservations necessary.

NORWAY: *Restaurant Akershus* — This all-you-care-to-eat Norwegian smorgasbord features a hot and cold buffet of fish, meats, and salads. The medieval decor sets the tone of Old Norway. Beer (Ringnes), wine, and spirits are available. Open for lunch and dinner; reservations recommended.

CHINA: *Nine Dragons Restaurant* — Several traditional Chinese cooking styles are served in this formal Oriental dining room. Entrees are served as individual meals, not family-style dishes. Beer (Tsing Tao), wine, and spirits are available. Open for lunch and dinner; reservations recommended.

GERMANY: *Biergarten* — Diners seated at long communal tables select from a buffet of traditional German dishes in a huge Bavarian hall. German wines and beer (Beck's, in thirty-three-ounce steins) are served. Performances featuring musicians, yodelers, and folk dancers are scheduled throughout the day. Open for lunch and dinner; reservations necessary.

ITALY: *L'Originale Alfredo di Roma Ristorante* — This popular restaurant features Italian dishes, including the house specialty, Fettuccine Alfredo. The pasta is made fresh, and chicken, beef, and veal dishes are also served. Musicians sing Italian ballads during dinner. Beer, wine, and spirits are served. Open for lunch and dinner; reservations necessary.

JAPAN: *Teppanyaki Dining Room* — This large second-floor restaurant features *teppanyaki*-style cooking. Guests are seated at large communal tables, each with its own grill, where a stir-fry chef prepares the meal — a show in itself. The menu includes beef, chicken, and seafood, with stir-fried vegetables. Beer, wine, and spirits are served. Open for lunch and dinner; reservations necessary.

Tempura Kiku — In this small restaurant adjacent to Teppanyaki Dining, guests are seated at a U-shaped counter surrounding a tempura bar and grill, where they dine on batter-fried chicken, seafood, and vegetables. Beer, wine, and spirits are served. Open for lunch and dinner; no reservations.

MOROCCO: ***Restaurant Marrakesh*** — Traditional Moroccan cuisine is featured in this exotic dining room. Beef, lamb, fish, and chicken are prepared with a variety of aromatic spices and served with couscous. Musicians and belly dancers entertain guests during meals. Beer, wine, and spirits are served. Open for lunch and dinner; reservations recommended.

FRANCE: ***Chefs de France*** — Traditional French cuisine created by three of France's celebrated chefs is served in this busy, pleasant restaurant, which has expanded to incorporate Au Petit Café, doubling in size and adding an atrium-style dining area overlooking the World Showcase Promenade. The classically French menu incorporates fresh seafood from Florida. The wine list is French, of course, and beer and spirits are also served. Open for lunch and dinner; reservations necessary.

Bistro de Paris — Located above the Chefs de France, this restaurant serves French nouvelle cuisine in a romantic and intimate setting. French wines, beer, and spirits are served. Open for dinner only (lunch may be offered during peak-attendance times); reservations necessary.

UNITED KINGDOM: ***Rose & Crown Dining Room*** — This handsome lagoonside restaurant serves cottage pie, roast prime rib, and fish and chips. Guests may sit outside on the terrace overlooking the lagoon, an especially good location for viewing the IllumiNations performance. Spirits, wine, and a selection of ales on tap are available. Open for lunch and dinner; reservations necessary.

CANADA: ***Le Cellier*** — In this large but cozy restaurant designed to resemble a wine cellar, guests select from hearty Canadian dishes such as Tortierre Pie (a traditional pork pie), chicken and meatball stew, and poached salmon. Cafeteria-style service with Canadian wine and beer (La Batt's). Open for lunch and dinner; no reservations. *Le Cellier may be changed to a full-service Canadian steakhouse.*

✳

CAFES AND LOUNGES

The international pavilions at the World Showcase have refreshment stands that serve snacks and fast food. Those listed below are especially pleasant and make ideal rendezvous spots. For before-dinner cocktails, try the serene Matsu No Ma Lounge in Japan or the lively Rose & Crown Pub in the United Kingdom.

MEXICO: ***Cantina de San Angel*** — This outdoor cafe on the World Showcase Lagoon serves burritos and tostadas, frozen Margaritas, beer, coffee, and hot chocolate. ☕️ 🍸

NORWAY: ***Kringla Bakeri og Kafé*** — This pleasant cafe offers open-face sandwiches, pastries, and beer. Its shaded outdoor location is perfect for an afternoon or evening rest stop. ☕️ 🍸

GERMANY: ***Sommerfest*** — Cold German beers and wines, along with such traditional snacks as soft pretzels and bratwurst, are available at this outdoor cafe. ☕️ 🍸

Weinkeller — There's a wine-tasting bar in this lively shop. On a warm day, it is an ideal place to cool off while sampling the wines of Germany. No seating. 🍸

U.S.A.: ***Liberty Inn*** — Located next to the American Adventure, this large, light-filled counter-service restaurant serves all-American hamburgers, hot dogs, and fried chicken. ☕️ 🍸

JAPAN: *Matsu No Ma Lounge* — This serene second-floor cocktail lounge has an excellent view of the World Showcase and is a great place to cool off on a hot day. The full bar serves hot sake, Japanese beer, and cocktails, as well as sashimi, sushi, and green tea. ⊺

Yakitori House — This little counter-service restaurant, serving Japanese-style beef and chicken, is hidden on the left side of the Japanese pavilion behind the pagoda and a small shop. It has an indoor seating area and a restful outdoor seating area with umbrellas at the tables. 🍽⊺

FRANCE: *Boulangerie Pâtisserie* — This popular shop bakes its pastry on the premises and serves strong French-roast coffee that guests can enjoy at outdoor tables in a picturesque Parisian-style courtyard. The lines here are often impossibly long. 🍽

La Maison du Vin — Guests can sample and buy the fine wines of France in this handsome wine shop. No seating. ⊺

UNITED KINGDOM: *Rose & Crown Pub* — This busy public house, a beloved hangout of World Showcase veterans, has several fine ales on tap. Guests who order snacks or drinks at the bar can carry them to the outdoor terrace adjacent to the Rose & Crown Dining Room. 🍽⊺

✳

SERVICES

WORLDKEY INFORMATION SERVICE: This interactive information and restaurant-reservation system is headquartered at Innoventions East in Future World. Visitors should arrive early in the day to make restaurant reservations. There is also a WorldKey Information Service kiosk in front of the Germany pavilion for visitors entering through the International Gateway. The system's simple-to-use touch-screen computer terminals offer detailed information about all of Epcot, including schedules for the day's events and shows. By touching the words *Call Attendant,* visitors can speak directly to a Guest Relations representative to make restaurant reservations.

REST ROOMS: Public rest rooms are located at Norway, Germany, U.S.A., Morocco, the United Kingdom, the International Gateway, and at the Odyssey Center, just past the Mexico pavilion on the walkway to Future World. There are quieter, fairly deserted rest rooms at the Rose & Crown Pub (United Kingdom), Matsu No Ma Lounge (Japan), and San Angel Inn Restaurante (Mexico).

TELEPHONES: Public telephones are located at the International Gateway and near all the public rest rooms in the World Showcase. Telephones are also located near the rest rooms in the cooler, quieter restaurants in Mexico, Japan, and Morocco.

MESSAGE CENTER: The Message Center is located at Guest Relations in Innoventions East in Future World. The Message Center is on a network shared by the Magic Kingdom and Disney-MGM Studios. Here, visitors can leave and retrieve messages for one another and exchange messages with companions visiting elsewhere. Anyone can phone in a message by calling (407) 824-4321.

FILM AND TWO-HOUR EXPRESS DEVELOPING: Film is available in at least one shop in every pavilion. Drop-off points for two-hour express developing are at Mexico (Artesanías Mexicanas), U.S.A. (Heritage Manor Gifts), Canada (Northwest Mercantile), and the International Gateway (World Traveler). Developed pictures can be picked up in the Kodak Camera Center at Epcot's Entrance Plaza or delivered to any Walt Disney World resort.

CAMERA RENTAL: Video camcorders, replacement batteries, and 35mm cameras are sold and rented in the World Traveler at the International Gateway and in the Kodak Camera Center at Epcot's Entrance Plaza. Replacement batteries for video cameras are also available at Die Weinachts Ecke in Germany. Rented equipment may be returned to a Kodak Camera Center in any major theme park.

MAIL DROPS: Mail drops are located at the following pavilions: Mexico, China, Germany, U.S.A., and the United Kingdom. A postage stamp machine is located near the lockers at Epcot's Entrance Plaza.

BANKING: There is an automated teller machine (ATM) outside Epcot's Main Gate, near Showcase Plaza, and at the WorldKey Information Service kiosk near Germany. There is an American Express cash machine outside Epcot's Main Gate, near the Guest Relations window. Personal checks up to about $25 can be cashed at Guest Relations in Innoventions East at Future World.

LOCKERS: There are lockers at the International Gateway; near the Kodak Camera Center at Epcot's Entrance Plaza; and at the Bus Information Center, just outside Epcot's Entrance Plaza.

PACKAGE PICKUP: Visitors can forward purchases free of charge to Showcase Gifts at the International Gateway or to the Gift Stop, outside of Epcot's Main Gate, and pick them up as they leave the park. Allow two to three hours between purchase and pickup. Guests staying at a Walt Disney World resort can have packages delivered to their hotel.

FIRST AID: The first-aid office is adjacent to the Odyssey Center, near the Mexico pavilion where Future World meets the World Showcase. Aspirin and other first-aid needs are dispensed free of charge. Over-the-counter medications are available at Disney Traders at Showcase Plaza. They are not on display and must be requested at the counter.

VISITORS WITH DISABILITIES: A complimentary guidebook for guests with disabilities is available at Guest Relations in Innoventions East in Future World. All attractions in the World Showcase have wheelchair access; however, visitors must leave their wheelchairs to ride Maelstrom in Norway.

WHEELCHAIR RENTALS: Wheelchairs can be rented at the International Gateway; outside of Epcot's Main Gate at the Gift Stop; and inside Epcot's Entrance Plaza in Future World. Electric Convenience Vehicles can be rented at Epcot's Entrance Plaza on a first-come, first-served basis. Replacement batteries, if needed, will be brought to your vehicle if you alert a Cast Member.

VISITORS WITH HEARING IMPAIRMENTS: A written text of Epcot's attractions is available at Guest Relations in Innoventions East in Future World. Assistive listening devices for some Epcot attractions are also available there. A telecommunications device for the deaf (TDD) is available in The AT&T Global Neighborhood behind Spaceship Earth. Hearing aid–compatible and amplified telephones are located throughout Epcot.

VISITORS WITH SIGHT IMPAIRMENTS: Tape players, touring cassettes that describe the park, and guidebooks in Braille are available at Guest Relations in Innoventions East in Future World.

FOREIGN LANGUAGE ASSISTANCE: Epcot maps are available in Spanish, French, Portuguese, German, and Japanese. Personal translator units (PTUs) that offer French, Spanish, and German translations of some of the Epcot attractions and presentations are available at Guest Relations in Innoventions East at Future World. The Walt Disney World Foreign Language Center can answer questions, help with travel arrangements, and offer assistance in a number of languages to visitors who call between between 8:30 AM and 9 PM (407 824-7900).

ATTRACTIONS

ATTRACTIONS

Half-Day Tours at the World Showcase

The afternoon and evening tours are designed to let visitors sample the best of the World Showcase in four to five hours, including lunch or dinner in one of the World Showcase restaurants. The Around-the-World in a Day Tour, below, is most pleasant in milder temperatures (October through March). The World Showcase at Night tour can be used year-round. You may not have time to see everything listed in the tours, but you will have a quality experience if you follow these guidelines: ❶ Never pass up an attraction if you can walk right in without a line. ❷ Do not wait in lines longer than fifteen minutes *unless* it is for an attraction you know you will enjoy. ❸ Don't hurry through the pavilions just to see them all. Forget about schedules, let yourself become distracted, indulge your interests, let the magic find you.

AROUND-THE-WORLD IN A DAY TOUR

Four to five hours — October through March — including lunch.
Well in advance of this tour, reserve a late lunch at 1 PM or later at a World Showcase restaurant.
If you do not have reservations on the day of your tour, call Same Day Reservations after 10 AM (939-3463).

⬇ Arrive at Epcot's Entrance Plaza or at the International Gateway at about 11 AM. Pick up an entertainment schedule, and check the special events occurring in the pavilions. You can base your tour on events that interest you, or surrender to the sights and sounds that grab your attention.

⬇ Proceed to the World Showcase promenade. If you do not have a lunch reservation or you prefer a light meal, plan to eat at a self-service restaurant such as Kringla Bakeri og Kafé in Norway or Tempura Kiku in Japan. Most of the international pavilions have a casual counter-service cafe.

⬇ Start your tour of the international pavilions in either direction, depending on your lunch destination and any special events you wish to see. It can take several hours to circle the lagoon while sightseeing. As you visit the pavilions, take in some of the following highlights that interest you:

- ◆ **Mexico** — live music, shops, and EL RIO DEL TIEMPO
- ◆ **Norway** — shops and MAELSTROM
- ◆ **China** — WONDERS OF CHINA film presentation, live acrobatic performances, architecture, gardens, and shops
- ◆ **Germany** — railroad garden, live music, shops, and wine tasting at Weinkeller
- ◆ **Italy** — architecture and live music, theater, or other street entertainment
- ◆ **U.S.A.** — crafts exhibits, VOICES OF LIBERTY and THE AMERICAN ADVENTURE, and if there is a show and time permits, the AMERICA GARDENS THEATRE
- ◆ **Japan** — gardens, shops, and street entertainment
- ◆ **Morocco** — shops, architecture, and courtyard musicians
- ◆ **France** — IMPRESSIONS DE FRANCE film presentation, shops, and street entertainment
- ◆ **United Kingdom** — shops, street theater, and Rose & Crown Pub for refreshments
- ◆ **Canada** — Victoria Gardens and O CANADA! film presentation

⬇ Pause your tour in time to arrive at your lunch destination about ten minutes early.

⬇ After lunch, continue your tour of the World Showcase until you're back where you began. ◆

THE WORLD SHOWCASE AT NIGHT TOUR

Four to five hours — year-round — including dinner.
Make a dinner reservation well in advance of this tour at one of the World Showcase restaurants.
If you do not have reservations on the day of your tour, call Same Day Reservations after 10 AM (939-3463).
If you prefer an early dinner, reserve a table at 6 PM or before.
If you prefer a late dinner, reserve about ninety minutes before IllumiNations begins (usually at 9 PM).
If you've seen IllumiNations and would like to experience the World Showcase late in the evening
after the crowds have all gone, make the latest possible dinner reservation.

- Arrive at the World Showcase after 4 PM. Pick up an entertainment schedule, which lists the show times for live performances and IllumiNations.

- If you're having an early dinner, start your tour in the direction closest to the pavilion where you will be dining. If you have a late dinner reservation, walk in the opposite direction. If you do not have a reservation or prefer a light meal, plan to eat at a counter-service cafe, such as Yakitori House in Japan, Cantina de San Angel in Mexico, or Kringla Bakeri og Kafé in Norway. (You can also try to be seated in the restaurant of your choice without a reservation. Seating is sometimes available at Restaurant Marrakesh in Morocco, Biergarten in Germany, and Nine Dragons in China.)

- Take your time as you tour the international pavilions. It can take several hours to circle the World Showcase Lagoon and visit the attractions, and as night falls, the lighting is charming. Watch for special entertainment events and take in some of the following highlights that interest you:

  - **Mexico** — live music, shops, and EL RIO DEL TIEMPO
  - **Norway** — shops and MAELSTROM
  - **China** — live acrobatic performances, shops, and WONDERS OF CHINA film presentation
  - **Germany** — railroad garden, street entertainment, shops, and wine tasting at Weinkeller
  - **Italy** — architecture, shops, and live music, theater, or other street entertainment
  - **U.S.A.** — THE AMERICAN ADVENTURE and, if there is a performance scheduled and time permits, the AMERICA GARDENS THEATRE
  - **Japan** — art exhibit, shops, and refreshments at the Matsu No Ma Lounge
  - **Morocco** — shops, architecture, courtyard musicians, and street entertainment
  - **France** — IMPRESSIONS DE FRANCE film presentation, shops, and street artists
  - **United Kingdom** — shops, street entertainment, and Rose & Crown Pub for refreshments
  - **Canada** — Victoria Gardens (if daylight) and O CANADA! film presentation.

- One-half hour before ILLUMINATIONS is scheduled to begin, find a viewing spot at the edge of the World Showcase Lagoon. The following locations offer some of the best views:

  - Along the promenade near Mexico or Norway
  - Along the promenade near Canada or the United Kingdom
  - From the bridges or the parks between the United Kingdom and France.

- After IllumiNations (or your late dinner), you may want to let the crowds rush out while you linger and stroll along the World Showcase promenade to see the international pavilions tranquil, empty, and romantically lit. You'll hear the theme of each country's music as you walk past. ◆

ATTRACTIONS

ATTRACTIONS

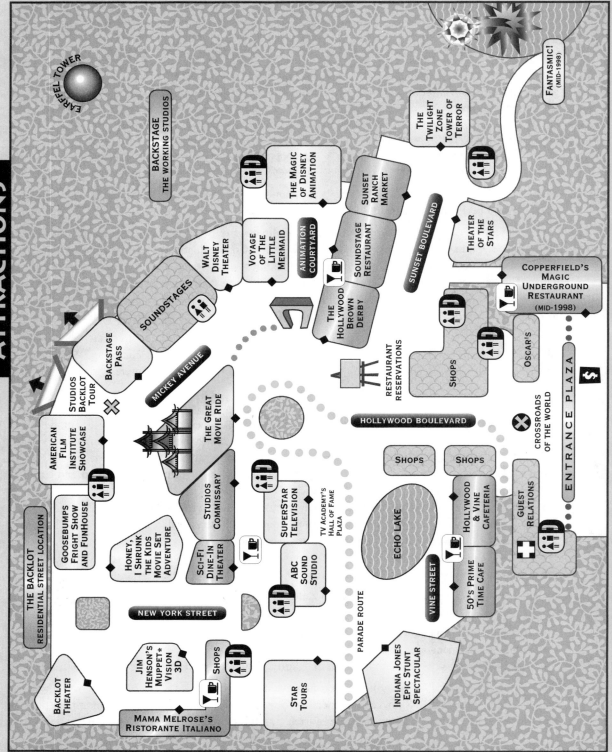

EARFFEL TOWER

BACKSTAGE
THE WORKING STUDIOS

FANTASMIC!
(MID-1998)

THE MAGIC OF DISNEY ANIMATION

THE TWILIGHT ZONE TOWER OF TERROR

SUNSET RANCH MARKET

ANIMATION COURTYARD

SUNSET BOULEVARD

THEATER OF THE STARS

VOYAGE OF THE LITTLE MERMAID

WALT DISNEY THEATER

SOUNDSTAGE RESTAURANT

THE HOLLYWOOD BROWN DERBY

COPPERFIELD'S MAGIC UNDERGROUND RESTAURANT
(MID-1998)

SOUNDSTAGES

BACKSTAGE PASS

STUDIOS BACKLOT TOUR

MICKEY AVENUE

RESTAURANT RESERVATIONS

SHOPS

OSCAR'S

ENTRANCE PLAZA

THE GREAT MOVIE RIDE

AMERICAN FILM INSTITUTE SHOWCASE

HOLLYWOOD BOULEVARD

CROSSROADS OF THE WORLD

GOOSEBUMPS FRIGHT SHOW AND FUNHOUSE

STUDIOS COMMISSARY

SUPERSTAR TELEVISION

SHOPS

SHOPS

THE BACKLOT
RESIDENTIAL STREET LOCATION

HONEY, I SHRUNK THE KIDS MOVIE SET ADVENTURE

SCI-FI DINE-IN THEATER

ABC SOUND STUDIO

TV ACADEMY'S HALL OF FAME PLAZA

ECHO LAKE

HOLLYWOOD & VINE CAFETERIA

GUEST RELATIONS

NEW YORK STREET

PARADE ROUTE

VINE STREET

50'S PRIME TIME CAFE

BACKLOT THEATER

JIM HENSON'S MUPPET* VISION 3D

SHOPS

STAR TOURS

INDIANA JONES EPIC STUNT SPECTACULAR

MAMA MELROSE'S RISTORANTE ITALIANO

DISNEY-MGM STUDIOS

Disney-MGM Studios offers visitors two distinct movie-making experiences: On one hand, it offers the aura and ambience of Hollywood's most glamorous era, and entertains visitors with rides, tours, live performances, restaurants, and shops that reflect the exciting world of television and motion picture entertainment. On the other hand, it provides a glimpse into the nuts and bolts of film and television production, and gives visitors access to Disney's working studios with tours that explore sound, animation, special effects, and editing. Disney-MGM Studios is the most dynamic of the major theme parks, as it continues to expand in many directions simultaneously. Because it is a working studio, it is also the creative center of Walt Disney World. The park is approaching its ten-year anniversary in 1999, and it is being groomed with major enhancements for the event. You may not hear as much about it, but many of the most exciting plans and projects on Disney's drawing board are slated to happen here.

WHEN TO GO: The best times to visit are early in the morning when the park opens, and after 3 PM. On weekdays, television shows and movies are often in production on the soundstages. Visitors who would like to view a film production or join a television show audience (or even appear as guests) should check at Guest Relations, just inside the park entrance. Tickets are available on a first-come, first-served basis; call 407 560-4651 for show times and information. Disney-MGM Studios generally closes earlier than the other major theme parks, except on nights that fireworks shows are scheduled. After Fantasmic! debuts in fall 1998, the park will stay open late every night, year-round. Opening, closing, and event times vary; call Disney Information (407 824-4321) for details. As you enter the park, be sure to pick up an entertainment schedule at the Crossroads of the World kiosk. Check the Guest Information Board, located at the junction of Hollywood and Sunset Boulevards, which lists attraction wait times and special events. Restaurant reservations can also be made there.

HOW TO GET THERE: The parking lot at Disney-MGM Studios is free to guests staying at a Walt Disney World resort (other visitors are charged about $6). The parking lot is serviced by trams. Buses travel between Disney-MGM Studios, Epcot, Downtown Disney, the Transportation and Ticket Center (TTC), and most Walt Disney World resorts. Water launches service the following resorts: Dolphin, Swan, BoardWalk, Yacht Club, and Beach Club.

ATTRACTIONS

★★★★ DON'T MISS IT!   ★★★ GOOD ENTERTAINMENT   ★★ MILDLY AMUSING   ★ OF LIMITED APPEAL

ENJOYED MOST BY:

A ADULTS   T TEENS   C CHILDREN   Y THE YOUNG AT HEART

EMOTIONAL AGE GROUPS • SEE PAGE 21

THE GREAT MOVIE RIDE ★★★★ A T Tucked into the Chinese Theater, this ride takes visitors on a multimedia journey through the history of the movies. Movie props and costumes are on display in the lobby, including a carousel horse from *Mary Poppins* and one of the three pairs of ruby slippers made for *The Wizard of Oz*. Visitors ride a large tram past spectacular sets featuring live talent, Audio-Animatronics figures, and convincing special effects that re-create detailed scenes from

ATTRACTIONS

such popular films as *The Wizard of Oz, Public Enemy, Alien,* and *Raiders of the Lost Ark.* The ride ends with a grand finale of clips from Academy Award–winning films. Duration: 20 minutes.

SUPERSTAR TELEVISION ★★★ A T Y Television visual effects are explored in this audience-participation attraction. Volunteers are selected during the preshow to act as stand-ins. They perform on the set against a special blue backdrop that allows a professional video editor to "key" them into scenes from popular ABC television shows. In the often hilarious finished product, shown on overhead monitors, the volunteers appear to be part of the show. Duration: 30 minutes.

ABC SOUND STUDIO ★★★ A T C Sound effects — the work of film crew members known as Foley artists — are the focus in this attraction. Volunteers are selected to create sound and special audio effects for a short animated film. A cartoon is shown without sound, and it's up the novice "sound technicians" to lay down a sound track on cue, in order to bring out its dramatic and humorous moments. The finished product is both informative and amusing, mistakes and all. The show engages the younger set, who will recognize the cartoon characters from ABC television, but the clever demonstration involves all ages in humorous hands-on hijinks. Duration: 15 minutes.

STAR TOURS ★★★★ A T *Star Wars* robots R2D2 and C3PO are employees of a travel agency booking visitors on a brief intergalatic tour. With special effects and spectacular imagery, visitors are hurtled through space at the speed of light in a ship run amok in this humorous scenario, nearly colliding with a giant ice crystal and caught in the crossfire of laser-wielding fighter ships. The spacecraft, which is actually a modified flight simulator, tilts and rocks dramatically during the show, which is not for those prone to motion sickness. *Plans are underway for a new story line, also based on new scenes from the expanded* Star Wars *film series.* Duration: 6 minutes.

GOOSEBUMPS HORRORLAND FRIGHT SHOW AND FUNHOUSE ★★★ T C Y Based on the best-selling thriller series for kids, Goosebumps is both a show and an attraction. A ragged sideshow of creepy characters that looks like it blew in overnight is staged five times daily from a deserted loading dock on New York Street. Meanwhile, visitors who venture inside the HorrorLand FunHouse find themselves in a dizzying maze of mirrors amid scary props and eerie effects.

JIM HENSON'S MUPPET*VISION 3D ★★★★ A T C This brilliantly conceived multimedia attraction is a favorite among Disney theme park fans. Visitors wear special glasses as they watch the escapades at Muppet Labs when Waldo, a new character symbolizing 3-D, is unleashed. Combining an amusing 3-D film with live Muppets, pyrotechnics, and a number of other special effects designed to evoke a you-are-there feeling, this attraction appeals to both young people and adults. *This attraction may be replaced in the near future; one plan in the works is a virtual reality experience based on the flying carpet ride in the animated film* Aladdin. Duration: 25 minutes.

HONEY, I SHRUNK THE KIDS MOVIE SET ADVENTURE ★ C This elaborate playground, based on the film *Honey, I Shrunk the Kids,* resembles a gigantic backyard filled with huge blades of grass and monstrously large ants. While the oversized props are interesting because of their scale, this playground was really designed for the children who pack the place. No time limit.

THE WALT DISNEY THEATER ★★ A This theater presents the behind-the-scenes view of the most recent Disney movies and how they were made. The films are filled with fascinating details and the air-conditioned theater is a nice break on a hot day, but you may want to skip it if the lines are long. Shows change periodically with new Disney releases. Duration: Approximately 25 minutes.

VOYAGE OF THE LITTLE MERMAID ★★★ A C Y This charming attraction features scenes from the Disney movie *The Little Mermaid*. Special effects simulate rippling water overhead to evoke a sense of being under the sea. Visitors unfamiliar with the movie may wish to simply enjoy the lively music and performances by colorful, cheerful denizens of the sea. On hot days, it's an ideal place to sit down and cool off — in fact, the audience is misted occasionally, in keeping with the watery theme. Shows are scheduled continuously. Duration: 15 minutes.

THE TWILIGHT ZONE TOWER OF TERROR ★★★★ A T Visitors pass through the lobby of the abandoned, lightning-seared Hollywood Tower Hotel and enter the hotel library, where Rod Serling tells the tale of guests who mysteriously vanished from the elevator during a storm long ago. Beyond the library, the next stop is.... the boiler room. Here, visitors are loaded onto a battered freight elevator, and travel upward into the abandoned hotel. At one stop, they catch a glimpse of the missing guests; at another, the whole car moves forward into an elevator shaft from "another dimension." The doors open briefly to a view high above the park before the elevator suddenly plunges, then reascends for another drop. The drop and ascent sequence is programmable, so the ride differs from time to time. Cutting-edge special effects and the programmable design make this a not-to-be-missed attraction. The thrill can be taxing, however, and health restrictions apply. Duration: 10 minutes.

✳

LIVE SHOWS AND SPECIAL EVENTS

Live entertainment, celebrity appearances, and extemporaneous happenings occur daily throughout Disney-MGM Studios. Along the boulevards, visitors encounter zany Hollywood characters who involve them in Hollywood-related antics and altercations. Check the entertainment schedule for events and show times.

INDIANA JONES EPIC STUNT SPECTACULAR ★★★ A T C This live-action show dramatically demonstrates the work of stunt designers and performers. Several audience members are preselected to act as "extras." Professional stunt performers reenact familiar scenes from the Indiana Jones movies, falling from buildings and dodging threatening boulders, fiery explosions, and out-of-control trucks. The fascinating explanation of the secrets behind the stunts does not reduce their excitement or sense of realism. For the best view, arrive at least twenty minutes early and find a seat in the upper center. Shows are scheduled continuously throughout the day. Duration: 30 minutes.

THEATER OF THE STARS ★★★★ A C Y This shaded outdoor amphitheater on Sunset Boulevard is reminiscent of the famed Hollywood Bowl. Here, talented singers and dancers, top-flight choreography and stage direction, elaborate sets, and imaginative costumes combine to create memorable productions. The shows are generally based on popular Disney animated films, and they change periodically. Performances are scheduled throughout the day. Duration: Approximately 20 minutes.

BACKLOT THEATER ★★★ A C Y This outdoor theater presents live shows based on recent Disney films. The productions feature singing and dancing performers, elaborate costumes, distinctive sets, and special effects, which enhance the story line and charm both adults and children. Recent productions include *The Hunchback of Notre Dame,* and shows generally reflect the latest Disney releases, such as *Legend of Mulan.* In warm months, the early shows and those at the end of the day are the best ones to catch, since the Backlot Theater can become uncomfortably hot at midday. Duration: Approximately 35 minutes.

FEATURE PARADE ★★★ Ⓒ Ⓨ Disney-MGM Studios parades are unique extravaganzas employing ornately designed floats, giant figures, live performers, elaborate costumes, and music, sound, and unexpected special effects. The parades change from time to time to reflect the theme of recently released Disney films, such as the Hercules "Zero to Hero" Victory Parade. They are held twice in the summer, at about 11:30 AM and 3:30 PM, and once daily, at about 1 PM, during the rest of the year. The parade route is less crowded near Star Tours. Duration: Approximately 15 minutes.

SORCERY IN THE SKY ★★★ Ⓐ Ⓣ Ⓒ On nights when the park is open late, visitors can see the Sorcery in the Sky fireworks show, which takes its theme from Mickey Mouse's role as the sorcerer's apprentice in *Fantasia*. The pyrotechnics light the sky with multicolored bursts and fountains of glittering sparks, and leave visitors cheering for more. The best viewing spot is at the intersection of Hollywood and Sunset Boulevards. Duration: Approximately 10 minutes. *In the Fall (1998), this long-running fireworks show will be replaced by Fantasmic!*

FANTASMIC! ★★★★ Ⓐ Ⓣ Ⓒ Evolving out of the sensational nighttime attraction of the same name at California's Disneyland, this multimedia event takes place in its own seven-thousand-seat amphitheater every night beginning in fall 1998. The amphitheater, which provides standing room for another three thousand guests, is the largest at any Disney theme park. It hugs the shore of a man-made lagoon, which encircles a forty-foot mountain where much of the drama unfolds. The story is a monumental mythology of the eternal struggle between good and evil that takes place in the dreams and fantasies of a serious-minded mouse: Mickey Mouse, to be exact. The show mixes projected animations, live performers, enchanting music from Disney classics, and spectacular effects including fireworks, jet fountains, water screens, lasers, dense fog, soaring flames, and the largest Audio Animatronics villain ever created. The show closes on a festive note as good prevails and the Steamboat Willie Riverboat emerges from behind the island, sailing past with all the Disney Characters onboard. Be prepared to be dazzled. The above ratings are based on Disneyland's Fantasmic! There are two shows every night. Duration: Approximately 25 minutes.

TOURS

STUDIOS BACKLOT TOUR ★★★ Ⓐ Ⓣ Ⓒ This tour presents an overview of movie making, and begins at a special-effects water tank for a demonstration of how sea battles and storm sequences are created. Visitors then board trams and head off for a truly informative behind-the-scenes look at motion picture production while riding past costume and scenery shops, warehouses filled with props, and Residential Street sets that are used as backdrops in television shows. The tour highlight has long been Catastrophe Canyon, where visitors feel the searing heat from an exploding tanker truck and, if sitting on the left side, are splashed by the waters of a flash flood. *There are plans to change the tour's thrill scene; one concept among those on the drawing board is based on* Journey to the Center of the Earth. Tours are continuous. Duration: 35 minutes.

BACKSTAGE PASS ★★ Ⓐ Ⓣ This walking tour presents a more in-depth view of motion picture production than the Backlot Tour. The tour's theme is generally based on a recent Disney live-action production. For example, it may begin with a look at props and special effects, such as a visit to Jim Henson's Creature Shop where many of the animal puppets from *101 Dalmatians* were created. On the soundstages, visitors may see an actual production, if a film is being shot that day. One soundstage may hold an entire set used for filming a recent Disney movie. The tour presents very little opportunity to sit down and relies heavily on overhead videos for explanatory narration. It is much more interesting when there is a production underway on the soundstages, so before signing up, check at Guest Relations. Tours are continuous. Duration: Approximately 25 minutes.

THE MAGIC OF DISNEY ANIMATION ★★★ A Y After leaving the waiting area, which has displays of classic and current animation cels, visitors enter a theater for a highly entertaining and informative film about animation starring Robin Williams and Walter Cronkite, and then tour Disney's working animation studio, where artists create future animated features. The various activities going on are explained on overhead monitors. Tours are continuous. Duration: Approximately 30 minutes.

SPECIAL INTEREST TOUR: *Inside Animation* ★★★ A T This popular tour offers a behind-the-scenes look inside the animation studios where Disney features are actually made. Visitors learn how to create animation cels, and even paint a Mickey Mouse cel of their own. Tours depart at 9:30 AM from the Bus Information Building outside the studio's turnstiles usually on Tuesdays and Thursdays. Reservations are required and should be made six weeks in advance through WDW Tours (407 939-8687). For visitors sixteen years old and older; tour cost is about $45. Duration: 2½ hours.

✳ FULL-SERVICE RESTAURANTS

Any visitor can make restaurant reservations up to sixty days in advance. Same-day reservations can be made at Hollywood Junction, located at the intersection of Hollywood and Sunset Boulevards, or at the restaurant itself. Smoking is not permitted. See "Restaurants," page 157, for reviews and reservation information.

THE HOLLYWOOD BROWN DERBY: Caricatures of famous personalities line the walls of this elegant, bustling restaurant. Steaks, seafood, pasta, and salads, including the house specialty, Cobb salad, are featured, along with a selection of specialty desserts. Beer, wine, and spirits are served, as are espresso and cappuccino. Open for lunch and dinner; reservations necessary.

SOUNDSTAGE RESTAURANT: Character Buffets are served in this restaurant resembling a busy, working production studio, with props and sets from recent Disney films. There are separate buffet bars for salads, hot entrees, and desserts. Beer, wine, and spirits are served. Open for breakfast and lunch; reservations necessary. (See "Dining Events," page 207.)

SCI-FI DINE-IN THEATER: Under a twinkling night sky, rows of booths shaped like vintage convertibles create a drive-in movie setting, complete with car-side speakers and a big screen showing classic science fiction and horror film clips. This is a popular restaurant for families with young children. Burgers and specialty dishes such as The Towering Terror — half a smoked chicken with citrus barbecue sauce — are the order of the day. Beer and wine are served. Open for lunch and dinner; reservations necessary.

50'S PRIME TIME CAFE: Decorated with fifties-style kitchens and dinette tables, this entertaining restaurant airs sitcoms of the period on black and white televisions, and serves such delectables as Uncle Giovanni's Pasta and Granny's Pot Roast. Soda fountain treats are also featured. Beer, wine, and spirits are available. Open for lunch and dinner; reservations necessary.

ATTRACTIONS

HOLLYWOOD & VINE CAFETERIA: Located on Vine Street, next door to the 50's Prime Time Cafe, this cafeteria-style restaurant is designed in a chromium blend of Art Deco and Diner Classic. Featured entrees include barbecued ribs, chicken, and a variety of salads. Beer and wine are available. Open for breakfast and lunch (and seasonally for dinner); no reservations.

MAMA MELROSE'S RISTORANTE ITALIANO: Loud good humor and basil-flavored olive oil for dipping bread into create a trattoria ambience in this restaurant, which features Italian cuisine and thin-crust pizzas baked in brick ovens. Beer, wine, and spirits are served, as are espresso and cappuccino. Open for lunch and dinner; reservations necessary.

COPPERFIELD'S MAGIC UNDERGROUND: Here's an opportunity to dine in a magician's workshop surrounded by props and tricks of the trade. Guests are immersed in interactive magic and illusions as they dine on pasta, steaks, satay, and pizza and other eclectic entrees. Beer, wine and spirits are served, as are espresso and cappuccino. Open for lunch and dinner; reservations necessary. The restaurant is accessible from both inside and outside the park. Opening mid-1998.

CAFES AND LOUNGES

Refreshment stands that serve snacks and fast food all day are located throughout Disney-MGM Studios. Those listed below are especially pleasant and make ideal rendezvous spots. For before-dinner cocktails, try The Catwalk Bar or the lively and surreal Tune In Lounge.

SUNSET RANCH MARKET: This pleasant outdoor food court on Sunset Boulevard is designed as a farmer's market, with umbrella-shaded tables, a tiny victory garden, and a small stage for special performances and events. Fruit, snacks, specialty hot dogs, and frozen yogurt treats are available here, as are coffee, beer, and wine coolers. 🍺Y

THE CATWALK BAR: Filled with props, lights, and production equipment, this pleasant, secluded bar is in the scaffolding above the Soundstage Restaurant and serves a limited selection of appetizers. Fine California wines, beer, and spirits are available, as are espresso and cappuccino. 🍺Y

TUNE IN LOUNGE: Located next to the 50's Prime Time Cafe, this bar serves up beer, wine, and spirits, along with appetizers and sitcoms, in a classic fifties environment complete with black and white TVs and Naugahyde couches. 🍺Y

STUDIOS COMMISSARY: Located next to the Chinese Theater, this large counter-service eatery has a streamlined contemporary decor and a display of Emmy awards earned by Disney productions. Snacks and fast food, including cold sandwiches, are served here, as are beer and coffee. 🍺Y

SERVICES

REST ROOMS: Public rest rooms are located throughout Disney-MGM Studios. The rest rooms at the foot of Sunset Boulevard, between the Theater of the Stars and The Twilight Zone Tower of Terror, are rarely crowded. Visitors can also find cool and quiet rest rooms at the Studios Commissary, the Tune In Lounge, The Hollywood Brown Derby, and The Catwalk Bar.

TELEPHONES: Public telephones are located throughout Disney-MGM Studios. The most secluded outdoor phones are those near the first-aid office at the Entrance Plaza and those by the rest rooms near The Twilight Zone Tower of Terror. The phones near the rest rooms at Mama Melrose's Ristorante Italiano and the Studios Commissary are not only quiet, but air-conditioned.

MESSAGE CENTER: The Message Center is located in Guest Relations at the Entrance Plaza. The Message Center is on a computer network also shared by Epcot and the Magic Kingdom. Here, visitors can leave and retrieve messages for one another and exchange messages with companions visiting elsewhere. Anyone can phone in a message by calling (407) 824-4321.

PACKAGE PICKUP: Visitors can forward purchases free of charge to the Package Pickup window, located at the Entrance Plaza, and pick them up as they leave the park. Guests staying at a Walt Disney World resort may have packages delivered to their hotel.

FILM AND TWO-HOUR EXPRESS DEVELOPING: Film is available at most Disney-MGM Studios shops. Drop-off points for express developing are at the Darkroom, on Hollywood Boulevard, and at the Disney Studio Store, next to Voyage of The Little Mermaid. Developed film may be picked up at the Darkroom or delivered to any WDW resort. The Darkroom also offers one-hour developing.

CAMERA RENTAL: Video camcorders and replacement batteries are available at the Darkroom on Hollywood Boulevard. Rented cameras can be returned to the Kodak Camera Center in any theme park.

MAIL DROPS: Mail can be dropped in the antique mailbox on Hollywood Boulevard near the Darkroom, and at the Guest Relations counter. There is a stamp machine next to Oscar's Classic Car Souvenirs.

BANKING: There is an automated teller machine (ATM) outside the turnstiles to the Entrance Plaza. Personal checks up to about $25 can be cashed at Guest Relations, located inside the Entrance Plaza.

LOCKERS: Lockers are located at Oscar's Classic Car Souvenirs at the Entrance Plaza. Larger luggage lockers are located at the Bus Information Building, outside the turnstiles.

FIRST AID: The first-aid office is at Disney-MGM Studios' Entrance Plaza, next to Guest Relations. Aspirin and other first aid is dispensed free of charge. Over-the-counter medications are available at Golden Age Souvenirs, near SuperStar Television. They must be requested at the counter.

VISITORS WITH DISABILITIES: A guidebook for guests with disabilities is available at Guest Relations, located at the Entrance Plaza. Most attractions at Disney-MGM Studios have wheelchair access; however, visitors must leave their wheelchairs to ride Star Tours and The Twilight Zone Tower of Terror.

WHEELCHAIR RENTALS: Wheelchairs can be rented at Oscar's Classic Car Souvenirs on Hollywood Boulevard, just inside the Main Gate. A limited number of Electric Convenience Vehicles are also available on a first-come, first-served basis, so get there early. Replacement batteries, if needed, will be brought to your vehicle if you alert a Cast Member.

VISITORS WITH HEARING IMPAIRMENTS: A written text of Disney-MGM Studios' attractions is available at Guest Relations, near the Entrance Plaza. Assistive listening devices are also available there for the Voyage of The Little Mermaid, ABC Sound Studio, Indiana Jones Epic Stunt Spectacular, Muppet*Vision 3D, Backlot Theater, Walt Disney Theater, SuperStar Television, The Magic of Disney Animation, Theater of the Stars, and the Sci-Fi Dine-In Theater Restaurant. A telecommunications device for the deaf (TDD) is also available at Guest Relations. Hearing aid–compatible and amplified telephones are available throughout the park.

ATTRACTIONS

VISITORS WITH SIGHT IMPAIRMENTS: Tape players and touring cassettes that describe the park are available at Guest Relations, located at Disney-MGM Studios' Entrance Plaza. A Braille map of the park is located on a pedestal in front of Guest Relations.

FOREIGN LANGUAGE ASSISTANCE: Park maps are available in Spanish, French, Portuguese, German, and Japanese at Guest Relations at Disney-MGM Studios' Entrance Plaza. The Walt Disney World Foreign Language Center can answer questions, help with travel arrangements, and offer assistance in a number of languages to visitors who call between between 8:30 AM and 9 PM (407 824-7900).

Half-Day Tours at Disney-MGM Studios

The morning and evening tours are designed to let visitors sample the best of Disney-MGM Studios in five to six hours, including a lunch or dinner in one of the park's restaurants. Both tours work during crowded park conditions; the evening tour is designed around Disney-MGM Studio's fireworks shows. You may not have time to visit every attraction listed on the tours, but you will have a quality experience if you follow these guidelines: ❶ Never pass up an attraction if you can walk right in without a line. ❷ Do not wait in lines longer than fifteen minutes *unless* it is for an attraction you know you will enjoy. ❸ Do not tour here on Early Entry days (usually Sunday and Wednesday) unless you are entering early to take advantage of that uncrowded ninety minutes. ❹ The attractions are great, but be aware that the theme park itself is an attraction, filled with unique characters and spontaneous entertainment that just might include you in an unforgettable magic moment. Be open to your surroundings.

MORNING IN MOVIELAND TOUR

Five to six hours — year-round — including lunch.
Well in advance of your tour, reserve a late lunch (1:30 PM) at one of the Disney-MGM Studios restaurants.

⬇ Arrive at Disney-MGM Studios' Entrance Plaza at least one half hour before the scheduled opening time. (The park usually opens one half hour before the announced opening time.)

⬇ When the park opens, pick up an entertainment schedule at the Crossroads of the World kiosk, then head over to Sunset Boulevard and walk to the end of the street to catch the one-of-a-kind thrill attraction, **THE TWILIGHT ZONE TOWER OF TERROR.**

⬇ Walk back to the intersection of Hollywood and Sunset boulevards. If you need a lunch reservation, stop at the restaurant desk to reserve lunch for 1:30 PM or later.

⬇ Head toward the Chinese Theater, just ahead, to begin your tour in a clockwise direction. Visit any of the following attractions that interest you in this order:

- ◆ **THE GREAT MOVIE RIDE**
- ◆ **STAR TOURS** (if you like thrill rides and are not prone to motion sickness)
- ◆ **JIM HENSON'S MUPPET*VISION 3D**
- ◆ **STUDIOS BACKLOT TOUR**
- ◆ **THE MAGIC OF DISNEY ANIMATION**
- ◆ **THE FEATURE PARADE** (when it is scheduled before lunch).

- Plan to arrive at your lunch destination ten minutes early.
- If you continue touring after lunch, take in some of the popular attractions you may have m
- **If the weather is hot, visit the indoor attractions:** THE WALT DISNEY THEATER ◆ VOYAGE OF THE LITTLE MERMAID ◆ SUPERSTAR TELEVISION ◆ ABC SOUND STUDIO.
- **If the weather is pleasant, visit some of the outdoor attractions:** INDIANA JONES EPIC STUNT SPECTACULAR ◆ BACKLOT THEATER ◆ THEATER OF THE STARS.

NIGHT OF THE STARS AFTERNOON AND EVENING TOUR

Five hours — year-round (on nights where there are fireworks shows) — including dinner.
Make dinner reservations well in advance of this tour.
Book a seating no later than ninety minutes before the fireworks show is scheduled to begin.
If you do not have reservations on the day of your tour, call Same Day Reservations (939-3463) at 10 AM.

- Arrive at Disney-MGM Studios' Entrance Plaza just after 3 PM, and pick up an entertainment schedule listing the show times for live performances and the Nighttime Fireworks or FANTASMIC!
- If there is a second performance of the FEATURE PARADE (scheduled for about 3:30 PM during peak seasons), either find a place to see it or quickly head down Sunset Boulevard to THE TWILIGHT ZONE TOWER OF TERROR. (Parade times can mark the shortest lines of the day here.)
- Stop at Hollywood Junction, at the intersection of Hollywood and Sunset Boulevards. If you need a dinner reservation, pick a time that lets you finish your meal before the fireworks begin.
- Study the Attractions Tip Board and note the wait times for rides listed below. Eliminate any with very long waits; you can pick them up later after the crowd thins out for dinner. Tour counterclockwise, visiting any of the following attractions that interest you. Your tour will be interrupted for dinner.
- **On Hot or Busy Afternoons:** ◆ THE MAGIC OF DISNEY ANIMATION ◆ VOYAGE OF THE LITTLE MERMAID ◆ THE WALT DISNEY THEATER ◆ THE GREAT MOVIE RIDE ◆ SUPERSTAR TELEVISION ◆ ABC SOUND STUDIO ◆ JIM HENSON'S MUPPET*VISION 3D ◆
- **In Mild Weather and Uncrowded Conditions:** ◆ THE GREAT MOVIE RIDE ◆ INDIANA JONES EPIC STUNT SPECTACULAR ◆ STAR TOURS ◆ JIM HENSON'S MUPPET*VISION 3D ◆ THE BACKLOT THEATER ◆ STUDIOS BACKLOT TOUR ◆ THEATER OF THE STARS ◆
- Pause in your tour in order to arrive at your dinner destination ten minutes early.
- After dinner, resume your tour. Now is the time to visit the attractions you haven't seen, especially ◆ STAR TOURS ◆ THE TWILIGHT ZONE TOWER OF TERROR ◆ THE GREAT MOVIE RIDE ◆
- If tonight's fireworks show is SORCERY IN THE SKY, about fifteen minutes before it is scheduled to begin, find a viewing spot anywhere near the intersection of Hollywood and Sunset Boulevards.
- If FANTASMIC! is showing, head over to the amphitheater at the end of Sunset Boulevard at least thirty minutes before it is scheduled to begin and find a place to sit down.
- After the show, you may wish to browse through the shops along Hollywood Boulevard (they stay open late) or find an empty bench and people-watch while the crowds rush out. ◆

ATTRACTIONS

ATTRACTIONS

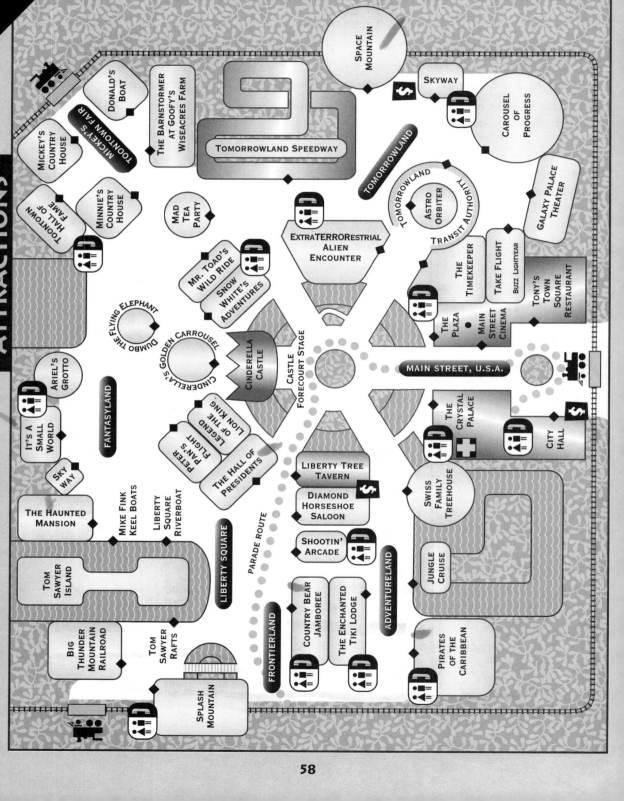

MAGIC KINGDOM

The Magic Kingdom, a replica of California's Disneyland, was the first theme park built at Walt Disney World more than a quarter-century ago. It covers about one hundred acres (nearly twenty more than Disneyland). The park opened with six theme lands: Main Street, U.S.A., Adventureland, Frontierland, Liberty Square, Fantasyland, and Tomorrowland, which was recently transformed into an imaginary "city of the future" based on visions from the past. A seventh theme land was added to the park in 1988, in honor of Mickey Mouse's sixtieth birthday. In 1996, it was completely redesigned for Walt Disney World's 25th Anniversary celebration. It is now called Mickey's Toontown Fair and is one place where visitors can be certain to meet Disney Characters. The Magic Kingdom attractions are similar to Disneyland's, but each park has several that are unique. While Sleeping Beauty Castle is the centerpiece at Disneyland, Cinderella Castle stands at the heart of the Magic Kingdom. The Magic Kingdom enchants children and triggers a delightful nostalgia in adults, especially avid Disney fans.

WHEN TO GO: The least crowded times of year to visit the Magic Kingdom is while schools are in session, and not during the summer months or holidays. Even during off-peak seasons, it's a good idea to arrive early in the morning, at least one half hour before the official opening time. Crowds also thin out after 4 PM, when parents are herding their exhausted children toward the exit. **There are no significant discounts on theme park admissions at any time of year (see "Admissions," page 9, and "Discount Travel Tips," page 17), but you can still make sure you get the best value for your vacation dollars. During off-peak seasons (fall through spring) the Magic Kingdom closes early on weekdays (unlike Epcot), so if you're spending only one day at the Magic Kingdom, be sure to go on a weekend, especially Saturday, when the park has the longest hours and the SpectroMagic parade and Fantasy in the Sky fireworks are offered.** Opening, closing, and event times vary throughout the year, so check ahead with Disney Information (407 824-4321).

HOW TO GET THERE: The vast Magic Kingdom parking lot is free to guests staying at any Walt Disney World resort (other visitors are charged about $6). The parking lot is serviced by trams that carry visitors to the Transportation and Ticket Center (TTC), the hub for all Walt Disney World transportation. Water launches and monorails transport visitors from the TTC to the park entrance. Water launches also service the Magic Kingdom from Discovery Island, River Country, and the following resorts: Fort Wilderness, Wilderness Lodge, Polynesian, and Grand Floridian. Sleek monorails that glide overhead on nearly fourteen miles of track connect the Magic Kingdom to the following resorts: Contemporary, Polynesian, and Grand Floridian. Monorails also run between the TTC and Epcot. Buses travel between the Magic Kingdom and all Walt Disney World resorts and theme parks, and drop passengers at the park entrance.

IN-PARK TRANSPORTATION: Several transportation options are available in each part of the Magic Kingdom. Visitors can travel down Main Street in horse-drawn trolleys, jitneys, bell-clanging fire trucks, colorful double-decker buses, and purring antique cars. Between Fantasyland and Tomorrowland, visitors can ride the Skyway, an aerial gondola that provides a sweeping view of the Magic Kingdom. The Walt Disney World Railroad, with authentic steam engine–powered trains, circles the park continuously and can be boarded from stations at Main Street, U.S.A., Frontierland, and Mickey's Toontown Fair.

ATTRACTIONS

★★★★	★★★	★★	★
DON'T MISS IT!	GOOD ENTERTAINMENT	MILDLY AMUSING	OF LIMITED APPEAL

ENJOYED MOST BY:

A ADULTS	T TEENS	C CHILDREN	Y THE YOUNG AT HEART

EMOTIONAL AGE GROUPS • SEE PAGE 21

MAIN STREET, U.S.A.: From its entryway beneath the train station to its view of Cinderella Castle in the distance, Main Street, U.S.A., is the first environment visitors encounter as they enter the Magic Kingdom. It is a picture-perfect turn-of-the-century town. Visitors can take care of banking needs in a traditional setting; drop by City Hall for entertainment schedules and restaurant reservations; browse through a wide variety of specialty shops (including The Chapeau, featuring the monogrammed mouse ears made famous by the Mouseketeers, and the Main Street Athletic Shop, offering sports-themed merchandise and apparel); peer into the old-time Harmony Barber Shop, where men can get haircuts (call 407 824-6550 for an appointment); and take a break to people-watch in the Town Square, a pleasant plaza with benches, shade, and periodic live musical entertainment.

CITY HALL INFORMATION CENTER: Maps, entertainment schedules, and other information are available at the podium in front of City Hall, and a helpful staff inside operates a Message Center for visitors and makes resort, guided tour, and restaurant reservations. City Hall is also a good rendezvous point for visitors traveling in groups.

MAIN STREET CINEMA ★★ A Y A recent presentation at this old-fashioned movie theater is *Mickey's Big Break,* which seamlessly mixes real-life footage with cartoon animation and features Mickey Mouse, Disney CEO Michael Eisner, and a host of big-screen stars. The theater is air-conditioned but has no seats. Films run continuously. Duration: Approximately 15 minutes.

WALT DISNEY WORLD RAILROAD, MAIN STREET STATION ★★ A C Four open-air trains, pulled by whistle-blowing steam-puffing engines, travel the Walt Disney World Railroad on a mile-and-a-half tour of the park. Fans of the Grand-Canyon-and-dinosaur diorama for which California's Disneyland is noted may be disappointed, since it is absent here, but this leisurely trip through the lush foliage lining the track, coupled with views of most of the theme lands, is still well worth the ride. Visitors can board and disembark at Main Street, as well as at Frontierland and Mickey's Toontown Fair. The trains run every four to seven minutes. Duration: Approximately 20 minutes for the entire circuit.

ADVENTURELAND: At the end of Main Street, off to the left, Adventureland welcomes visitors into a tropical fantasy that is a blend of Africa, the Caribbean, Asia, the South Seas, and a bit of New Orleans. The dense jungle foliage and the mysterious rustles, squawks, and cries create an exotic atmosphere. Some Adventureland attractions are scheduled for refurbishing and remodeling, and almost every day brings a change.

JUNGLE CRUISE ★★★ A C Y A lighthearted reminder of the Bogart-Hepburn classic film *The African Queen,* this boatride attraction takes visitors on a steamy adventure cruise down some of the world's great rivers — the Amazon, Congo, Nile, and Mekong — with a detour through the cavernous interior of a mysterious Asian temple. Guides deliver witty, pun-laced narrations about the rivers and their denizens, all the while protecting visitors from the clearly fake local hostiles and wild animals along the riverbank. Exotic jungle plants, cascading waterfalls, updated Audio-Animatronics figures, and amusing special effects all add up to a truly comic adventure. There are generally very long lines for this attraction; the shortest wait is just before the park closes. Duration: 9 minutes.

PIRATES OF THE CARIBBEAN ★★★★ A T C This attraction begins in the underground catacombs of a mysterious stone fortress, where visitors board boats for a ride through a coastal settlement under attack by a band of raucous, rum-sotted pirates. After floating through dimly lit passages with unexpected drops (some in complete darkness), visitors are treated to humorous vignettes of attacking ships with shots exploding overhead, buildings on fire, rooms heaped with treasure, and high-spirited drunken debauchery. The elaborate sets, rich costuming, and sophisticated Audio-Animatronics and special effects make this a must-see attraction. Duration: 9 minutes.

SWISS FAMILY TREEHOUSE ★ C Y This multilevel walkthrough attraction invites visitors to tour the home of the storybook shipwrecked family. Built into a giant replica of a banyan tree draped with real Spanish moss, this is the ultimate fantasy treehouse, complete with cozy bedrooms perched in the limbs to an intricate plumbing system that provides running water in every room! There are many stairs to climb and almost always lots of kids enthusiastically exploring the novel rustic abode. Duration: Approximately 15 to 20 minutes.

THE ENCHANTED TIKI LODGE ★★ Y In the newest version of this long-lived attraction, the familiar Audio-Animatronics cast of singing birds is joined by the feathered stars of recent Disney animated features, namely, Iago from *Aladdin,* and Zazu from *The Lion King*. With Iago and Zazu's 'help,' the bird show gets hip to modern times with an updated roster of sing-along tunes. Die-hard fans of this attraction can still count on the presence of a satisfying selection of groan-eliciting puns. Visitors may leave the show at any time through the exit at the far side of the theater. This was the first Disney attraction to use Audio-Animatronics figures, and the dimly lit lodge is always a pleasant place to relax and cool off on a hot day. Duration: 20 minutes.

FRONTIERLAND: Beyond Adventureland lies the rough-and-tumble American frontier of the nineteenth century, the world of Davy Crockett, Mark Twain, and the miners of the Gold Rush. Here, stone, clapboard, and split-log structures evoke the distinct frontiers of the East, the Midwest, and the Southwest. Two of the three Magic Kingdom roller-coaster thrill rides are located in Frontierland.

BIG THUNDER MOUNTAIN RAILROAD ★★★★ A T On this roller-coaster ride, visitors travel through a Gold Rush–era mountain mining town on what soon becomes a runaway train. The roller coaster relies on side-to-side, rather than up-and-down, motion, but it's fast nonetheless. Creative special effects and scenery, including crashing rocks, rushing waterfalls, flapping bats, braying donkeys, and a flooded mining town make for a lively experience. Many visitors consider this ride to be even more fun and enchanting at night. Duration: 4 minutes.

COUNTRY BEAR JAMBOREE ★★★ C Y Nearly two dozen Audio-Animatronics bears make for lively antics at this performance in Grizzly Hall. Henry, the show's emcee, introduces the bears, who tell tall tales, crack corny jokes, and perform musical numbers. Many of the show's players, including popular favorite Big Al, have been updated. The show and decor are changed throughout the year to reflect seasonal holidays. Duration: 15 minutes.

FRONTIERLAND SHOOTIN' ARCADE ★ **T** **C** This attraction puts an electronic spin on the traditional carnival shooting gallery. Using replica buffalo rifles (fitted with infrared beams instead of bullets), visitors shoot at frontier-motif targets in a Tombstone Territory setting. Through the magic of special effects, "hit" targets twist, howl, or trigger a secondary humorous effect. Don't spend too long aiming; there are no prizes and rifles are programmed to provide a specified number of either shots *or* minutes of service, whichever comes first. Kids flock to this arcade, which requires spending money in the form of small change. Duration: 25 shots for 50 cents.

SPLASH MOUNTAIN ★★★★ **A** **T** **C** The Disney classic, *Song of the South,* provides the theme of this water-chute roller coaster. Amid the antics of Brer Rabbit, Brer Fox, Brer Bear, and their friends, visitors are swept along in log boats on a half-mile journey through bayous, gardens, swamps, and caves. Sudden unexpected drops (some in complete darkness) and slow, lazy drifts alternately startle and lull visitors until they confront Brer Fox, in a quandary about throwing Brer Rabbit into the briar patch. From there, the ride goes downhill, literally, plunging almost five stories to splash into the giant briar patch below. The outstanding Audio-Animatronics and sets in this attraction, as well as the pacing and sound track, show Disney wizardry at its most creative. Expect to get fairly wet on the ride. As for visitors who have stopped to watch the action from the bridge above, every third ride vehicle splashes a cascade of water over the chute's edge to drench them. Souvenir photos of riders are snapped during the plunge. Duration: 12 minutes.

TOM SAWYER ISLAND ★★ **C** **Y** This attraction evokes the Missouri frontier of Mark Twain's famed character, and it appeals to youngsters with plenty of energy to burn. Ferried back and forth to the island on rafts, visitors can spelunk in a spooky cave, wobble across a barrel bridge, walk along mysterious winding paths, inspect a working windmill and waterwheel, and explore the Fort Sam Clemens stockade. The island is often filled with free-wheeling children, but in the late afternoon it can provide a pleasant and relaxing interlude. The island closes at sundown. No time limit.

WALT DISNEY WORLD RAILROAD, FRONTIERLAND STATION ★★ **A** **C** With its open boarding platform and large wooden water tank, this rustic Old West railroad station artfully creates the mood of nineteenth-century train travel. Of the three stops on the Walt Disney World Railroad, this one is the busiest. Duration: Approximately 20 minutes for the entire circuit.

LIBERTY SQUARE: Liberty Square re-creates a New England town at the time of the American Revolution. The buildings are accurate in architectural detail, right down to their leather-hinged shutters hanging slightly askew. A reproduction of the Liberty Bell, cast at the same foundry as the original, hangs in the square, and a huge one-hundred-year-old live oak nearby is hung with thirteen metal lanterns representing the light of freedom in each of the original colonies.

LIBERTY SQUARE RIVERBOAT ★★ **A** **Y** The brand-new *Liberty Belle,* a replica steam-powered stern-wheeler, actually rides on an underwater rail on a pleasant, sedate journey around Tom Sawyer Island. Sights en route include a burning cabin, Fort Sam Clemens, and pioneering props along the shore. The boat leaves on the hour and the half hour and there are often Disney Characters on all levels of the ship mingling with visitors. Duration: 20 minutes.

MIKE FINK KEEL BOATS ★ **T** **C** **Y** The small squat boats on this water ride evoke a backwoods journey. Like the Liberty Square Riverboat, the keelboats circle Tom Sawyer Island, gliding past various riverbank sights that tell the legends of the pioneers who settled the frontier. This attraction operates when the weather is warm and closes at sundown. Duration: 20 minutes.

THE HALL OF PRESIDENTS ★★★ A The show opens with a 70mm film (narrated by author Maya Angelou) showcasing the U.S. Constitution and selected historical events that shaped its amendments. As the film ends, a curtain rises to reveal an Audio-Animatronics representation of all forty-two U.S. Presidents in a startlingly lifelike tableau. Rustles fill the air when a roll call begins, and each figure responds to his name as the others nod, turn to look, or shift restlessly. Clinton checks his watch while Lincoln speaks and later gives a speech of his own, the show's first-ever by a living president. This attraction's tone is more serious than most at the Magic Kingdom, but its sophisticated Audio-Animatronics (plus the sit-down air-conditioned theater) make it worthwhile, especially for first-time visitors. Duration: 23 minutes.

THE HAUNTED MANSION ★★★★ A T C This eighteenth-century red-brick mansion, which creaks, groans, and moans with eerie sounds is Liberty Square's most popular attraction. Visitors pass by a town graveyard with wretchedly punned tombstone epitaphs, to be welcomed into the house by a creepy, supercilious butler and led into a waiting area decorated with some very unusual family portraits. Visitors then board ride vehicles that carry them off on a dark and spooky tour of the mansion. Ghosts dance, and rattles, rustles, and screams fill the air, while quirky humor permeates the ongoing narration. The many clever sets and props, and unusual visual effects make The Haunted Mansion a favorite attraction of many visitors. Duration: 9 minutes.

FANTASYLAND: A potpourri of carousel horses, colorful banners, wacky rides, and fairy-tale encounters, Fantasyland is the theme land that best reflects the young-at-heart side of Walt Disney's imagination. The appealing Alpine-village setting with its half-timbered buildings and festive tentlike structures spreads out behind Cinderella Castle, the Magic Kingdom's beautiful centerpiece. Although most of the attractions in Fantasyland are designed with children in mind, visitors of all ages will enjoy taking in the sights.

ARIEL'S GROTTO ★ C This walkthrough attraction is a fanciful re-creation of Ariel's underwater home from the Disney movie, *The Little Mermaid*. Brightly colored anemones and sea creatures perched on large rocks squirt visitors as they walk around on the padded surface, and Ariel herself makes frequent appearances inside a rocky cave. Duration: No time limit.

CINDERELLA'S GOLDEN CARROUSEL ★★ C Y Sparkling with mirrors, gilded decorations, painted scenes from the movie *Cinderella,* and beautifully detailed horses, this elegant merry-go-round is a true classic. Riders are carried back in time in leisurely, pleasant circles. No two horses are alike, and the carrousel is especially pretty and evocative at twilight. Duration: 2 minutes.

DUMBO THE FLYING ELEPHANT ★★ C In this fancifully detailed version of a kiddie carnival ride, visitors in sixteen big-eared Dumbo-shaped gondolas circle slowly with gentle lifts and drops around a golden crown. Adults can bypass this ride without missing anything special, but it is irresistible to the very young. Duration: 2 minutes.

IT'S A SMALL WORLD ★★★ Y Boats carry visitors on a whimsical water journey through a world populated by dolls representing children of every nationality. The moving dolls, dressed in elaborate folk costumes, sing the verses to "It's A Small World" in the language of the culture they represent. Although the tune is difficult to shake off, visitors seem to come away happy (or perhaps mesmerized by the repetitive expressions of the designers' good intentions). Long lines move quickly here (and during parades, you can walk right on). On a hot day, this ride can be a godsend — it's a long, relaxing air-conditioned respite. Duration: 11 minutes.

ATTRACTIONS

LEGEND OF THE LION KING ★★ C Y This stage show is based on the popular animated movie, *The Lion King*. Visitors meet a sleepy Rafiki (the baboon, played by a live performer) and are shown the *Circle of Life* movie short before entering a sit-down theater where selected scenes from the film are re-created with Rafiki, large puppets, special effects, and animation clips. Don't sit too close — the elevated stage can partially block views. Duration: about 30 minutes.

MAD TEA PARTY ★★ T C Y Inspired by *Alice in Wonderland,* this attraction features giant madly spinning pastel-painted teacups on a whirling ride that is not for the weak of stomach. The Mad Tea Party is really a fairly simple ride that has been dressed up Disney style. Children and teens are its greatest fans. Duration: 2 minutes.

MR. TOAD'S WILD RIDE ★★ C Y This wacky drive takes visitors through barn doors, chicken coops, a fireplace, and on a collision course with an oncoming train. Adults who expect the word *wild* to have a meaning other than "silly" will be disappointed, although Mr. Toad definitely has a lot of loyal fans. Duration: 3 minutes.

PETER PAN'S FLIGHT ★★★ C Y Set in Never-Never Land, this whimsical attraction takes visitors for a flight in miniature versions of Captain Hook's pirate ship. The ride starts high above the rooftops of London and dips down from time to time into settings that re-create scenes from *Peter Pan.* Although designed to amuse children, Peter Pan's Flight is surprisingly delightful and even leaves adults with a happy glow. Duration: 4 minutes.

SKYWAY TO TOMORROWLAND ★★ A T C An Alpine chalet houses this cable car ride to Tomorrowland. Open-air gondolas give visitors a spectacular bird's-eye view of the Magic Kingdom. Each car holds only a few people and no specific scenario demands attention, so visitors who are comfortable with heights can just relax and enjoy the terrific view. Duration: 5 minutes.

SNOW WHITE'S ADVENTURES ★ C Y This ride takes visitors in wooden mining cars past sets depicting scenes from the Disney animated classic (some enhanced with Audio-Animatronics figures). Originally designed to tell the story through Snow White's terrified eyes, the attraction was toned down in 1994 to make the wicked witch less scary and include the heroine in some new, more colorful scenes. The result lacks the unique "you-are-there" feel of the original, and most visitors will find little to enchant them. Duration: 2 minutes.

MICKEY'S TOONTOWN FAIR: Mickey's Toontown Fair is a riot of brightly colored buildings and tents that look as though they were cut out of a cartoon and set in a small country town. This is where Disney-Character devotees will find Mickey, Minnie, and their friends and neighbors.

THE BARNSTORMER AT GOOFY'S WISEACRES FARM ★★ C Y This big red barn filled with bric-a-brac, airplane parts, and funny Audio-Animatronics chickens houses a kid-sized roller coaster with cars decorated as bright blue biplanes. This fairly mild ride is very popular with children and the wait is ridiculously long. Duration: Approximately 1 minute.

DONALD'S BOAT ★ C The *S.S. Daisy*, Donald Duck's leaky cartoonlike boat, is a popular play area. The boat spouts water from its smokestack and floats on a padded surface that spurts up fountains and squirts visitors as they step on certain spots. No time limit.

MICKEY'S COUNTRY HOUSE ★★ C Y Mickey's bright yellow house, with props and furnishings familiar to Disney cartoon lovers, is clearly the home of a sports enthusiast. Visitors exit at the rear and pass through Mickey's garden filled with whimsical and amusing plants. Just beyond is the large yellow-and-purple striped Judge's Tent, where Mickey Mouse fans have the chance to meet Mickey, take photographs, and collect autographs. No time limit.

MINNIE'S COUNTRY HOUSE ★★ C Y Hearts are everywhere at Minnie's pink-and-lavender house, including the gazebo, where visitors can meet Minnie, take photographs, and collect autographs when she's home. The frilly furnishings and props inside the house attest to Minnie's romantic feminine nature, and visitors can hear a special message from her by pushing the button on her answering machine. No time limit.

TOONTOWN HALL OF FAME ★ C Y In this large tentlike structure, visitors can shop for collectibles and take photographs and collect autographs from Disney Characters in three classic categories: Disney Princesses, Disney Villains, and Mickey's Pals. No time limit.

WALT DISNEY WORLD RAILROAD, TOONTOWN FAIR STATION ★★ A C The circus-tent look and bright blue color of this train station reflect the cartoon-fantasy tone of Mickey's Toontown Fair. Disney Characters can often be seen here greeting visitors or waving good-bye to them. Duration: Approximately 20 minutes for the entire circuit.

TOMORROWLAND: Tomorrowland, which had a facelift in 1994, is now a sci-fi city-of-the-future as envisioned by the machine-age dreamers of the past, evoking a sense of comic-book surrealism. Visitors strolling on the walkway from Main Street pass under an arch of rich-hued and jumbled metal rods, elements repeated in sculptures and building details. Sleek glass kiosks and oddly angular palm trees sprout out of the pavement; the architecture is retro-moderne, with an offbeat color scheme accented by vividly colored graphics and neon lights. As part of the facelift, most attractions in Tomorrowland were revamped or replaced with new ones.

ASTRO ORBITER ★★ T C Color-splashed rockets spin, dip, and lift riders in circles as they rush past giant planets. Though striking and imaginative, this spiffed-up version of the StarJets carnival ride is designed primarily to thrill youngsters. Duration: 2 minutes.

CAROUSEL OF PROGRESS ★★★ A Y Visitors seated on a revolving turntable watch Audio-Animatronics figures depict lifestyles from the early 1900s through the not-too-distant future. In each humorous scene, the husband marvels at the age's technological advancements, while his family puts them to use with unexpected results. The attraction begins with a historical film about Walt Disney. Duration: 22 minutes.

THE EXTRATERRORESTRIAL ALIEN ENCOUNTER ★★★ A T Visitors are greeted with a sales pitch and demo of XS Tech's new teletransporter. A technical glitch in the demo slightly sizzles the fuzzy alien beamed from one cylinder to another. Visitors are then invited to observe a real interplanetary teletransport and are firmly harnessed in their seats. This demo, too, is botched, circuits blow, and an alien monster breaks loose in the darkness. Frightening sounds and scary effects attest to the monster's destructiveness. Visitors, stuck in their seats, can hear it move closer and closer, until it is so near they can feel its breath and sense it pulling at their harness. This attraction utilizes sophisticated psychological effects. It terrifies young children and sensitive adolescents and delights ten-year-old boys and thrill-seekers. Duration: Approximately 20 minutes.

SKYWAY TO FANTASYLAND ★★ A T C This overhead cable car travels high above the Magic Kingdom, connecting Tomorrowland to Fantasyland. Each open-air gondola holds only a few people and affords spectacular views of the Magic Kingdom. Duration: 5 minutes.

ATTRACTIONS

SPACE MOUNTAIN ★★★★ A T This unique roller-coaster ride through the cosmos is housed in a huge spired and domed structure visible throughout the Magic Kingdom and beyond. The moment visitors enter the sleek spaceport's futuristic environment, they are caught up in the excitement. Once on board, they are hurtled through mostly dark space, illuminated occasionally by flashing comets, colorful bursts, and whirling galaxies. Distinctive special effects, the creative use of darkness, and two roller coasters running concurrently make this attraction a must-try experience. The thrill can be taxing, however, and health restrictions apply. Duration: 3 minutes.

TAKE FLIGHT ★ A Y This attraction takes visitors on a narration-free journey through the history of modern aviation. The attraction uses giant pop-up books as opening and closing motifs, and mixes props with special you-are-there visual effects. *This attraction may be replaced with a ride based on Buzz Lightyear from the Disney movie,* Toy Story. Duration: 5 minutes.

THE TIMEKEEPER ★★★ A T In this large theater, an intertemporal-tour planner named Timekeeper sends visitors on a wacky trip through time with his multiple-lensed assistant Nine-Eye. The results of Timekeeper's sloppy temporal technique are depicted in a Circle-Vision 360 film, which ricochets visitors through the centuries, brings them face to face with Jules Verne, and then swoops them off on a time-travel adventure. This attraction is adapted from *Le Visionarium* at Disneyland Paris, with the addition of Audio-Animatronics robots. The theater accommodates several hundred visitors, so waits are seldom long. Visitors must stand for the show. Duration: 18 minutes.

TOMORROWLAND SPEEDWAY ★ T C Y Visitors get behind the wheel of miniature gasoline-powered cars that travel less than seven miles per hour along one of four parallel tracks. This noisy attraction seems to belong more in Fantasyland than Tomorrowland. It thrills young kids and a few grown men, as well. Duration: Less than 5 minutes, depending on crowd and driving speed.

TOMORROWLAND TRANSIT AUTHORITY ★★ A T Visitors board an elevated-track tram for a narrated tour of Tomorrowland. It travels just about ten miles per hour above, alongside, and through several attractions, including Space Mountain. Duration: 10 minutes.

SPECIAL EVENTS AND LIVE ENTERTAINMENT

Live entertainment events are scheduled throughout the day at the Magic Kingdom. As you enter the park, stop at City Hall and pick up an entertainment schedule, which also shows the parade routes. When planning a trip, you can also call Walt Disney World Information a month or two ahead (407 824-4321).

DIAMOND HORSESHOE SALOON REVUE: *Frontierland* ★★ Y Songs and dances from the Gay Nineties entertain visitors of all ages in this Old West saloon. Visitors can lounge at the long bar or sit at tables scattered throughout this lively and popular saloon. The show runs continuously from about 10:30 AM to 5:30 PM. Counter-service snacks, sandwiches, and beverages are available for purchase to enjoy during the show. Duration: Approximately 40 minutes.

AFTERNOON PARADE: *Frontierland, Liberty Square, and Main Street, U.S.A.* ★★★ C Y This large-scale extravaganza, which changes themes from time to time, is a festive Magic Kingdom treat every afternoon, usually at 3 PM. The parade features dancers and stilt-walkers in flashy costumes. Disney Characters interact with visitors, providing mini performances along the way. The crowds are lighter in Frontierland than on Main Street. Duration: Approximately 20 minutes.

SPECTROMAGIC: *Frontierland, Liberty Square, and Main Street, U.S.A.* ★★★★ A T C
At selected nights throughout the year, this magical parade of elaborate floats wends its way through the Magic Kingdom. Twinkling lights dance in perfect synchronicity to original music, while hologram illusions and smoke combine to complete the dazzling show. The parade attracts huge crowds, especially along Main Street, where viewers gather as much as an hour before it begins. The parade is best watched from Frontierland or Liberty Square, where the crowds are thinner. On busy nights when the parade is held twice, the later one attracts smaller crowds. Duration: Approximately 18 minutes.

FANTASY IN THE SKY FIREWORKS ★★★★ A T C At selected times throughout the year, usually when Magic Kingdom hours are extended to 9 PM or later, fireworks burst above Cinderella Castle, preceded by Tinker Bell's dramatic flight across the sky from a castle tower to Tomorrowland. The show is best watched from the walkway from Tomorrowland to Main Street, where crowds are thinner than on Main Street (the Plaza Pavilion's terrace is usually empty at this time). Visitors interested in the fireworks only, and not Tinker Bell's flight, will find that Mickey's Toontown Fair makes an ideal, uncrowded vantage point. While the show is not an elaborate spectacle, its nostalgia value is priceless. Duration: Approximately 6 minutes.

CASTLE FORECOURT STAGE: *Main Street, U.S.A.* ★★ Y At this outdoor gathering spot in front of Cinderella Castle (facing Main Street), visitors can enjoy a variety of musical and theatrical shows featuring Disney Characters from recent film releases, as well as guest artists. Shows usually run about 15 minutes.

GALAXY PALACE THEATER: *Tomorrowland* ★ T C Live entertainment ranging from rock groups to brass bands to Disney Character skits is staged in this large open-air theater. These performances attract different age groups, depending on the type of show. During the day, shows run about 20 minutes; evening performances are usually longer.

TOUR: *Keys to the Kingdom* ★★★ A Departing daily from City Hall at about 10 AM, this walking tour is an informative and entertaining way for visitors to learn about the history of Walt Disney World, see highlights of the Magic Kingdom, and catch a glimpse of some of the backstage areas and underground "utilidors." Attractions visited may vary with the season, but often include the Tomorrowland Transit Authority, It's A Small World, The Haunted Mansion, Country Bear Jamboree, and Pirates of the Caribbean. The tour is limited to fifteen people who must be age sixteen and over. Reservations for the tour, which fills quickly, should be made as far in advance as possible through Walt Disney World Tours (407 939-8687). If space is available, visitors without reservations can sign up for the tour at City Hall; about $45, excluding food. Duration: Approximately 4 hours.

✳

FULL-SERVICE RESTAURANTS

Restaurant reservations may be made up to sixty days in advance by all Walt Disney World visitors. Same-day reservations can be made at City Hall or at the restaurant itself. No alcohol is served in the Magic Kingdom. Smoking is not permitted. See "Restaurants," page 157, for reviews and reservation information.

MAIN STREET, U.S.A.: *Tony's Town Square Restaurant* — The menu of this spacious restaurant with a sunny glassed-in patio and pleasant Victorian-style *Lady and the Tramp* decor offers waffles, eggs, and pancakes in the morning, and pasta, pizza, and other Italian dishes throughout the day. Espresso and cappuccino are served. Open for breakfast, lunch, and dinner; reservations suggested.

The Plaza Restaurant — This light and airy restaurant with pleasant, fanciful Art Nouveau decor is generally busy throughout the day. The menu features a selection of hot entrees, sandwiches, hamburgers, salads, and ice cream specialties. Espresso, cappuccino, and café mocha are served. Open for lunch and dinner; no reservations.

The Crystal Palace — This replica of a Victorian conservatory, with a circular atrium and skylights throughout, offers all-you-care-to-eat buffet-style Character Meals. At breakfast, egg dishes, French toast, and a breakfast lasagna are featured. Lunch includes soups, salads, pastas, and sandwiches. At dinner, chicken, beef, fish, and pasta dishes are offered. Open for breakfast, lunch, and dinner; reservations suggested.

LIBERTY SQUARE: *Liberty Tree Tavern* — With its low lighting, plank floors, and giant fireplace, this friendly restaurant has a comfortable colonial ambience. At lunch, the menu features New England clam chowder, large salads, roast turkey, and sandwiches. The Character Dinner includes chicken, steak, and special sausages. Open for lunch and dinner; reservations required.

FANTASYLAND: *Cinderella's Royal Table* — This restaurant high up in Cinderella Castle has a medieval elegance and fantasy decor. Cinderella herself makes appearances here from time to time. At the Character Breakfast, waffles, pancakes, and egg dishes are featured. Salads, sandwiches, roast beef, seafood, and chicken dishes are served at lunch and dinner. Open all day; reservations required.

✳

CAFES

There are refreshment stands throughout the Magic Kingdom that serve snacks and fast-food meals. A few, listed below, are pleasant rest and rendezvous stops. No alcohol is served in the Magic Kingdom.

MAIN STREET, U.S.A.: *Main Street Bake Shop* — Freshly baked cookies, cakes, pastries, and tarts are available to eat at small, cozy tables in a turn-of-the-century tearoom. ☕

ADVENTURELAND: *El Pirata y El Perico* — This fast-food stand serves sandwiches, snacks, and the only tacos in the Magic Kingdom, which visitors can enjoy at nearby umbrella-shaded tables. ☕

Sunshine Tree Terrace — Perched along the passage way to Frontierland, this is the place for fresh fruits, fruit juice, and nonfat frozen yogurt, as well as espresso and cappuccino. ☕

LIBERTY SQUARE: *Sleepy Hollow* — This fast-food eatery offers quick meals and vegetarian fare, including chili, sandwiches, and snacks, and a good view of the daily afternoon parade at the rail-side tables on its outdoor patio. ☕

FANTASYLAND: *The Pinocchio Village Haus* — This two-story Bavarian-styled restaurant features fast foods such as hot dogs, hamburgers, turkey sandwiches, and pasta salads. ☕

TOMORROWLAND: *Cosmic Ray's Starlight Cafe* — An outdoor terrace and large open room done in bright contemporary colors make comfortable places to take a break from touring. The cafe serves rotisserie chicken, hamburgers, sandwiches, and other fast food, along with entertainment such as Sonny Eclipse's tunes on the Astro Organ. ☕

ATTRACTIONS

SERVICES

REST ROOMS: Public rest rooms are numerous throughout the Magic Kingdom. On Main Street, the rest rooms to the right of City Hall, although crowded in the morning and evening, are relatively empty in the afternoon. Despite large crowds, there are rarely waits in the rest rooms located across from the Swiss Family Treehouse, in the breezeway between Adventureland and Frontierland. In Frontierland, the rest rooms located near the exit to Splash Mountain are generally uncrowded. In Fantasyland, the rest rooms behind the Enchanted Grove (near Mr. Toad's Wild Ride) usually remain uncrowded. In Tomorrowland, the least-crowded rest rooms are those by the Skyway to Fantasyland. For quieter accommodations, Liberty Tree Tavern has rest rooms upstairs, although most restaurant rest rooms are crowded during mealtimes.

TELEPHONES: Public telephones are located throughout the Magic Kingdom. The least busy are those near The Crystal Palace restaurant at the end of Main Street; at the exit to Pirates of the Caribbean in Adventureland; near the exit to Splash Mountain in Frontierland; behind the Enchanted Grove (near Mr. Toad's Wild Ride) in Fantasyland; near the Skyway to Fantasyland in Tomorrowland; and at the Frontierland Railroad Station. To make quieter, air-conditioned calls, slip into a full-service restaurant (except Tony's Town Square Restaurant), where the telephones are located near the rest rooms.

MESSAGE CENTER: The Message Center is located at Guest Relations in City Hall on Main Street. The Message Center is on a network also shared by Epcot and Disney-MGM Studios. Here, visitors can leave and retrieve messages for one another and exchange messages with companions visiting elsewhere. Anyone can phone in a message by calling 407 824-4321.

FILM AND TWO-HOUR EXPRESS DEVELOPING: Film is available at shops and kiosks throughout the Magic Kingdom. Drop-off points for express developing are at the Newsstand and the Kodak Camera Center on Main Street; at the Crow's Nest in Adventureland; at the Kodak Kiosk in Fantasyland, across from Cinderella's Golden Carrousel; at Kodak's Funny Photos in Mickey's Toontown Fair; and at Geiger's Counter in Tomorrowland. Developed pictures may be picked up at the Kodak Camera Center on Main Street or delivered to any Walt Disney World resort.

CAMERA RENTAL: Video camcorders, replacement batteries, and 35mm cameras are available at the Kodak Camera Center on Main Street. Rented equipment may be returned to a Kodak Camera Center in any major theme park.

MAIL DROPS: Mail drops are located at the Newsstand, in front of City Hall and Tony's Town Square Restaurant, and here and there on both sides of Main Street; across from the Swiss Family Treehouse in Adventureland; across from the Country Bear Jamboree in Frontierland; and across from the Tomorrowland Speedway in Tomorrowland. Stamps may be purchased on the lower level of the Main Street Railroad Station, and at City Hall and the Emporium, both located on Main Street.

BANKING: Although once provided on Main Street, there are no longer full banking services in the Magic Kingdom. Automated teller machines (ATMs) are located under the Main Street Railroad Station near the lockers; across from the Swiss Family Treehouse in Adventureland; near the Diamond Horseshoe Saloon Revue, in the breezeway between Adventureland and Frontierland; and at the Tomorrowland Arcade. Personal checks of about $25 can be cashed at City Hall on Main Street.

ATTRACTIONS

ATTRACTIONS

LOCKERS: Lockers are located on the lower level of the Main Street Railroad Station. Oversized packages may be left at Package Pickup, located outside City Hall on Main Street.

PACKAGE PICKUP: Visitors can forward purchases free of charge to Package Pickup, located near City Hall on Main Street, and pick them up as they leave the park. Guests staying at a Walt Disney World resort may have packages delivered to their hotel.

FIRST AID: The first-aid station is located just past The Crystal Palace, at the end of Main Street. Aspirin and other first-aid needs are dispensed free of charge. Over-the-counter medications are available at the Emporium, on Main Street. They are not on display and must be requested at the counter.

VISITORS WITH DISABILITIES: A free guidebook for guests with disabilities is available at the Guest Relations window in the Entrance Plaza and at City Hall, on Main Street. Visitors with disabilities should note that the monorail stop at the Contemporary resort is not accessible to wheelchairs. Most attractions at the Magic Kingdom have wheelchair access, but there are a number of exceptions. For these, special arrangements can usually be made to transfer visitors from wheelchairs into the ride vehicle. Inquire at City Hall. Areas along the Magic Kingdom parade route are designated for visitors in wheelchairs. Ask at City Hall for these locations, available on a first-come, first-served basis.

WHEELCHAIR RENTALS: Wheelchairs and a limited number of Electric Convenience Vehicles can be rented at the Stroller Shop, in the Entrance Plaza. All rentals are on a first-come, first-served basis, so get there early. Replacement batteries, if needed, will be brought to you if you alert a Cast Member.

VISITORS WITH HEARING IMPAIRMENTS: Assistive listening devices, written descriptions of the Magic Kingdom's attractions, and a telecommunications device for the deaf (TDD) are available at City Hall, on Main Street. Hearing aid–compatible and amplified telephones can be found throughout the Magic Kingdom.

VISITORS WITH SIGHT IMPAIRMENTS: Tape players with Braille buttons, touring cassettes describing the park, and Braille guidebooks with maps and descriptions of attractions are available at City Hall, on Main Street.

FOREIGN LANGUAGE ASSISTANCE: Park maps in French, Spanish, German, Japanese, Portuguese, and a few other languages are available at City Hall, on Main Street. The Walt Disney World Foreign Language Center (407 824-7900) can help with travel plans and offer assistance in a number of languages to visitors who call between 8:30 AM and 9 PM.

✳

ON THE DRAWING BOARD

There are always plans on the drawing board for new attractions throughout Walt Disney World, but until construction actually begins, these plans have a way of changing or becoming delayed. At the time of publication, an overall revamping of Fantasyland was being scheduled .

TOMORROWLAND: *Buzz Lightyear Attraction* — Timeworn Take Flight may be replaced by a new attraction featuring the Buzz Lightyear character from the popular Disney movie, *Toy Story*. Take Flight's basic ride system will be left in place, but upgraded with an interactive concept, such as a ride-through computer game with vehicle mounted firing devices that keep scores. Tentatively called Buzz Lightyear's Star Command, the new attraction is expected to open during 1998.

Half-Day Tours at the Magic Kingdom

The morning and evening tours that follow are designed to let visitors sample the best of [...] Kingdom in four to five hours, including a lunch or dinner in one of the Magic Kingdom restau[...]. Magic Kingdom Morning Tour is designed for lower-attendance times: September throug[...] [...]arch. The Lights & Magic Afternoon and Evening Tour is designed for peak-attendance times when the Magic Kingdom is open late and there are fireworks shows (June through August, and on Saturday nights and holidays throughout the year). You may not have time to visit every attraction listed on the tours, but you will have a quality experience if you follow these guidelines: ❶ Never pass up an attraction that you can walk in without a line. ❷ Do not wait in lines longer than twenty minutes *unless* it is for an attraction you know you will enjoy. ❸ Do not visit the Magic Kingdom during the day on Early Entry days (usually Monday, Thursday, and Saturday) unless you are entering early to take advantage of that uncrowded ninety minutes. ❹ Don't race blindly from attraction to attraction; at the Magic Kingdom, especially, the most memorable moments happen in the simplest places. Look around; keep an open heart.

> NOTE: If you want to visit the Magic Kingdom in the morning during a crowded time, one good strategy is to reserve the popular Keys to the Kingdom tour, which leaves City Hall about 10 AM, then arrive very early and hurry to the attractions that are *not* included on the tour. (Keys to the Kingdom may not be offered during some peak periods.) Reserve well ahead of time through Walt Disney World Tours (407 939-8687), and ask which attractions will be visited to plan your strategy.

✳

MAGIC KINGDOM MORNING TOUR

Four to five hours — September through March (except holiday periods) — including lunch.
Well in advance, reserve lunch at 1 PM or later at Cinderella's Royal Table, Liberty Tree Tavern, or
Tony's Town Square Restaurant — or plan to eat at a counter-service restaurant or back at your resort.

⬇ Arrive at the Magic Kingdom Entrance Plaza one half hour before the scheduled opening time. (The gates often open about one half hour before the announced opening time.)

⬇ Take in the sights along **Main Street, U.S.A.**, which opens before the rest of the park. If you do not have lunch reservations, stop at City Hall and book a table for 1 PM or later. Time your Main Street browsing so that you arrive at the walkway to **Tomorrowland** when the rest of the park opens.

⬇ Tour the park counterclockwise and visit, in the order below, any of the following attractions that interest you (skip lines longer than 20 minutes and return at night or two hours before closing):

◆ **Tomorrowland** ◆ SPACE MOUNTAIN ◆ THE EXTRATERRORESTRIAL ALIEN ENCOUNTER (if scary attractions appeal to you) ◆ THE TIMEKEEPER ◆

◆ **Mickey's Toontown Fair** ◆ A quick twenty minute stroll for the young at heart through MICKEY'S COUNTRY HOUSE ◆ MINNIE'S COUNTRY HOUSE ◆ THE BARNSTORMER AT GOOFY'S WISEACRES FARM (if the mood strikes and the wait is no more than 10 minutes) ◆

◆ **Fantasyland** ◆ IT'S A SMALL WORLD (if you're feeling young at heart or just want to cool off) ◆ PETER PAN'S FLIGHT ◆

◆ **Liberty Square** ◆ THE HAUNTED MANSION ◆ LIBERTY SQUARE RIVERBOAT (for a change of pace) ◆ THE HALL OF PRESIDENTS (if U.S. history interests you) ◆

ATTRACTIONS

 ◆ **Frontierland** ◆ SPLASH MOUNTAIN ◆ BIG THUNDER MOUNTAIN RAILROAD (if you like thrill rides and the lines are not too long) ◆
 ◆ **Adventureland** ◆ PIRATES OF THE CARIBBEAN ◆ JUNGLE CRUISE ◆

Arrive at your lunch destination ten minutes early. If you skipped attractions you want to experience, return about two hours before closing, or come back for evening events if the park is open late.

✳

LIGHTS & MAGIC AFTERNOON AND EVENING TOUR

Four to six hours — June through August (plus holidays and Saturday nights) — including dinner.
Reserve an early dinner well in advance of this tour at Cinderella's Royal Table, Liberty Tree Tavern, or Tony's Town Square Restaurant. If you prefer a late dinner, let the reservationist know that you want to see SpectroMagic and would like to finish dinner before the first parade begins.
If you do not have reservations on the day of your tour, call Same Day Reservations (939-3463) at 10 AM.

Arrive at the Magic Kingdom Entrance Plaza at 4 PM. Pick up an entertainment schedule, which lists the show times for live performances, SpectroMagic, and the fireworks show.

As you make your way toward **Adventureland**, take in the sights along **Main Street, U.S.A.**

Tour the park clockwise and visit, in the order below, any of the following attractions that interest you (your tour will be interrupted for dinner and SpectroMagic; just continue where you left off):

 ◆ **Adventureland** ◆ JUNGLE CRUISE ◆ PIRATES OF THE CARIBBEAN ◆
 ◆ **Frontierland** ◆ SPLASH MOUNTAIN ◆ BIG THUNDER MOUNTAIN RAILROAD (if you like roller coasters) ◆
 ◆ **Liberty Square** ◆ THE HAUNTED MANSION ◆ THE HALL OF PRESIDENTS (if U.S. history interests you) ◆
 ◆ **Fantasyland** ◆ IT'S A SMALL WORLD ◆ PETER PAN'S FLIGHT (both for the young at heart) ◆ SKYWAY TO TOMORROWLAND (if you don't mind heights) ◆
 ◆ **Tomorrowland** ◆ THE EXTRATERRORESTRIAL ALIEN ENCOUNTER (if scary attractions appeal to you) ◆ SPACE MOUNTAIN (if you like roller coasters) ◆ THE TIMEKEEPER ◆ TOMORROWLAND TRANSIT AUTHORITY ◆
 ◆ **Mickey's Toontown Fair** ◆ If you're feeling young at heart, backtrack to tour MICKEY'S COUNTRY HOUSE ◆ MINNIE'S COUNTRY HOUSE ◆ THE BARNSTORMER AT GOOFY'S WISEACRES FARM (if it looks like fun and the line is short) ◆

If it fits your plans, take the WALT DISNEY WORLD RAILROAD back to the Main Street Station or on to Frontierland for the SPECTROMAGIC parade.

Within one half hour before the start of SPECTROMAGIC, secure a viewing spot along the parade route. Or, skip the 9 PM parade to take advantage of the shorter lines in Tomorrowland and elsewhere. You can catch the second parade, if one is scheduled tonight.

After the parade passes your viewing spot, pick up your tour where you left off.

On nights when it is held, be sure to stay for the FANTASY IN THE SKY fireworks show, which is scheduled after SpectroMagic. There are often good viewing locations from the walkway between Tomorrowland and Main Street, U.S.A., and on the terrace of the Plaza Pavilion. ◆

DISNEY'S BOARDWALK

Capturing the turn-of-the-century atmosphere of Atlantic City's Boardwalk, Disney's BoardWalk is a bustling waterfront complex with restaurants, entertainment, and specialty shops fronting a quarter-mile stretch of Crescent Lake. On the wood-slatted BoardWalk Promenade, performers entertain passersby, artists sketch caricatures of visitors and create wax sculptures of their hands, and colorful carts offer unique souvenirs, snacks, and beverages. When the sun goes down, the midway lights come up, transforming the BoardWalk into a re-creation of the early amusement parks designed for the pleasure of adults, rather than children. Aromas waft from the restaurants and music spills from the clubs. With two hotels perched above the shops and restaurants — the informal yet elegant BoardWalk Inn and the homey BoardWalk Villas — Disney's BoardWalk is both an atmospheric recreation area and a vacation destination resort. It is also fast becoming a favorite evening-out destination among frequent visitors.

WHEN TO GO: The most crowded and festive times at the clubs are Friday and Saturday nights, when local residents join the ranks of visitors. Most BoardWalk shops are open from 9 AM until 1 AM, and most restaurants are open throughout the day. The sports-oriented ESPN Club is open from 11:30 AM until 1 AM (until 2 AM on weekends). For information on scheduled events at ESPN Club, call the club's podium (407 939-1177). Jellyrolls and Atlantic Dance, the nightclubs at Disney's BoardWalk, are open from about 7 PM until 2 AM. Hours vary with the season. For entertainment information, call the Atlantic Dance hotline (407 939-2444).

HOW TO GET THERE: Disney's BoardWalk is located in the Epcot Resorts Area. Parking is available at the BoardWalk's Guest Parking Lot on Epcot Resorts Boulevard. Valet parking and taxi service are also available. Water launches travel between Disney's BoardWalk, Disney-MGM Studios, and the World Showcase at Epcot, as well as the following resorts: Swan, Dolphin, Yacht Club, and Beach Club. Buses travel between Disney's BoardWalk and most theme parks. Disney's BoardWalk is within walking distance of the International Gateway to the World Showcase at Epcot. It is also within walking distance of the following resorts: Swan, Dolphin, Yacht Club, and Beach Club.

ADMISSIONS AND RESTRICTIONS: Admission to Disney's BoardWalk is free, although the nightclubs may levy a modest cover charge (about $5). Florida law prohibits serving alcohol to anyone under twenty-one, and visitors must be twenty-one to enter Jellyrolls and Atlantic Dance. Unless otherwise noted, smoking is not permitted at the restaurants.

✳

CLUBS & ENTERTAINMENT

ATLANTIC DANCE: With the giant sign "DANCE HALL" glowing from its rooftop and terraces looking out over the waters of Crescent Lake, Atlantic Dance captures the sleek elegance of the high-class casino dance clubs popular in the 1920s and thirties. Just past a foyer adorned with stylish supergraphics is the club's main area, where a ten-piece band on a raised stage performs dance hits from the 1940s to the nineties. Lights sparkle across the wooden dance floor, reflected from double mirrored balls overhead; the mood is sophisticated and romantic. A sweeping staircase leads to a second-floor balcony overlooking the dance area furnished with small tables with carved-back chairs

ATTRACTIONS

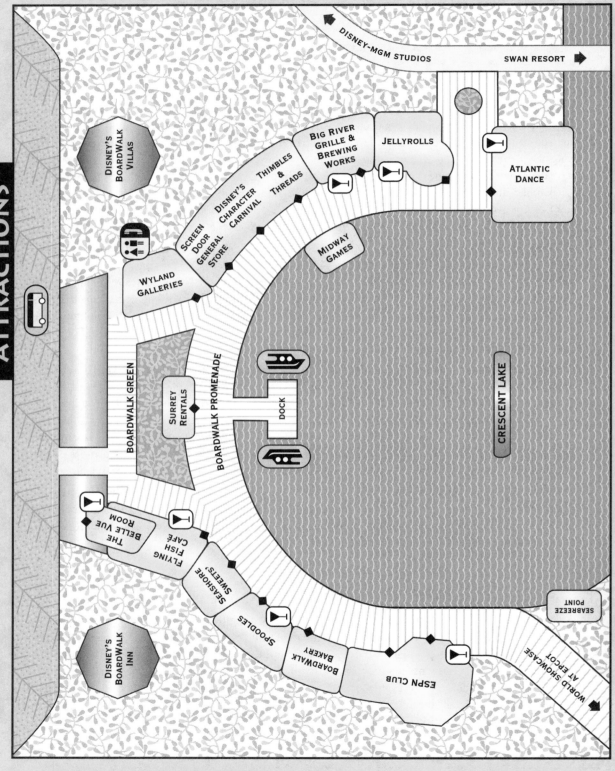

DISNEY-MGM STUDIOS

SWAN RESORT

DISNEY'S BOARDWALK VILLAS

BIG RIVER GRILLE & BREWING WORKS

THIMBLES & THREADS

JELLYROLLS

ATLANTIC DANCE

DISNEY'S CHARACTER CARNIVAL

SCREEN DOOR GENERAL STORE

MIDWAY GAMES

WYLAND GALLERIES

BOARDWALK GREEN

CRESCENT LAKE

SURREY RENTALS

BOARDWALK PROMENADE

DOCK

THE BELLE VUE ROOM

FLYING FISH CAFE

SEASHORE SWEETS?

SPOODLES

BOARDWALK BAKERY

DISNEY'S BOARDWALK INN

ESPN CLUB

SEABREEZE POINT

WORLD SHOWCASE AT EPCOT

and a few comfortable loveseats. French doors open out onto the terraces overlooking Crescent Lake, which offer views of IllumiNations fireworks. Large bars with marble tops and dramatically lit mirrors can be found on both floors. Beer, wine, and spirits are served, including specialty martinis. Snacks such as Iced Jumbo Shrimp, Flat Bread Pizza, and an assortment of mini desserts called Sweet Samplers are available. A selection of imported cigars, mostly Honduran, is also offered. Atlantic Dance opens at 8 PM and has a modest cover charge (about $5). A club pass, good for one year for two people, is available for about $32. No one under the age of twenty-one may enter.

ESPN CLUB: A giant arm and barbell above the door and a basketball hoop for pick-up games at the entrance signal this complex, the ultimate in entertainment for sports enthusiasts. More than seventy video monitors scattered throughout the club (including the rest rooms) carry a dazzling array of sports events. In the evenings and any time that popular events are telecast, fans can be heard cheering on their favorites. The friendly exuberance is contagious, and even if you have little interest in sports, you can have a good time. ESPN Club has three main areas:

THE SIDELINES: In this large sports bar, video monitors overhead and inset into wood-paneled walls show a constant stream of televised events. Plaques, pictures, awards, and large murals add to the sports theme, as do the servers costumed in uniforms patterned after those of referees. Guests can seat themselves at the Penalty Box Bar or sit at tables where they can switch on an audio feed for sports events on the monitors. Four computer terminals near the entrance allow guests to explore ESPNNet on the World Wide Web. Appetizers, hot dogs, hamburgers, and sandwiches are served, as are sports-themed specialty drinks. Smoking is permitted.

SPORTS CENTRAL: Located to the left of the main entrance, this multisided room with the look of a basketball court is ESPN Club's main dining area and also a fully equipped television and radio broadcast studio. Tables are arranged in tiers, and face a video wall and small sound stage. The room is hung with video monitors, and a huge overhead scoreboard displays the latest scores. Live ESPN and ESPN2 sports wrap-ups, sports-oriented talk shows, and programs such as "SportsCenter" are beamed from Sports Central by satellite to worldwide feeds. Guests can dine as they watch the broadcasts in progress or live-action sports events on the monitors.

THE YARD: Chipped-brick walls, aluminum siding, and black chain-link fencing create a clean, well-lit version of a gritty urban environment at this large arcade, which features interactive and virtual-reality sports and adventure games. The Yard is popular with visitors bent on challenging themselves and each other.

JELLYROLLS: At this rambunctious club, a rounded storefront welcomes guests into a room with the look of an old warehouse. Beer-company banners hang from wooden beams above a large sunken seating area with tables and chairs, and a higher level with bar-stool seating runs around three sides of the club. On a raised stage, musicians at a pair of pianos play and sing classic rock tunes and attempt to outdo each other with their dancing digits and improvisational comedy routines. The club's enthusiastic guests need little encouragement to participate in the banter, suggesting tunes and sometimes singing along. The keyboard antics of the gifted performers are reflected on large mirrors at the back of the stage. Beer, wine, and spirits are served, including a rotating list of thirty-two-ounce specialty drinks. Popcorn is also available. Jellyrolls opens about 7 PM and has a modest cover charge (about $5). No one under twenty-one may enter.

SURREY RENTALS: Visitors can enjoy the BoardWalk Promenade's sights as they are pedaled along in large wicker vehicles modeled on the rolling chairs of Atlantic City's Boardwalk. Baskets seat two, and a ride from one end of the Promenade to the other costs about $6. Visitors who would like to combine sightseeing with a little exercise can rent four-wheeled surreys with striped-canvas tops to pedal along the BoardWalk Promenade and over to the nearby Yacht and Beach Club resorts. Surreys seating four adults and two children cost about $12 for one half hour; those seating six adults and two children cost about $15. Basket tours and surreys are available on a first-come, first-served basis; no reservations are taken. Surrey Rentals is open from 11 AM until 10 PM.

SHOPS & STOPS

THE BELLE VUE ROOM: This 30s-era lounge is just off the upstairs lobby of the BoardWalk Inn. With its period tables and comfortable couches tucked among bookcases filled with curios and antique radios playing broadcasts of the era, The Belle Vue Room is a romantic spot for a quiet talk, or to watch a sunset or play a game of chess or backgammon on a rainy afternoon. Beer, wine, and spirits are served, as are coffee, tea, espresso, and cappuccino. Open from 11 AM until midnight.

BOARDWALK BAKERY: Muffins, croissants, cakes, and a variety of other fresh-baked goods and snacks are available here, along with soft drinks, coffee, espresso, and cappuccino. Guests can enjoy their purchases sidewalk cafe–style at the bakery's outdoor tables. It's a great place to grab an early breakfast on the way to Epcot. Open from 6:30 AM until 10 PM.

DISNEY'S CHARACTER CARNIVAL: Distinguished by its multicolored striped awnings, this store offers Disney-themed merchandise such as hats, accessories, stuffed animals, and a wide variety of tee-shirts and children's apparel.

SCREEN DOOR GENERAL STORE: Designed as an old-fashioned general store, the Screen Door carries Disney-themed dishes and cooking utensils, gifts, sundries, snacks, and a limited selection of groceries and frozen foods. The store also stocks several types of beer, wine, and spirits, as well as mixers, bar accessories, and cigarettes.

SEASHORE SWEETS': "Miss America" is the theme at this brightly lit haven for guests with a sweet tooth. Portraits of many of the pageant's winners decorate the shop, which offers ice cream, saltwater taffy, and a variety of candies, along with lemonade, coffee, espresso, and cappuccino. Open from 11 AM until 2 AM.

THIMBLES & THREADS: This small shop stocks a selection of seasonal resort wear (swimsuits in summer, sweaters and sweatshirts in winter) and accessories for men and women. Golf clothing with Disney motifs from Nike Golf and Titleist by Corbin is also available, along with golf balls, tees, and other golf accessories.

WYLAND GALLERIES: Wood veneers, pillars, and curving surfaces create a sleek showcase for unique, often dramatic sculptures, paintings, books, and furnishings that feature a marine-mammal environmental theme. Works by Wyland, considered the leading marine-life artist in America, are featured here, along with selected pieces from other environmental artists. All gallery items are limited editions. Open daily from 10 AM until 11 PM.

*

FULL-SERVICE RESTAURANTS

Any visitor can make restaurant reservations up to sixty days in advance. Same-day reservations can be made at the restaurant itself. See "Restaurants," page 157, for reviews and reservation information.

BIG RIVER GRILLE & BREWING WORKS: The rich smell of malt greets guests as they enter this microbrewery/restaurant. A glassed-in area behind the bar houses the microbrewery's huge stainless steel vats. As they watch the brewmasters at work, guests can choose from five brews produced on the premises, or order a special tasting sampler of all of them. The restaurant serves steak, chicken, and seafood, and homemade sausages are featured. Both indoor and outdoor seating is available. Wine and spirits are also served. Open from 11 AM until 2 AM; no reservations.

ESPN CLUB SPORTS CENTRAL: ESPN Club serves food in two areas: The Sidelines sports bar, filled with dozens of monitors playing a variety of sports events, and Sports Central, a broadcast studio where occasional live interviews with sports figures are beamed to ESPN's worldwide feeds. Tables are arranged in tiers with views of the video wall's televised sports events and other goings-on. The menu features sandwiches and hearty entrees. Beer, wine, and spirits are served, as are espresso and cappuccino. Open from 11:30 AM until 1 AM (2 AM on weekends); no reservations.

FLYING FISH CAFÉ: Blue flying fish, rendered in glowing neon, welcome guests to this unique, sophisticated restaurant on the BoardWalk Green. Whimsical flying fish and large murals pay tribute to the midway rides of an earlier era at Atlantic City's Boardwalk. Guests can dine at individual tables or, if they prefer, at the copper-tiled counter facing the kitchen's open grill. Fresh seafood, steaks, and chicken are on the menu, along with grilled and sautéed vegetables. Beer, wine, and spirits are served, as are espresso and cappuccino. Open for dinner from 6 PM until 11 PM; reservations recommended.

SPOODLES: A hodgepodge of mismatched furniture and tableware create a casual setting for this noisy family-style restaurant. The open kitchen serves up pizza and tapas, appetizer-sized dishes served in whatever order they emerge from the kitchen. The restaurant also has outdoor seating, with views of Crescent Lake and the BoardWalk Promenade. Beer, wine, and spirits are served as are coffee, espresso, and cappuccino. Spoodles is open for breakfast and for all-day dining from 7 AM until 10 PM; reservations recommended.

*

SERVICES

REST ROOMS: Rest rooms can be found inside or near all of the BoardWalk's restaurants and nightclubs. The ones at ESPN Club feature monitors with sports events. There are also public rest rooms located in the breezeway just off the BoardWalk Green to the left of Wyland Galleries.

TELEPHONES: Public telephones are located inside or near all of the BoardWalk's rest rooms, but the quietest are those at Atlantic Dance. The outdoor telephones in the breezeway just off the BoardWalk Green to the left of Wyland Galleries are quiet and uncrowded in the evenings.

BANKING: An automated teller machine (ATM) is located on the Green, near the Wyland Galleries. ◆

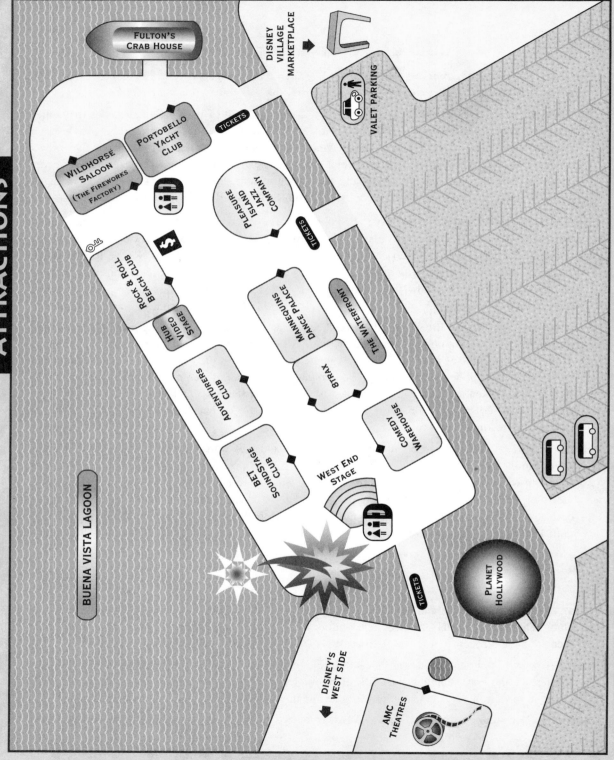

FULTON'S CRAB HOUSE

DISNEY VILLAGE MARKETPLACE →

VALET PARKING

WILDHORSE SALOON (THE FIREWORKS FACTORY)

PORTOBELLO YACHT CLUB

TICKETS

PLEASURE ISLAND JAZZ COMPANY

TICKETS

ROCK & ROLL BEACH CLUB

HUB VIDEO STAGE

MANNEQUINS DANCE PALACE

8TRAX

THE WATERFRONT

ADVENTURERS CLUB

BET SOUNDSTAGE CLUB

WEST END STAGE

COMEDY WAREHOUSE

BUENA VISTA LAGOON

PLANET HOLLYWOOD

TICKETS

DISNEY'S WEST SIDE ←

AMC THEATRES

ATTRACTIONS

PLEASURE ISLAND
AT DOWNTOWN DISNEY

Pleasure Island is a six-acre enclave of upbeat, sophisticated evening entertainment. It is located in the center of Downtown Disney, between the shops at Disney Village Marketplace and the supper clubs and concert halls at Disney's West Side. By day, you can shop in the Island's trendy stores, have lunch at one of several good restaurants, or catch a matinee at the 24-screen movie theater complex. At night, however, Pleasure Island is transformed: Limousines line up at the entrances, the streets fill with party-goers, and the nightclubs open their doors. At midnight, there's a splashy New Year's Eve celebration and fireworks show, and the partying continues into the wee hours. Every night on Pleasure Island is a street party, often with special entertainment events, visiting performers, or seasonal celebrations.

WHEN TO GO: Pleasure Island's clubs are open from between 7 and 8 PM until 2 AM, the shops are open from 10 AM until 1 AM, and the AMC Theatres screen films from 10 AM until 1 AM (until 2 AM on weekends). The most crowded nights are Thursday (when Walt Disney World Cast Members receive a discount on admissions) and Friday and Saturday, when local residents join the ranks of Walt Disney World visitors. To sample all of the Island's legendary nightlife, you'll need to get an early start; some clubs get rolling as early as 7:45 PM. Club entertainment changes frequently. For special entertainment events, contact Disney Theme Park Information (407 824-4321). As you enter Pleasure Island, pick up an entertainment schedule, which lists performance times at the clubs. For information on the evening's feature films and show times, call the AMC Theatres (827-1300).

HOW TO GET THERE: Pleasure Island is located at Downtown Disney in the Disney Village Resorts Area. There's free parking in the lots at Pleasure Island and at nearby Disney Village Market-place and the West Side. Starting at 5:30 PM, valet parking is available. Walt Disney World buses travel at night between all Walt Disney World resorts and theme parks and Pleasure Island. Shuttle service is also available from most area hotels. Water launches service the following resorts: Old Key West, Dixie Landings, and Port Orleans. Taxi service is available. Friday and Saturday nights draw huge crowds, and it can be very difficult to park at Pleasure Island.

ADMISSIONS AND RESTRICTIONS: From 10 AM until 7 PM daily, Pleasure Island is free and only the shops and eateries are open. After 7 PM, admission is charged (about $20) and visitors wear wrist bands that allow them into the clubs. Pleasure Island admission is included with Length of Stay Passes and some Multiday Passes. Movie-Island combo tickets are also available. **At most times of year, guests who present a receipt from a full-service restaurant at Disney Village Marketplace, Pleasure Island, or any Walt Disney World resort will receive a 20 percent discount on Pleasure Island admission for that same evening. Be sure to ask!**

$AVE

After 7 PM, no one under eighteen is permitted on Pleasure Island or inside the clubs without an accompanying adult, except in Mannequins, which prohibits anyone under the age of twenty-one. Visitors over eighteen need a picture ID (valid passport, U.S. driver's license, or foreign driver's license with a backup ID). Florida law prohibits serving alcohol to anyone under twenty-one. Alcoholic beverages may be consumed anywhere on Pleasure Island as long as they are carried in plastic cups, which are conveniently placed at club exits. Smoking is not permitted inside some clubs.

ATTRACTIONS

NIGHTCLUBS

MANNEQUINS DANCE PALACE: Featuring dazzling light and sound shows and on-stage dance performances, this club is the most popular gathering spot on Pleasure Island. It draws the twenty- to thirty-something locals, and is also is a favorite among Disney Cast Members. The dance floor is a giant moving turntable that fills quickly as professional DJs on high-tech sound equipment spin contemporary music. Beer, wine, and spirits are served, as are specialty drinks. Mannequins opens at 8 PM, on weekends lines form at the club door. No one under the age of twenty-one may enter, except during dance shows, when minors escorted by Cast Members may visit. Dance performances with special sound and light effects are scheduled several times each night, and it's well worth the effort to catch one. Check the entertainment schedule for show times.

8TRAX: This continually reinvented club has an urban-industrial ambience and is very popular among visitors in their late teens and early twenties. The superior (and very loud) sound system pumps out disco hits from the seventies at the volume they were meant to be enjoyed. Visitors can perch on stools overlooking the pipe-railed dance floor or tucked into intimate alcoves created by black chain-link panels. 8TRAX opens at 8 PM. Beer, wine, and spirits are served.

COMEDY WAREHOUSE: Every night, Pleasure Island visitors crowd into this large multilevel room and settle onto stools for solid comedy entertainment. Talented house comedians with a musician sidekick expertly improvise hilarious skits and routines that play heavily off the audience — and the audience loves every minute of it. Even though the routines are set, the improvisation keeps the regulars coming back. Well-known comedians also put in occasional appearances. Beer, wine, and spirits are served, as well as specialty drinks and a limited selection of snacks and appetizers. On busy nights, lines form at the door up to an hour before the thirty-five-minute shows, which begin around 7:30 PM. The first show is the easiest to get into, and the third show is timed to get guests back out on the street for the New Year's Eve show. Check the entertainment schedule for show times. Smoking is not permitted in this club.

BET SOUNDSTAGE CLUB: Jazz, rhythm and blues, soul, and hip-hop share the stage at this waterfront club, replacing the long-running Neon Armadillo Music Saloon. Owned by Black Entertainment Television, BET SoundStage Club features live performances from local and well-known artists in urban contemporary and traditional music styles. Video screens show a continuous stream of music videos and concerts by popular performers. The sophisticated lighting and great acoustics create the ideal atmosphere for visitors who love to dance and for those who want to listen. A limited menu of barbecued specialties and appetizers is offered. Beer, wine, and spirits are available. BET SoundStage Club opens at 8 PM. Check the entertainment schedule for show times.

ADVENTURERS CLUB: This take-off on a 1930s British explorers club, entered from above on a memorabilia-filled balcony that overlooks the main room, revolves around a group of regular "club members," delightfully eccentric performers who mingle with visitors and embroil them in altercations. The setting is a series of parlors furnished with Victorian-style sofas and love seats, and a long bar, whose barstools rise and lower subtly and unexpectedly at the whim of the bartender. The club appeals to anyone who likes to sit back and watch the goings-on, and it draws a core of regulars who like to participate in the interactive comedy. Beer, wine, and spirits are served, including such specialty drinks as the Kungaloosh, a frozen blend of fruit juices laced with rum and blackberry brandy. A limited selection of snacks is also available. The Adventurers Club opens at 7 PM, and every hour or so, quirky shows and lectures are presented in the club's Library, complete with a haunted organ. Check the entertainment schedule for show times. Smoking is not permitted in this club.

ROCK & ROLL BEACH CLUB: Visitors climb an outside stairway lined with surfboards and enter this dance club on the third floor. Below are two levels of bars, pool tables, and video games; the stage and dance floor are on the ground floor. Live bands perform contemporary and classic rock, and DJs spin a mean mix between sets. The atmosphere is relaxed and casual, and the music is full-volume. The crowd is split between late teens and twenty-somethings, who come to dance, and older visitors, who like to listen to good rock-and-roll music. Beer, wine, and spirits are served, and pizza is sold whole or by the slice. The Rock & Roll Beach Club opens at 7 PM, and the forty-five-minute live sets start at about 8 PM. Check the entertainment schedule for show times.

PLEASURE ISLAND JAZZ COMPANY: In a casual circular room decorated with steamer trunks and the paraphernalia of traveling musicians, visitors can enjoy live jazz, blues, and classic jam sessions featuring local, national, and international performers. The club appeals to jazz lovers of all ages, and many locals show up when a favorite group is appearing. Beer, wine, and spirits are served, with a special focus on wines and champagnes by the glass. This is a nice spot for an impromptu light meal of the appetizer-sized dishes featured here, including Grilled Mahi-Mahi with Tomato-Basil Creme Sauce and Beef Tenderloin with Port Wine Sauce and Onion Straws. The club also features an assortment of desserts and specialty coffee drinks. The Pleasure Island Jazz Company opens at 8 PM, and live sets start at about 8:30 PM. Check the entertainment schedule for show times.

WILDHORSE SALOON: This high-energy club occupies what was once the Fireworks Factory, and is the hot spot for country-western music fans. Live performances from up-and-coming bands, as well as nationally known country artists, are regularly scheduled and pack the house with a friendly, boisterous crowd. Between sets, jockeys play the best in music and video for two- or ten-stepping to the latest hits on the large dance floor. Free hour-long dance classes, taught by professional country dancers, are offered on select nights each week. The action starts at about 7 PM. Check the entertainment schedule for dance class and show times. The Wildhorse Saloon also has a restaurant that is open from about 4 PM until midnight. (See "Restaurants," page 195.)

✳

EVENTS AND ENTERTAINMENT

AMC THEATRES: The AMC movie theaters are located at Disney's West Side, just outside the entrance to Pleasure Island behind the West End Stage. Twenty-four screens (including sixteen with Continental stadium seating) show first-run movies, and all have Sony Digital Surround Sound. Recalling the glamor of the film industry's heyday, two theaters feature balcony seating and three-story-high viewing screens. **The lowest-priced movie tickets are available to all visitors for shows between 4 and 6 PM. Guests staying at a Walt Disney World resort also receive a 30 percent discount on movie tickets throughout the evening (after 6 PM) with their resort ID.** To avoid long lines or to secure space at popular films or movie premiers, visitors can charge tickets up to three days before the show (827-1311). Call the theater (827-1300) for movie listings and show times.

➡ **WEST END STAGE:** Framed by shiny high-tech lighting trusses and massive speakers, this huge outdoor performance platform presents live music that gets guests moving and keeps them jumping all night long, culminating with a flashy New Year's Eve countdown. Talented local bands and guest artists appear in concert nightly, beginning around 7:30 PM. Visitors who wish to avoid the dense crowd near the stage can watch the performances on the Hub Video Stage, an outdoor wall of twenty-five large video monitors. The Hub Video Stage also features live performances from time to time. Check the entertainment schedule for show times and events.

➡ **NEW YEAR'S EVE STREET PARTY:** Every night, a loud and lively New Year's Eve party materializes at Pleasure Island. At about 11:30 PM, visitors step out of the clubs and fill the streets for this Pleasure Island laser-and-light show tradition that takes place on the West End Stage. Professional dancers in sexy costumes power through a slick, complex routine to hard-driving music and motivate the crowd for the countdown to midnight. New Year's erupts with fireworks and confetti, and sometimes the street party continues with a live band.

➡ **THE WATERFRONT:** This area stretches along the shore between Mannequins and 8TRAX near the main gate to Pleasure Island. On weekends, entertainment events often appear here along with food booths that serve a variety of cuisines. The Waterfront is also used for seasonal festivals and special celebrations. Check the entertainment schedule for current events.

✳

FULL-SERVICE RESTAURANTS

Pleasure Island is located in the center of Downtown Disney, which puts it in the midst of the best dining area at Walt Disney World, where most restaurants are privately owned and nationally known. On one side, at Disney Village Marketplace, the very popular Rainforest Cafe is perched on the waterfront, just a pleasant stroll away. On the other side of Pleasure Island, at West Side, there are several dining choices, including Bongos Cuban Cafe serving tasty Cuban and Caribbean dishes in a cabaret setting, and the extraordinary Wolfgang Puck Cafe, offering dining inside or lagoon side.

The restaurants listed below can be entered from outside Pleasure Island and do not require an admission ticket to enjoy. All have smoking areas. See "Restaurants," page 157, for reviews and reservation information.

FULTON'S CRAB HOUSE: Fresh seafood, including crab and lobster, is the specialty at this huge restaurant located aboard a replica nineteenth-century riverboat. Diners are seated at tables on the riverboat's three decks, many with pleasant views of Buena Vista Lagoon. Beer, wine, and spirits are served. Open for dinner from 5 PM until midnight; reservations recommended.

PORTOBELLO YACHT CLUB: Guests can enjoy Italian specialties, fresh seafood, and a variety of oven-fired thin-crust pizzas in one of several spacious dining areas featuring yachting trophies and other maritime mementos. Beer, wine, and spirits are served, as are excellent espresso and cappuccino. Open for lunch from 11:30 AM; dinner from 5 PM until midnight; reservations recommended.

WILDHORSE SALOON/FIREWORKS FACTORY: This country western music and dance club, the former Fireworks Factory, has a separate restaurant featuring an "unbridled barbecue" of mesquite smoked ribs, chicken, and beef, along with large salads and hamburgers. Beer, wine and spirits are served. Open for dinner from 5 PM until midnight. Reservations for groups only.

PLANET HOLLYWOOD: A razzle-dazzle, star-studded ambience greets guests as they enter this restaurant, where they can enjoy tasty classic American dishes including hamburgers, pizza, and inventive entrees. This is the place for great desserts, including a distinctive apple strudel made from a recipe created by Arnold Schwarzenegger's mother. Beer, wine, and spirits are served, as are espresso and cappuccino. Open from 11 AM until 2 AM; no reservations.

✳

CAFES AND LOUNGES

A number of refreshment stands and shops scattered around Pleasure Island serve fast-food meals and snacks. The lounges listed below are the most pleasant for a sit-down respite from the clubs. They stay open late and make good rendezvous spots for visitors who want to club-hop separately and meet up later.

FULTON'S STONE CRAB LOUNGE: The curved window wall of this lounge offers a marvelous view of Lake Buena Vista. The dark wood trim and the subdued lighting at night gives this spacious, casual area an intimate atmosphere. During the day, light entrees and appetizers are available here, including many kinds of shellfish, fish, and salads. The full bar has an extensive assortment of liquors and wines. 🍸

PORTOBELLO YACHT CLUB BAR: Warm, dark mahogany paneling and polished brass fixtures create a pleasant, clubby atmosphere. The full bar features an extensive array of grappas and good Italian wines. Appetizers include Quattro Fromaggi Pizza, Antipasto Assortito, Calamaretti Fritti, and Carpaccio (thinly sliced raw sirloin with oak-roasted mushrooms, romano cheese, and red onions with lemon oil). Walt Disney World's most potent espresso and cappuccino are found here. 🍸

PLANET HOLLYWOOD: Dinner lines at this ultra-busy restaurant disappear around 10 PM, and after an evening of club-hopping at Pleasure Island, visitors can grab a late supper here or take in the trendy scene from one of its two friendly bars. 🍸

✳

SERVICES

REST ROOMS: All restaurants and clubs have rest rooms. An uncrowded public rest room is located between the Wildhorse Saloon and the Portobello Yacht Club. The rest rooms at the top of the stairs in the Wildhorse Saloon are quiet as well as uncrowded.

TELEPHONES: Outdoor public telephones are located near the rest rooms between the Portobello Yacht Club and the Wildhorse Saloon, and also near the rest rooms behind the West End Stage. There are telephones near the rest rooms in all restaurants and clubs, but the quietest phones are those at the Pleasure Island Jazz Company.

BANKING: An automatic teller machine (ATM) and a change machine are located under the stairs that lead up to the Rock & Roll Beach Club entrance.

LOCKERS: Lockers can be found in the Rock & Roll Beach Club, Mannequins Dance Palace, 8TRAX, and the BET SoundStage Club. There are outdoor lockers across from the Wildhorse Saloon.

VISITORS WITH DISABILITIES: All areas of Pleasure Island are wheelchair accessible, and all multi-level clubs have elevators.

Pleasure Island Club-Hopping Tour

This tour is designed to let first-time visitors sample the best of Pleasure Island in a single evening. To create your own custom vacation at Walt Disney World, combine this tour with a morning tour at any other theme park. For example, combine the evening tour at Pleasure Island with a morning tour and lunch at Disney-MGM Studios. Use the afternoon to relax and enjoy your resort.

Five to six hours — year-round — including dinner.
Plan an early dinner (about 6 PM) at the Wildhorse Saloon, Portobello Yacht Club, or Fulton's Crab House.
You can generally walk in at that time, but make reservations if they are being taken.
If you wish to dine at Planet Hollywood, which does not take reservations,
you will need to be in line no later than 5 PM.

⬇ If you arrive early and are dining at one of the Pleasure Island restaurants, you may enter Pleasure Island beforehand for a quick overview tour of the shops and attractions. At the entrance gate, pick up an entertainment schedule listing the evening's show times and events. Proceed to your selected restaurant for your 6 PM dinner.

⬇ If you are dining at Planet Hollywood, you will need to be in line at the restaurant about 5 PM.

⬇ After dinner, stroll through the nearest entrance to Pleasure Island. Buy a ticket if you need one.

⬇ Start your early tour of the clubs, and include some of the following entertainment:

◆ **COMEDY WAREHOUSE** — for an improv comedy performance; the first show starts at about 7:15 PM and has the shortest lines of the evening.

◆ **MANNEQUINS DANCE PALACE** — for the not-to-be-missed high-energy light, sound, and dance show that begins around 9 PM; stand near the front of the dance floor for a good view of the performance, or upstairs for a glimpse of the technical aspects of the show.

◆ **ADVENTURERS CLUB** — to settle in and eavesdrop on the club members' altercations or catch one of the offbeat performances in the adjacent library.

◆ **WILDHORSE SALOON** — for live music and lively country-western dancing; go early if you want to learn the latest dance steps.

◆ **PLEASURE ISLAND JAZZ COMPANY** — to catch a set of live jazz and sample the outstanding appetizers.

◆ **ROCK & ROLL BEACH CLUB** — to dance to R&R hits performed by a live band, or try your hand at a game of pool or pinball.

◆ **8TRAX** — for a "disco fever" experience straight from the seventies or **BET SOUNDSTAGE** for some savvy urban contemporary hits along with the hottest dance styles.

⬇ At about 11:30 PM, work your way through the crowd toward the West End Stage to see the sizzling show that kicks off the **NEW YEAR'S EVE STREET PARTY**.

⬇ If you plan to party on, return to your favorite club or head over to The West Side for the following:

◆ **PLANET HOLLYWOOD LOUNGES** — for a nightcap among the incredible movie props

◆ **BONGOS CUBAN CAFE** — to sample appetizers and cool Latin-style cabaret entertainment

◆ **AMC THEATRES** — for a late-night first-run feature. ◆

DISNEY'S WEST SIDE
AT DOWNTOWN DISNEY

Disney's West Side is the latest addition to the waterfront shopping and entertainment complex at Downtown Disney, which also includes Pleasure Island and Disney Village Marketplace. A hip, eclectic place with trendy restaurants, performance halls, and television broadcast facilities, the West Side is Walt Disney World's cultural crossroads, an entertainment venue for visiting artists and top-name performers, and an enclave, as well, for celebrity-owned restaurants and nightclubs. Wolfgang Puck displays his culinary genius in his new West Side restaurant, offering his cooking wizardry in a casual cafe setting overlooking Buena Vista Lagoon. Bongos Cuban Cafe, a smart supper club created by pop star Gloria Estefan, features Latin music and Cuban cuisine in a spicy Caribbean setting. House of Blues, the famous concert club of musical worship, created by Isaac Tigrett and Dan Aykroyd, offers regional Louisiana cuisine for Gospel Brunches and dinner, and top musical talent in concert every night. The internationally acclaimed Cirque du Soleil is making West Side their permanent home, performing their circus magic five days a week in a sensational performance hall designed just for the show.

WHEN TO GO: Most West Side restaurants are open all day. The AMC Theatres show films from 10 AM until 1 AM (2 AM on the weekends). The shops are open from 10 AM until 11 PM. The most crowded nights are Friday and Saturday, when local residents come out to join the fun. Concert tickets can be reserved directly from the clubs, or in some cases, purchased from Ticketmaster. For a listing of entertainment events and information on reservations, call Walt Disney World Information (407 824-4321). For films and show times at the AMC Theatres, call 827-1300.

HOW TO GET THERE: Disney's West Side is located in the Disney Village Resorts Area. It runs along the shore of Buena Vista Lagoon next to Pleasure Island. The large Downtown Disney parking lot is free. Buses travel between most resorts and theme parks and Downtown Disney. Water launches service the following resorts: Dixie Landings, Port Orleans, and Old Key West. Valet parking is available nearby starting at about 5:30 PM. Taxi service is available.

ADMISSIONS AND RESTRICTIONS: Admission to Disney's West Side is free, and there are no age restrictions. Each nightclub or show has its own age policies and ticket price or cover charge.

ENTERTAINMENT EVENTS

AMC THEATRES: AMC Theatres is frequented by visitors to both West Side and Pleasure Island. Twenty-four screens (including sixteen with Continental stadium seating) show first-run movies all day. Two of the larger theaters, used for new releases and first-run premiers, recall the splendor and luxury of the movie palaces from an earlier era, with three-story-tall screens and balcony seating. **The lowest-priced movie tickets are available to all visitors for shows between 4 and 6 PM. Guests staying at a Walt Disney World resort may also receive a 30 percent discount on movie tickets throughout the evening (after 6 PM) with their resort ID. Be sure to ask!** To avoid long lines or to secure space at popular films or movie premiers, visitors can charge tickets up to three days before the show (827-1311). Call the theater (827-1300) for movie listings and show times.

$AVE

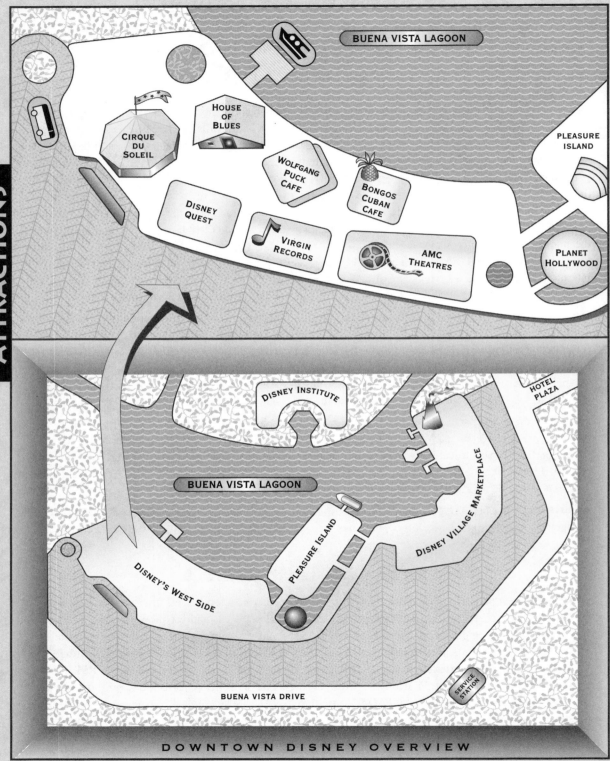

ATTRACTIONS

BUENA VISTA LAGOON

PLEASURE ISLAND

CIRQUE DU SOLEIL

HOUSE OF BLUES

WOLFGANG PUCK CAFE

BONGOS CUBAN CAFE

DISNEY QUEST

VIRGIN RECORDS

AMC THEATRES

PLANET HOLLYWOOD

DISNEY INSTITUTE

HOTEL PLAZA

BUENA VISTA LAGOON

PLEASURE ISLAND

DISNEY VILLAGE MARKETPLACE

DISNEY'S WEST SIDE

SERVICE STATION

BUENA VISTA DRIVE

DOWNTOWN DISNEY OVERVIEW

CIRQUE DU SOLEIL: The curtain rises late in 1998 on this spectacular stage extravaganza featuring more than seventy talented performers in a not-to-be-missed mix of big-top circus acts with original music, fantastic costumes, and innovative choreography. The show will be staged twice daily, five days a week, in a 1,650-seat theater that resembles a circus tent on the outside and a great performance hall inside.

VIRGIN RECORDS MEGASTORE: This vast three-story music store, a retail spin-off of the London-based recording label, features thousands of music and video titles along with books and software. For shoppers, there are more than three hundred listening stations, video viewing stands, and computer terminals. Virgin also has a small concert stage above the entrance, and a trendy cafe serving coffeehouse specialties. Open from 10 AM.

DISNEY QUEST: Like Innoventions in Future World, this cutting edge amusement center and multilevel arcade boasts the latest in gaming technology, including an interactive play area with laser tag, virtual reality adventures, and the latest grand-scale arcade games. Disney Quest is designed to be the ideal safe hangout for teens age twelve to twenty. Admission may be charged.

✳

ENTERTAINMENT DINING

BONGOS CUBAN CAFE: Cuban-style cuisine and live entertainment energize this festive dinner club created by pop star Gloria Estefan and her husband Emilio. A three-story pineapple growing up through the multilevel building sets the Caribbean mood, and as guests dine, a Latin guitar trio performs. On weekends, a Cuban band puts on a lively, upbeat performance, followed by a late-night cabaret where guests can drop in and sample appetizers while they take in the show. Beer, wine, and spirits are served. Open for lunch and dinner from 11 AM until 2 AM; no reservations.

HOUSE OF BLUES: Performances by top musicians are a nightly event at this combination restaurant and concert hall. The club's television studio and radio broadcast facilities make this the West Side's hot spot of sensational musical happenings. Visitors can purchase tickets for scheduled concerts, or drop to dine on Louisiana's Delta cuisine. The House of Blue's popular Gospel Brunch with live entertainment occurs daily. Beer, wine, and spirits are served. Open for brunch from 10:30 AM; dinner from 5 PM; concerts begin about 9 PM. Advance reservations are a must for both Gospel Brunches and performances; no reservations for dinner. (See "Dining Events," page 209.)

PLANET HOLLYWOOD: This restaurant serves up trendy music and the razzle dazzle of Hollywood movies along with tasty dishes served in jumbo portions, ranging from hamburgers and pizza to creative seasonal entrees. Beer, wine, and spirits are served, along with excellent cappuccino and espresso. Open from 11 AM until 2 AM; no reservations. (See "Restaurants," page 182.)

WOLFGANG PUCK CAFE: Internationally renowned chef Wolfgang Puck brings his unique cuisine to Downtown Disney. This relaxed two-story cafe, with soft lighting and snazzy decor, is a showcase of imaginative California cuisine and specialty pizzas that guests can enjoy while seated inside or outdoors overlooking the lagoon. Beer, wine, and spirits are served, as are cappuccino and espresso. In a separate area, Wolfgang Puck Express offers take-out delicacies. Open all day from 11 AM until 2 AM; no reservations. (See "Restaurants," page 196.) ◆

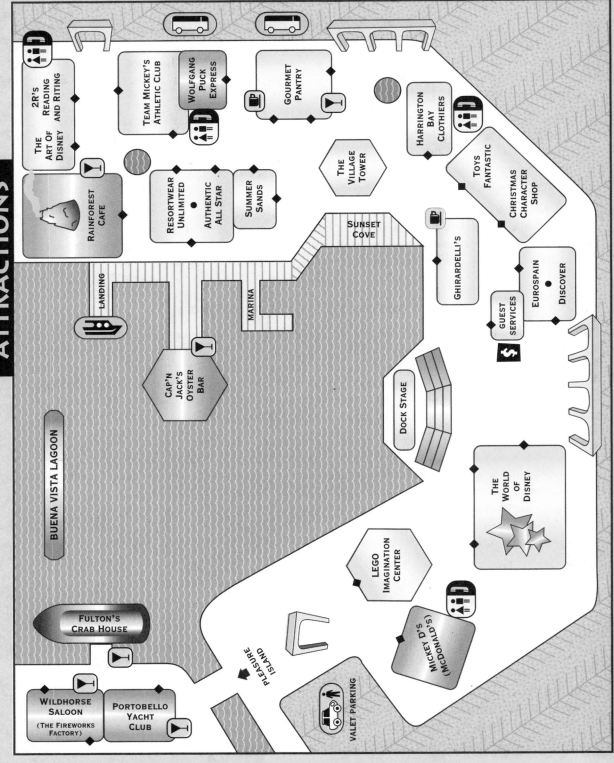

ATTRACTIONS

2R'S READING AND RITING

THE ART OF DISNEY

TEAM MICKEY'S ATHLETIC CLUB

WOLFGANG PUCK EXPRESS

GOURMET PANTRY

HARRINGTON BAY CLOTHIERS

TOYS FANTASTIC

CHRISTMAS CHARACTER SHOP

RAINFOREST CAFE

RESORTWEAR UNLIMITED

AUTHENTIC ALL STAR

SUMMER SANDS

THE VILLAGE TOWER

SUNSET COVE

GHIRARDELLI'S

GUEST SERVICES

EUROSPAIN DISCOVER

$

LANDING

MARINA

CAP'N JACK'S OYSTER BAR

DOCK STAGE

BUENA VISTA LAGOON

THE WORLD OF DISNEY

LEGO IMAGINATION CENTER

FULTON'S CRAB HOUSE

PLEASURE ISLAND

MICKEY D'S (MCDONALD'S)

WILDHORSE SALOON (THE FIREWORKS FACTORY)

PORTOBELLO YACHT CLUB

VALET PARKING

DISNEY VILLAGE MARKETPLACE
AT DOWNTOWN DISNEY

Disney Village Marketplace is a shopping and entertainment center with the atmosphere of a picturesque waterfront town. It's perched on the shoreline of Buena Vista Lagoon along with the rest of Downtown Disney, which includes Pleasure Island and Disney's West Side. At the Marketplace, visitors can stroll along the pleasant waterfront promenade, studded with fanciful topiaries and fountains; relax in one of several restaurants or lounges; or explore the many shops and boutiques offering name-brand clothing, specialty foods, special-interest gifts, and Disney collectibles. **Magic Kingdom Club cardholders and visitors using special American Express Vacation Packages may receive a 10 percent discount on most merchandise sold in the shops. Remember to use your cards!** Disney Village Marketplace is also the site of several annual events, holiday celebrations, and ongoing crafts demonstrations, and has a recreational marina for boating and fishing and as well as outdoor play areas and fountains for children.

WHEN TO GO: Disney Village Marketplace shops are open every day from 9:30 AM until about 11 PM. It is always busy, but parking is much easier before lunch. For information on special-event schedules, call Disney Village Marketplace Guest Services (407 828-3058).

HOW TO GET THERE: Disney Village Marketplace is in the Disney Village Resorts Area. Free parking is available. The Marketplace is within walking distance of the Disney Institute and the Hotel Plaza resorts. Walt Disney World buses travel between all resorts and theme parks and Disney Village Marketplace. Water launches service the following resorts: Dixie Landings, Port Orleans, and Old Key West. Valet parking is available near Pleasure Island starting at about 5:30 PM.

SHOPS

THE WORLD OF DISNEY: With ten themed shopping areas, The World of Disney is the largest Disney store in the world. The Great Hall and Rotunda form the core of this huge flow-through market filled with more Disney merchandise than has ever been amassed under one roof. From luggage to sleepwear to jewelry to videos to toys, nothing has been left out in an effort to attract even the most judicious consumer. The largest selection ever of Disney-character apparel for any age can be found here, as well as costumes, sportswear, and high fashion. This store is always busy, but it is least crowded during the first hour it is open in the morning.

LEGO IMAGINATION CENTER: A sea serpent rising from Buena Vista Lagoon and a number of other giant fanciful sculptures built with LEGO's interlocking blocks mark the site of this new superstore with a focus on creativity. The very latest LEGOs are featured here, along with hundreds of other items from LEGO's international product line. The store features a hands-on demonstration area with products that visitors of all ages can try before they buy, and a whimsical outdoor playground where children can burn off energy in imaginative ways.

DISCOVER: Living topiary and bonsai, rocks and crystals, and nature-oriented books and gifts fill this pleasant natural-wonders shop. Garden-lovers will find seeds and bulbs, birdhouses, gardening

ATTRACTIONS

books and tools, sun hats, and an array of tee-shirts and tote bags featuring nature-themed designs. The shop also offers herbal bathing products and cosmetics, and a large menagerie of exotic stuffed animals such as giraffes, gorillas, lion cubs, and frogs.

EUROSPAIN: Eurospain offers a vast array of collectibles from around the world, all displayed in uniquely designed showcases. The shop stocks a selection of Austrian and Italian crystal, Goebels miniatures, ceramic masks, music boxes, porcelain figurines, and a variety of crystal and enameled jewelry. Crafts demonstrations include glass blowing and engraving.

CHARACTER CHRISTMAS SHOP: Year-round, the Character Christmas Shop is one of the most popular stores at Disney Village Marketplace. One-of-a-kind Christmas ornaments, collectibles, Nativity scenes, recordings of Christmas music, cards, garlands, wreaths, clothing, animated figures, Christmas Disney-character ornaments and lights, and almost anything else required for the Christmas season can be found here. Personalization is also available.

TOYS FANTASTIC: This Disney-Mattel collaboration stocks what is possibly the most complete selection of Barbie dolls and Barbie-doll paraphernalia anywhere. Mattel's Hot Wheels and truck-loads of accessories are also featured here.

GHIRARDELLI'S ICE CREAM SODA FOUNTAIN AND CHOCOLATE SHOP: This haven for ice cream–lovers and chocolate connoisseurs, reminiscent of a turn-of-the-century soda "shoppe," features San Francisco's well-known Ghirardelli chocolates. The sweet and soothing treats here include old-fashioned malts, milk shakes, floats, huge ice cream sundaes, and, of course, chocolate in almost every imaginable form.

HARRINGTON BAY CLOTHIERS: With its pleasant masculine decor, this store provides a peaceful oasis for the shopping weary. Men's brand-name casual and dress fashions are featured, and accessories, tote bags, windbreakers, ties, and golf wear are also available.

THE VILLAGE TOWER: This octagonal shop is open on all sides and is the showcase store for special events and seasonal activities at Disney Village Marketplace. During those times, The Village Tower becomes a merchandising outlet for the featured event, such as the Festival of the Masters art show. At other times, the store's selection is dedicated exclusively to name-brand athletic shoes and sportswear. In the summer, fun-in-the-sun merchandise is featured. The shop's inventory is completely overhauled several times a year.

GOURMET PANTRY: One side of this store is a culinary collectors' paradise, with a dizzying variety of gourmet cookware, utensils, and cookbooks. The other side houses a deli counter stocked with cheese, cold meats, salads, and Italian sandwiches sold by the inch. Gourmet Pantry also has a liquor and wine department; a tobacco shop featuring premium cigars, pipe tobacco, and smoking accessories; a Candy Shoppe; and a bakery that offers muffins, pastries, cookies, and gourmet coffees brewed strong enough to get shoppers back on their feet. Shaded tables are scattered about outside. Gourmet Pantry (828-3486) provides free delivery service to the Walt Disney World resorts.

RESORTWEAR UNLIMITED: In the summer months, this is the place to find women's casual wear, sun hats, sandals, sunglasses, and one of the largest selections of swimwear at Walt Disney World. During the winter months, jackets, slacks, and sweaters are also featured. The shop also carries sneakers, low-heeled dress shoes, and costume jewelry.

- **SUMMER SANDS:** This small shop sells bathing suits, a variety of watertoys, jewelry featuring seashells and aquatic mammals, and a typical assortment of Florida accessories: sunglasses, sun block and other sun-related skin care products, big hats, and straw bags in assorted sizes and colors.

- **AUTHENTIC ALL STAR:** This shop showcases hats, jackets, tee-shirts, sweatshirts, and other merchandise emblazoned with the logos and emblems of popular sports teams and the Official All Star Cafe, the celebrity-athlete-owned restaurant located at Disney's Wide World of Sports.

- **TEAM MICKEY'S ATHLETIC CLUB:** This popular store features a huge selection of sports accessories and apparel (most festooned with the Disney insignia), such as golfing sweaters and bags, baseball jerseys and jackets, bowling shirts and bags, rugby and polo shirts, bicycling gear, aerobics outfits, and warm-up suits. In the athletic shoe department, a set of bleachers that faces a wall of video monitors showing sports events all day long is a great spot for shopping-weary sports fans to sit down, cool off, and relax.

- **THE ART OF DISNEY:** This gallery's selection of upscale Disney collectibles and original works of art based on Disney themes is a not-to-be-missed display that includes sculptures, animation cels, mosaics, paintings, blown glass, and furniture. Prices above $10,000 are not unusual.

- **2R'S READING AND RITING:** The Art of Disney opens onto this pleasant, busy bookstore, which features current bestsellers among its range of titles for children and adults. Stationery, videos, magazines, audiotapes and CDs, and Disney software and CD-ROMs are also available here. A walk-up coffee bar in the store serves espresso and cappuccino. ☕

ACTIVITIES, EVENTS, AND LIVE ENTERTAINMENT

Live entertainment and seasonal events are scheduled throughout the year at Disney Village Marketplace. These include the Classic Car show in June, the Boat Show in October, the Festival of the Masters art show in November, and tree-lighting ceremonies and carolers during the Christmas season. Many of the Marketplace shops feature daily demonstrations by guest artisans. For current entertainment schedule call Disney Village Marketplace Guest Services (407 828-3058).

- **DOCK STAGE:** The Dock Stage is located in an open plaza at the edge of Buena Vista Lagoon. Throughout the year, it is the site of jazz concerts, special holiday celebrations, high school band competitions, and a wide variety of other live entertainment.

- **BOATING AT CAP'N JACK'S MARINA:** This busy marina has been downsized with the development of Downtown Disney, but it still rents canopy boats, pontoon boats, and zippy Water Sprites to visitors who would like to take a spin on Buena Vista Lagoon or explore the bayoulike Village Waterways and tour the themed resorts in the Disney Village Resorts Area (see "Boating & Marina," page 218). Cap'n Jack's Marina is open daily from 10 AM until sundown.

- **FISHING AT CAP'N JACK'S MARINA:** Popular guided fishing tours depart from here daily in search of largemouth bass. Reservations for the two-, three-, or four-hour catch-and-release excursions should be made in advance by calling Cap'n Jack's Marina (407 828-2461). Visitors who wish to test their fishing skills from the dock can rent old-fashioned cane poles at the Marina. Bait is provided. (See "Fishing," page 223.)

ATTRACTIONS

⊙ **SUNSET COVE:** This waterfront area is a pleasant spot to sit, relax, and watch the watercraft come and go from the nearby dock, or munch on takeout snacks from the Gourmet Pantry or Ghiradelli's. A refreshment stand nearby also serves a variety of beverages.

✳

FULL-SERVICE RESTAURANTS

All visitors to Walt Disney World can make advance reservations for any restaurant at Disney Village Marketplace that accepts them. See "Restaurants," page 157, for reviews and reservation information. Unless otherwise noted, smoking is not permitted in the restaurants.

RAINFOREST CAFE: A huge 'active' volcano distinguishes this spacious tropical-jungle-themed restaurant with cascading waterfalls, aquariums, and sounds of thunder and rain. Guests can enjoy steaks, chicken, seafood, pasta, pizza, and salads with unique flavor combinations. Fruit juices and smoothies, beer, wine, and spirits are served, as are espresso and cappuccino. Open all day from 10 AM until 11 PM Sunday through Thursday (until midnight Friday and Saturday). No reservations.

CAP'N JACK'S OYSTER BAR: Occupying a pier out in the lagoon, this restaurant offers diners a great water view from any table. The restaurant attracts a lively crowd for clams and oysters on the half shell, shrimp cocktails, crab cakes, lobster, and pasta. Beer, wine, and spirits are served. Open all day. Visitors who just want to snack can simply walk in and seat themselves at the bar. No reservations.

FULTON'S CRAB HOUSE: Crab, lobster, and other fresh seafood are the specialties at this huge restaurant aboard a replica nineteenth-century riverboat. Diners are seated at tables on the riverboat's three decks, many with pleasant views of Buena Vista Lagoon. Beer, wine, and spirits are served. Open for dinner from 5 PM until midnight; reservations recommended.

PORTOBELLO YACHT CLUB: Guests enjoy Italian entrees, fresh seafood, and oven-fired thin-crust pizzas in spacious dining areas featuring yachting trophies and other maritime mementos. Beer, wine, and spirits are served, as are excellent espresso and cappuccino. Open for lunch from 11:30 AM; dinner from 5 PM until midnight; reservations recommended.

WILDHORSE SALOON/FIREWORKS FACTORY: A full menu of "unbridled barbecue" at this Pleasure Island restaurant and country western club features mesquite smoked chicken ribs, and beef, along with meal-sized salads and hamburgers. Guests can hear country-western tunes filtering in from the Wildhorse Saloon's stage and dance floor. Pleasure Island admission is not required in the restaurant. Beer, wine and spirits are served. Open for dinner from 5 PM until midnight. No reservations.

✳

CAFES AND LOUNGES

Several counter-service restaurants and lounges at Disney Village Marketplace serve fast-food meals and snacks. Those listed below are especially pleasant and make good rendezvous spots for visitors who want to shop separately and meet up later.

GHIRARDELLI'S ICE CREAM SODA FOUNTAIN AND CHOCOLATE SHOP: Here, ice cream–lovers and chocoholics can take a break from shopping and indulge their sweet tooth with sundaes, floats, milk shakes, and candies. Coffee and espresso are also served. ▟

DISNEY VILLAGE MARKETPLACE

GOURMET PANTRY: Step up to the bakery and check out the selection of freshly brewed specialty coffees lined up along the back wall. A long deli counter offers take-out sandwiches and snacks. There are pleasant shaded tables scattered outside the shop. ☕

WOLFGANG PUCK EXPRESS: This counter-service restaurant features California cuisine such as rotisserie chicken, pizzas, specialty pastas, grilled seasonal vegetables, and distinctive desserts. Mineral water, beer, and wine are served, as are espresso and cappuccino. ☕🍸

MICKEY D'S: The expanded menu here at the world's largest McDonald's restaurant features several healthier items along with the traditional fast-food fare. Soft drinks and coffee are served. ☕

CAP'N JACK'S OYSTER BAR: The hexagonal copper bar in this lively restaurant is known for its tasty frozen strawberry Margaritas. This convivial bar is a great place to meet fellow visitors while enjoying a quick pick-me-up or to sit back for a long, relaxing view of the sunset over Buena Vista Lagoon. Coffee and espresso are served as well. ☕🍸

RAINFOREST CAFE'S MAGIC MUSHROOM JUICE & COFFEE BAR: Guests at this lively tropical-themed bar can enjoy appetizers infused with a multicultural influence as they sit beneath a giant mushroom on fanciful barstools representing jungle animals. The full-service bar serves fresh fruit and vegetable juices (which can be ordered with or without spirits), espresso, cappuccino, and a variety of specialty coffee beverages. ☕🍸

FULTON'S STONE CRAB LOUNGE: This lounge's curved and fully windowed wall gives guests a marvelous view of Lake Buena Vista. The dark wood trim and the subdued lighting at night lend a casual yet intimate atmosphere to the spacious area. During the day, several kinds of shellfish, seafood, and salads are served as appetizers and light meals. The full bar features an extensive assortment of liquors and wines. ☕🍸

PORTOBELLO YACHT CLUB BAR: Warm, dark mahogany paneling and polished brass fixtures create a pleasant, clubby atmosphere here. The full bar features an array of grappas and good Italian wines. Appetizers include Quattro Formaggi Pizza, Antipasto Assortito, and Calamaretti Fritti. Some of Walt Disney World's most potent espresso and cappuccino can be found here. ☕🍸

HOT TIPS

DISNEY SHOPPING TIPS: Unique Disney merchandise is spread throughout Walt Disney World's theme parks and resorts. If you see something you like, you will probably not run into it again. It's smarter to buy when you can, and return it if you must. ***Returning's easy! If you have the receipt, you can return your purchase anywhere at Walt Disney World, including your own hotel gift shop. How do you know when Disney merchandise has been marked down? Look for prices ending in "99." If you see that shirt you want marked $12.99, grab it, because it's probably discontinued. For authentic Disney merchandise at rock-bottom prices, head over to Character Warehouse, a short drive away.***

GUEST SERVICES: Disney Village Marketplace Guest Services desk is one of the most helpful at Walt Disney World. Resort guests can drop their purchases at Guest Services for gift wrapping or for free delivery to their hotel. After 8 PM, Guest Services is the only location at Walt Disney World where late-arriving visitors can buy theme park tickets and avoid those long lines in the morning. ◆

TYPHOON LAGOON

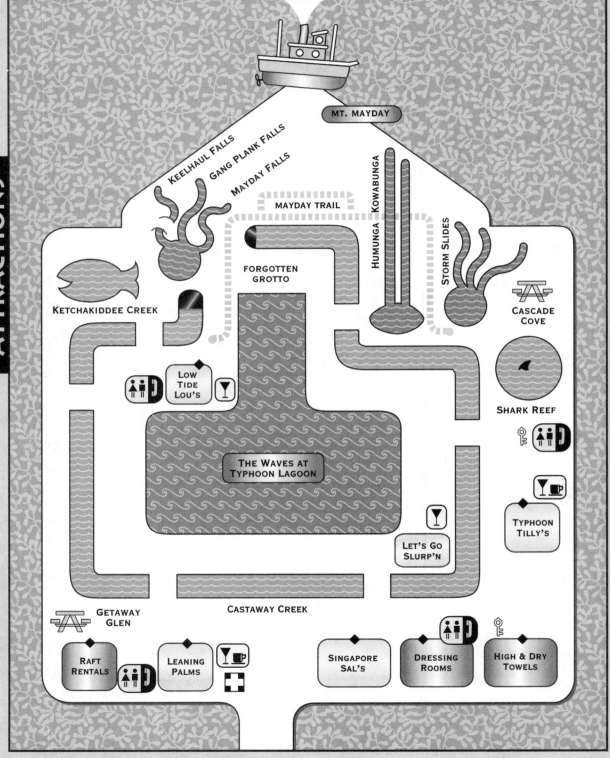

ATTRACTIONS

MT. MAYDAY

KEELHAUL FALLS
GANG PLANK FALLS
MAYDAY FALLS
MAYDAY TRAIL

HUMUNGA KOWABUNGA

STORM SLIDES

FORGOTTEN GROTTO

KETCHAKIDDEE CREEK

CASCADE COVE

LOW TIDE LOU'S

SHARK REEF

THE WAVES AT TYPHOON LAGOON

TYPHOON TILLY'S

LET'S GO SLURP'N

GETAWAY GLEN

CASTAWAY CREEK

RAFT RENTALS

LEANING PALMS

SINGAPORE SAL'S

DRESSING ROOMS

HIGH & DRY TOWELS

TYPHOON LAGOON

Typhoon Lagoon is an imaginatively designed fifty-six-acre theme park devoted to water play, with white-water rafting, snorkeling, waterslides, body surfing atop the largest machine-made waves in the world, and a long, lazy float down the meandering creek encircling the park. Depending on where their adventures take them, visitors can enjoy white sand beaches, shady coves, waterfalls, and misty rain forests. According to Disney legend, the lagoon was once the site of a peaceful fishing village that was devastated by a raging typhoon. The *Miss Tilly* shrimp boat was neatly deposited on top of Mt. Mayday, the Placid Palms restaurant became the Leaning Palms, and a steamship moored at Shark Reef was permanently overturned. Part of the fun of Typhoon Lagoon is finding other telltale signs of the storm.

WHEN TO GO: Typhoon Lagoon is open year round, except from mid-November through December when it is closed for refurbishing. Operating hours vary throughout the year, so call Typhoon Lagoon Information (407 560-4141) to find out about opening and closing times. During peak-attendance times (April through September) and weekends year-round, it is essential to arrive before opening time (about 9 AM), since the park fills to capacity by about 10:30 AM and is closed to new arrivals until mid afternoon. During low-attendance times (October through March), mornings can be cool, so plan to visit in the afternoon, when Typhoon Lagoon provides a welcome respite from the frenzy of the theme parks. The park closes about 6 PM in cool months and at 8 PM during the summer. Brief tropical rain showers are common in the summer months, usually in the late afternoon. During a storm, swimmers are chased from the water to wait it out, and many simply leave for the day. Once the storm passes, the park empties significantly, making a post-storm visit worthwhile. If the weather looks uncertain, call Disney Weather (824-4104) for details.

HOW TO GET THERE: Typhoon Lagoon is in the Disney Village Resorts Area, not far from Downtown Disney. Free parking is available in the Typhoon Lagoon parking lot. Buses service Typhoon Lagoon from the Walt Disney World resorts, the major theme parks, Downtown Disney, and the Transportation and Ticket Center.

ADMISSION: Adult admission is about $26 per day (about $20 for children). Admission to Typhoon Lagoon is included with Length of Stay Passes and some Multiday Passes. **At times during the summer months and Spring Break, when the park is open late, twilight admission prices may be offered. If you are arriving after about 3 PM, you can save as much as 30 to 50 percent on admission costs! These special savings are not announced, always be sure to ask.**

✳

ATTRACTIONS

THE WAVES AT TYPHOON LAGOON: The centerpiece of the park is the 2½-acre lagoon and its famous wave maker, which creates impressive six-foot surfing waves. The machine also produces gentle bobbing waves perfect for floating on inner tubes, which are available for rent. The two types of waves alternate for an hour at a time all day long; surfing waves usually start on the even hours. Near the lagoon, a blackboard with the surf report gives information on the water temperature, weather, and alternating surf conditions. *Miss Tilly,* the former shrimp boat atop Mt. Mayday, gives a hoot and sprays a fifty-foot plume of water in the air every half hour, so visitors who are waiting for that first big curl can keep track of the time while experiencing other attractions.

CASTAWAY CREEK: Giant turquoise inner tubes draped with relaxed swimmers are swept along in the currents of Castaway Creek for a lazy thirty-minute float around the perimeter of the park. At the five entrances at different points along the fifteen-foot-wide creek, visitors can wait for an empty tube to float by or grab one of the tubes stacked nearby for the taking. Visitors may also simply swim or drift along with the currents of the three-foot-deep creek if they wish. The currents are strong enough to keep floaters moving, and lifeguards along the way keep an eye on things. Rafters struggling to dodge flotsam and jetsam create laughing and bumping logjams. Where Castaway Creek passes through a misty rain forest, the going is slow enough to permit floaters-by to read the labels on the tropical trees and shrubs. A waterfall soaks all who pass under Mt. Mayday, so leave hats and cameras behind.

SHARK REEF: Before entering the reef, be sure to visit the underwater viewing station. Fashioned as the boiler room of a half-sunken, overturned steamship, its windows reveal snorkelers swimming among the fish in the water above. The water in Shark Reef is salty and unheated to accommodate the Caribbean sea life. Those who wish to swim with the fish get life vests, snorkels and masks, and a five-minute lesson in using them. Then it's off for a shower and a brief swim across the lagoon, which has two islands, loads of interesting fish, and several small sharks. Since Shark Reef is kept cooler than the rest of Typhoon Lagoon, it's a great place to really chill out on hot days.

HUMUNGA KOWABUNGA: Thrill-seeking waterslide enthusiasts will be thoroughly satisfied by the terrifyingly steep and fast descent on these two slides: about a fifty-foot drop in less than thirty seconds. Clothing with rivets or buckles is not allowed, and one-piece bathing suits are advised for women; sliding in thong-style suits may result in friction burns. Riders hit the water hard at the bottom, so nose plugs are also a good idea. The steepness of the slide is hidden from those in line by cleverly planted bushes. There are viewing bleachers at the bottom. You must be physically fit to ride this daring attraction.

STORM SLIDES: These three body slides are tamer than those at Humunga Kowabunga, but still pretty exciting. Riders can choose from the Stern Burner, Jib Jammer, and Rudder Buster, all of which deliver more or less the same ride. Instead of a straight downward descent, these slides take riders on a circuitous corkscrew route through caves and waterfalls. The pool at the bottom is just deep enough to cushion landings (although they can be abrupt enough to wrench off the top of a two-piece bathing suit). There are viewing bleachers at the bottom.

MAYDAY FALLS: Mayday Falls offers a twisty, speedy, bumps-and-ridges tube ride. The tubes are for single riders only, and riders are timed at the top and urged out at the bottom by lifeguards. Mayday Falls is slightly faster than Keelhaul Falls.

GANG PLANK FALLS: Extra-large tubes that hold up to four people zip along speedily down the chute. Although this is the tamest of the three raft rides, in the process of shoving them off, the lifeguards duck every raft under a nearby waterfall, thoroughly soaking the occupants.

KEELHAUL FALLS: The tube ride down Keelhaul Falls is slower than the one down Mayday Falls, but it plunges into a pitch-black tunnel about halfway down. This is a real thrill and completely unexpected, since riders are hurtling along with no clue as to what's coming next. Riders end up safely at the common landing pool, where they quickly exit.

KETCHAKIDDEE CREEK: This little-kids-only area is specially designed for children and their parents. An assortment of scaled-down water rides similar to those found throughout the park are offered here, along with floating toys and a little waterfall. It's a happy, noisy area.

※

REFRESHMENT STANDS AND PICNIC AREAS

The refreshment stands at Typhoon Lagoon serve snacks and fast-food meals all day, although the lines can be quite long. Snack and beverage carts throughout the park sell beer and soft drinks, and guests may bring food and beverages into the park, but no glass containers or alcoholic beverages. There are no cooking facilities.

LEANING PALMS: The largest refreshment stand, Leaning Palms, is to the left of the main entrance. Pizza, hamburgers, hot dogs, salads, and turkey, tuna, and chicken sandwiches are sold here, along with soft drinks, milk shakes, beer, and coffee. Eating areas with shaded tables are nearby.

TYPHOON TILLY'S GALLEY & GROG: Located on the far right side of the lagoon, this large refreshment stand has two separate walk-up counters. Both sides offer snacks, beverages, and ice cream, but the left counter, which opens earlier in the day, serves hot dogs and sandwiches, as well as beer and coffee. There are shaded tables nearby, or diners can picnic on the sand at Cascade Cove. Typhoon Tilly's may be closed during slow seasons.

LET'S GO SLURP'N: This thatch-roofed beach shack serves a limited supply of snacks, as well as beer, wine coolers, and spirits, including frozen fruit drinks.

LOW TIDE LOU'S: This small beach shack near the entrance to Gang Plank Falls sells foot-long hot dogs and grilled cheese sandwiches as well as soft drinks, draft beer, wine coolers, and frozen rum punch, all of which can be enjoyed in the quaint shelter nearby. Low Tide Lou's is near Ketchakiddee Creek, so the noise level can be fairly high.

GETAWAY GLEN PICNIC AREA: This picnic area with many tables and play areas is on the left side of the lagoon near Leaning Palms. A volleyball net is permanently installed, but there is plenty of room for eating as well as playing. Overhanging shelters provide a shady break from the sun, and mist from the rain forest keeps things cool on windy days.

CASCADE COVE PICNIC AREA: Cascade Cove is located between Shark Reef and Castaway Creek on the right side of the lagoon. Chaise lounges, wooden tables, and shady overhangs create a welcome picnic spot. Cascade Cove is larger than Getaway Glen, but fills up rapidly because of its proximity to Typhoon Tilly's.

※

SERVICES

REST ROOMS: Public rest rooms are located near Typhoon Tilly's snack bar, the Leaning Palms snack bar, and at the base of Gang Plank Falls, close to Low Tide Lou's snack bar. All the rest rooms can get quite crowded in the afternoons. The rest rooms at the Dressing Rooms are the largest.

ATTRACTIONS

ATTRACTIONS

TELEPHONES: Public telephones are located outside the Dressing Rooms near Singapore Sal's and adjacent to all rest rooms. The phones inside the Dressing Rooms offer a shady spot for making calls. Those at Typhoon Tilly's are generally available.

TOWELS: Towels can be rented at High & Dry Towels, located to the right of the entrance walkway.

CHANGING ROOMS & SHOWERS: The Dressing Rooms, located next to Singapore Sal's, have many shower/changing rooms. Since all rest rooms in the park have shower cubicles, visitors can also use them to change, and most are less crowded than those at the Dressing Rooms.

LOCKERS: Keys to lockers near the Dressing Rooms or near Typhoon Tilly's can be rented at High & Dry Towels. Specify the location that you prefer.

WATERTOYS: Life vests are available free of charge at High & Dry Towels. Tubes for the bobbing waves in Typhoon Lagoon can be rented at Castaway Creek Raft Rentals. During busy times, tubes are also rented on the beach. Visitors are not permitted to bring their own equipment into the park.

FIRST AID: The first-aid station is located to the left of the main entrance, near the Leaning Palms snack bar. Aspirin and other first-aid needs are dispensed free of charge.

VISITORS WITH DISABILITIES: Wheelchairs may be rented just inside the entrance gate to Typhoon Lagoon, although only a limited number are available. All pathways are wheelchair accessible, and there is a ramp to the viewing station in Shark Reef. Most of the thrill rides may be inappropriate for people with serious disabilities, but Castaway Creek and the gentler bobbing waves in Typhoon Lagoon can be ideal.

✳

TYPHOON LAGOON TIPS

❗ During high-attendance times, there is always a long line for rental towels and locker keys. Bring your own towel, if you can, and leave valuables behind. If you must have a locker, get in this line when the park first opens and ask for a key to the lockers near Typhoon Tilly's.

❗ Establish a "camp" by claiming a picnic table or lounge chair and leaving your towels, shoes, and belongings on top. At Typhoon Lagoon, this signals to all that it is occupied. Try to choose a site in the shade or under a shelter, which will keep your belongings dry in a sudden downpour and protect you against overexposure to the sun. If you want to work on your tan, you can always find a place in the sun.

❗ During the summer months, Typhoon Lagoon is a tempting destination, but the crowds can make it difficult. A good time to visit is after 4 PM, when parents are taking their tired kids back to their hotels and others are leaving to pursue dinner plans. Late afternoon is an enchanting time at Typhoon Lagoon, which often stays open until 8 PM. The park takes on a tropical remoteness, and lines to the attractions are short or nonexistent, so you can frolic to your heart's content or simply plop down in a lounge chair under the swaying palms with a wine cooler.

❗ Many WDW resort coffee shops will prepare a box lunch, so you can eat well and avoid the long lines at refreshment stands. Purchase drinks at one of the Typhoon Lagoon beverage carts.

Half-Day Tour at Typhoon Lagoon

The half-day tour that follows is designed to allow first-time visitors to experience the best of Typhoon Lagoon in three to four hours. During peak seasons, this tour works best either in the early morning or late in the afternoon (3 or 4 PM). In cool seasons, the tour works best in the early afternoon (1 PM). Visitors on the Peak Season Morning Tour can buy a fast-food lunch inside the park, bring a box lunch from their hotel coffee shop, or plan to lunch at 1 PM or later at their hotel or a restaurant in nearby Disney Village Marketplace. Visitors on the Peak Season Late Afternoon Tour may want to eat at the park and stay until closing (8 PM), or plan a late dinner elsewhere. Visitors on the Cool Season Early Afternoon Tour should eat lunch before they arrive.

✳

MORNING OR AFTERNOON AT THE LAGOON

Three to four hours.
Peak Season Morning Tour (9 AM) — April through September — lunch optional.
Peak Season Late Afternoon Tour (3 or 4 PM) — April through September — does not include dinner.
Cool Season Early Afternoon Tour (1 PM) — October through March — does not include lunch.
On the Peak Season Morning Tour, reverse the order of the numbered attractions to avoid long lines.

⬇ Pack a tote bag with sun block and a hat or visor. Wear your bathing suit under your clothes. If you have a towel, bring it rather than waste time in the towel line.

⬇ If you are on the Morning Tour, arrive at the entrance to Typhoon Lagoon about twenty minutes before the park officially opens. Call Typhoon Lagoon Information (560-4141) or check with Guest Services in your resort for opening times.

⬇ When you enter the park, get in the line to rent towels and a locker (if you need them) at High & Dry Towels. Request a locker near Typhoon Tilly's.

⬇ Set up camp in one of the sheltered coves near Typhoon Tilly's. On the Afternoon Tours you may need to wait and watch for the perfect site to appear, as visitors begin to leave.

⬇ Proceed to ❶ CASTAWAY CREEK. There is an entrance close to Typhoon Tilly's. Grab one of the extra tubes stacked here or look for an empty one floating by. Use the Water Tower as your exit landmark and take off down the creek for a revolution or two around the park.

⬇ After you leave Castaway Creek, walk over to the ❷ SHARK REEF viewing station for an underwater view. Then go topside to gear up and join the snorkeling tour of Shark Reef.

⬇ When you're done at Shark Reef, climb the stairs to Humunga Kowabunga, and turn off halfway up on MAYDAY TRAIL. Follow the trail across Mt. Mayday and behind Forgotten Grotto for a bird's-eye view of Typhoon Lagoon. Mayday Trail ends near ❸ KEELHAUL FALLS, where you can catch a white-water raft ride (or grab a beverage at Low Tide Lou's).

⬇ If Keelhaul Falls whets your appetite for thrills, backtrack to ❹ STORM SLIDES and ride the spiraling water chutes. Daredevils can take the terrifying plunge at ❺ HUMUNGA KOWABUNGA.

⬇ Relax and ride the bobbing waves or body surf in TYPHOON LAGOON (check the wave schedule in front of the Lagoon). The eruption of Mt. Mayday (every half hour) will tell you when surf's up. ◆

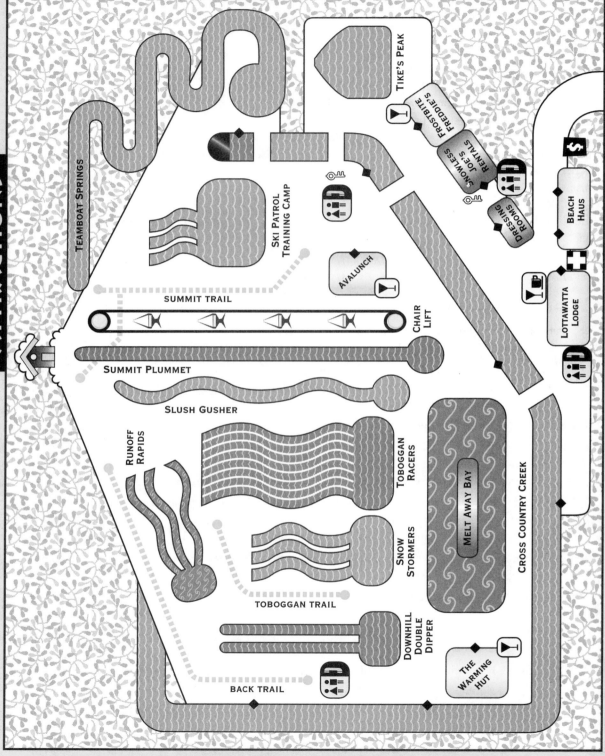

ATTRACTIONS

TEAMBOAT SPRINGS

TIKE'S PEAK

FROSTBITE FREDDIE'S

SNOWLESS JOE'S RENTALS

DRESSING ROOMS

SKI PATROL TRAINING CAMP

AVALUNCH

SUMMIT TRAIL

CHAIR LIFT

SUMMIT PLUMMET

SLUSH GUSHER

RUNOFF RAPIDS

TOBOGGAN RACERS

MELT AWAY BAY

SNOW STORMERS

TOBOGGAN TRAIL

CROSS COUNTRY CREEK

DOWNHILL DOUBLE DIPPER

BACK TRAIL

THE WARMING HUT

BEACH HAUS

LOTTAWATTA LODGE

BLIZZARD BEACH

Blizzard Beach, Walt Disney World's new water park, blends the wintery elements of a snowy landscape with the pleasures of frolicking under the warm Florida sun. Adventurous visitors can enjoy plunging waterslides and exciting tube and raft rides, while the more sedate can relax with around-the-park floats, beach picnics, and a stroll to Mt. Gushmore's summit for a bird's-eye view of the park. The Disney yarn about Blizzard Beach is that a capricious Mother Nature set a snowstorm raging on Florida's Mt. Gushmore one day, inspiring developers to create an alpine snow park. When the climate returned to normal and the ice and snow began melting, so did the developers' dreams. As they surveyed their dismal situation, they noticed an alligator having fun sliding down the mountain slopes in the slush. The 'gator's good time gave the developers a brilliant idea: Rather than offering visitors snow-based activities like skiing and sledding, why not use the snow-park equipment to take advantage of the melting ice and provide challenging water sports instead? Blizzard Beach was the result.

WHEN TO GO: Blizzard Beach is open year-round, except from January to mid-February when it may be closed for maintenance. Operating hours vary throughout the year. To find out about opening and closing times, call Blizzard Beach Information (407 560-3400). During peak-attendance times (April through September), it is essential to arrive before opening time (about 9 AM), since the park restricts new arrivals when its parking lot fills, usually by 11 AM. During low-attendance times (October through March), mornings can be cool, so plan your visit to Blizzard Beach in the early afternoon as a relaxing break from the theme parks. The park closes about 5 PM in the cool months, and about 8 PM during the summer. In the summer months, Florida has brief tropical rain showers, usually in the late afternoon. During a storm, swimmers are chased from the water to wait it out, and many leave for the day. After the storm passes, the park empties significantly, making a post-storm visit highly desirable. If the weather looks uncertain, call Disney Weather (824-4104) for details.

HOW TO GET THERE: Blizzard Beach is in the Animal Kingdom Resorts Area, not far from Disney-MGM Studios. Free parking is available in the Blizzard Beach parking lot. Buses service Blizzard Beach from the Walt Disney World resorts, the major theme parks, Downtown Disney, and the Transportation and Ticket Center.

ADMISSION: Adult admission is about $28 per day (about $22 for children). Admission to Blizzard Beach is included with Length of Stay Passes and some Multiday Passes. **At times during the summer months and Spring Break, when the park is open late, twilight admission prices may be offered. If you are arriving after about 3 PM, you can save as much as 30 to 50 percent on admission costs! These special savings are not announced, so be sure to ask.**

✳

ATTRACTIONS

◗ **CROSS COUNTRY CREEK:** Relaxed riders on giant inner tubes drift along in the currents of Cross Country Creek for a pleasant thirty-minute float around the perimeter of Blizzard Beach. Cross Country Creek may seem like a dull ride on first glance, but the alpine landscaping, occasional swift stretches, and a trip through a spooky cave of melting "ice" lend a bit of spice to the excursion. There

ATTRACTIONS

are several entrances at different points along the creek where visitors can wait for an empty tube to float by or grab one of the tubes that stack up early or late in the day. Swimmers may also enter without tubes; the currents are strong enough to keep things moving.

CHAIR LIFT: Visitors can walk to the top of Mt. Gushmore or board the zany, colorful Chair Lift to reach the following attractions: Summit Plummet, Slush Gusher, and Teamboat Springs. Riders on cable cars with mock skis attached beneath enjoy a sweeping view on their ascent. The trip is very slow, and riders must exit quickly at the top. The Chair Lift is a one-way ride — the only way back down from the top of Mt. Gushmore is on the Summit Trail or the Toboggan Trail.

SUMMIT PLUMMET: Billed as the fastest waterslide on earth, Summit Plummet will delight thrill-seeking enthusiasts. The one-tenth-mile course starts at the "ski jump" perched on Mt. Gushmore's summit. At speeds over fifty miles per hour, riders free fall more than one hundred feet into a pool at the foot of the mountain. Viewers looking up will also get a thrill as they watch riders "vanish" from the slopes into a cloud of mist. Only physically fit people are allowed on the ride, which is over in less than a minute.

SLUSH GUSHER: At ninety feet, Slush Gusher is touted as the world's tallest waterslide. Although not quite as daunting an experience as Summit Plummet, Slush Gusher takes riders on a roller-coaster-like descent through a "wintery" canyon landscape. Riders are positioned feet first, on their backs, with arms and legs crossed, and actually become airborne on parts of this ride. Only physically fit people are allowed on the ride, which should be avoided by those with back problems.

SNOW STORMERS: Visitors ride rafts on one of three side-by-side slalom courses that zigzag down the mountainside. The challenge for rafters is to try to avoid bumping into the flags and "ski gates" as they speed down.

TOBOGGAN RACER: Riders lie face down on toboggan-shaped rafts with front handles for a thrilling head-first plunge down Mt. Gushmore on one of eight side-by-side waterslides. Lifting the handles speeds the descent; to maintain control, push down when approaching the bottom.

DOWNHILL DOUBLE DIPPER: This recent addition to the park's wild slides drops 50 feet as riders on inner tubes race against each other down one of two side-by-side waterslides, reaching speeds of up to twenty-five miles per hour. The tubes are for single riders only.

RUNOFF RAPIDS: Three separate waterslides at Runoff Rapids, on Mt. Gushmore's back face, offer bumps-and-ridges inner tube rides for singles, doubles, and threesomes. One of the waterslides plunges riders into a twisty, pitch-black pipe slide.

TEAMBOAT SPRINGS: Extra-large inner tubes that hold up to five people zip over cascades down a twisting one-quarter-mile-long flume, the longest of its kind anywhere.

MELT AWAY BAY: Nearly the size of a football field, Melt Away Bay with its white sand beach is located at the bottom of Mt. Gushmore. "Snow" from the mountain, "liquefied" by the warm Florida climate, cascades into the bay. The bay's wave-making machine, not nearly as dynamic as Typhoon Lagoon's, creates gentle Caribbean-style swells for swimmers, floaters, and splashers. The beach is packed with lounge chairs, but the shade value of the covered picnic tables makes them the most coveted and convenient hangouts.

SKI PATROL TRAINING CAMP: Designed primarily for pre-teens, the Training Camp offers three separate activities:

MOGUL MANIA: Mogul Mania offers a bumpy inner tube descent over a knobby, snow-lined water field. The tubes are for single riders only.

THIN ICE TRAINING COURSE: The challenge here is to walk across a swimming pool on floating, bobbing chunks of ersatz "ice" while holding onto an overhead cargo net.

SKI PATROL SHELTER: Riders hang on to a suspended T-bar at Fahrenheit Drop and glide out before dropping into an "icy" pool. The fast slide at Frozen Pipe Springs exits into the same pool.

TIKE'S PEAK: Specially designed for small children and their parents, this enchanting kids-only area offers a miniaturized Mt. Gushmore with selected scaled-down water rides similar to those found on the mountain. Squirting fountains add to the activity at this happy but noisy area. Visitors seeking quiet relaxation should be sure to camp elsewhere.

✳

REFRESHMENT STANDS AND PICNIC AREAS

The refreshment stands at Blizzard Beach serve snacks and fast-food meals. Beverage carts near Melt Away Bay and across from Snowless Joe's Rentals sell ice cream, soft drinks, and beer. You may bring food and beverages into the park, but no glass containers or alcoholic beverages. There are no cooking facilities.

LOTTAWATTA LODGE: The largest refreshment stand, Lottawatta Lodge, is located near the park's entrance. Designed with a ski lodge look, the walk-up counter offers salads, hamburgers, hot dogs, pizza, and sandwiches, along with soft drinks, frozen fruit drinks, beer, wine coolers, and coffee. Tables on the partially shaded terrace offer great views of the action at Blizzard Beach. ♨ Y

FROSTBITE FREDDIE'S FROZEN FRESHMENTS: Tucked around the corner from Snowless Joe's Rentals, this refreshment stand offers soft drinks, frozen fruit drinks, wine coolers, and spirits. There are shaded tables in front of the stand. Y

AVALUNCH: Located near Tike's Peak, this food stand offers hot dogs, nachos, snacks, and ice cream, as well as soft drinks, beer, and wine coolers. There are shaded tables nearby. Y

THE WARMING HUT: This snow-covered snack shack on the far side of Melt Away Bay offers counter-service hot dogs, turkey legs, snacks, and ice cream, along with soft drinks, frozen fruit drinks, beer, and wine coolers. There are shaded tables nearby. Y

PICNIC SPOTS: Unlike Typhoon Lagoon, picnic spots are hard to find at Blizzard Beach. Your best bet is to arrive well before opening time and rush to stake a claim at one of the covered picnic tables surrounding Melt Away Bay. Do not pass Go: Do this first.

✳

SERVICES

REST ROOMS: Public rest rooms are located at the Dressing Rooms near the park's entrance, and near Lottawatta Lodge, Avalunch, and The Warming Hut. Rest rooms can get quite crowded. The rest rooms at the Dressing Rooms are the largest; those at The Warming Hut are the least crowded.

ATTRACTIONS

ATTRACTIONS

TELEPHONES: Public telephones are located just outside the park's entrance, outside the Dressing Rooms near the park's entrance, and near all the rest rooms. The phones at Lottawatta Lodge are generally available. Those at The Warming Hut offer a quiet location for making calls.

BANKING: There is an automated teller machine (ATM) just outside the park's entrance, on the left.

TOWELS: Towels can be rented at Snowless Joe's Rentals, near the park's entrance.

SHOWER & CHANGING AREA: The Dressing Rooms near the park's entrance have the only indoor showers at Blizzard Beach.

LOCKERS: Keys to the day lockers near the Dressing Rooms or near the rest rooms at Avalunch can be rented at Snowless Joe's Rentals.

WATERTOYS: Life vests are available free of charge (with a deposit) at Snowless Joe's Rentals. Visitors may bring flotation aids, such as water wings and flotation belts, but no masks or fins.

FIRST AID: The first-aid station is located near Lottawatta Lodge. Aspirin and other first-aid needs are dispensed free of charge.

VISITORS WITH DISABILITIES: A limited number of wheelchairs are available just inside the entrance gate to Blizzard Beach. Most ground-level pathways are wheelchair accessible. The Chair Lift has a wheelchair car, and wheelchairs (but not visitors) are placed in it to return to the bottom. Most of the waterslides are off-limits to people with serious physical disabilities, but Teamboat Springs, Cross Country Creek, and the bobbing waves of Melt Away Bay are ideal for just about everyone.

✳

BLIZZARD BEACH TIPS

! During high-attendance times in the warm months, long lines for rental towels and locker keys will greet you. If you are planning to visit on a crowded day, wear your bathing suit under your clothes, bring your own towel, do not bring valuables or anything else you would want to store, and focus first on locating a place to "camp." Good, shady spots are limited. If you *do* need a locker, make it a point to get to the park well before opening time and get into the locker line first thing. There can be very long lines at the refreshment stands, as well. Most resort coffee shops will prepare a box lunch for you to take into Blizzard Beach so you can avoid the lines. Many visitors also bring along beverages in small coolers.

! Establish a "camp" by claiming an umbrella-covered lounge chair or one of the shaded picnic tables. Leave your towels and other belongings scattered on top to signal that the chair or table is occupied. The picnic tables that have shade covers will keep your towels and clothing dry in a sudden downpour (common in the warm months) and protect you from overexposure to the sun.

! The Florida sun is very hot and can give you a nasty sunburn, but its effects are especially powerful at Blizzard Beach, with its all-white, reflective "snow." To protect yourself, bring along a tee-shirt to wear with your bathing suit; you can wear the shirt on the slides and when swimming.

! During the summer months, Blizzard Beach is a tempting destination, but crowds can make it difficult. A smart time to visit is after 3 PM on days when the park stays open until 7 PM or later. The crowds that arrived at opening time are starting to leave. Summer afternoon downpours, which last only a half hour or so, also drive crowds away.

Half-Day Tour at Blizzard Beach

The half-day tour that follows is designed to allow first-time visitors to experience the best of Blizzard Beach in three to four hours. This tour works best in the early morning during warm months and in the afternoon year-round.

✳

MORNING OR AFTERNOON AT BLIZZARD BEACH

Three to four hours. This tour does not include meals.
Peak Season Morning Tour (9 AM) — April through September — lunch optional.
Peak Season Late Afternoon Tour (3 or 4 PM) — April through September — does not include dinner.
Cool Season Early Afternoon Tour (1 PM) — October through March — does not include lunch.
On the Peak Season Morning Tour, reverse the order of the numbered attractions to avoid long lines.

⬇ Pack a tote bag with sun block and a hat or visor. Wear your bathing suit under your clothes. If you don't need a locker and have a towel, you might want to bring it and not waste time in line.

⬇ If you are on the Morning Tour, arrive at the entrance to Blizzard Beach one half hour before the park officially opens (between 9 and 10 AM). Call Blizzard Beach Information (560-3400) for opening and closing times, which vary with the season.

⬇ As you enter the park, you can rent towels and lockers if you need them at Snowless Joe's Rentals.

⬇ Find a shady spot on the far side of Melt Away Bay, beyond The Warming Hut, and set up camp.

⬇ Proceed to ❶ CROSS COUNTRY CREEK. There is an entrance close to The Warming Hut. Grab one of the extra tubes stacked here or look for an empty one floating by and take off down the creek for a float or two around the park. When you're ready for action, exit where you entered.

⬇ Grab an inner tube at the Tube Pick-Up Station and head up the Back Trail to ❷ DOWNHILL DOUBLE DIPPER for a steep drop down one of the park's newer waterslides at speeds up to twenty-five miles per hour.

⬇ Grab an inner tube at the Tube Pick-Up Station and climb the winding Back Trail to ❸ RUNOFF RAPIDS for a white-knuckle tube ride down the back side of Mt. Gushmore.

⬇ Grab a raft at the Mat Pick-Up Station and climb the Toboggan Trail to ❹ SNOW STORMERS to test your raft slalom skills, then grab another raft and ascend Toboggan Trail again for the downhill challenge at ❺ TOBOGGAN RACERS.

⬇ Ride the Chair Lift to the summit of Mt. Gushmore — on busy days it may be faster to climb the steps of Summit Trail to the top — and take a wild tube ride down ❻ TEAMBOAT SPRINGS.

⬇ Return to the top of Mt. Gushmore on the Chair Lift or climb the Summit Trail to the top, where thrill seekers can head for ❼ SLUSH GUSHER to sample this very steep waterslide.

⬇ If you are now ready for your big-time water adventure, head back to the top of Mt. Gushmore for the terrifying airborne plunge at ❽ SUMMIT PLUMMET.

⬇ Take a well-deserved rest and ride the bobbing waves in MELT AWAY BAY or relax on the beach to work on your tan and watch all the goings-on. ◆

ATTRACTIONS

FORT WILDERNESS & RIVER COUNTRY

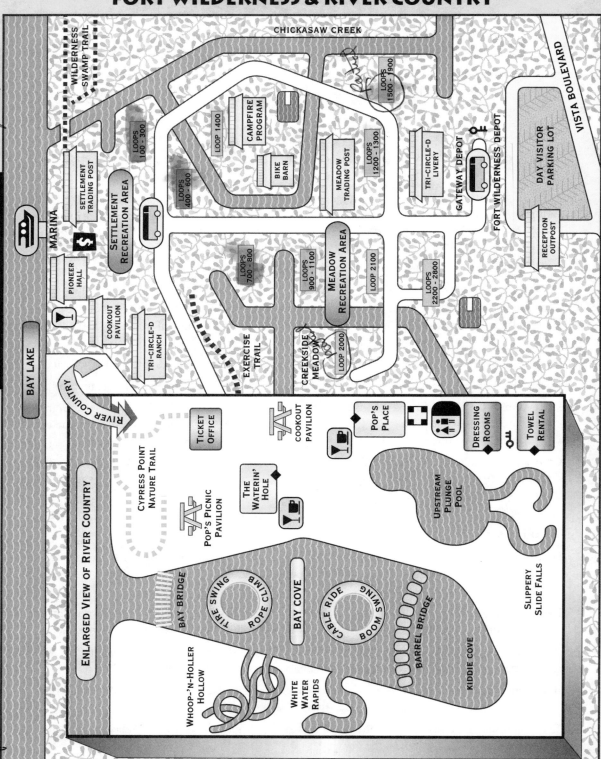

ATTRICTIONS

preferred

1700 - 2000 precluded

full

CHICKASAW CREEK

WILDERNESS SWAMP TRAIL

LOOPS 1500 - 1900

LOOP 1400

CAMPFIRE PROGRAM

LOOPS 100 - 300

LOOPS 400 - 600

BIKE BARN

LOOPS 1200 - 1300

TRI-CIRCLE-D LIVERY

GATEWAY DEPOT

FORT WILDERNESS DEPOT

VISTA BOULEVARD

DAY VISITOR PARKING LOT

SETTLEMENT TRADING POST

SETTLEMENT RECREATION AREA

MEADOW TRADING POST

RECEPTION OUTPOST

MARINA

LOOPS 700 - 800

LOOPS 900 - 1100

MEADOW RECREATION AREA

LOOP 2100

LOOPS 2200 - 2800

PIONEER HALL

BAY LAKE

COOKOUT PAVILION

TRI-CIRCLE-D RANCH

EXERCISE TRAIL

CREEKSIDE MEADOW

LOOP 2000

RIVER COUNTRY

ENLARGED VIEW OF RIVER COUNTRY

CYPRESS POINT NATURE TRAIL

TICKET OFFICE

COOKOUT PAVILION

POP'S PLACE

DRESSING ROOMS

TOWEL RENTAL

POP'S PICNIC PAVILION

THE WATERIN' HOLE

UPSTREAM PLUNGE POOL

BAY BRIDGE

TIRE SWING

ROPE CLIMB

BAY COVE

CABLE RIDE

BOOM SWING

BARREL BRIDGE

KIDDIE COVE

SLIPPERY SLIDE FALLS

WHOOP-'N-HOLLER HOLLOW

WHITE WATER RAPIDS

FORT WILDERNESS & RIVER COUNTRY

Fort Wilderness offers visitors an old-fashioned country getaway: swimming, boating, picnicking, hiking, horseback riding, fishing, and just kicking back in a 700-acre cypress- and pine-wooded recreation area and campground. This carefully maintained wilderness area is also a Walt Disney World resort, where guests can camp in tents, hook up RVs, or stay in one of the resort's permanent trailer homes (see "Camping at Fort Wilderness," page 113, and "Disney's Fort Wilderness Resort and Campground," page 136). It is not unusual to spot native white-tailed deer, raccoons, opossums, and armadillos; the wetlands are also home to indigenous waterfowl, including egrets, heron, and pelicans.

Fort Wilderness has three main recreation complexes: MEADOW RECREATION AREA in the center of the park, where meandering waterways attract both canoers and anglers and where bike paths lead off in every direction; SETTLEMENT RECREATION AREA at the edge of Bay Lake, with a busy marina and white sand beach, a nature trail, a small ranch, and a restaurant; and RIVER COUNTRY at Bay Lake, a Disney-designed version of an old-fashioned swimming hole, complete with waterslides and beaches. Throughout Fort Wilderness, visitors will find swimming pools, bicycle trails, volleyball nets, tennis courts, shuffleboard, fishing, waterskiing, horseback-riding, and live entertainment in the evenings.

WHEN TO GO: Fort Wilderness is open year-round, and there are activities, attractions, and entertainment suitable for every type of weather. At the Fort Wilderness Marina, boats may be rented from 10 AM until sundown. At the Bike Barn, recreational equipment may be rented or borrowed from 8 AM until sundown. Closing times vary with the season.

River Country is open year-round, except for October, when it is closed for maintenance. During holidays and peak-attendance months (April through August), the water park is packed, but during low-attendance periods (September through March), it can be a welcome break from the hectic theme parks. Opening and closing times at River Country vary throughout the year, so check ahead by calling River Country Information (407 824-2760). River Country may close on very cold days or during lightning storms. If the weather looks uncertain, call Disney Weather (824-4104) for details.

HOW TO GET THERE: Fort Wilderness is in the Magic Kingdom Resorts Area, adjacent to Bonnet Creek Golf Club, and extends from Vista Boulevard to the shores of Bay Lake. The Fort Wilderness Marina is serviced by ferry from the Magic Kingdom, Discovery Island, and the Contemporary resort. Walt Disney World buses service Fort Wilderness from the Wilderness Lodge resort and the Transportation and Ticket Center. Visitors who are driving can reach Fort Wilderness by following the signs to the Magic Kingdom Resorts Area and then to Fort Wilderness — or they can take a shortcut and enter by way of Vista Boulevard. The Fort Wilderness Day Visitor Parking Lot is free to guests staying at a Walt Disney World resort (other visitors are charged about $6 to enter the area).

IN-PARK TRANSPORTATION: The Fort Wilderness roads are reserved for its own buses, which operate daily from 7 AM until 2 AM. Bus routes are posted at all bus stops. (Passenger cars and recreational vehicles are allowed on the roads only to reach campsites, and there is no parking at the Fort Wilderness attractions.) Visitors arriving by car can park in the Fort Wilderness Day Visitor Parking Lot and proceed to one of the two bus stops there, depending on their destination: The bus stop marked "Gateway Depot" is for the express bus to River Country; the smaller bus stop marked "Fort Wilderness Depot" makes local stops at the campsite loops and the Meadow and Settlement

Recreation Areas, as well as River Country. Guests who want to get around Fort Wilderness at their own pace can rent bicycles or electric carts at the Bike Barn, located in the Meadow Recreation Area. The electric carts hold up to four passengers and plug in for continuous recharging at scores of outlets throughout Fort Wilderness (see "Electric Cart Rentals," page 112).

ADMISSION: Fort Wilderness is free to all visitors at Walt Disney World. Admission to River Country water park is about $19 for adults (about $15 for children). Admission to River Country is included with Length of Stay Passes and some Multiday Passes.

✳

SETTLEMENT RECREATION AREA

The Settlement Recreation Area borders Bay Lake and encompasses the Fort Wilderness Marina and beach; Pioneer Hall, where the nightly Hoop-Dee-Doo Musical Revue dinner show is held; and the Tri-Circle-D Ranch. At the Settlement Trading Post, visitors can buy gifts, sundries, groceries, sandwiches, and beverages including beer, wine, and a limited selection of spirits. River Country is a short walk away.

FORT WILDERNESS MARINA: The marina is situated on Bay Lake, in the center of Fort Wilderness's long, lovely white sand beach. At the marina, visitors can rent motorboats and sailboats or join waterskiing or fishing excursions. (See "Sports," page 213.) At the beach, visitors can swim or simply relax in lounge chairs under umbrellas or in the shade of the nearby trees. Lockers are available at the marina to store belongings, and the nearby Beach Shack provides refreshments and cold beer. The Fort Wilderness Marina is open every day from 10 AM until sundown.

WILDERNESS SWAMP TRAIL: The Wilderness Swamp Trail, about two miles long, offers a gentle nature hike among the local flora and fauna. Only the sounds of nature break the silence along the trail, which begins behind the Settlement Trading Post. The trail meanders through the forest, crosses the sun-drenched grassy banks of the Fort Wilderness waterways, and skirts the wetlands — populated by egrets, herons, and other native waterfowl — before plunging back into the deep shade of the overgrown forest canopy. The array of swamp ferns, saw palmetto, ancient cypress hung with Spanish moss, and colorful berries and flowers creates a semitropical paradise for nature-lovers.

WILDERNESS EXERCISE TRAIL: This one-mile (round trip) path begins across from the Tri-Circle-D Ranch and links Fort Wilderness to Disney's Wilderness Lodge. Exercise stations along the way cue fitness enthusiasts through stretches, lunges, chin-ups, and other activities that add up to a serious workout. The trail winds through a deeply shaded pine forest, lush with ferns and palmettos. Twittering birds, shy marsh rabbits, deep shadows, and silence inspire a soothing sense of isolation and privacy. The trail turns back at Disney's Wilderness Lodge.

TRI-CIRCLE-D RANCH: This stable and corral houses the horses used in the Magic Kingdom parades, and the Blacksmith Shop where their hooves are tended. A small museum inside the Horse Barn displays photographs of Walt Disney and his beloved horses. Outside, the horses are bathed and groomed, much to their pleasure. Horse enthusiasts will enjoy close-up views of the beautiful Percherons that pull the trolleys along Main Street, and the elegant steeds with elaborately braided manes that are featured in some parades and special events. At the Blacksmith Shop, visitors can watch the horses being shod and their hooves being dressed.

➡ **PETTING FARM:** This corral at the Tri-Circle-D Ranch is filled with chickens, turkeys, rabbits, goats, ducks, and some very beautiful and well-cared-for ponies. Interestingly, the Petting Farm, with its hands-on opportunities, attracts as many adults as children.

✳

MEADOW RECREATION AREA

The Meadow Recreation Area lies in the center of Fort Wilderness and offers access to the Fort Wilderness waterways and bicycle trails. This area encompasses the Bike Barn, where visitors can rent bicycles, boats, electric carts, fishing gear, and tennis equipment; and the Meadow Recreation Complex, which offers swimming, tennis, volleyball, and shuffleboard. The Meadow Trading Post sells gifts, sundries, groceries, sandwiches, soups, and beverages, including beer and wine. On hot afternoons, visitors can come inside to cool off and play a game of checkers, or they can picnic by the creek at the tree-shaded tables out back.

➡ **CANOEING, KAYAKING, AND PEDAL BOATING:** The grassy banks and tree-canopied waterways of Fort Wilderness are home to a variety of native waterfowl and fish. Visitors may tour the waterways by canoe, pedal boat, or kayak, and are welcome to fish for bass and bream. The Bike Barn rents boats from 8 AM until sundown. Boaters are given a map of the waterway system and can take a picnic lunch along on their adventure. (See "Boating," page 221.)

➡ **BICYCLING:** The nine miles of roads and trails in Fort Wilderness are ideal for bicycle expeditions. Bikers must contend with occasional traffic on the paved roads, but the extensive trail system was designed with bicycles in mind. The trails meander along waterways, past beaches and wetlands, through shady forests, and across bridges and boardwalks. The Bike Barn rents bicycles and tandem bikes from 8 AM until sundown. Bikers are provided with a map of the bike trails and roads of Fort Wilderness. (See "Bicycling," page 217.)

➡ **CANAL FISHING:** Fishing in the waterways at Fort Wilderness is one of the hidden pleasures at Walt Disney World. Anglers can walk along the shores or rent canoes, pedal boats, or kayaks and paddle to any fishing spot that appeals to them. The Meadow Trading Post sells lures and bait, and visitors who do not have their own gear can rent cane poles at the Bike Barn. The fishing rule at Fort Wilderness is catch and release. (See "Fishing," page 225.)

✳

RIVER COUNTRY ATTRACTIONS

River Country, a water park located just a short walk from the Settlement Recreation Area, is modeled on the imaginary "swimming hole" that Huck Finn might have enjoyed. Visitors pay admission at the gate, and once inside, they can rent lockers and towels and settle into lounge chairs around the pool or on the sandy beach. There are a number of waterslides and water activities here, but River Country has a gentler, more nature-oriented atmosphere than either Typhoon Lagoon or Blizzard Beach. It is one of the most relaxing spots at Fort Wilderness, and it's a great place to do absolutely nothing. Two snack bars, Pop's Place and the smaller Waterin' Hole, offer hamburgers, hot dogs, sandwiches, salads, ice cream, beer, wine, and coffee.

➡ **BAY COVE:** Bay Cove, an inlet of Bay Lake, is bordered on one side by a large beach and on the other by a hill with waterslides. It features good, old-fashioned water play at River Country, complete

ATTRACTIONS

with the Boom Swing, Rope Climb, Tire Swing, and Cable Ride. Two rickety bridges, Barrel Bridge and Bay Bridge, span the Cove and lead swimmers to the water-play equipment in the center and to the tube rides and body slides at Raft Rider Ridge on the far shore.

WHOOP-'N-HOLLER HOLLOW: Across Bay Cove from the beach is Whoop-'n-Holler Hollow, where swimmers can climb to two thrilling corkscrewing waterslides. One is longer than the other, but both are fast. The slides twist and turn and wind around each other, finally depositing riders, with a splash, into Bay Cove. This attraction is big with the kids and the lines move quickly.

WHITE WATER RAPIDS: Despite its name, this is actually a leisurely inner-tube ride among gentle currents and calm pools. Riders cross Barrel Bridge and plop onto inner tubes atop Raft Rider Ridge. They meander down a 330-foot-long contoured chute, sometimes revolving in a slow whirlpool, before being gently washed into Bay Cove.

UPSTREAM PLUNGE POOL AND SLIPPERY SLIDES: This crystal-clear 330,000-gallon swimming pool is heated in winter and is surrounded by lounge chairs, where most of the adults at River Country are busy relaxing. Slippery Slide Falls, at the back of the pool, offers two steeply angled waterslides for the adventurous youngsters who flock to them. The slides end with a thrilling free-fall splash landing.

CYPRESS POINT NATURE TRAIL: This short but tranquil wooden boardwalk meanders through the wetlands at the edge of Bay Lake. Old-growth bald cypress trees provide shade, and egrets fish among the water reeds. Aviaries tucked into the moss-hung bayous house hawks and other rehabilitated birds that are no longer able to survive in the wild. Few visitors ever find the trail, which is set apart from River Country. See the map on page 106 for the location.

EXCURSIONS AND TOURS

WATERSKIING EXCURSION: Waterskiers enjoy ideal conditions on the smooth surface of Bay Lake. Skiers can bring their own equipment or use the skis, Scurfers, or Hydraslides provided. Excursion boats carry up to five skiers and leave from the Fort Wilderness Marina throughout the day. Guides will also pick up skiers from other Magic Kingdom resorts. Waterskiing excursions must be booked in advance, and cost about $100 per hour. (See "Waterskiing," page 242.)

FORT WILDERNESS TRAIL RIDE: The Tri-Circle-D Livery maintains a herd of well-trained quarter horses, paints, and Appaloosas for cowboy-guided trail rides. Groups of up to twenty take this gentle ride-at-a-walk through the shady pine forest. The Tri-Circle-D Livery is adjacent to the Fort Wilderness Guest Parking Lot. The trail ride leaves four times daily, and reservations are required (824-2832). Cost is about $20 for forty-five minutes. (See "Horseback Riding," page 234.)

FISHING EXCURSION: Anglers can try their luck reeling in largemouth bass, bluegill, and other fish from Bay Lake, the largest natural lake at Walt Disney World. The Fort Wilderness Marina offers two-hour fishing excursions several times daily, although the catch tends to be better early in the morning. Anglers can use their own equipment or that provided on the boat; the fishing rule is catch and release. No fishing license is required. Excursions must be booked in advance, and cost about $170. (See "Fishing," page 223.)

✳ EVENTS AND LIVE ENTERTAINMENT

Many of the activities at Fort Wilderness, such as hayrides, Disney movies, and campfire ente presented with younger guests in mind, but they are enjoyed by adults as well.

ELECTRICAL WATER PAGEANT: This shimmering light show appears on Seven Seas Lagoon and Bay Lake every night. A thousand-foot-long string of barges transports an intricate and dynamic light and music show past the Polynesian, Grand Floridian, Contemporary, Wilderness Lodge, and Fort Wilderness resorts. King Neptune presides over the dancing images of sea life that come alive in animated lights and are reflected across the black waters of the Bay Lake. The show is brief, approximately seven minutes, but enchanting nonetheless. The Electrical Water Pageant reaches Fort Wilderness at about 9:45 PM. The best viewing location is at the Fort Wilderness Marina and beach.

HOOP-DEE-DOO MUSICAL REVUE: This popular dinner show is held three times nightly in rustic Pioneer Hall, which was recently updated. Colorfully dressed entertainers rely heavily on audience participation for a song-and-dance performances laced with puns, broad humor, and groan-inducing punch lines. Reservations are difficult to get, so book well in advance. (See "Dining Events," page 208.) Walk-up seating and same-day reservations are occasionally available through Pioneer Hall (824-2858).

HAYRIDES: Visitors can enjoy a casual, old-fashioned hayride on a horse-drawn wagon twice each night, all year-round. The hayride departs from Pioneer Hall and travels through the pine forest and along the beach. No reservations are taken and riders are welcome aboard on a first-come, first-served basis. Hayrides are scheduled at 7 PM and 9:30 PM, and riders should plan to arrive at Pioneer Hall at least fifteen minutes before departure time. The ride lasts about forty-five minutes and costs about $6 for adults and about $4 for children.

CAMPFIRE PROGRAM: Visitors can join Chip 'N Dale to toast marshmallows and sing favorite and familiar tunes at this campfire show. Disney cartoons and feature films are shown after dark. Hot dogs, snacks, popcorn, soft drinks, beer, and canned frozen daiquiris may be purchased at the campfire's Chuck Wagon. **Visitors who would enjoy a memorable night of free, laid-back entertainment, off the beaten path but undeniably Disney, should head on over. During the summer months, two Disney features are sometimes shown under the stars.** The campfire happens nightly at the amphitheater in the forest near the Bike Barn in the Meadow Recreation Area. Show times vary with the season. Call 824-2742 for details. During rainy evenings, activities usually become a "Porch Jam" at the Meadow Trading Post.

ALL-AMERICAN BACKYARD BARBECUE: Staged seasonally, between April and October, this all-you-care-to-eat buffet dinner and country dance features live musical entertainment and visits from Disney Characters at the Cookout Pavilion between River Country and Fort Wilderness. Barbecued chicken and pork ribs, hot dogs, corn on the cob, baked beans, corn bread, and dessert (usually a fruit cobbler or strawberry shortcake) are served, along with soft drinks, beer, and wine. The barbecue gets started about 6 PM and costs about $40 for adults and $30 for children. This is a unique setting for family birthdays. Reservations can be made up to sixty days in advance through Disney Dining Reservations (407 939-3463). For same-day reservations call 939-3463 after 10 AM.

ATTRACTIONS

ATTRACTIONS

DINING HALL & SALOON

Sandwiches, snacks, and picnic supplies are available at the Settlement Trading Post and the Meadow Trading Post. There are several snack bars in River Country that serve hamburgers and sandwiches as well. The establishments below are located at Pioneer Hall in the Settlement Recreation Area, which is the heart of Fort Wilderness. The Hoop-Dee-Doo Musical Revue dinner show is staged here nightly.

TRAIL'S END BUFFETERIA: Fried chicken, spaghetti, hamburgers, hot dogs, pizza, casseroles, soups, and a salad and fruit bar are offered in this casual cafeteria filled with tables and rustic props. The restaurant's late-night pizza buffet and pizza to go are popular with campers. Open for breakfast, lunch, and dinner; no reservations.

CROCKETT'S TAVERN: In this frontier-style saloon bedecked with Davy Crockett memorabilia, guests may perch at the bar or take their beverages outside to enjoy while sitting in comfortable rockers on the large wraparound porch. Crockett's Tavern is a popular (some say mandatory) stop for guests on their way to the Hoop-Dee-Doo Musical Revue. Beer, wine, and spirits are served.

SERVICES

BANKING: An automated teller machine (ATM) can be found near the rest rooms at Pioneer Hall.

REST ROOMS: Rest rooms are located at the Meadow Trading Post, Settlement Trading Post, Pioneer Hall, and Reception Outpost in the Fort Wilderness Day Visitor Parking Lot, and by the first-aid office in River Country. Air-conditioned comfort stations, complete with rest rooms, laundromats, showers, ice dispensers, and telephones, are located near all bus stops and campsite loops throughout Fort Wilderness.

TELEPHONES: Telephones can be found at the Gateway Depot bus stop in the Fort Wilderness Guest Parking Lot; at the comfort stations throughout the Fort Wilderness campsite locations; at Pioneer Hall and the Settlement Trading Post in the Settlement Recreation Area; and at the Meadow Trading Post in the Meadow Recreation Area.

ELECTRIC CART RENTALS: Any visitor can rent an electric cart by the day or overnight for use in Fort Wilderness. Electric carts carry up to four passengers and cost about $25 for the day, or about $40 for overnight. They run up to an hour (depending on the number of passengers) before needing a recharge at one of the plug-in recharging posts located throughout Fort Wilderness and in front of all attractions there. Electric carts are stabled at the Bike Barn in the Meadow Recreation Area, which is open from 8 AM until sundown. Guests must be at least age eighteen to rent, age sixteen to drive. Reservations are required and can be made up to a year in advance (407 824-2742).

LOCKERS: Lockers are located at the Fort Wilderness Marina, River Country, and Meadow Recreation Area, and at the Gateway Depot bus stop in the Fort Wilderness Guest Parking Lot.

VISITORS WITH DISABILITIES: Wheelchairs, which must be reserved in advance through Guest Services (407 824-2900), are available at the Reception Outpost in the Fort Wilderness Guest Parking Lot. Guests can also rent electric carts for use in Fort Wilderness by making same-day reservations at the Bike Barn (824-2742).

CAMPING AT FORT WILDERNESS

Camping at Fort Wilderness, whether in a travel trailer, recreational vehicle, or tent, is by far the most economical way to visit Walt Disney World and enjoy the privileges of staying at a Disney resort. Moreover, it's a great way to enjoy the pleasures of the great outdoors as only Disney can do it. *Trailer Life,* a noted camping magazine, has rated Fort Wilderness campground the best in the United States.

CAMPSITES: Fort Wilderness is divided up into loops, or camping areas (see the "Fort Wilderness Map," page 106, for locations). Campsite categories include Partial Hookups (water and electricity), Full Hookups (water, electricity, sanitary disposal), and Preferred Campsites, which include cable television (bring your own cable). All sites have asphalt pads large enough for RVs, although guests bringing a Class A recreational vehicle should request a wider campsite. Campsites are surrounded by shrubbery and trees that provide relative privacy, and have a grill and picnic table for cookouts.

FACILITIES: Each loop has its own air-conditioned comfort station with showers, laundry, ice, and telephones. Campers should bring along a flashlight, insect repellant, charcoal, matches, an extension cord, a clothesline cord, rolls of quarters for laundry, laundry detergent, and a drinking water hose.

LOOPS: The most popular campsites are the Preferred sites close to the marina, beach, Trail's End Buffeteria, River Country, and Settlement Trading Post (loops 100 through 500 and 700). Also popular are the Full Hookup campsites near the Meadow Trading Post, campfire program, swimming pool, tennis courts, and Bike Barn, where electric golf carts, bikes, boats, and fishing equipment can be rented (loops 600 and 800 through 1600). Campsite loops 1700 through 2000 are near the Meadow Trading Post, but are more secluded. They border on the loops for the Wilderness Homes permanent trailers. (See "Fort Wilderness Resort and Campground," page 136.) Partial Hookup campsites are in loops 1500 and 2000. Pets are allowed to stay with their owners on loops 1600 through 1900.

SPECIAL CAMPSITES: Groups of twenty or more can camp in Creekside Meadow, a secluded area reserved exclusively for large parties. Guests settling here can also rent camping gear, such as tents and cots. For reservations, call Fort Wilderness Group Camping Reservations (407 939-7807).

For smaller groups or individuals, there is one rustic cabin on loop 1200 that costs only a bit more than a full-hookup campsite. The cabin sleeps five in two sets of bunk beds and has electricity and a front porch swing; it does not have heat, air-conditioning, a toilet, water, or linens. It also can be reserved through Fort Wilderness Group Camping Reservations (407 939-7807).

TRANSPORTATION: Except for getting to and from campsites, no cars are allowed inside Fort Wilderness. There is internal bus transportation although many guests also rent bicycles or electric golf carts to get around (see "Electric Cart Rentals," Page 112).

✳

PETS AT WALT DISNEY WORLD: Pets are allowed to stay with their owners in Fort Wilderness for about $3 per night. Pets must be kept on a leash, and should be kennelled during the day if owners leave their campsite. There is a kennel located near the entrance of Fort Wilderness, as well as at each major theme park. All kennels are members of the American Boarding Kennel Association and have facilities for cats and dogs. Among other frequent visitors at the Disney kennels are rodents, ferrets, birds, and nonvenomous snakes, who are all welcome when in their own carrier. Kennels charge about $6 per day, or about $10 for twenty-four hours. Be sure to bring a copy of your pets' vaccination record, or you will not be allowed to board them. Call 407 824-6568 for more information. ◆

ATTRACTIONS

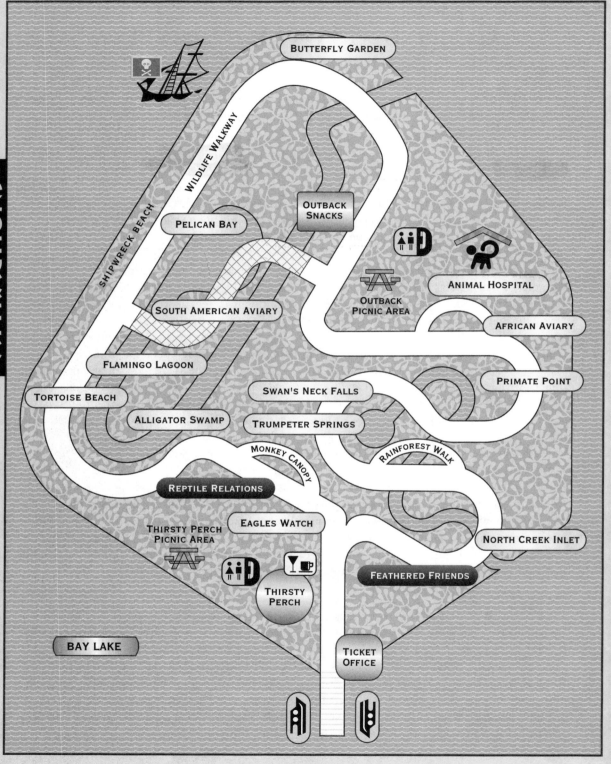

ATTRACTIONS

BUTTERFLY GARDEN

WILDLIFE WALKWAY

SHIPWRECK BEACH

PELICAN BAY

OUTBACK SNACKS

OUTBACK PICNIC AREA

ANIMAL HOSPITAL

SOUTH AMERICAN AVIARY

AFRICAN AVIARY

FLAMINGO LAGOON

PRIMATE POINT

TORTOISE BEACH

SWAN'S NECK FALLS

ALLIGATOR SWAMP

TRUMPETER SPRINGS

MONKEY CANOPY

RAINFOREST WALK

REPTILE RELATIONS

THIRSTY PERCH PICNIC AREA

EAGLES WATCH

NORTH CREEK INLET

THIRSTY PERCH

FEATHERED FRIENDS

BAY LAKE

TICKET OFFICE

DISCOVERY ISLAND

Discovery Island is an idyllic escape into nature from the more structured entertainments at Walt Disney World. This natural eleven-acre island, in the middle of Bay Lake, was originally planned by Disney as a *Treasure Island* adventure. To create a lush forest environment, the island was landscaped with native trees, palms, and bamboo, along with hundreds of tropical specimen plants from around the world. A white sand beach was added, and a wrecked wooden sailing ship was transported here from the Florida coast to lend atmosphere. Aviaries were built and stocked with a wide variety of exotic birds, from elegant demoiselle cranes to flashy scarlet ibises. As the island ecology evolved and more wildlife arrived and thrived — both imported species and local volunteers — the *Treasure Island* concept was dropped and Discovery Island became a nature park. In 1979, it was accredited by the American Association of Zoological Parks and Aquariums, and it regularly exchanges animals with zoos throughout the world. Today, this sanctuary is home to more than 125 species of birds, reptiles, and mammals, including endangered species and disabled wildlife such as Galapagos tortoises, brown pelicans, and the American bald eagle.

At Discovery Island, visitors can stroll through the tropical foliage along a winding three-quarter-mile path, picnic on the white sand beach, pause beside a stream with gurgling cascades, and come face-to-face with a variety of birds and animals at almost every turn. Peacocks and rabbitlike Patagonian cavies, along with waterfowl native to the area, are among the many animals that roam freely on Discovery Island. Almost an acre of the island is enclosed in nearly invisible fine green netting, creating one of the largest walkthrough aviaries in the United States — so large that visitors often do not realize they are inside an enclosure. There are only a few places to sit down along the shady paths, so visitors should be comfortable with walking the three-quarter-mile distance.

WHEN TO GO: Discovery Island opens every day at 10 AM and closes between 5 PM and 7 PM, depending on the season. It is delightful at any time of day. The best month to visit is November, before Thanksgiving, when the weather is cool and the island is virtually deserted. Discovery Island, however, is seldom crowded at any time. Nesting season lasts from February through September, and from about mid-February to mid-March, the island is closed for refurbishing (and perhaps to give the wildlife a vacation from people). For current schedules, call Walt Disney World Information (407 824-4321) or Discovery Island Information (407 824-2875). If the weather looks uncertain on the day you go, call Disney Weather (824-4104) for details.

HOW TO GET THERE: The only way to reach Discovery Island is on the ferries that depart every twenty minutes from the Magic Kingdom Dock, the Fort Wilderness Marina, and the Marina Pavilion at the Contemporary resort. The last ferries leave for Discovery Island at about 4 PM, although ferries do stop to pick up Discovery Island visitors until the park closes. Before boarding ferries, hold onto your hats or tie them on, so the breezes don't blow them overboard. Visitors are not permitted to dock rental boats at Discovery Island.

ADMISSION: Adult admission to Discovery Island is about $14 (about $8 for children). Discovery Island admission is included with Length of Stay Passes and some Multiday Passes. Tickets may be purchased at Guest Services in any Walt Disney World resort or at the Discovery Island ticket office. Ferries to Discovery Island are complimentary for all visitors.

LIVE EXHIBITS

Signs scattered around Discovery Island tell you about the animals you might see. Discovery Island changes from day to day as plants grow and bloom and birds and animals mature, breed, and give birth. Many island residents hide in the foliage, and you can find animals at almost every turn. As you enter, pick up a brochure, which describes some of the birds and animals, and lists the schedule for the animal shows. Follow the path to the right after you leave the Discovery Island Dock.

DISCOVERY ISLAND PATH: The three-quarter-mile Discovery Island Path directs visitors in a roughly counter-clockwise direction around the island. It first enters an area known as Parrots Perch, where the island's bird shows are staged. This is the home of brightly plumaged macaws, cockatoos, and some of the other colorful birds that perform in the shows. The large trees here provide shade and nesting homes during mating season.

NORTH CREEK INLET: At the approach to North Creek Inlet, visitors pass the Birds of the Islands exhibit, which includes palm cockatoos from New Guinea. The path crosses a flowing island stream where it empties into Bay Lake, then turns to enter a dense forest of tropical plants, palms, and flowering hibiscus. The path meanders back and forth across a series of footbridges, passing a stand of Senegal date palms and many other specimen plants along the way. North Creek Inlet is also home to golden lion tamarins, a tree-dwelling yellow-furred monkey from the American tropics.

TRUMPETER SPRINGS: This area includes a small, tropically landscaped Rainforest Walk, and is home to a pair of beautiful black-necked swans, as well as to the large white trumpeter swans, known for their distinctive call. These fairy-tale birds, the largest of the swans, have been nearly hunted out of existence. In spring, great white egrets nest in the treetops at Trumpeter Springs. Farther along the path is the habitat of the Fishing Cat, a feline native to Southeast Asia that swims to catch its favorite food.

SWAN'S NECK FALLS: At Swan's Neck Falls, visitors can enjoy cascading waterfalls and spot a variety of waterfowl fishing in the pools below. Graceful Chilean flamingos, lighter in color than the familiar bright pink Caribbean flamingos, are some of the occupants here.

PRIMATE POINT: After passing through a grove filled with different varieties of bamboo from many parts of the world, including vivid green golden bamboo, visitors arrive at Primate Point. A number of small mammals reside here, including the endangered ring-tailed lemur from Madagascar, with a foxlike face and monkeylike body.

AFRICAN AVIARY: Just past Primate Point is the African Aviary, home to the African crowned cranes, named for their distinctive head feathers, and the Ethiopian yellow-billed hornbills, who seem to spend the entire day grooming themselves.

ANIMAL HOSPITAL AND NURSERY: The colorful wood-shingled Animal Hospital and Nursery has walk-up windows where visitors can look into various animal-care facilities. In the nursery, animals orphaned in the wild are cared for around the clock until they can be released back into the wild or incorporated into exhibits. The operating room, also visible by window, is where animals undergo surgery for injuries. Visitors can watch the goings-on in the lab, too, where blood

ATTRACTIONS

samples are studied to help diagnose animal diseases. The lab also houses an X-ray machine used for diagnosing internal problems and bone fractures. This powerful machine is capable of X-raying a five-hundred-pound Galapagos tortoise. (Hmm... you don't want to stand too close to the window when one of those guys steps onto the table — the rays must be pretty intense.)

BUTTERFLY GARDEN: This addition between South Creek Inlet and Shipwreck Beach is expected to draw a colorful variety of local and migrating butterflies by using trees and flowering plants that are specially selected to attract them.

SOUTH AMERICAN AVIARY: Just beyond the Animal Hospital, visitors can enter the South American Aviary, which is devoted to that continent's birds and waterfowl. Covering almost an acre, this huge walkthrough aviary is home to a colorful population, including one of the largest U.S. breeding colonies of the scarlet ibis. These birds, distinctively plumaged in an almost Day-Glo red from a diet high in carotenes, were described by the early Spanish explorers as being covered in blood. Visitors pass through the aviary on elevated walkways high above the lagoons and nesting areas of the waterfowl. Tall trees reach through the top of the enclosure, creating the remarkable illusion of open sky. The aviary exits at the beach.

PELICAN BAY: The brown pelican is the state bird of Florida, and those that are sheltered here are among the permanently disabled birds on Discovery Island, unable to survive in the wild. Once threatened with extinction due to the effects of the pesticide DDT, the brown pelican is now protected by federal law, and its population is slowly recovering. In the late afternoon, about 4 PM, animal caretakers feed the pelicans, which is an entertainment event in itself.

WILDLIFE WALKWAY: The Wildlife Walkway skirts a lush tropical forest as it follows the island's white sand beach. As visitors stroll along, they have a chance to see many of Central Florida's native birds in the wild, including herring gulls, American coots, herons, egrets, and large turkey vultures. The path leads to the far end of the island, where the *Hispaniola* is beached. This wrecked single-masted schooner was salvaged from the Florida Keys and offers a vivid example of the shipmaking craft of the eighteenth century. The waters of Bay Lake lap on the beach, and visitors may leave the path to lounge on the sand or walk barefoot at the water's edge.

FLAMINGO LAGOON: This shady lagoon across from the beach is home to a breeding colony of Caribbean flamingos, recognized by their distinctive bright pink plumage and awkward grace. The Caribbean flamingos have adapted to the presence of humans, unlike their cousins, the Florida flamingos, which have not been seen in the wild since about 1920.

TORTOISE BEACH: Along the sandy beach of Discovery Island, Galapagos tortoises from the islands off the coast of Ecuador have found a new resort. Weighing up to five hundred pounds and with lifespans of up to 150 years, these great lumbering beasts are now a rare and endangered species. When the weather is cold, they move into the Tortoise Shelter. Large windows let visitors look inside, and a small exhibit gives visitors a close look at an unusual reptile or amphibian on display.

ALLIGATOR SWAMP: This picturesque grotto is home to a number of American alligators. The population of these Florida natives, once declining because of the dictates of fashion and encroaching development, is now on the increase. Also in the swamp is the rare broadnose caiman, a petite alligator that is virtually extinct in the wild.

ATTRACTIONS

➡ **MONKEY CANOPY:** As the path continues toward the dock, it passes the Monkey Canopy, where visitors can see white-fronted marmosets, cotton-top tamarins, red-handed tamarins, and titi monkeys.

➡ **EAGLES WATCH:** Just beyond the Monkey Canopy is Eagles Watch, where visitors can get an up-close look at the bald eagle residing there. The eagle, seriously injured when it arrived, has a permanent home here because its injuries made it unable to be rehabilitated and returned to the wild.

✴

EDUTAINMENT

Animal shows are scheduled several times daily at Discovery Island. Pick up an entertainment schedule at the Discovery Island ticket office for exact show times. Shows may be cancelled due to inclement weather.

➡ **FEATHERED FRIENDS:** Visitors sit on shaded benches to watch this pleasant, often funny show featuring the antics of tame macaws, cockatoos, and parrots. During the show, the parrot wranglers describe the special-care and captive-breeding programs for Discovery Island's many exotic, colorful birds. Next, the island's birds of prey are introduced, including a red-tailed hawk, a large owl, and a king vulture, and visitors have a chance to see these remarkable birds up close and learn about their feeding and mating habits. Visitors are encouraged to ask questions about the birds while learning more about the wildlife rehabilitation and protection programs at Discovery Island. Four shows daily, beginning at about 11:30 AM. Duration: Approximately 30 minutes.

➡ **REPTILE RELATIONS:** Visitors can sit in the shade on hand-hewn log benches or stand off to the side to watch this informative reptile show, staged near Alligator Swamp. An animal handler gives visitors a close-up look at a number of interesting reptiles and amphibians, including a small but toothy American alligator, a vivid green iguana from the treetops of the rain forest, and a gopher tortoise that burrows as deep as thirty feet underground. Other performers in the show include an indigo snake and a friendly Burmese python that literally hangs out with the crowd. Four shows daily, beginning at about 11 AM. Duration: Approximately 25 minutes.

➡ **NATIVE NEIGHBORS:** During summer months, visitors gather at the same location where the Feathered Friends show is held for an informative and up-close look at many of Florida's native birds and animals. Visitors learn where to look for these creatures and how to identify them, and have the chance to ask questions about their feeding and mating habits. One show daily, beginning at about 4:30 PM. Duration: Approximately 20 minutes.

➡ **EDUCATIONAL TOURS:** The Discovery Island Education Department offers learning tours for visitors of all ages. Tours change seasonally and should be reserved at least six weeks in advance (407 934-2651). The two listed below are for groups of eight to fifteen persons age sixteen and over.

DISCOVERY CLUB: Visitors on a behind-the-scenes walking tour of the island learn how zoological parks address issues of animal and habitat conservation, and get to meet many of the island's residents. The tour lasts approximately three hours; about $20 per person.

BREAKFAST WITH THE BIRDS: After an early-morning birdwatching expedition on Bay Lake, visitors enjoy a Continental breakfast on Discovery Island, get to meet some of the island's feathered residents, and learn about endangered bird species on a behind-the-scenes walking tour. The tour lasts approximately three hours; about $40 per person.

✳

REFRESHMENT STANDS AND PICNIC AREAS

Two refreshment stands offer light meals and snacks, and Discovery Island has a number of picnic areas for those who bring their own food. The picnic spots are pleasant rest stops and rendezvous points.

THIRSTY PERCH: The largest snack bar on the island, Thirsty Perch is located near the Discovery Island Dock and offers sandwiches, snacks, soft drinks, coffee, and beer, as well as a selection of nature-oriented publications and souvenirs. Visitors can purchase food and beverages at Thirsty Perch, which they may consume anywhere on the island, provided they do not litter or offer food to the animals or birds, who are quite well fed. 🍴 🍸

THIRSTY PERCH PICNIC AREA: Located on the beach just beyond Thirsty Perch, this area has a dozen or so picnic tables. A thick grove of bamboo to one side provides shelter, and picnickers can watch the ferries dock as they eat. Egrets, cranes, peahens, and peacocks mingle with picnickers and provide entertainment. Don't miss the majestic bald eagle at Eagles Watch, located behind Thirsty Perch. Trash containers and rest rooms are nearby.

OUTBACK SNACKS: This small snack stand is located just beyond the Animal Hospital, and offers a limited selection of sodas, bottled water, chips, and candy. There are shaded tables across the path.

OUTBACK PICNIC AREA: Just across the path from Outback Snacks, this picnic area is tucked into a secluded glade. Several picnic tables are set on thick grass under the shade of tall palms. The Outback Picnic Area is located in the center of the island and is filled with the sounds of birds. Trash containers and rest rooms are nearby.

WILDLIFE WALKWAY AND SHIPWRECK BEACH: Visitors who bring along a towel or ground cloth will find the white sands of Shipwreck Beach a fine spot for a picnic. Visitors can take off their shoes and walk along the water's edge, but swimming is not permitted. Wildlife Walkway divides the beach from the forest and leads to the shipwrecked *Hispaniola*. This area provides lovely views of Bay Lake and the resorts on the far shore. Trash containers are nearby; the nearest rest rooms are by Outback Snacks and by Thirsty Perch.

TOURING TIP: It is not a good idea to let any of the roaming birds or animals eat from your hand. They are not tame and, in fact, are well fed. The animal caretakers are very knowledgeable and friendly, so do ask questions if you spot them tending the animals.

✳

SERVICES

REST ROOMS: Public rest rooms are located behind Thirsty Perch and across from Outback Snacks in the Outback Picnic Area.

TELEPHONES: Public telephones are located behind Thirsty Perch and next to the Outback Picnic Area.

FILM: A wide variety of film is available for sale at Thirsty Perch.

VISITORS WITH DISABILITIES: All of Discovery Island is wheelchair accessible, and a limited number of wheelchairs are available free of charge at the dock. Some, but not all, of the ferries have wheelchair access, so visitors needing assistance may need to wait for a properly outfitted ferry.

Getaway Tour at Discovery Island

The tour that follows is designed to allow first-time visitors to experience the best of Discovery Island in three hours, as a midday getaway. To create your own custom vacation at Walt Disney World, you can combine the Nature Walk and Picnic with an afternoon and evening tour at one of the theme parks.

NATURE WALK AND PICNIC

Three hours — year round — including a picnic lunch.

- If you are planning to bring a picnic, ask your hotel coffee shop to pack one for you. You can buy beverages at Discovery Island and picnic at a shady table or in the sun on the white sand beach.

- Catch a ferry to Discovery Island at about 11:45 AM. (Ferries depart every twenty minutes from the Magic Kingdom Dock, Fort Wilderness Marina, and Marina Pavilion at the Contemporary resort.)

- On arriving at Discovery Island, pick up an entertainment schedule at the ticket office and stop by Thirsty Perch to purchase beverages for your picnic, if you wish.

- Step over to the DISCOVERY ISLAND PATH and bear to the right (counter-clockwise). Follow the path to Parrots Perch, an animal-show staging area.

- Grab a seat for the 12:30 PM performance of the FEATHERED FRIENDS show to watch the beautiful trained tropical birds and meet some of the birds of prey that live on Discovery Island.

- When the show ends, continue down the path toward NORTH CREEK INLET. Enjoy the sights and sounds as you walk along past TRUMPETER SPRINGS, SWAN'S NECK FALLS, PRIMATE POINT, and the AFRICAN AVIARY. You'll also see many fascinating tropical plants in these areas.

- Stop at the ANIMAL HOSPITAL on your right and peek into the nursery and treatment rooms.

- If you would like to picnic in a secluded grassy glade, stop at the Outback Picnic Area, just ahead, for lunch. If you prefer to picnic on the beach, continue on.

- Bear left toward the SOUTH AMERICAN AVIARY. Enter the large enclosed aviary and stroll through on the elevated walkways. You will see a variety of graceful South American waterfowl.

- Leave the aviary and turn right toward PELICAN BAY for a look at Florida's endangered state bird.

- Continue on up the WILDLIFE WALKWAY for a shoreside stroll to the shipwrecked *Hispaniola*. If it is open, proceed to the BUTTERFLY GARDEN for a look at its seasonal visitors. If you're planning to picnic at the beach, choose a spot on the sand for your picnic.

- Turn around and head toward FLAMINGO LAGOON and over to TORTOISE BEACH, on your right, for a look at the enormous slow-moving Galapagos tortoises.

- Continue on to ALLIGATOR SWAMP, for a view of its large and fearsome-looking residents, then head toward the rustic benches on your right for the 2 PM REPTILE RELATIONS show, starring a number of engaging and toothsome creatures from around the world.

- After the show, head to MONKEY CANOPY for a look at its residents' antics, and to EAGLES WATCH for a rare, up-close look at a bald eagle, before returning to the Discovery Island Dock. ◆

DISNEY'S ANIMAL KINGDOM

The creation of Animal Kingdom is Disney's most ambitious theme park venture ever, and is a fitting tribute to Walt Disney's original inspiration for much of his greatest work: "I have learned from the animal world," he said, "and what anyone will learn who studies it, is a renewed sense of kinship with the earth and all its inhabitants." Disney's Animal Kingdom celebrates the animals of the present, the past, and the imagination in an innovative mix of attractions and open-habitat zoo. Many of the concepts at work in the design of the park are meant to engage visitors as participants as well as spectators, bringing a new dimension of reality to the Disney Experience. At five hundred acres, Animal Kingdom is almost five times the size of the Magic Kingdom, and is the largest physical zoo anywhere in the world. Like the Magic Kingdom, the attractions are clustered into environments, or "lands," that branch off from a central hub. A monumental Tree of Life, on the scale of Epcot's Spaceship Earth, is Animal Kingdom's signature icon, visible from great distances. Animal Kingdom will expand in phases through the end of this century, as new animal habitats are opened through colossal feats of land engineering. It is interesting to note that this land is already home to many species, including otters, frogs, egrets, heron, and deer. What actually seems to be taking place here is a controlled experiment in rapid evolution, exploring the possibility of a delicate but functional balance among man, animals, and the forces of nature, as each finds a place in this new Garden of Eden.

WHEN TO GO: In the wild, the day begins when the sun rises and ends when it sets, and the park hours at Animal Kingdom follow suit. This should be your first clue that this is not just a theme park. The Rainforest Cafe, which can be entered from outside the park, opens for breakfast at 6 AM.

HOW TO GET THERE: Disney's Animal Kingdom is tucked into an undeveloped area in the southwest quadrant of Walt Disney World. Buses travel between Animal Kingdom and all Walt Disney World resorts. Because of the enormous physical scale of Animal Kingdom, the visitors experience is structured much like a journey. Boats provide transportation up-river and between lands. A steam train travels across the African plains to Conservation Station, headquarters for animal care and species survival at Animal Kingdom, and an interactive information center for visitors.

✳ ATTRACTIONS

Animal Kingdom will be in the creation process for years to come. It is Disney's first living park and as such, will continually evolve. What follows is a description of the first phase, which opens mid- to late 1998.

➡ **THE OASIS:** Animal Kingdom is entered through Oasis Gardens, which is designed to quickly set the "story" in motion. Here visitors are immersed in a lush, dreamlike natural paradise of grottos, glades, waterfalls, and animals, as they make their way toward the wooden bridge that spans Discovery River. On the other side is Safari Village, the central crossroads of Animal Kingdom.

◆ **RAINFOREST CAFE:** A thundering waterfall cascades into a misty cloud at the entrance to this nature-themed restaurant. Seated among Audio-Animatronics monkeys and elephants, guests dine on casual and creative international dishes. Fresh fruit juices and smoothies, beer, wine, and spirits are served, as are espresso and cappuccino. Open all day from 6 AM until park closing.

➤ **SAFARI VILLAGE:** Encircled by Discovery River and canopied by the massive Tree of Life, Safari Village is the island hub of Animal Kingdom and the departure point for all journeys.

◆ **TREE OF LIFE:** This huge tree towering majestically above the bustling village looks convincingly real from a distance. Viewed up close, however, hundreds of hand-carved animals seem to be growing out of its trunk and branches. Inside the tree is a unique multimedia theater that delivers superior 3-D and sensory effects. The premiere performance is *Bugs,* a computer-animated look at life from a insect's point of view, based on a Disney movie of the same name.

◆ **DISCOVERY RIVER CRUISE:** This river-to-adventure boat ride not only entertains but also provides transportation to the park's themed lands. On the way up-river, the boat passes treacherous Dragon Rocks, steaming geysers, prehistoric beasts, and fantasy creatures.

➤ **DINOLAND, U.S.A.:** The look of Dinoland has been described as a "quirky roadside attraction," and its mood is undeniable one of dinosaur-mania. This is where you can find that Triceratops in every color, size, and flavor. Also at Dinoland are attractions that let visitors envision life on earth as it was millions of years ago.

◆ **COUNTDOWN TO EXTINCTION:** Visitors join a scientific expedition to journey 65 million years into the past. In this eerie primeval world, they quickly find themselves in an exciting close encounter with the dinosaurs, and then experience a breathtaking escape seconds before a hurtling comet collides with the earth — the cataclysmic event that brought about the extinction of the dinosaurs. This attraction features spectacular special effects, the latest generation of Audio-Animatronics, and motion simulators that not only move up, down, and sideways, but also travel along on tracks.

◆ **BONEYARD:** This imaginative playground, geared to the younger set, looks like an exaggerated paleontological dig and features distinctively designed slides, swings, and inventive climbing equipment built out of giant dinosaur "bones."

◆ **CRETACEOUS TRAIL:** A shady primordial forest provides a cool green environment on this nature walk back through time. As always, there are a few surprises along the way.

◆ **THEATER IN THE WILD:** Live stage shows are presented daily in this fifteen-hundred-seat amphitheater. In the works is an original stage show based on the animated feature *The Lion King.*

➤ **AFRICA:** Visitors arrive at the modern-day African town of Harambe, which lies on the edge of the savannah. Herds of zebras, giraffes, lions, elephants, and other African species, including several that are endangered, freely roam the landscape of forests, rivers, and open plains.

◆ **KILIMANJARO SAFARI:** Canopied safari vehicles depart for a rainy-season tour of the rugged African countryside and a glimpse of the animals that dwell there. When the safari comes across a band of poachers at work, the journey turns into a harrowing high-speed chase over roads washed out by landslides and flash floods, and across a crocodile-infested river spanned by a collapsing bridge.

◆ **GORILLA FALLS EXPLORATION TRAIL:** This nature trek meanders through the habitats of the lowland gorillas and offers an underwater view of hippos and a walk-through aviary of exotic birds.

◆ **WILDLIFE EXPRESS TO CONSERVATION STATION:** This steam train excursion crosses the African savannah to Conservation Station, the back-country headquarters for all wildlife care at Animal Kingdom. An interactive learning and information center shows visitors how they can help the animals they've just met from continuing on the path to certain extinction. ◆

HOTELS

The hotel you choose will ultimately become part of the vacation memories you'll return home with. Often visitors select out-of-the-way, low-cost hotels with few services or transportation options. They imagine themselves in the theme parks all day, returning to the hotel only to sleep at night — an exhausting and stressful strategy. The ideal hotel is a convenient one that you can easily return to for a swim or snooze, continuing your tour later, refreshed and ready for fun. This chapter is filled with great hotels and tips on how to make them fit your budget. There are three categories of hotels to choose from:

OFF-SITE HOTELS: Numerous hotels surround Walt Disney World, ranging from luxury resorts to shabby motels. Many provide shuttle service to the major attractions, but if you want to see and do a lot, you'll need a car. Among the best values in this category are the mostly suites hotels within five minutes of Walt Disney World. They are very spacious, usually with mini-kitchens, and are priced reasonably. Many include breakfast. See "Off-Site Hotels & Suites," page 152, for descriptions.

PARTNER HOTELS AT WALT DISNEY WORLD: There are ten independently-operated resorts inside Walt Disney World: seven near Downtown Disney, two in the Epcot Resorts Area, and one near the Magic Kingdom. They offer great locations, good transportation, and other Walt Disney World privileges, including discounts and advance reservation for golf, and free taxis to the golf courses. Most are moderately priced and all are reviewed in the pages that follow.

DISNEY-OWNED RESORTS: All sixteen Walt Disney World Resorts have charming themed environments, a warm embrace of Disney magic that continues twenty-four hours a day. Guests at Disney-owned resorts are afforded certain privileges, including early admission to a different theme park each day; free parking or transportation to the theme parks; and resort ID charge cards good in shops and restaurants. Accommodations range from campsites to luxury vacation homes and everything in between.

RATINGS & COSTS

The ratings in the hotel reviews that follow are based on four criteria: ATMOSPHERE (quality, comfort, and creativity); SERVICE (promptness, attitude, and knowledge); FRESHNESS (cleanliness and newness of the rooms); and VACATION VALUE (how much you get for what you actually pay), as shown:

★★★★	★★★	★★	★
SUPERIOR IN EVERY WAY	BETTER THAN MOST	SATISFACTORY	SUB-STANDARD

The hotels in all categories span a wide range of costs, depending on the hotel's amenities and location (see "Guide to Hotel Features," page 124). The hotel reviews show the starting price of a standard (non-view) room, averaged across peak and value seasons, excluding taxes (about 11 percent), as follows:

$ – UNDER $90
$$ – $91 TO $150
$$$ – $151 TO $200
$$$$ – $201 TO $250
$$$$$ – $251 TO $300
$$$$$$ – $301 TO $400
♛ – OVER $400

MONEY $AVING PAGE

GUIDE TO HOTEL FEATURES

This chart compares the features of the Walt Disney World resorts, including ❶ A location close to parks and stores, and convenient for quick trips back to the room from most parks; ❷ transportation choices to parks and restaurants, including walking; ❸ services such as fitness centers, child care, room service, and the number of recreation facilities, such as boating and bicycling; ❹ the number of full-service restaurants accessible either by foot or by monorail.

● A WORLD OF CHOICES	◔ MANY POSSIBILITIES	◎ LIMITED OPTIONS	○ RESTRICTED BY COMPARISON

HOTEL	Overall Quick Convenient Location	Walking and Transportation Options	Hotel Services and Recreation	On Site and Nearby Dining Options	Standard Room Starting Price
Buena Vista Palace Resort & Spa	◎	◎	◔	◔	$$
Courtyard by Marriott	◎	◎	○	◔	$$
Disney's All-Star Resorts	○	○	○	○	$
Disney's Beach Club Resort	◔	◔	◔	◔	$$$$$
Disney's BoardWalk Inn	◔	◔	◔	◔	$$$$$
Disney's BoardWalk Villas	◔	◔	◔	◔	$$$$
Disney's Caribbean Beach Resort	○	○	◎	◎	$$
Disney's Contemporary Resort	◔	◔	◔	◔	$$$$
Disney's Coronado Springs Resort	○	○	◎	◎	$$
Disney's Dixie Landings Resort	○	○	◎	◎	$$
Disney's Fort Wilderness Campground	○	○	◎	○	$
Disney's Grand Floridian Beach Resort	◔	◔	◔	◔	$$$$$$
Disney's Old Key West Resort	○	○	◔	○	$$$$
Disney's Polynesian Resort	◔	◔	◔	◔	$$$$$
Disney's Port Orleans Resort	○	○	◎	◎	$$
Disney's Wilderness Lodge	○	○	◔	◔	$$$$
Disney's Yacht Club Resort	◔	◔	◔	◔	$$$$$
DoubleTree Guest Suites Resort	◎	◎	○	◔	$$$
Grosvenor Resort	◎	◎	○	◔	$$$
The Hilton Resort	◎	◎	○	◔	$$$
Hotel Royal Plaza	◎	◎	○	◔	$$
Shades of Green	○	◎	◎	○	$
Travelodge Hotel	◎	◎	○	◔	$$
The Villas at the Disney Institute	○	◎	◔	○	$$$$
Walt Disney World Dolphin	◔	◔	◔	◔	$$$$
Walt Disney World Swan	◔	◔	◔	◔	$$$$

VALUE SEASON HOTEL RATES

$AVE

Value seasons vary year to year, but generally the lowest hotel rates tend to occur during the following times:

◆ **DISNEY'S BUDGET RESORTS:** January through Mid-February ● Late August through Mid-December

◆ **DISNEY'S BETTER RESORTS:** January through Mid-February ● Early July through Mid-December

◆ **SWAN, DOLPHIN, AND HILTON RESORTS:** January ● May through December

◆ **GROSVENOR RESORT:** Mid-April through December

◆ **OTHER HOTEL PLAZA RESORTS:** January through Mid-February ● Late August through Mid-December

◆ **OFF-SITE HOTELS SUPER-VALUE MONTHS:** January ● September

Smart✓

WALT DISNEY WORLD HOTEL MAP

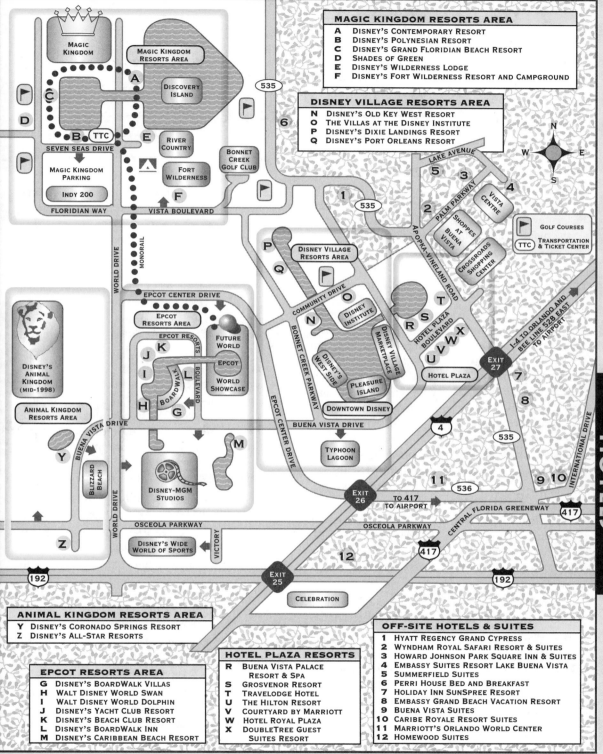

MONEY $AVING PAGE

BUENA VISTA PALACE RESORT & SPA

A Privately Owned Hotel

1900 Buena Vista Drive, Lake Buena Vista, Florida 32830
Telephone (407) 827-2727 • Fax (407) 827-6034
Websites: www.bvpalace.com — www.ten-io.com/disney-vha

★★★	★★★★	★★★★	★★★★
ATMOSPHERE	SERVICE	FRESHNESS	VACATION VALUE

LOCATION: The Buena Vista Palace Resort & Spa is one of seven independently owned Hotel Plaza Resorts located on Walt Disney World property, within walking distance to Downtown Disney. The hotel provides shuttle bus service to the major Walt Disney World attractions.

AMBIENCE: Large fountains mark the entrance to this imposing and majestic mirror-paneled high-rise hotel. The Buena Vista Palace is situated on twenty-seven acres of open land and pine forest and boasts its own private lagoon. The elegant multilevel lobby encircles a twenty-seven-story atrium. The guest rooms have private balconies and have recently been refurbished. The Palace Suites, in an adjacent low-rise building, offer spacious suites with separate bedrooms and mini kitchens. Extensive spa facilities, about nine thousand luxurious square feet, offer guests a complete spa experience during their vacation. The Buena Vista Palace Resort & Spa ranks as one of the top five resorts in the United States.

RATES: Standard rooms 💲💲. Crown-Level concierge rooms 💲💲💲💲 (including Continental breakfast, appetizers, no-host cocktails, and special room amenities). Palace Suites 💲💲💲💲 (including separate bedroom, refrigerator, wet bar, two baths, and in-room coffeemaker). Rates vary with the season.

AMENITIES: Twenty-four-hour room service, mini bar, in-room safe, hair dryer, turndown service, voice mail, pay-per-view movies, and valet parking.

RESTAURANTS: *The Outback* — Steak and seafood dinners, Australian-style cuisine.

Arthur's 27 — Elegant Continental dining in an award-winning rooftop restaurant.

Watercress Cafe & Bake Shop — Breakfast, lunch, and dinner, with soup and salad bar.

RECREATION: Two pools, lap pool, marina, tennis, volleyball, jogging path, full-service spa and fitness center, exercise classes, steam room, sauna, massage, and whirlpools.

HOTEL TRANSPORTATION: Walk or bus to Downtown Disney. Bus to Epcot, Disney-MGM Studios, the Magic Kingdom, Typhoon Lagoon, Disney's BoardWalk, and Blizzard Beach. For transportation to other destinations or resorts, connect to destination buses at Downtown Disney. Taxi service available.

FEATURES: The full-service Spa at the Buena Vista Palace offers visitors a complete range of treatments and massage in an elegant setting. (See "Spas," page 226.) **Readers can receive a 50 percent discount on spa treatments! (See "Vacation Discount Coupons!" page 272.)**
 Alamo is conveniently located here for visitors who might like to rent a car during their stay.

DRAWBACKS: Buses to minor attractions and other resorts can be inconvenient from here.

HOT TIPS: The resort offers vacation packages that include hotel accommodations, some meals, theme park admission, and other amenities. Call the hotel directly (800 327-2990) for a brochure.
 Buena Vista Palace offers room discounts to many travel clubs, including Meritz Exclusively Yours, AAA, and Orlando Magicard, which offers the best discount at about 20 percent.

MAKING RESERVATIONS: Call the hotel's toll-free number (800 327-2990) and ask about special promotional rates. Reservations may also be made through Walt Disney World Central Reservations Office (407 934-7639).

HOTELS

COURTYARD BY MARRIOTT

A MARRIOTT HOTEL
1805 HOTEL PLAZA BOULEVARD, LAKE BUENA VISTA, FLORIDA 32830
TELEPHONE (407) 828-8888 • FAX (407) 827-4623
WEBSITE: www.ten-io.com/disney-vha

★★	★★	★★	★★
ATMOSPHERE	SERVICE	FRESHNESS	VACATION VALUE

LOCATION: Courtyard by Marriott is one of seven independently owned Hotel Plaza Resorts located on Walt Disney World property near Downtown Disney. The hotel provides shuttle bus service to the major Walt Disney World attractions.

AMBIENCE: This recently renovated high-rise hotel with a six-story garden wing has a modern white-stuccoed exterior, roofed with traditional terra-cotta mission tile. Inside, the fourteen-story atrium lobby has glass elevators that transport guests to the upper floors. A thatch-roofed bar at the back of the lobby, umbrella-shaded tables, and a small fountain to one side evoke a cool Caribbean mood. The turquoise-, coral-, and sand-colored guest rooms have standard but comfortable hotel-style furnishings with tropical accents. All rooms have balconies, many with views of Walt Disney World.

RATES: Standard rooms 💲💲. Rates vary with the season.

AMENITIES: Room service, in-room safe, hair dryer, coffeemaker, pay-per-view movies, daily newspaper, and in-room Nintendo. Refrigerator available on request for a fee.

RESTAURANTS: *Courtyard Cafe & Grille* — American-style buffet and a la carte breakfast, lunch, and dinner.

Village Deli — New York–style deli sandwiches, pizza, frozen yogurt, and take-out menu for lunch, dinner, and late-night snacks.

RECREATION: Two pools, jogging path, fitness center, and whirlpool.

HOTEL TRANSPORTATION: Walk or bus to Downtown Disney. Bus to the Magic Kingdom, Disney-MGM Studios, Epcot, Typhoon Lagoon, Blizzard Beach, and Disney's BoardWalk. For transportation to other theme parks or resorts, connect to destination buses at Downtown Disney. Taxi service available.

FEATURES: Courtyard Club members can earn points, have free local phone calls, and receive room discounts.

Visitors planning to tour the parks early in the morning can order espresso, cappuccino, and pastries from the lobby coffee bar to take along.

DRAWBACKS: Guests relying on hotel buses to reach minor attractions or other resorts may find them inconvenient from here. The parking lot can be overcrowded during peak seasons.

HOT TIPS: Higher floors offer sweeping views. Request a room that faces Pleasure Island for a view of its nightly fireworks display.

Courtyard by Marriott offers discounts to many organizations, including the American Association of Retired Persons. **AAA members receive a 10 percent discount on rooms.**

Courtyard by Marriott offers a number of vacation packages that include accommodations, theme park admission, some meals, and other travel amenities. To receive a brochure, call the hotel's toll-free number (800 223-9930).

A rental car can save considerable commuting time from this location.

MAKING RESERVATIONS: First call Courtyard Central Reservations (800 321-2211), then call the hotel and compare rates (800 223-9930). Reservations may also be made through WDW Central Reservations Office (407 934-7639). **Be sure to ask about special promotional rates, which could cut room costs up to 40 percent, depending on the day of arrival.**

HOTELS

SAVE

DISNEY'S ALL-STAR RESORTS

DISNEY'S ALL-STAR SPORTS RESORT
1701 WEST BUENA VISTA DRIVE
LAKE BUENA VISTA, FLORIDA 32830
TELEPHONE (407) 939-5000

DISNEY'S ALL-STAR MUSIC RESORT
1801 WEST BUENA VISTA DRIVE
LAKE BUENA VISTA, FLORIDA 32830
TELEPHONE (407) 939-6000

★	★★	★★	★★★
ATMOSPHERE	SERVICE	FRESHNESS	VACATION VALUE

LOCATION: Disney's budget All-Star Resorts is located in the Animal Kingdom Resorts Area. Nearby attractions include Blizzard Beach water park, Disney's Wide World of Sports, Disney-MGM Studios, and Disney's Animal Kingdom, opening in 1998. The resort complex encompasses three themed hotels: Disney's All-Star Sports Resort, Disney's All-Star Music Resort, and Disney's All-Star Movies Resort, scheduled to open in early 1999.

AMBIENCE: This huge resort complex is made up of twenty three-story buildings with exterior corridors. The otherwise plain block structures are distinguished by massive, light-hearted, corporate pop sculpture — huge red paper cups of Coca-Cola attached to the All-Star Sports Resort's Home Run Hotel and gigantic cans of Spalding tennis balls fastened to the Center Court Hotel. The All-Star Music Resort wears larger-than-life trombones, jukeboxes, and electric guitars. The exterior theme of each building is carried over to its pool area. The guest rooms themselves are small and sparsely furnished.

RATES: Standard rooms 🅢.

AMENITIES: Voice mail, in-room safe, pizza delivery, and refrigerator on request for a fee.

RESTAURANTS: *End Zone Food Court* (All-Star Sports Resort) — Counter service; open all day.
The Intermission Food Court (All-Star Music Resort) — Counter service; open all day.

RECREATION: Two pools located at each resort complex, jogging path.

WDW PUBLIC TRANSPORTATION: Bus to all theme parks, including the Magic Kingdom, Epcot, Disney-MGM Studios, Blizzard Beach, Typhoon Lagoon, and Downtown Disney. To reach other destinations or resorts, bus to the Transportation and Ticket Center (TTC) or to Downtown Disney and connect to destination buses. Taxi service available.

FEATURES: Pools are open until midnight and are designed to reflect each resort's theme. For example, at Disney's All-Star Sports Resort, the pools are shaped like a baseball diamond.

The hotel provides the advantages of staying in a Disney resort to visitors on limited budgets.

DRAWBACKS: During peak seasons, buses to the Magic Kingdom can be slow; buses to distant resorts and dining events are very inconvenient.

It can be a very long trek from the guest rooms to the food courts — some rooms are more than a quarter-mile away.

The hotel has no full-service restaurants and attracts mainly young families and students.

The price is right but the atmosphere is much like a Disney-style housing project; the rooms are minuscule and the windows do not open.

HOT TIPS: For locations near the bus stops and food courts, request a room in Surf's Up! at the All-Star Sports Resort, and in Calypso at the All-Star Music Resort. For the quietest, most secluded rooms, request an upper-floor room with a forest view in Country Fair at the All-Star Music Resort.

A rental car will save a lot of commuting time from this location and is essential for visitors who want to see all that Walt Disney World has to offer or who would like to dine in full-service restaurants at other resorts.

MAKING RESERVATIONS: Call WDW Central Reservations Office (407 934-7639). Ask about special rates and seasonal vacation packages.

DISNEY'S BEACH CLUB RESORT

A DISNEY-OWNED HOTEL

1800 EPCOT RESORTS BOULEVARD, LAKE BUENA VISTA, FLORIDA 32830
TELEPHONE (407) 934-8000 • FAX (407) 934-3850
WEBSITE: www.disneyworld.com

★★★	★★★	★★★★	★★★
ATMOSPHERE	SERVICE	FRESHNESS	VACATION VALUE

LOCATION: Disney's Beach Club Resort is one of seven hotels in the Epcot Resorts Area. It is located within walking distance of the International Gateway to the World Showcase at Epcot. It faces Crescent Lake and shares a white sand beach and harbor waterfront with Disney's Yacht Club Resort.

AMBIENCE: This sky blue multilevel resort was designed by architect Robert Stern and patterned after the fashionable New England seacoast–style resorts of the nineteenth century. It shares resort amenities with the more formal Yacht Club located next door. It has sporty, casual decor, from the 1927 Chevrolet taxi parked in front, to the striped wicker furnishings and caged finches in the lobby. Guest rooms are cheerful and light, furnished in beach-style pink and white cabana stripes and gauzy curtains. Many rooms have verandas or small balconies that overlook the hotel's white sand beach on Crescent Lake.

RATES: Standard rooms 💲💲💲💲.

AMENITIES: Twenty-four-hour room service, mini bar, hair dryer, daily newspaper, in-room safe, voice mail, and valet parking.

RESTAURANTS: *Cape May Cafe* — Character Breakfast buffet and clambake dinner buffet. Lobster is available on a separate menu.
Beaches and Cream — Breakfast and all-day hamburgers and soda fountain specialties.

RECREATION: Pool, white sand beach, mini water park, marina, tennis, jogging path, volleyball, lawn bowling, croquet, fitness center, sauna, steam room, fitness classes, fitness training, whirlpool, and massage.

WDW PUBLIC TRANSPORTATION: Walk or water launch to the World Showcase at Epcot and Disney's BoardWalk. Water launch to Disney-MGM Studios. Bus to Typhoon Lagoon, the Magic Kingdom, Blizzard Beach, and Disney Village Marketplace and Pleasure Island at Downtown Disney. To reach other destinations or resorts, bus to the Transportation and Ticket Center (TTC) or Downtown Disney and connect to destination buses. Taxi service is available.

FEATURES: In terms of location, the Beach Club has it all. It is conveniently located for guests primarily interested in Epcot and Disney-MGM Studios, and is a short, scenic walk to Disney's BoardWalk for shopping, fine restaurants, and evening entertainment.
    Stormalong Bay, the resort's own mini water park, is one of the best recreation features at any Walt Disney World resort.

DRAWBACKS: Buses to minor attractions and other resorts can be inconvenient from here.

HOT TIPS: The rooms on the fifth floor were originally designated as concierge rooms, so they are a bit more spacious and generous in comforts. Most upper-floor rooms have balconies. If the weather is cool, you may want to request a "full balcony" room, which has outdoor seating.
    Standard rooms that face the front, but that are not directly over the parking portico, are a good value. Rooms located at the far end of the hotel (with numbers ending 11 to 30), although a bit of a trek from the lobby, offer pleasant views of the forest or the quiet pool, and have fast access by foot to the International Gateway to the World Showcase at Epcot. Many rooms sleep five.

MAKING RESERVATIONS: Call WDW Central Reservations Office (407 934-7639). Ask about special rates and seasonal vacation packages.

HOTELS

DISNEY'S BOARDWALK INN

A DISNEY-OWNED HOTEL

2101 EPCOT RESORTS BOULEVARD, LAKE BUENA VISTA, FLORIDA 32830
TELEPHONE (407) 939-5100 • FAX (407) 939-5150
WEBSITE: www.disneyworld.com

★★★	★★★★	★★★★	★★
ATMOSPHERE	SERVICE	FRESHNESS	VACATION VALUE

LOCATION: Disney's BoardWalk Inn is one of seven hotels in the Epcot Resorts Area. It is located at Disney's BoardWalk, a short distance from Disney-MGM Studios and within walking distance of the International Gateway to the World Showcase at Epcot. The hotel sits above Disney's BoardWalk Promenade, overlooks Crescent Lake, and shares a lobby and a large outdoor terrace with Disney's BoardWalk Villas, a Disney Vacation Club resort.

AMBIENCE: Disney's BoardWalk Inn is built on several levels that rise above and extend behind Disney's BoardWalk, a bustling promenade reminiscent of the Atlantic City Boardwalk of the 1930s. The hotel's design recalls the cheerful, casual luxury of turn-of-the-century Eastern Seaboard summer resorts. The moderate-sized guest rooms have balconies with French doors and are decorated with rosebud-patterned rugs, comfortable beach house–style furnishings, and curtains printed with soft images of vintage postcards. The hotel also has a number of charming two-story "honeymoon cottages" with small gardens and private entrances.

RATES: Standard rooms 💲💲💲💲. Concierge service rooms 👑 (including Continental breakfast, private lounge, afternoon snacks, evening cordials and desserts, bathrobes, and other room amenities). Honeymoon Cottages 👑. Rates vary with the season.

AMENITIES: Twenty-four-hour room service, bathrobes, hair dryer, daily newspaper, turndown service (on request), in-room safe, voice mail, and valet parking.

RESTAURANTS: The hotel is served by several restaurants along Disney's BoardWalk, including Spoodles, ESPN Club, Flying Fish Café, and Big River Grille & Brewing Works.

RECREATION: Quiet pool, mini water park, bicycling, tennis, jogging path, croquet, fishing, fitness center, sauna, steam room, outdoor whirlpool, and massage.

WDW PUBLIC TRANSPORTATION: Walk or water launch to the World Showcase at Epcot. Water launch to Disney-MGM Studios. Bus to the Magic Kingdom, Blizzard Beach, Typhoon Lagoon, and Pleasure Island and Disney Village Marketplace at Downtown Disney. To reach other destinations or resorts, bus to the Transportation and Ticket Center (TTC) or Downtown Disney and connect to destination buses. Taxi service available.

FEATURES: This full-amenity resort is conveniently located for guests primarily interested in Epcot, Disney-MGM Studios, and the nightlife and clubs on the BoardWalk Promenade.

The Belle Vue Room off the lobby is a pleasant place to watch a sunset or play a quiet game of checkers or backgammon on a rainy afternoon.

DRAWBACKS: The resort stretches over half the BoardWalk. Request a close-in room if you wish to be near the lobby and valet parking areas.

While the hotel is nice and well located, many guests feel it is too expensive for what they get.

HOT TIPS: The rooms overlooking Crescent Lake and the BoardWalk Promenade offer a bustling, brightly lit view. If that's not what you are looking for, request a room overlooking the gardens or the quiet-pool area.

MAKING RESERVATIONS: Call WDW Central Reservations Office (407 934-7639). Ask about special rates and seasonal vacation packages.

DISNEY'S BOARDWALK VILLAS

A DISNEY VACATION CLUB TIMESHARE

2101 EPCOT RESORTS BOULEVARD, LAKE BUENA VISTA, FLORIDA 32830

TELEPHONE (407) 939-5100 • FAX (407) 939-5150

WEBSITE: www.disneyworld.com

★★★	★★★	★★★★	★★★
ATMOSPHERE	SERVICE	FRESHNESS	VACATION VALUE

LOCATION: Disney's BoardWalk Villas is one of seven hotels in the Epcot Resorts Area. It is located at Disney's BoardWalk, a short distance from Disney-MGM Studios and within walking distance of the International Gateway to the World Showcase at Epcot. The hotel sits above Disney's BoardWalk Promenade, overlooks Crescent Lake, and shares a lobby and a large outdoor terrace with Disney's BoardWalk Inn.

AMBIENCE: Painted in shades of cream and terracotta and sporting festive striped awnings, Disney's BoardWalk Villas extends above and behind Disney's BoardWalk, an entertainment complex of restaurants, clubs, and shops that curves around Crescent Lake. Accommodations are designed to be "vacation homes." Studios have wet bars, and one-, two-, and three-bedroom suites have full kitchens. All units have comfortable beach house–style furnishings and French doors that open onto small balconies.

RATES: Studios 💲💲💲 (including wet bar, refrigerator, microwave, and coffeemaker). One-bedroom vacation homes 💲💲💲💲. Two-bedroom vacation homes 💲💲💲💲💲. Three-bedroom vacation homes ♛. All vacation homes except studios have fully equipped kitchens, laundry facilities, wide-screen televisions, and VCRs. Rates vary with the season.

AMENITIES: Twenty-four-hour room service, coffeemaker, daily newspaper, in-room safe, hair dryer, turndown service (on request), voice mail, and valet parking.

RESTAURANTS: The hotel is served by several restaurants along Disney's BoardWalk, including Spoodles, ESPN Club, Flying Fish Café, and Big River Grille & Brewing Works.

RECREATION: Quiet pool, mini water park, bicycling, tennis, jogging path, croquet, fishing, fitness center, sauna, steam room, outdoor whirlpool, and massage.

WDW PUBLIC TRANSPORTATION: Walk or water launch to the World Showcase at Epcot. Water launch to Disney-MGM Studios. Bus to the Magic Kingdom, Blizzard Beach, Typhoon Lagoon, and Pleasure Island and Disney Village Marketplace at Downtown Disney. To reach other destinations or resorts, bus to the Transportation and Ticket Center (TTC) or Downtown Disney and connect to destination buses. Taxi service available.

FEATURES: The resort is conveniently located for guests primarily interested in Disney-MGM Studios and Epcot, as well as the nightlife and clubs on the BoardWalk Promenade.

For young-at-heart guests, the resort's carnival-themed pool area, Luna Park, has a roller-coaster waterslide and a whimsical poolside bar.

DRAWBACKS: The resort stretches over half the BoardWalk. Request a close-in room if you wish to be near the lobby and valet parking areas.

The studios seem a little cramped; the suites, while more expensive, offer a better value.

HOT TIPS: The rooms overlooking the Board-Walk Promenade and Crescent Lake offer a view of the midway and Epcot fireworks.

Disney's BoardWalk Villas is also a Disney Vacation Club timeshare resort. Units not used by timeshare owners are available to guests as full-service hotel accommodations.

MAKING RESERVATIONS: Call WDW Central Reservations Office (407 934-7639). Ask about special rates and seasonal vacation packages.

HOTELS

DISNEY'S CARIBBEAN BEACH RESORT

A DISNEY-OWNED HOTEL
900 CAYMAN WAY, LAKE BUENA VISTA, FLORIDA 32830
TELEPHONE (407) 934-3400 • FAX (407) 934-3288
WEBSITE: www.disneyworld.com

★★★	★★	★★★	★★★
ATMOSPHERE	SERVICE	FRESHNESS	VACATION VALUE

LOCATION: Disney's Caribbean Beach Resort is one of seven hotels in the Epcot Resorts Area. The buildings of the resort encircle forty-acre Barefoot Bay, a series of three lakes created for the resort's exclusive use. From Disney's Caribbean Beach Resort it is a short drive to Epcot, Disney-MGM Studios, Typhoon Lagoon, and Downtown Disney.

AMBIENCE: Built as Walt Disney World's first budget resort, the sprawling Caribbean Beach Resort consists of clusters of pitched-roof two-story buildings painted in very bright colors. Each area has a pool and is surrounded with expertly designed tropical landscaping. Instead of a formal lobby, the resort welcomes guests at its modest freestanding Customs House, where overhead fans and wicker settees set a tropical note. The limited-amenity guest rooms, with soft toned wood furnishings, are functional and cozy. Most resort activities are centered at Old Port Royale, on one side of Barefoot Bay.

RATES: Standard rooms 💲💲. Rates remain the same year round.

AMENITIES: Mini bar, coffeemaker, voice mail, and pizza delivery to rooms.

RESTAURANTS: *Old Port Royale* — Food court with six counter-service restaurant serving breakfast, lunch, and dinner.

Captain's Tavern — Dinner featuring prime rib and American cuisine.

RECREATION: Seven pools, white sand beach, marina, bicycling, jogging path, nature walk, volleyball, and whirlpool.

WDW PUBLIC TRANSPORTATION: Disney's Caribbean Beach Resort has its own internal bus system. Bus to all theme parks, including the Magic Kingdom, Disney-MGM Studios, Epcot, Blizzard Beach, Typhoon Lagoon, and Downtown Disney. To reach other destinations or resorts, bus to the Transportation and Ticket Center (TTC) or Downtown Disney and connect to destination buses. Taxi service available.

FEATURES: Parrot Cay, a small island in the middle of Barefoot Bay, has a fantasy Spanish-fort playground, a tropical nature walk, and an aviary stocked with colorful birds.

DRAWBACKS: The resort is especially popular among families with young children, making it an all-day noisy experience at the main pool.

Because the resort sprawls over two hundred acres, it can be a long trek from guest rooms to the food court at Old Port Royale.

Buses to minor attractions and other resorts can be inconvenient from this location. Guests who are primarily interested in the Magic Kingdom may find the commute tedious.

HOT TIPS: To select a room close to Old Port Royale, request Trinidad North, next door, or Jamaica, just across the bridge. For isolation, request Trinidad South, which has a quiet pool and secluded beach.

The rooms on the second floor afford the most privacy. Some of the remote building locations can provide a romantic tropical setting.

If you would like to be near Parrot Cay island, request a room in Jamaica or Aruba.

A rental car can speed commuting time to the theme parks from this location, and is essential if frequently visiting other resorts.

MAKING RESERVATIONS: Call WDW Central Reservations Office (407 934-7639). Ask about special rates and seasonal vacation packages.

HOTELS

DISNEY'S CONTEMPORARY RESORT

A DISNEY-OWNED HOTEL
4600 NORTH WORLD DRIVE, LAKE BUENA VISTA, FLORIDA 32830
TELEPHONE (407) 824-1000 • FAX (407) 824-3539
WEBSITE: www.disneyworld.com

★★★	★★★★	★★★	★★★
ATMOSPHERE	**SERVICE**	**FRESHNESS**	**VACATION VALUE**

LOCATION: Disney's Contemporary Resort is one of six hotels in the Magic Kingdom Resorts Area. It is conveniently located on the monorail line that serves the Magic Kingdom and Epcot. It has a long white sand beach and sweeping views of Bay Lake.

AMBIENCE: The elongated pyramidal structure of this resort has a futuristic look overall. The minimalist-style first-floor lobby is strictly functional, with angular furniture in stylish colors and sleek modern art. The main lobby is actually located on the Concourse level, where the monorail glides through the hotel's glass-and-steel atrium. The resort's outdoor pool area was recently enlarged and a waterslide added. The tower rooms and suites are decorated in sophisticated neutrals and streamlined furniture. The three-story garden wing rooms are spacious, but set at some distance from the lobby. All rooms have a balcony or patio.

RATES: Garden wing standard rooms 🍴🍴🍴. Tower rooms 🍴🍴🍴🍴. Tower concierge suites 👑 (including Continental breakfast, evening wine and cheese, and special room amenities). Rates vary with the season.

AMENITIES: Twenty-four-hour room service, in-room safe (tower rooms), daily newspaper, voice mail, and valet parking.

RESTAURANTS: *California Grill* — The dinner menu changes daily in this trendy rooftop restaurant with an open kitchen. The food preparation is part of the show.

Chef Mickey's — Character buffet for breakfast and dinner.

Concourse Steakhouse — Breakfast, lunch, and dinner featuring steak and prime rib.

RECREATION: Three pools, white sand beach, marina, waterskiing, parasailing, tennis, volleyball, shuffleboard, jogging path, fitness center, sauna, whirlpool, fitness training, and massage.

WDW PUBLIC TRANSPORTATION: Walk to the Magic Kingdom. Monorail to the Magic Kingdom, the Transportation and Ticket Center (TTC), and Epcot. Water launch to Discovery Island, Fort Wilderness, and River Country. Bus to all other attractions and Downtown Disney. Taxi service available.

FEATURES: In this most tennis-oriented of the Walt Disney World resorts, the Racquet Club offers practice courts and personal instruction.

The hotel has an outdoor viewing platform on the fifteenth floor, which is great for watching the Magic Kingdom fireworks.

This hotel has many unique transportation options, including direct ferry service from its marina to Discovery Island and Fort Wilderness.

DRAWBACKS: Buses to minor attractions or other resorts for dining events can be inconvenient from here. Guests must change trains at the TTC for monorails to Epcot.

HOT TIPS: Tower rooms are the most popular, convenient, and expensive. Higher-floor rooms facing the Magic Kingdom have a view of the fireworks show. Many rooms sleep five persons.

Garden wing rooms, although less expensive, are a distance from the lobby; request a location close in. The rooms on the first floor facing Bay Lake are popular because they have sliding glass doors that open onto private patios.

MAKING RESERVATIONS: Call WDW Central Reservations Office (407 934-7639). Ask about special rates and seasonal vacation packages.

HOTELS

DISNEY'S CORONADO SPRINGS RESORT

A DISNEY-OWNED HOTEL

 1000 WEST BUENA VISTA DRIVE, LAKE BUENA VISTA, FLORIDA 32830
TELEPHONE (407) 939-1000 • FAX (407) 939-0425
WEBSITE: www.disneyworld.com

★★★★	★★★	★★★★	★★★★
ATMOSPHERE	SERVICE	FRESHNESS	VACATION VALUE

LOCATION: Disney's Coronado Springs Resort is located in the Animal Kingdom Resorts Area. Nearby attractions include Blizzard Beach, Disney's Wide World of Sports, and Disney's Animal Kingdom, opening in 1998.

AMBIENCE: This handsomely designed resort combines the stately architectural styles of Colonial Mexico with the rustic simplicity of the American Southwest. The landscaping varies from desert oasis to tropical jungle and three distinct clusters of hotel buildings with pools encircle the resort's private lake: the Cabanas, two-story Mexican-style lakefront bungalows; the Ranchos, secluded rustic stucco buildings with pleasant courtyards and fountains; and the Casitas, a bright festive village of three- and four-story buildings roofed in Spanish terracotta. Guest rooms have whitewashed walls, ceiling fans, and colorful Southwestern-themed furnishings. The hotel's large, impressive lobby and common areas have high open-beam ceilings with elaborate detailing. Coronado Springs was designed to be a moderately priced convention hotel, as well as a family vacation resort.

RATES: Standard rooms 💲💲💲. Rates vary with the season.

AMENITIES: Room service, coffeemaker, hair dryer, in-room safe, valet parking, and voice mail. Refrigerator on request for a fee.

RESTAURANTS: *Maya Grill* — Breakfast and dinner featuring wood-fire grilled specialties highlighting Southwest-style cuisine.

Pepper Market — This upscale food court has the look of a festive Mexican market and offers traditional American and Mexican dishes. Guests are seated by servers; open all day.

RECREATION: Three pools, mini water park, white sand beach, marina, volleyball, bicycling, jogging path, nature walk, fitness center, whirlpool, and massage.

WDW PUBLIC TRANSPORTATION: Walk or bus to Blizzard Beach. Bus to Epcot, the Magic Kingdom, Disney-MGM Studios, Downtown Disney, and Typhoon Lagoon. To reach other destinations or resorts, bus to the Transportation and Ticket Center (TTC) and connect to destination buses. Taxi service available.

FEATURES: This new limited-amenity resort provides the ambience and privileges of staying in a Disney resort to visitors on somewhat restricted budgets. Because of the hotel's focus on convention travelers, services here may be above average for a budget-priced resort.

The resort's pleasantly themed pool and mini water park has been designed to look like a tropical archeological "Dig Site." It is dominated by a large Mayan pyramid with waterslides.

DRAWBACKS: Guests relying on buses to reach minor attractions or other resorts for dining events may find them inconvenient from here.

The rooms have no private balconies, although the windows can be opened.

HOT TIPS: The Cabanas are oriented to fifteen-acre Lago Dorado and have picturesque views; request a lake view. For locations near the food court and restaurant, request a Casitas room near the lobby. The Ranchos are closest to the resorts themed pool and recreation area. Upper-floor rooms offer the most privacy.

MAKING RESERVATIONS: Call WDW Central Reservations Office (407 934-7639). Ask about special rates and seasonal vacation packages.

DISNEY'S DIXIE LANDINGS RESORT

A DISNEY-OWNED HOTEL

1251 DIXIE DRIVE, LAKE BUENA VISTA, FLORIDA 32830
TELEPHONE (407) 934-6000 • FAX (407) 934-5777
WEBSITE: www.disneyworld.com

★★★	★★	★★★	★★★★
ATMOSPHERE	SERVICE	FRESHNESS	VACATION VALUE

LOCATION: Disney's Dixie Landings Resort is one of four hotels in the Disney Village Resorts Area. It is connected by waterway and carriage path to the nearby Port Orleans resort and by waterway to Disney Village Marketplace and Pleasure Island at Downtown Disney.

AMBIENCE: The rustic bayous and antebellum mansions of the Old South are re-created at Dixie Landings. The large, sprawling resort has two sections. On one side is Alligator Bayou, with its two-story Cajun-style brick or stucco lodges sporting wide front porches and rough-hewn railings, all set in a dense moss-hung pine forest. On the other side is Magnolia Bend, with elegant three-story plantation manors set apart by fountains, sweeping lawns, and weeping willows. The Sassagoula River loops through the resort, and in the center is the reception area, designed as a riverboat depot, circa 1880. The rooms in this limited-amenity resort are decorated simply in soft neutral colors; furnishings in the Bayou rooms are more rustic than in the Magnolia rooms. Guest rooms have a vanity-dressing area with two pedestal sinks.

RATES: Standard rooms $$. Rates vary with the season.

AMENITIES: Voice mail and pizza delivery to rooms. Refrigerator on request for a fee.

RESTAURANTS: *Boatwright's Dining Hall* — Breakfast and dinner featuring Cajun specialties.
Colonel's Cotton Mill — Food court with five counter-service restaurants for breakfast, lunch, and dinner, housed in an old cotton mill.

RECREATION: Five pools, theme pool, marina, bicycling, jogging path, whirlpool, and an old-fashioned fishing hole.

WDW PUBLIC TRANSPORTATION: Bus or water launch to Downtown Disney. Bus to all theme parks, including the Magic Kingdom, Epcot, Blizzard Beach, Disney-MGM Studios, and Typhoon Lagoon. To reach other destinations or resorts, bus to the Transportation and Ticket Center (TTC) or Downtown Disney and connect to destination buses. Taxi service available.

FEATURES: The resort is conveniently located for guests interested in golfing at Walt Disney World. The Bonnet Creek Golf Club is just a short distance away.

Guests may rent their own boats at the marina and commute by water to Downtown Disney and to other Disney Village resorts.

DRAWBACKS: This budget-priced hotel is very popular with young families, especially during peak seasons. If you're seeking a quiet, romantic setting, request Alligator Bayou lodge 38.

Buses to minor attractions and other resorts can be very inconvenient from this location.

HOT TIPS: This limited-amenity resort offers an excellent value for the price. Upgrade to a river-view room and you'll have a luxury setting for a fraction of the cost of Walt Disney World's premier resorts. Many rooms sleep five persons.

The most popular locations are those close to the common areas and lobby. If you prefer a plantation home, request a room in Oak Manor; for a more rustic setting, request Alligator Bayou lodges 14, 18, or 27.

A rental car can save commuting time from this location, especially when visiting other resorts.

MAKING RESERVATIONS: Call WDW Central Reservations Office (407) 934-7639). Ask about special rates and seasonal vacation packages.

HOTELS

DISNEY'S FORT WILDERNESS RESORT AND CAMPGROUND

4820 N. FORT WILDERNESS TRAIL, LAKE BUENA VISTA, FLORIDA 32830
TELEPHONE (407) 824-2900 • FAX (407) 824-3508

Ratings for One-Bedroom Wilderness Trailer Homes:

★★★	★★★	★★	★★★
ATMOSPHERE	SERVICE	FRESHNESS	VACATION VALUE

LOCATION: Disney's Fort Wilderness Resort and Campground is one of six hotels in the Magic Kingdom Resorts Area. It stretches from Vista Boulevard to the shores of Bay Lake.

AMBIENCE: This lush 700-acre pine forested campground is ideal for visitors who enjoy the rustic outdoors. There are about 780 campsites for tents or for recreational vehicles, and about 400 fully appointed one-bedroom trailers. Fort Wilderness offers a peaceful, natural setting to return to after a hectic day at the theme parks and is itself a Walt Disney World attraction (see "Fort Wilderness & River Country," page 107).

RATES: Wilderness Homes (fully equipped one-bedroom trailers) 💲💲💲💲. Campsites with full hookups 💲. Campsites with partial hookups 💲. Rates vary with the season.

AMENITIES: Wilderness Homes include a full kitchen, cable TV, voice mail, housekeeping services, daily newspaper, and outdoor grill. Full-hookup campsites include sanitary disposal, water, cable TV outlet, electricity, and outdoor grill. Partial-hookup campsites include water, electricity, and outdoor grill. All campsite loops have air-conditioned rest rooms, showers, ice makers, laundry facilities, and telephones. (See also "Camping at Fort Wilderness," page 113.)

RESTAURANTS: *Trail's End Buffeteria* — Cafeteria service for breakfast, lunch, and dinner, and late-night pizza to eat in or take out.

RECREATION: Pool, lap pool, marina, white sand beach, volleyball, basketball, tetherball, shuffleboard, jogging path, nature trail, tennis, bicycling, horseback riding, waterskiing, fishing, canoeing, hayrides, petting farm, and evening campfire and movies.

WDW PUBLIC TRANSPORTATION: Bus stops can be found throughout Fort Wilderness, which has its own internal bus system to all campsites and local attractions. (There is no public parking inside Fort Wilderness or at River Country.) Bikes and electric carts can also be rented for use within the resort. Walk or bus to River Country. Water launch to the Magic Kingdom, Discovery Island, and the Contemporary resort. To reach all other theme parks, bus or water launch to the Transportation and Ticket Center (TTC) and transfer to destination buses or monorails.

FEATURES: Fort Wilderness offers daily entertainment events, including the Hoop-Dee-Doo Musical Revue dinner show, hayrides, and a nightly campfire program with movies.

Two on-site convenience stores, Settlement Trading Post and Meadow Trading Post, carry a limited supply of groceries and prepared foods.

DRAWBACKS: Disney transportation to most attractions is very time consuming from here.

In the summer expect mosquitoes, afternoon thundershowers, and very hot weather.

HOT TIPS: A car is essential at this location, especially during the hot rainy season. Guests may drive to and from their campsites to all Walt Disney World attractions.

The most desirable Wilderness Home locations are on loops 2500 and 2700 near the pool. The most desirable campsites are on loops 100 through 500, near the marina and River Country. Pets are allowed to stay with their owners in loops 1600 through 1900.

MAKING RESERVATIONS: Call WDW Central Reservations Office (407 934-7639). **Lower weekly rates are available. Be sure to ask.**

HOTELS

DISNEY'S GRAND FLORIDIAN BEACH RESORT

A DISNEY-OWNED HOTEL
4401 FLORIDIAN WAY, LAKE BUENA VISTA, FLORIDA 32830
TELEPHONE (407) 824-3000 • FAX (407) 824-3186
WEBSITE: www.disneyworld.com

★★★★	★★★★	★★★★	★★★★
ATMOSPHERE	SERVICE	FRESHNESS	VACATION VALUE

LOCATION: Disney's Grand Floridian Beach Resort is one of six hotels in the Magic Kingdom Resorts Area. It is conveniently located on the monorail line that serves the Magic Kingdom and Epcot. It faces Seven Seas Lagoon and is adjacent to Disney's Wedding Pavilion.

AMBIENCE: The most elegant and expensive of the Walt Disney World resorts, this rambling, romantic Victorian-style hotel is fashioned after the grand seaside resorts of the 1890s. With its white banisters and railings, paned glass windows, peaked red-shingled roofs, and formal flower and shrub gardens, this resort is a favorite with honeymooners. Its spacious and luxurious stained-glass-domed lobby has ornate wrought-iron elevators, potted trees, and clusters of intimately placed settees where guests can sit and enjoy the ongoing live music in the common areas. The guest rooms are handsomely decorated, and each has a patio or balcony. The Grand Floridian features a deluxe full-service spa.

RATES: Standard rooms . Concierge service rooms (including Continental breakfast, afternoon snacks, evening cordials and appetizers, and special room amenities). Rates vary with the season.

AMENITIES: Twenty-four-hour room service, mini bar, in-room safe, hair dryer, bathrobes, daily newspaper, voice mail, and valet parking.

RESTAURANTS: *Victoria & Albert's* — Very elegant, award-winning candlelight dinner; prix-fixe menu.
Narcoossee's — Lunch and dinner featuring New Floridian cuisine on the waterfront.
1900 Park Fare — Buffet-style breakfast and dinner; Disney Characters drop by.

Grand Floridian Cafe — Breakfast, lunch, and dinner featuring Florida-style cuisine.

RECREATION: Pool, white sand beach, marina, waterskiing, clay tennis courts, jogging path, volleyball, fitness center, fitness training, spa, sauna, steam room, whirlpool, and massage.

WDW PUBLIC TRANSPORTATION: Monorail or water launch to the Magic Kingdom. Monorail to the Transportation and Ticket Center (TTC) and Epcot. Monorail or water launch to the Magic Kingdom to transfer to water launch to Discovery Island, Fort Wilderness, and River Country. Bus to Downtown Disney. Monorail to the TTC to transfer to destination buses for all other attractions. Taxi service available.

FEATURES: The Grand Floridian has all the upscale features of a great premier hotel. Late for a dinner reservation? Just tell the valet and you'll be whisked off in a cab or private car.
A wonderful afternoon tea is served from 3 until 6 PM in the Garden View Lounge.
Guests can select from a range of treatments at the Grand Floridian's new full-service spa.

DRAWBACKS: Guests relying on buses to reach minor attractions or distant resorts for dining events may find them inconvenient.

HOT TIPS: While all the rooms are graciously appointed, the rooms on the upper floors are more private. Many rooms sleep five persons.
The lagoon-view rooms are the most popular, but the rooms overlooking the central courtyard convey the enchantment of the Victorian-themed architecture, especially at night.

MAKING RESERVATIONS: Call WDW Central Reservations Office (407 934-7639). Ask about special rates and seasonal vacation packages.

HOTELS

DISNEY'S OLD KEY WEST RESORT

A DISNEY VACATION CLUB TIMESHARE
1510 NORTH COVE ROAD, LAKE BUENA VISTA, FLORIDA 32830
TELEPHONE (407) 827-7700 • FAX (407) 827-7710
WEBSITE: www.disneyworld.com

★★★★	★★★	★★★	★★★
ATMOSPHERE	SERVICE	FRESHNESS	VACATION VALUE

LOCATION: Disney's Old Key West Resort is one of four hotels in the Disney Village Resorts Area. The resort is connected by waterway to Disney Village Marketplace and Pleasure Island at Downtown Disney.

AMBIENCE: The casual village atmosphere of Key West with a dash of Caribbean flair is the theme here, complete with a landmark lighthouse at the edge of the resort's private lagoon. Charming tin-roofed two- and three-story buildings, in pastel-colored clapboard with ornate white trim and picket fences, line the winding streets of the village. The accommodations feel like spacious vacation homes and are furnished in shades of apricot, aqua, and celadon, colors used throughout the resort exteriors. All rooms have balconies that overlook waterways, golf greens, or woodlands. Clustered around the lagoon at the center of the resort is a small lobby, an inviting library, and recreational facilities and services.

RATES: Studios 💲💲💲 (including a wet bar, refrigerator, microwave, and coffeemaker). One-bedroom vacation homes 💲💲💲💲💲. Two-bedroom vacation homes ♛. Two-story, three-bedroom vacation homes ♛. All units except studios have fully equipped kitchens, laundry facilities, wide-screen televisions, and VCRs. Rates vary with the season.

AMENITIES: In-room safe, VCR, videocassette library, pizza delivery to rooms, and voice mail.

RESTAURANTS: *Olivia's Cafe* — Breakfast, lunch, and dinner featuring Floridian cuisine.

RECREATION: Four pools, small white sand beach, tennis, volleyball, shuffleboard, marina, bicycling, jogging path, fitness center, sauna, whirlpool, and massage.

WDW PUBLIC TRANSPORTATION: Bus or water launch to Disney Village Marketplace and Pleasure Island at Downtown Disney. Bus to all theme parks, including the Magic Kingdom, Epcot, Disney-MGM Studios, Typhoon Lagoon, and Blizzard Beach. To reach other destinations or resorts, bus to the Transportation and Ticket Center (TTC) or Downtown Disney and connect to destination buses. Taxi service available.

FEATURES: The resort is conveniently located for guests interested in golfing at WDW. The resort also offers golfing vacation packages.

Guests may rent their own boats and commute by water to Disney Village Marketplace and other Disney Village resorts.

DRAWBACKS: Although Walt Disney World buses operate throughout this sprawling resort, guests relying on buses to reach minor attractions or to travel to other resorts for dining events may find them time-consuming and inconvenient.

HOT TIPS: A rental car is a must for guests who want to see it all or visit other resorts.

Room locations that are close to the recreation area and lobby are in buildings 12, 13, and 14. Buildings 11 and 15 are secluded, but still close to the common areas. Buildings 20, 34, 37, and 45 are near bus stops. Building 55 has a romantic water view and is farthest from the lobby .

Disney's Old Key West Resort is actually a Disney Vacation Club timeshare and a member of several timeshare exchange programs. Units not used by timeshare owners are available to guests as full-service hotel accommodations.

MAKING RESERVATIONS: Call WDW Central Reservations Office (407 934-7639). Ask about special rates and seasonal vacation packages.

HOTELS

DISNEY'S POLYNESIAN RESORT

A DISNEY-OWNED HOTEL
1600 SOUTH SEAS DRIVE, LAKE BUENA VISTA, FLORIDA 32830
TELEPHONE (407) 824-2000 • FAX (407) 824-3174
WEBSITE: www.disneyworld.com

★★★★	★★	★★★	★★
ATMOSPHERE	SERVICE	FRESHNESS	VACATION VALUE

LOCATION: Disney's Polynesian Resort is one of six hotels in the Magic Kingdom Resorts Area. It is conveniently located on the monorail line that serves the Magic Kingdom and Epcot, and it has a long white sand beach that fronts Seven Seas Lagoon.

AMBIENCE: This aptly named resort is situated in a fabulous tropical garden. Guest rooms are patterned after South Pacific lodges, long two- and three-story buildings spanned by heavy wooden beams. The hotel buildings spaced across the expertly landscaped grounds each have pleasant garden or water views. The atrium lobby wraps around a lush tropical garden with blooming orchids. Guest rooms have ceiling fans and batik bed canopies. Most upper-floor rooms have balconies. Some rooms sleep five persons.

RATES: Standard rooms 💲💲💲💲. Royal Polynesian concierge-service rooms 💲💲💲💲💲 (including Continental breakfast, mid-afternoon snacks, evening wine and appetizers, no-host cocktails, and other amenities). Rates vary with the season.

AMENITIES: Room service, in-room safe, daily newspaper, voice mail, and valet parking.

RESTAURANTS: *Coral Isle Cafe* — Breakfast, lunch, and dinner; American and Asian dishes.

'Ohana — Daily Character Breakfast and Hawaiian-themed dinner served family style, featuring open-hearth grilled meats.

Polynesian Luau — Polynesian cuisine served family style at this popular Disney dinner show.

RECREATION: Two pools, white sand beach, marina, waterskiing, volleyball, and jogging.

WDW PUBLIC TRANSPORTATION: Monorail or water launch to the Magic Kingdom. Bus to Disney-MGM Studios and Blizzard Beach. Walk or monorail to the Transportation and Ticket Center (TTC) and change trains for Epcot or transfer to buses for all other theme parks or distant resorts. Monorail or water launch to the Magic Kingdom and transfer to the water launch to Discovery Island, Fort Wilderness, and River Country. Taxi service available.

FEATURES: Beautiful landscaped gardens with tropical plant specimens and flaming torches create an enchanting island atmosphere at night.

There are great views of the Electrical Water Pageant and the Magic Kingdom fireworks from the beach in front of the hotel.

Neverland Club, Walt Disney World's most popular child care program, provides dinner and entertainment for little ones.

Guests interested in golfing are within walking distance of the Magnolia and Palm golf courses.

DRAWBACKS: The Polynesian has been going through a long term of refurbishing and remodeling that sometimes occurs in occupied guest areas. Cast Members have an air of uncertainty, and service can be uneven.

HOT TIPS: Lagoon view rooms are very popular. For a secluded setting, request a room in Samoa, which is farthest from the lobby at the edge of the lagoon. Upper-floor rooms offer the most privacy. For the best value, reserve a garden view room, which can be upgraded after you arrive.

Concierge rooms are a good value for guests who spend considerable time at the hotel. The fireworks display from the lounge is wonderful.

MAKING RESERVATIONS: Call WDW Central Reservations Office (407 934-7639). Ask about special rates and seasonal vacation packages.

HOTELS

DISNEY'S PORT ORLEANS RESORT

A DISNEY-OWNED HOTEL
2201 ORLEANS DRIVE, LAKE BUENA VISTA, FLORIDA 32830
TELEPHONE (407) 934-5000 • FAX (407) 934-5353
WEBSITE: www.disneyworld.com

★★★	★★★	★★★	★★★
ATMOSPHERE	SERVICE	FRESHNESS	VACATION VALUE

LOCATION: Disney's Port Orleans Resort is one of four hotels in the Disney Village Resorts Area. It is connected by carriage path and waterway to the nearby Dixie Landings resort and by waterway to Disney Village Marketplace and Pleasure Island at Downtown Disney.

AMBIENCE: Port Orleans is designed to capture the atmosphere of the New Orleans French Quarter preparing for Mardi Gras. Beyond the large steel-and-glass atrium lobby is a courtyard where a Dixieland band entertains guests. The resort is arranged in a complex grid of cobblestone streets with names like Rue D'Baga and Reveler's Row. The three-story row house–style buildings, some in red brick and others painted in shades of peach, aqua, and French blue, mimic the diverse architectural styles of New Orleans. Ornate wrought-iron railings, varying rooflines, louvered shutters, French doors, and small front-yard gardens all amplify the atmosphere. At night, old-fashioned street lamps form soft pools of light among the magnolia and willow trees. The moderate-sized guest rooms have ceiling fans and are decorated simply in soft neutral colors. The small vanity area features two old-fashioned pedestal sinks.

RATES: Standard rooms 💲💲. Rates vary with the season.

AMENITIES: Voice mail and pizza delivery to rooms. Refrigerator on request for a fee.

RESTAURANTS: *Bonfamille's Café* — Breakfast and dinner featuring both Creole and American cuisine.

Sassagoula Floatworks and Food Factory — Mardi Gras–themed food court; open for breakfast, lunch, and dinner.

RECREATION: Theme pool, marina, bicycling, croquet, jogging path, and whirlpool.

WDW PUBLIC TRANSPORTATION: Bus or water launch to Downtown Disney. Bus to theme parks, including the Magic Kingdom, Epcot, Blizzard Beach, Disney-MGM Studios, and Typhoon Lagoon. To reach other destinations or resorts, bus to the Transportation and Ticket Center (TTC) or Downtown Disney and connect to destination buses. Taxi service available.

FEATURES: The resort is located near Bonnet Creek Golf Club for guests interested in golfing.

Guests may rent their own boats and commute by water to Disney Village Marketplace and Pleasure Island at Downtown Disney, as well as other Disney Village Resorts.

DRAWBACKS: This budget resort is geared to young families, and the fantasy-themed pool scene is designed primarily for the young at heart. Although priced the same, Dixie Landings, located next door, offers several quiet pools.

Buses to minor attractions and other resorts are very inconvenient from this location.

HOT TIPS: This limited-amenity resort offers a very good value for the price. Upgrade to a top-floor river-view room and you'll have a luxury view for a fraction of the cost of a premier resort. Port Orleans will reserve rooms with king-sized beds. For a quiet river-views, the best bets are buildings 1 and 6.

A rental car will save a lot of commuting time from this location, especially when visiting other resorts for restaurants or dining events.

MAKING RESERVATIONS: Call WDW Central Reservations Office (407 934-7639). Ask about special rates and seasonal vacation packages.

DISNEY'S WILDERNESS LODGE

A DISNEY-OWNED HOTEL
901 TIMBERLINE DRIVE, LAKE BUENA VISTA, FLORIDA 32830
TELEPHONE (407) 824-3200 • FAX (407) 824-3232
WEBSITE: www.disneyworld.com

ATMOSPHERE	SERVICE	FRESHNESS	VACATION VALUE
★★★★	★★★	★★★	★★

LOCATION: Disney's Wilderness Lodge is one of six hotels in the Magic Kingdom Resorts Area. The resort is located deep in the forested area on the southwest shore of Bay Lake, halfway between Disney's Contemporary Resort and Fort Wilderness.

AMBIENCE: Disney's Wilderness Lodge was inspired by the U.S. National Park lodges built in the early 1900s. The seven-story quarry-stone, pine-beamed building is surrounded by forest and filled with natural light. Dark wood furnishings and Native American design motifs give the hotel its rustic lodge-retreat atmosphere. The atrium lobby features unusual chandeliers of striking design, a massive rock fireplace, and two gigantic totem poles from the Pacific Northwest. A "warm" spring bubbling in the lobby appears to flow to the outdoor courtyard, where it is transformed into a waterfall that cascades into the resort's rock-carved swimming pools and spas. Nearby, a geyser modeled on Yellowstone's Old Faithful erupts frequently and dramatically. There are rooms overlooking the atrium lobby, but most accommodations are in the two long wings on either side of the resort's pool area.

RATES: Standard rooms $ $ $ $. Rates vary with the season.

AMENITIES: Room service, in-room safe, voice mail, and valet parking.

RESTAURANTS: *Whispering Canyon Cafe* — Hearty family-style breakfast and all-you-care-to-eat lunch, and dinner served with a rustic flair; meats are roasted, grilled, and barbecued.

Artist Point — Character Breakfast daily; dinner featuring Pacific Northwest cuisine and smoked-on-premises meats.

RECREATION: Pool, whirlpool, marina, white sand beach, waterskiing, bicycling, and jogging path.

WDW PUBLIC TRANSPORTATION: Water launch to the Magic Kingdom and Discovery Island. Walk or bus to Fort Wilderness and River Country. Bus to all other theme parks. For other destinations or resorts, bus to the Transportation and Ticket Center (TTC) and connect to destination buses or transfer to monorails for Epcot and the Magic Kingdom. Taxi service available.

FEATURES: The resort is adjacent to Fort Wilderness, which provides nature trails, bike paths, fishing, tennis, volleyball, horseback riding, and a particularly good jogging trail that meanders through a beautiful forested area, with exercise stations along the way. The hotel's large pool area is beautifully designed and very pleasant.

DRAWBACKS: The parking lot can be crowded and very dark at night, requiring a flashlight.

While the hotel common areas are huge, the guest rooms are very small and thin walls allow noise to enter from hallways and other rooms.

HOT TIPS: Upper rooms in the main lodge area offer the most privacy. Rooms on the top floor have balconies with solid walls that will ensure privacy, although they can block some views.

The lake-view rooms offer an unparalleled vista of Bay Lake and Discovery Island. The forest-view rooms provide peaceful seclusion.

Although the forest-view rooms face the Magic Kingdom, tall trees in front of some rooms can block views of the fireworks show.

MAKING RESERVATIONS: Call WDW Central Reservations Office (407 934-7639). Ask about special rates and seasonal vacation packages.

HOTELS

DISNEY'S YACHT CLUB RESORT

A DISNEY-OWNED HOTEL

1700 EPCOT RESORTS BOULEVARD, LAKE BUENA VISTA, FLORIDA 32830
TELEPHONE (407) 934-7000 • FAX (407) 934-3450
WEBSITE: www.disneyworld.com

★★★★	★★	★★★★	★★★
ATMOSPHERE	SERVICE	FRESHNESS	VACATION VALUE

LOCATION: Disney's Yacht Club Resort is one of seven hotels in the Epcot Resorts Area. It is located within walking distance of the International Gateway to the World Showcase at Epcot. It faces Stormalong Bay and shares a white sand beach and harbor waterfront with Disney's Beach Club Resort.

AMBIENCE: The rambling, New England–style gray and white Yacht Club, designed by architect Robert Stern, has rope-slung boardwalks and a picturesque lighthouse along its waterfront. Its motif is decidedly nautical and it shares resort amenities with the more casually appointed Beach Club, next door. The sophisticated yet comfortable lobby has dark wood floors, with tufted leather couches and bright brass fixtures. The recently refurbished guest rooms impart a home-away-from-home feeling, with white furniture, ceiling fans, and roomy balconies.

RATES: Standard rooms 💲💲💲💲. Concierge-service rooms 💲💲💲💲💲 (including Continental breakfast, afternoon snacks, evening wine, cordials, appetizers, and special room amenities). Rates vary with the season.

AMENITIES: Twenty-four-hour room service, mini bar, in-room safe, turndown service (on request), hair dryer, voice mail, and valet parking. In-room checkers and chess games on request.

RESTAURANTS: *Yacht Club Galley* — Breakfast buffet or a la carte; lunch and dinner with emphasis on New England specialties.

Yachtsman Steakhouse — Dinner featuring prime-cut steaks and a small selection of seafood and poultry dishes.

RECREATION: Pool, white sand beach, mini water park, marina, tennis, jogging path, lawn bowling, volleyball, croquet, fitness center, sauna, steam room, whirlpool, fitness classes, fitness training, and massage.

WDW PUBLIC TRANSPORTATION: Walk or water launch to the World Showcase at Epcot, and Disney's BoardWalk. Water launch to Disney-MGM Studios. Bus to Blizzard Beach, Typhoon Lagoon, the Magic Kingdom, and Pleasure Island and Disney Village Marketplace at Downtown Disney. For other destinations or resorts, bus to the Transportation and Ticket Center (TTC) or Downtown Disney and connect to destination buses. Taxi service available.

FEATURES: This full-amenity resort is conveniently located for guests primarily interested in Epcot and Disney-MGM Studios.

The Yacht Club's location between the Beach Club and the Dolphin hotel makes the amenities at either resort easily accessible.

Guests interested in nightlife will appreciate the easy access to Disney's BoardWalk, with its restaurants, shops, and entertainment.

Stormalong Bay, the resort's mini water park, is one of the best and most popular recreation facilities at any resort in Walt Disney World.

DRAWBACKS: During peak seasons, buses to the Magic Kingdom can be slow; buses to distant resorts and dining events are very inconvenient.

HOT TIPS: Rooms surrounding the "quiet pool" are popular and secluded. Upper-floor garden-view or standard rooms facing the entrance are a very good value. Reserve the lowest-priced room here; you can always upgrade after you arrive.

MAKING RESERVATIONS: Call WDW Central Reservations Office (407) 934-7639). Ask about special rates and seasonal vacation packages.

HOTELS

MONEY SAVING PAGE

DOUBLETREE GUEST SUITES RESORT

DOUBLETREE HOTELS CORPORATION
2305 HOTEL PLAZA BOULEVARD, LAKE BUENA VISTA, FLORIDA 32830
TELEPHONE (407) 934-1000 • FAX (407) 934-1008
WEBSITE: www.ten-io.com/disney-vha

★★	★★★	★★★	★★★
ATMOSPHERE	SERVICE	FRESHNESS	VACATION VALUE

LOCATION: DoubleTree Guest Suites Resort is one of seven independently owned Hotel Plaza Resorts located on Walt Disney World property near Downtown Disney. The hotel provides shuttle bus service to the major Walt Disney World attractions.

AMBIENCE: This contemporary mirror-glassed hotel is a quasi-pyramidal seven-story building. Its modern, comfortable lobby is decorated with large murals and bright color accents. Double-Tree is the only all-suites hotel inside Walt Disney World. The guest suites are generous in size and have been handsomely refurbished in soft pastel shades. Each suite has a kitchenette and separate bedroom.

RATES: One-bedroom suites 💲💲💲. Two-bedroom suites 💲💲💲💲. Rates vary with season.

AMENITIES: Room service, microwave, coffeemaker, refrigerator (unstocked), in-room safe, hair dryer, pay-per-view movies, video games, and three televisions (two color, one black and white) in each suite.

RESTAURANTS: *Streamers* — Large restaurant for a la carte and buffet breakfast. American-style dishes are offered at lunch and dinner.

RECREATION: Pool, whirlpool, tennis, fitness center, and jogging path.

HOTEL TRANSPORTATION: Shuttle bus to the Magic Kingdom, Epcot, Disney-MGM Studios, Downtown Disney, Typhoon Lagoon, Blizzard Beach, and Disney's BoardWalk. For transportation to other destinations or resorts, walk or bus to Downtown Disney and connect to destination buses. Taxi service available.

FEATURES: DoubleTree Guest Suites has been remodeled recently and is an excellent value for a suite at Walt Disney World. Each suite has a large living room that includes a dining area and limited kitchen facilities.

For grocery shopping, Gooding's Supermarket is within walking distance. The resort also has a small convenience store that stays open late.

DoubleTree Guest Suites participates in the American Express Membership Miles program.

The resort has a particularly pleasant free-form pool that is large enough for swimming laps. The Tropical Pool Bar serves lunch, and cocktails.

Budget is conveniently located here for visitors who might like to rent a car during their stay.

DRAWBACKS: Guests relying on hotel buses to reach minor attractions or other resorts for dining events may find them inconvenient from here.

HOT TIPS: Rooms with a pool view are very pleasant. Ground-floor rooms have sliding glass doors that open onto small patios. Walt Disney World-view rooms are popular room locations and the most frequently requested.

The hotel offers vacation packages that include accommodations, breakfast, and other amenities. For a brochure, call the hotel (407 934-1000).

DoubleTree Guest Suites offers discounts to members of several travel clubs, including the American Association of Retired Persons. **AAA members can receive a 20 percent discount on accommodations; be sure to ask.**

MAKING RESERVATIONS: First call DoubleTree Central Reservations (800 222-8733), then call the hotel directly and compare rates (407 934-1000). Reservations may also be made through Walt Disney World Central Reservations Office (407 934-7639). **Ask about special promotional rates, such as the SuiteSaver, which may have discounts of up to 40 percent.**

HOTELS

SAVE

GROSVENOR RESORT

A BEST WESTERN HOTEL
1850 HOTEL PLAZA BOULEVARD, LAKE BUENA VISTA, FLORIDA 32830
TELEPHONE (407) 828-4444 • FAX (407) 827-8230
WEBSITE: www.ten-io.com/disney-vha

★★★	★★★	★★★	★★★
ATMOSPHERE	SERVICE	FRESHNESS	VACATION VALUE

LOCATION: Grosvenor Resort is one of seven independently owned Hotel Plaza Resorts located on Walt Disney World property near Downtown Disney. Guests are provided with bus service to the major Walt Disney World attractions and can walk to Downtown Disney.

AMBIENCE: The stately, solid exterior of this nineteen-story high-rise hotel belies its warm, comfortable interior. The lobby decor is British Colonial, with dark green carpets, rattan furnishings, and understated chandeliers. Rooms in the Grosvenor's central tower have Walt Disney World views. The tower is flanked by garden wings with exterior corridors facing the landscaped recreation area and gardens, and Lake Buena Vista beyond.

RATES: Standard rooms 💲💲💲. Rates vary with the season. **Readers get a 50 percent discount on accommodations and a 10 percent discount when dining at Baskervilles. (See "Vacation Discount Coupons!" page 272.)**

AMENITIES: Room service, coffeemaker, daily newspaper, in-room safe, refrigerator, hair dryer, pay-per-view movies, VCR, video rentals, video camcorder rentals, and valet parking.

RESTAURANTS: *Crumpet's Cafe* — Lobby deli market for light snacks; open twenty-four hours.
Baskervilles — British-themed dining room serving buffet and a la carte breakfast, lunch, and dinner featuring prime rib.

RECREATION: Two pools, tennis, volleyball, basketball, handball, jogging path, fitness center, whirlpool, and massage.

HOTEL TRANSPORTATION: Walk or shuttle bus to Downtown Disney. Shuttle bus to the Magic Kingdom, Epcot, Disney-MGM Studios,

Typhoon Lagoon, Blizzard Beach, and Disney's BoardWalk. To reach all other destinations or resorts, connect to destination buses at Downtown Disney. Taxi service available.

FEATURES: The in-room VCRs allow guests to watch movies from the hotel's video library or review their own videos taken during the day.

On weekends, the very popular **MurderWatch Mystery Dinner Theatre** is held at Baskervilles, where guests are involved in solving a murder staged by professional actors (see "Dining Events," page 211). **Readers receive $5 off per person for the show and dinner! (See "Vacation Discount Coupons!" page 272.)**

Thrifty is conveniently located here for visitors who might like to rent a car during their vacation.

DRAWBACKS: Buses to some attractions and other resorts are inconvenient from this location.

Although newly remodeled, the low ceilings in some guest rooms can make them seem smaller than they are; the bathrooms are compact.

HOT TIPS: The garden-wing rooms facing the pool are popular. Tower rooms lack balconies but they offer good views of Walt Disney World.

The Grosvenor offers discounts to members of travel clubs, including the American Association of Retired Persons, AAA, Orlando Magicard, and Entertainment Publications.

The Grosvenor offers vacation packages that include accommodations, meals, and theme park admission. For a brochure, call 800 624-4109.

MAKING RESERVATIONS: First, call Reservations at Best Western (800 528-1234), then call the hotel and compare rates (800 624-4109). Ask about special promotional rates. Reservations may also be made through Walt Disney World Central Reservations Office (407 934-7639).

MONEY SAVING PAGE

THE HILTON RESORT

A HILTON HOTEL
1751 HOTEL PLAZA BOULEVARD, LAKE BUENA VISTA, FLORIDA 32830
TELEPHONE (407) 827-4000 • FAX (407) 827-3890
WEBSITES: www.hilton.com — www.ten-io.com/disney-vha

★★	★★	★★	★★
ATMOSPHERE	SERVICE	FRESHNESS	VACATION VALUE

LOCATION: The Hilton Resort is one of seven independently owned Hotel Plaza Resorts located on Walt Disney World property near Downtown Disney. The hotel provides bus service to the major Walt Disney World attractions.

AMBIENCE: This hotel, one of the largest in the Hotel Plaza area, is a sprawling medium highrise with wings that angle off to each side of the central structure. The hotel is situated on several acres of open land and has a duck pond and fountains in front. The angular lobby has a muted tropical decor, with brass-railed staircases, pink conch-shell wall sconces, and a fountain with long-legged birds made of sculptured metal. Saltwater fish swim in the large aquarium behind the long rose-colored marble reception desk. The recently renovated guest rooms are pleasantly decorated with peach and light yellow accents and sand-colored bedspreads. The hotel caters to business travelers and seminar attendees.

RATES: Standard rooms $$$. Tower Concierge rooms $$$$ (including Continental breakfast, all-day snacks, evening tea and petits fours, no-host cocktails, and special room amenities). Rates vary with the season.

AMENITIES: Twenty-four-hour room service, mini bar, voice mail, pay-per-view movies, and valet parking.

RESTAURANTS: *Finn's Grill* — Dinner featuring Floribbean-style seafood and steaks.

County Fair Ristorante — Breakfast, lunch, and Italian dinner a la carte or buffet, indoors or on the terrace.

Benihana — Steak and seafood dinners grilled and served at communal tables by Japanese teppan chefs.

RECREATION: Two pools, jogging path, fitness center, and sauna.

HOTEL TRANSPORTATION: Walk or bus to Downtown Disney. Bus to Epcot, the Magic Kingdom, Typhoon Lagoon, Disney-MGM Studios, Blizzard Beach, and Disney's BoardWalk. To reach other theme parks or resorts, connect to destination buses at Downtown Disney. Taxi service available.

FEATURES: Hilton Honors members can earn points and upgrade rooms.

Avis is conveniently located here for guests who might like to rent a car during their vacation.

DRAWBACKS: Guests relying on hotel buses to reach minor attractions or other resorts for dining events may find them inconvenient from here.

HOT TIPS: Most rooms have nice views, but be sure to put in a request for a room with a view of Walt Disney World and evening fireworks shows when making reservations.

The Hilton Resort offers vacation packages that include accommodations, daily breakfast, and theme park admission. Call the resort's toll-free number for a brochure (800 782-4414).

A rental car can save considerable commuting time from this location.

The Hilton offers AAA members significant discounts on rooms, often over 30 percent.

MAKING RESERVATIONS: First call Hilton Central Reservations (800 221-2424), then call the hotel and compare rates (800 782-4414). **Be sure to ask about special promotions, such as the Bounce-Back Weekend, which can save up to 40 percent on the room rate.** Reservations may also be made through Walt Disney World Central Reservations Office (407 934-7639).

HOTELS

$AVE

HOTEL ROYAL PLAZA

A PRIVATELY OWNED HOTEL
1905 HOTEL PLAZA BOULEVARD, LAKE BUENA VISTA, FLORIDA 32830
TELEPHONE (407) 828-2828 • FAX (407) 827-3977
WEBSITE: www.ten-io.com/disney-vha

★★	★	★★	★★★
ATMOSPHERE	SERVICE	FRESHNESS	VACATION VALUE

HOTELS

LOCATION: Hotel Royal Plaza is one of seven independently owned Hotel Plaza Resorts located on Walt Disney World property near Downtown Disney. The hotel provides bus service to the major Walt Disney World attractions.

AMBIENCE: Hotel Royal Plaza is perennially being remodeled or in the process of becoming something else — it might well be called the Hotel Royal Renovation. The high-rise hotel, with its pagoda-style roof and garden wing, is detailed in shades of rose and pure white. The lobby is usually remodeled with a Caribbean theme, and in the guest rooms, ceilings have been raised and the rooms enlarged. The guest rooms are tastefully furnished in pale pastels. All tower rooms and suites have small half-moon-shaped balconies; the higher floors offer sweeping views of Walt Disney World. The ground-level garden-wing rooms have been extended to provide private patios.

RATES: Standard rooms 💲💲. Rates vary with the season.

AMENITIES: Room service, mini bar, in-room safe, hair dryer, coffeemaker, VCR, videocassette library, and video camcorder rentals.

RESTAURANTS: *The Veranda* — Open all day until midnight for breakfast, lunch, and dinner featuring American cuisine.

Intermissions Lounge — Casual lounge that may become a dinner club. Open until 2 AM.

RECREATION: Pool, putting green, jogging path, tennis, shuffleboard, exercise room, sauna, and whirlpool.

HOTEL TRANSPORTATION: Walk or bus to Downtown Disney. Bus to the Magic Kingdom, Epcot, Disney-MGM Studios, Typhoon Lagoon, Blizzard Beach, and Disney's BoardWalk. To reach other theme parks or resorts, connect to destination buses at Downtown Disney. Taxi service available.

FEATURES: Intermissions offers a happy hour buffet and televised sporting events.

DRAWBACKS: Buses to smaller attractions and other resorts are inconvenient from this location.

Various parts of the hotel seem to be undergoing some sort of renovation, so be sure to request a room that has been recently renovated.

HOT TIPS: The most popular rooms are the higher-floor tower rooms with a view of Walt Disney World and the evening fireworks show at Pleasure Island. Also popular are the ground-floor poolside garden rooms.

For the best room value, request a premier room. Premier rooms cost about $30 more than standard rooms, but offer large, deep corner-style whirlpool tubs, which can be really great after a hard day in the theme parks.

Hotel Royal Plaza offers discounts to a number of travel clubs, including Entertainment Publications. AAA members can receive discounts of over 40 percent on rooms.

The Royal Plaza offers vacation packages that include accommodations, daily breakfast, theme park admission, and other amenities. Call the hotel for a brochure (800 248-7890).

A rental car can save considerable commuting time from this location.

MAKING RESERVATIONS: Call the Hotel Royal Plaza toll-free number (800 248-7890) and ask about promotional rates. Reservations may also be made through the Walt Disney World Central Reservations Office (407 934-7639).

SHADES OF GREEN

A U.S. ARMED FORCES RECREATION CENTER
1950 WEST MAGNOLIA/PALM, LAKE BUENA VISTA, FLORIDA 32830
TELEPHONE (407) 824-3400 • FAX (407) 824-3460
WEBSITE: http://image.redstone.army.mil/html/mwr/shades_green.html

★★	★★★	★★★	★★★★
ATMOSPHERE	SERVICE	FRESHNESS	VACATION VALUE

LOCATION: Shades of Green is one of six hotels in the Magic Kingdom Resorts Area. As a U.S. Armed Forces Recreational Center, its accommodations are available only to active and retired military personnel and their families; however, the restaurants and golf courses are open to all visitors. The resort is located adjacent to the Magnolia and Palm golf courses, in a quiet area that is a short drive from the Magic Kingdom.

AMBIENCE: This wood-shingled low-rise hotel seems set apart from the rest of Walt Disney World. The long entrance road winds through the two golf courses that surround the hotel. The lobby is a comfortable ranch-style room with rock walls and windows overlooking the pool and golf courses. Guest rooms are spacious quasi suites with a country-inn atmosphere enhanced by pine furnishings and are comfortable for larger families. All rooms feature balconies or patios with views of the pools, the golf courses, or the resort's lush landscaping. The resort is very low key and could be located anywhere — although the unmistakable whistle of the Walt Disney World Railroad trains at the Magic Kingdom can be heard from the grounds.

RATES: Standard rooms 💲. Rates increase based on military rank.

AMENITIES: Room service, voice mail, and valet parking.

RESTAURANTS: *The Garden Gallery* — A la carte breakfast and a dinner buffet with a different culinary theme every night.

Evergreens Sports Bar & Grill — Poolside restaurant serving snacks and light meals all day.

Back Porch Lounge — Lunch only, especially popular with the golf crowd.

RECREATION: Two pools, tennis, nature walk, fitness center, two PGA golf courses, pro shop, putting greens, and driving ranges.

HOTEL TRANSPORTATION: Shuttle bus to Blizzard Beach and Disney-MGM Studios. Bus to the Transportation and Ticket Center (TTC) to catch monorails to the Magic Kingdom and Epcot or to transfer to WDW buses to reach other destinations. Water launch from the Magic Kingdom to Discovery Island, Fort Wilderness, and River Country. Taxi service available.

FEATURES: All military personnel and their dependents receive discounts of about 10 percent on theme park admissions. Call Shades of Green Guest Services (407 824-1403).

During value seasons, guests staying at Shades of Green can enjoy a 50 percent discount on golf through Shades of Green Guest Services.

DRAWBACKS: Buses to distant attractions and other resorts for dining events can be inconvenient during peak seasons.

HOT TIPS: A rental car can save considerable commuting time from this location.

Shades of Green shuttle buses to and from the Transportation and Ticket Center (TTC) depart every 20 minutes until 2 AM.

Rooms 101 to 113 surround the "quiet pool," and rooms 301 to 313 on the top floor have sweeping fairway views.

If the hotel is fully booked, ask about overflow rooms. Military personnel are sometimes able to stay at other Disney-owned hotels at a moderate discount, if rooms are available.

MAKING RESERVATIONS: Military personnel and their families can book rooms by calling Shades of Green Reservations (407 824-3600).

HOTELS

TRAVELODGE HOTEL

FORTE HOTELS, INC.

2000 HOTEL PLAZA BOULEVARD, LAKE BUENA VISTA, FLORIDA 32830

TELEPHONE (407) 828-2424 • FAX (407) 828-8933

WEBSITE: www.ten-io.com/disney-vha

★★	★★★	★★	★★
ATMOSPHERE	SERVICE	FRESHNESS	VACATION VALUE

LOCATION: Travelodge Hotel is one of seven independently owned Hotel Plaza Resorts located on Walt Disney World property near Downtown Disney. The hotel provides shuttle bus service to the major Walt Disney World attractions.

AMBIENCE: The wide entrance portico of the Travelodge's eighteen-story tower leads to its tropically themed interior, done in the style of a Barbados plantation manor. The comfortable lobby is filled with plants, rattan furniture, and green faux-marble pillars. In the center, a circular staircase leads up to the meeting rooms on the mezzanine level. The hotel grounds and the large pool area are landscaped with lush tropical foliage. The nice-sized guest rooms are serene and pleasantly decorated in soft neutral colors. All rooms have balconies, and most, especially on the higher floors, have impressive views of Walt Disney World. The Travelodge has introduced Sleepy Bear's Den, a new guest room concept for families. Sleepy Bear rooms have child-sized furniture and kid-pleasing decor, a videocassette player with children's videos, a small refrigerator, and other amenities.

RATES: Standard rooms 💲💲. Sleepy Bear rooms 💲💲. Rates vary with the season.

AMENITIES: Room service, mini bar, in-room safe, coffeemaker, pay-per-view movies, hair dryer, and daily newspaper.

RESTAURANTS: *Parakeet Cafe* — Lobby deli serving light meals and snacks all day.

Traders Int'l Restaurant & Terrace — Breakfast and dinner, a la carte or buffet, indoors or outside on the patio.

RECREATION: Pool, jogging path.

HOTEL TRANSPORTATION: Walk or bus to Downtown Disney. Bus to the Magic Kingdom, Epcot, Disney-MGM Studios, Typhoon Lagoon, Blizzard Beach, and Disney's BoardWalk. To reach other destinations or resorts, connect to destination buses at Downtown Disney. Taxi service available.

FEATURES: Toppers Nite Club, located on the eighteenth floor, offers large-screen video entertainment until 2 AM and has sweeping views of Walt Disney World and the fireworks shows. Hotel guests receive discounts on drinks.

Members of Travelodge Business Break Club and Classic Travel Club (for seniors) receive room and rental car discounts.

DRAWBACKS: Guests who are looking for the recreational features of a full-scale resort will be disappointed here.

Buses to some smaller attractions and other resorts are very inconvenient from this location.

HOT TIPS: For the best room location, request a room with a view of Walt Disney World. The fireworks at Pleasure Island can be seen from the upper-floor guest rooms.

Travelodge offers discounts to several travel clubs, including Encore, Entertainment Publications, and the American Association of Retired Persons. **AAA members receive discounts of up to 40 percent on accommodations.**

MAKING RESERVATIONS: First call Travelodge Central Reservations (800 578-7878); we found they offered better discounts and promotional rates than the hotel itself. Then call the hotel and compare rates. Reservations may also be made through WDW Central Reservations Office (407 934-7639).

THE VILLAS AT THE DISNEY INSTITUTE

AVAILABLE TO ALL VISITORS AND THOSE ATTENDING THE DISNEY INSTITUTE
1901 BUENA VISTA DRIVE, LAKE BUENA VISTA, FLORIDA 32830
TELEPHONE (407) 827-1100 • FAX (407) 934-2741
WEBSITE: www.disneyinstitute.com

★★★	★★★	★★★	★★
ATMOSPHERE	SERVICE	FRESHNESS	VACATION VALUE

LOCATION: The Villas at the Disney Institute is one of four hotels in the Disney Village Resorts Area. Spread out across 250 acres of woodlands, waterways, and golf greens, the resort fronts Buena Vista Lagoon along with Downtown Disney. The campus of the Disney Institute is also located here, a learning center that offers unique educational vacation packages. (See "Disney Institute," page 248.)

AMBIENCE: This resort resembles a large country club and encompasses the fairways of Lake Buena Vista Golf Course. The facility is very spread out, with four distinct resort areas and interconnecting roadways. The dark brown Fairway Villas and Grand Vista Suites are scattered along tree-lined lanes or perched at the edge of the golf course. The tall Treehouses are isolated in a forested area, and some overlook the bayou-like waterways. Guests attending the Disney Institute stay in the Townhouses, which are within walking distance of Disney Village Marketplace, or in the cozy Bungalows at the edge of the Disney Institute's small lake.

RATES: Bungalow suites 💲💲💲 and one- and two-bedroom Townhouses 💲💲💲💲💲 (both with refrigerator, microwave, and coffeemaker). Three-bedroom Treehouse Villas 💲💲💲💲💲💲, two-bedroom Fairway Villas 💲💲💲💲💲💲, and large two- and three-bedroom Grand Vista Suites 👑 (all with fully equipped kitchens). Rates vary with the season. Accommodations are included for guests attending Disney Institute programs. (See "Disney Institute," page 248, for pricing and reservation information.)

AMENITIES: Room service, refrigerator, coffeemaker, microwave, voice mail, and valet parking.

RESTAURANTS: *Seasons* — Open for breakfast, lunch, and dinner. Cuisine changes frequently and sometimes features the talents of visiting chefs teaching at Disney Institute.

RECREATION: Six pools, nearby marina, tennis, bicycling, volleyball, jogging path, full-service spa and fitness center, PGA golf course, putting green, driving range, and pro shop.

WDW PUBLIC TRANSPORTATION: Walk, bus, or rent an electric cart to travel to Disney Village Marketplace at Downtown Disney. Bus to the Magic Kingdom, Epcot, Disney-MGM Studios, Blizzard Beach, and Typhoon Lagoon. To reach other theme parks or resorts, connect with destination buses at Downtown Disney. Taxi service available.

FEATURES: Electric carts may be rented for use both within the resort and at Downtown Disney.

DRAWBACKS: Guests who are relying on buses to reach minor attractions or other resorts for dining events may find them inconvenient.

HOT TIPS: The circular Treehouse Villas are ideal for secluded romantic getaways. Request a water view. The Grand Vista Suites, designed like spacious suburban homes, are ideal for smaller groups or large families.

Guests not enrolled at the Disney Institute can purchase tickets to dinner and evening performances or sign up for selected day programs.

Although Walt Disney World buses operate within the resort, a rental car is quite helpful from this location if your focus is on the theme parks.

MAKING RESERVATIONS: For hotel reservations only, call WDW Central Reservations Office (407 934-7639). For Disney Institute vacation packages, call 800 282-9282.

HOTELS

MONEY $AVING PAGE

WALT DISNEY WORLD DOLPHIN

A SHERATON HOTEL
1500 EPCOT RESORTS BOULEVARD, LAKE BUENA VISTA, FLORIDA 32830
TELEPHONE (407) 934-4000 • FAX (407) 934-4099
WEBSITE: www.swandolphin.com

★★★	★★★	★★★	★★★
ATMOSPHERE	SERVICE	FRESHNESS	VACATION VALUE

LOCATION: The Dolphin is one of seven hotels in the Epcot Resorts Area. It is located a short distance from the International Gateway to the World Showcase at Epcot. It faces Crescent Lake and shares a waterfront plaza, white sand beach, and recreational facilities with the Swan hotel.

AMBIENCE: The plaza entrance of this pyramid-shaped high-rise hotel features a multistory fountain that cascades down tiers of giant clam shells. The lobby is in a huge striped tent with a dolphin-motif fountain, and the nice-sized guest rooms have a fantasy tropical beach decor.

RATES: Standard rooms $$$$. Concierge rooms $$$$$ (including Continental breakfast, no-host cocktails, appetizers, and special room amenities). Rates vary with the season.

AMENITIES: Twenty-four-hour room service, mini bar, in-room safe, hair dryer, coffeemaker, turndown service, daily newspaper, voice mail, pay-per-view movies, and valet parking.

RESTAURANTS: Readers get a terrific $50 dining certificate for these restaurants! (See "Vacation Discount Coupons!" page 272.)

  Coral Cafe — Pleasant coffee shop with all-day dining; full-buffet breakfast and dinner.

  Juan & Only's — Dinner featuring traditional regional Mexican cuisine.

  Harry's Safari Bar & Grille — Steak and seafood dinners, and Sunday Character Brunch.

  Tubbi's Buffeteria — Cafeteria and convenience market; open twenty-four hours.

  Dolphin Fountain — Entertaining light dining, hamburgers, sandwiches, and ice cream and soda fountain treats.

  Cabana Bar & Grill — Light meals, snacks, and specialty drinks served poolside.

RECREATION: Pool, grotto pool, small beach, tennis, volleyball, jogging path, fitness center, sauna, steam room, whirlpool, fitness classes, fitness training, and massage.

WDW PUBLIC TRANSPORTATION: Walk or water launch to Disney's BoardWalk. Water launch to the World Showcase at Epcot and Disney-MGM Studios. Trams to Epcot run seasonally. Bus to the Magic Kingdom, Blizzard Beach, Typhoon Lagoon, and Downtown Disney. To reach other destinations or resorts, bus to the Transportation and Ticket Center (TTC) or Downtown Disney and connect to destination buses. Taxi service available.

FEATURES: Members of the ITT Sheraton Club earn points and may upgrade rooms.

  It's a short walk to Disney's BoardWalk for shopping, dining, dancing, and entertainment.

DRAWBACKS: Buses to the Magic Kingdom can be inconvenient during peak seasons.

  Only rooms with a balcony have windows that open; request one during the cooler seasons.

HOT TIPS: Members of AAA are offered discounts of up to 25 percent on rooms.

  The Dolphin offers vacation packages that include accommodations, some meals, theme park admissions, and other amenities. Call the hotel for a brochure (800 227-1500).

  The most popular room locations are those with views of IllumiNations or the pool area.

MAKING RESERVATIONS: First call Sheraton Central Reservations (800 325-3535), then call the hotel and compare rates (800 227-1500). Ask about special promotional rates. Reservations may also be made through Walt Disney World Central Reservations Office (407 934-7639).

HOTELS

$AVE

MONEY SAVING PAGE

WALT DISNEY WORLD SWAN

A WESTIN HOTEL
1200 EPCOT RESORTS BOULEVARD, LAKE BUENA VISTA, FLORIDA 32830
TELEPHONE (407) 934-3000 • FAX (407) 934-4499
WEBSITE: www.swandolphin.com

★★★	★★★	★★★	★★★
ATMOSPHERE	SERVICE	FRESHNESS	VACATION VALUE

LOCATION: The Swan is one of seven hotels in the Epcot Resorts Area. It is just a short distance from the International Gateway to the World Showcase at Epcot. It faces Crescent Lake and shares a waterfront plaza, white sand beach, and recreational facilities with the Dolphin hotel.

AMBIENCE: This contemporary high-rise hotel, designed by noted architect Michael Graves, is a standout example of entertainment architecture. The Swan's water-fantasy theme is expressed in soft splashes of turquoise and coral, which extend to the guest rooms. The large lobby is divided into smaller alcoves, giving an overall impression of privacy and sophistication. The Swan houses a large convention center, and the hotel has an adult atmosphere.

RATES: Standard rooms $\$\$\$$. Royal Beach Club concierge rooms $\$\$\$\$\$$ (including Continental breakfast, snacks and appetizers, no-host cocktails, and special room amenities). Rates vary with the season.

AMENITIES: Twenty-four-hour room service, mini bar, bathrobes, turndown service, in-room safe, daily newspaper, pay-per-view movies, voice mail, and valet parking.

RESTAURANTS: Readers get a terrific $50 dining certificate for these restaurants! (See "Vacation Discount Coupons!" page 272.)

⭐ *Palio* — Dinner featuring homemade pasta, brick-oven pizza, and light entertainment in an Italian trattoria.

⭐ *Garden Grove Cafe* — Family-style dining for breakfast and lunch.

⭐ *Gulliver's Grill* — Entertainment dining with Disney Characters or tableside magic.

⭐ *Splash Grill & Terrace* — Breakfast a la carte and buffet, and all-day light meals.

Kimonos — Evening and late-night cocktails, sushi, and Asian hors d'oeuvres.

RECREATION: Lap pool, grotto pool, small beach, tennis, jogging path, fitness center, sauna, whirlpool, and massage.

WDW PUBLIC TRANSPORTATION: Walk or water launch to Disney-MGM Studios and Disney's BoardWalk. Water launch to the World Showcase at Epcot. Bus to the Magic Kingdom, Blizzard Beach, Typhoon Lagoon, and Pleasure Island and Disney Village Marketplace at Downtown Disney. To reach other destinations or resorts, bus to the Transportation and Ticket Center (TTC) or Downtown Disney and connect to destination buses. Taxi service available.

FEATURES: Westin Premier club members earn points and may upgrade rooms.

The resort is conveniently located for guests who are primarily interested in Disney-MGM Studios and Epcot, and it is right next door to the nightlife at Disney's BoardWalk.

Fantasia Gardens, Walt Disney World's miniature golf complex, is located across the street.

DRAWBACKS: Buses to the Magic Kingdom can be inconvenient during peak seasons.

HOT TIPS: AAA members can get discounts of up to 25 percent on accommodations.

The Swan offers resort packages that include accommodations, some meals, and theme park admission. For brochures, call (407 934-3000).

MAKING RESERVATIONS: First call Westin Central Reservations (800 228-3000), then call the hotel and compare rates (800 248-7926). Ask about special promotional rates. Reservations may also be made through Walt Disney World Central Reservations Office (407 934-7639).

SAVE

HOTELS

OFF-SITE HOTELS & SUITES

The numerous hotels surrounding Walt Disney World range from low-budget motels to deluxe resorts to vacation homes for families or groups. The hotels listed below are primarily all-suites hotels. They were selected because they offer spacious accommodations and the welcome convenience of an in-room kitchen for about the cost of a moderate hotel room on Walt Disney World property. Suites offer exceptional value to larger families and small groups: They have separate bedrooms, the sitting rooms have foldout beds, and they sleep about six persons.

Most of the hotels below provide a time- and money-saving complimentary breakfast and free shuttles to and from the major theme parks, although renting a car is good idea when staying off property. They are all within a five-minute drive of Walt Disney World (see "Walt Disney World Hotel Map," page 125, for hotel locations). Also listed are two popular destination resorts that offer luxurious vacation experiences. The OVERALL VALUE RATINGS indicate the quality of the accommodations, as well as transportation, restaurant, and recreation options, in relation to the cost of a stay. The results are indicated as:

★★★★ **EXCELLENT OVERALL VALUE** ★★★ **GOOD VACATION VALUE** ★★ **FAIR VALUE**

PRICES: The rates shown in the reviews are the starting price of a standard room or suite averaged across peak and value seasons, without taxes (about 11 percent). For pricing codes, see page 123.

RESERVATIONS: As with all hotels at Walt Disney World, it is essential to make reservations as far in advance as possible. **Be sure to ask whether the hotel offers discounts to members of any travel clubs you may belong to, such as AARP, Entertainment, or the American Automobile Association. These travel club discounts can amount to as much as 50 percent at participating off-site hotels during value seasons. Hotel discounts are also available through the Orlando and the Kissimmee-St. Cloud convention and visitors bureaus.** (See "Discount Travel Tips," page 17.) **Some of these hotels, such as Summerfield Suites and Embassy Suites, offer their own discount vacation packages. To find out about these special offers, you must ask! The off-property hotels offer their deepest seasonal discounts during September and January ◆**

BUENA VISTA SUITES
14450 INTERNATIONAL DRIVE, LAKE BUENA VISTA, FL 32830

★★★ OVERALL VALUE *(The full-buffet breakfast is very convenient and a terrific money saver.)*

The suites in this seven-story hotel are large, handsomely decorated, and feature a separate living room, VCR, coffeemaker, microwave, and refrigerator. Deluxe suites have a king-size bed and whirlpool. Hotel amenities include a complimentary buffet breakfast daily, evening room service, pool, exercise room, whirlpool, and transportation to Walt Disney World. During busy times such as Spring Break, however, the clamor from the hallway can be heard in some of the suites.

LOCATION: Buena Vista Suites is located about 2.5 miles from the Epcot entrance to Walt Disney World.

AVERAGE RATES: Standard suites 💲💲, deluxe suites 💲💲💲. Rates vary with the season.

TELEPHONE: Hotel 407 239-8588. Hotel toll free 800 537-7737.

CARIBE ROYALE RESORT SUITES

14300 INTERNATIONAL DRIVE, ORLANDO, FL 32830

★★ OVERALL VALUE *(Convenient for vacationers, but also caters to business travelers.)*

The new Caribe Royale has over twelve hundred pleasantly decorated suites housed in three ten-story V-shaped towers surrounding a tropical lagoon–themed pool with a dramatic waterfall. The suites feature a separate living room, wetbar, coffeemaker, microwave, and refrigerator. Resort amenities include a restaurant, room service, pool, whirlpool, fitness centers, child care center, tennis, valet parking, complimentary full-buffet or Continental breakfast, and transportation to Walt Disney World.

LOCATION: Caribe Royale Resort Suites is located about three miles from the Epcot entrance to Walt Disney World.

AVERAGE RATES: Standard rooms 💲💲💲💲. Rates vary with the season.

TELEPHONE: Hotel 407 328-8000. Hotel toll free 800 823-8300.

EMBASSY GRAND BEACH VACATION RESORT AT LAKE BRYAN

8317 LAKE BRYAN BEACH BOULEVARD, ORLANDO, FL 32821

★★★★ OVERALL VALUE *(Terrific for groups; the largest family suites near Walt Disney World.)*

The Embassy Grand Beach Vacation Resort offers the largest accommodations in the Walt Disney World area. The four-story buildings of this all-suites resort are set beside a lake, creating a beach resort atmosphere. Suites feature three bedrooms, three baths, a large kitchen and dining area, a large screened porch, VCR, stereo, and three televisions. Resort amenities include a pool, exercise room, tennis, volleyball, and jet- and waterskiing. The hotel does not provide transportation to Walt Disney World.

LOCATION: Embassy Grand Beach Vacation Resort at Lake Bryan is located two miles from the Disney Village and Hotel Plaza entrance to Walt Disney World, and 2.5 miles from the Epcot entrance.

AVERAGE RATES: Three-bedroom suites 💲💲💲. Rates vary with the season.

TELEPHONE: Hotel 407 238-2800. Reservations toll free 800 341-4440.

EMBASSY SUITES RESORT, LAKE BUENA VISTA

8100 LAKE AVENUE, ORLANDO, FL 32836

★★★ OVERALL VALUE *(This atrium-style hotel offers a soothing, restful respite from the theme parks.)*

This six-story hotel features comfortable two-room suites with microwave, refrigerator, coffeemaker, wet bar, and VCR. Resort amenities include a complimentary full-buffet breakfast and cocktails and beverages in the evenings, indoor-outdoor pool, room service, exercise room, sauna, tennis, volleyball, shuffleboard, and transportation to Walt Disney World. There is a child care center on the premises, and the hotel has been designed to provide exceptional accessibility for visitors with disabilities.

LOCATION: Embassy Suites Resort, Lake Buena Vista is located one mile from the Disney Village and Hotel Plaza entrance to Walt Disney World.

AVERAGE RATES: Standard suites 💲💲💲. Rates vary with the season.

TELEPHONE: Hotel 407 239-1144. Hotel toll free 800 257-8483. Central reservations 800 362-2779.

HOTELS

HOLIDAY INN SUNSPREE RESORT, LAKE BUENA VISTA

13351 STATE ROAD 535, LAKE BUENA VISTA, FL 32830

★ ★ ★ OVERALL VALUE *(Great for family trips or for parents mixing business with pleasure.)*

Three low-rise vivid pink hotel buildings enclose the tropically landscaped pool area. The rooms are spacious and have kitchenettes. Some feature a new concept called Kid Suites, an enclosed mini room inside the parents' suite, with bunk beds, TV, VCR, video games, and table and chairs. Hotel amenities include a fitness center, whirlpools, room service, full-service restaurant, and transportation to Walt Disney World. A fully licensed child care and activity center is on the premises.

LOCATION: Holiday Inn SunSpree Resort, Lake Buena Vista is located less than one mile from the Disney Village and Hotel Plaza entrance to Walt Disney World.

AVERAGE RATES: Standard rooms 💲, Kid Suites 💲💲. Rates vary with the season.

TELEPHONE: Hotel 407 239-4500. Central reservations 800 465-4329.

HOMEWOOD SUITES

3100 PARKWAY BOULEVARD, KISSIMMEE, FL 34746

★ ★ ★ OVERALL VALUE *(Rooms close to the main office have easier access at breakfast and at night.)*

This inviting all-suites hotel consists of seven two- and three-story buildings. The suites include one-bedroom/one-bath, two-bedroom/one-bath, and two-bedroom/two-bath layouts, and offer plenty of sprawl space, with a separate living room and a fully equipped kitchen. Hotel amenities include a complimentary Continental breakfast daily featuring muffins made on the premises; a pool, whirlpool, and fitness center; complimentary grocery shopping service; and transportation to Walt Disney World.

LOCATION: Homewood Suites is located about two miles from the Magic Kingdom entrance to Walt Disney World.

AVERAGE RATES: One-bedroom suites 💲💲, two-bedroom suites 💲💲.

TELEPHONE: Hotel 407 396-2229. Hotel toll free 800 255-4543. Central reservations 800 225-5466.

HOWARD JOHNSON PARK SQUARE INN & SUITES

8501 PALM PARKWAY, LAKE BUENA VISTA, FL 38330

★ ★ OVERALL VALUE *(Request a room near the courtyard pool to avoid long walks in the corridors.)*

The Howard Johnson Park Square Inn & Suites has two low-rise buildings, and features both moderate-sized suites and standard rooms. The suites include a separate sitting area, microwave, refrigerator, coffeemaker, and wet bar. Hotel amenities include two pools, a whirlpool, a full-service restaurant, and transportation to the Magic Kingdom, Epcot, and Disney-MGM Studios. Although the decor could use a renovation, this family-oriented hotel it is very conveniently located and very affordable.

LOCATION: Howard Johnson Park Square Inn & Suites is about one block from the Disney Village and Hotel Plaza entrance to Walt Disney World.

AVERAGE RATES: Standard rooms 💲, suites 💲💲. Rates vary with the season.

TELEPHONE: Hotel 407 239-6900. Hotel toll free 800 635-8684. Central reservations 800 654-2000.

HOTELS

PERRI HOUSE, A BED & BREAKFAST INN

10417 CENTURION COURT, LAKE BUENA VISTA, FL 32830

★★★ OVERALL VALUE *(A unique vacation site with friendly hosts and a lovely, secluded pool.)*

Perri House is the closest bed-and-breakfast inn to Walt Disney World. Hosts Nick and Angie Perri built and decorated this charming country home, which includes twenty acres of natural preserve for many species of native birds. The inn has six unique guest rooms with private baths and entrances, a pool and spa, and an extensive library on area attractions. A complimentary Continental breakfast is served daily. Transportation to Walt Disney World is not provided.

LOCATION: Perri House is located less than one mile from the Disney Village and Hotel Plaza entrance to Walt Disney World.

AVERAGE RATES: Bed-and-breakfast rooms 💲💲.

TELEPHONE: Hotel 407 876-4830. Hotel toll free 800 780-4830. E-mail: perrihse@iag.net.

SUMMERFIELD SUITES HOTEL, LAKE BUENA VISTA

8751 SUITESIDE DRIVE, ORLANDO, FL 32836

★★ OVERALL VALUE *(No special views here. Rooms on the ground floor are the most convenient.)*

Set amid tall palms and lush tropical plantings, this 150-unit all-suites hotel consists of eight low-rise buildings with exterior corridors. The one- and two-bedroom suites sleep between four and eight people and have a fully equipped kitchen, dining area, and living room with VCR. The two-bedroom suites have two bathrooms. Hotel amenities include a daily Continental breakfast buffet, exercise room, whirlpool, swimming pool, and transportation to Walt Disney World.

LOCATION: Summerfield Suites Hotel, Lake Buena Vista is located approximately one-half mile from the Disney Village and Hotel Plaza entrance to Walt Disney World.

AVERAGE RATES: One-bedroom suites 💲💲💲, two-bedroom suites 💲💲💲💲. Rates vary with the season.

TELEPHONE: Hotel 407 238-0777. Reservations toll free 800 833-4353.

WYNDHAM ROYAL SAFARI RESORT & SUITES

12205 APOPKA-VINELAND ROAD, ORLANDO, FL 32836

★★★ OVERALL VALUE *(This spiffed up budget hotel is a good value for cost-conscious visitors.)*

This former Days Inn has been renovated and transformed into an African-themed family hotel in keeping with Disney's Animal Kingdom. The hotel's tropically landscaped courtyard pool is surrounded by a quartet of six-story buildings. Accommodations include both standard guest rooms and moderate-sized suites, complete with separate bedrooms and a mini kitchens. Resort amenities include a pool and water slide, full-service restaurant, room service, and transportation to Walt Disney World.

LOCATION: Wyndham Royal Safari Resort & Suites is located one block from the Disney Village and Hotel Plaza entrance to Walt Disney World.

AVERAGE RATES: Standard rooms 💲, suites 💲💲. Rates vary with the season.

TELEPHONE: Hotel 407 239-0444. Reservations toll free 800 423-3297.

HOTELS

PREMIER DESTINATION RESORTS

The Hyatt Regency Grand Cypress and Marriott's Orlando World Center are considered among the top destination resorts in the world. They provide a luxury vacation experience, with on-site recreation options such as golf and horseback riding. Both premier resorts are just minutes from Walt Disney World.

HYATT REGENCY GRAND CYPRESS
ONE GRAND CYPRESS BOULEVARD, ORLANDO, FL 32836

★★★★ OVERALL VALUE *(This romantic hotel is nestled next to WDW, yet it's a world unto itself.)*

The Hyatt Regency Grand Cypress is a dramatic eighteen-story atrium building situated on fifteen hundred acres of forest and landscaped recreation areas. Even-numbered hotel rooms generally face Disney property and have views of the theme parks and fireworks; odd-numbered rooms overlook the forest and greenways. Standard guest rooms are very compact, yet pleasant, and each features a balcony, mini bar, and pay-per-view movies. This self-contained resort has five full-service restaurants and twenty-four-hour room service. Recreational facilities include a huge free-form grotto swimming pool; a full-service spa and health club; a day care center; and youth camps. Scattered over the resort are tennis and racquetball courts; an eighteen-hole PGA golf course; stables, corrals, and trails for horseback riding; and a lake with canoes, sailboats, and paddle boats. For an additional charge, the resort offers transportation to Walt Disney World and other area attractions.

LOCATION: Hyatt Regency Grand Cypress is located less than one mile from the Disney Village and Hotel Plaza entrance to Walt Disney World.

AVERAGE RATES: Standard rooms 💲💲💲💲, Regency Club concierge rooms 💲💲💲💲💲 (including Continental breakfast, evening cocktails, health club, and other amenities). Rates vary with the season.

TELEPHONE: Hotel 407 239-1234. Central reservations 800 233-1234.

MARRIOTT'S ORLANDO WORLD CENTER
WORLD CENTER DRIVE, ORLANDO, FL 32821

★★★ OVERALL VALUE *(The suites overlooking the lagoon have views of the WDW fireworks shows.)*

Marriott's Orlando World Center has over fifteen hundred elegant rooms and suites in a twenty-seven-story central tower flanked by tiered wings. The hotel, situated on 205 landscaped acres, surrounds a tropical lagoon–themed pool complex. Rooms range in size from moderate to spacious and feature a balcony or patio, mini bar, coffeemaker, in-room safe, and pay-per-view movies. Resort amenities include five full-service restaurants, twenty-four-hour room service, pools, whirlpools, a health club, massage, a child care center, volleyball, basketball, miniature golf, tennis, and an eighteen-hole golf course. For an additional charge, the hotel offers transportation to Walt Disney World. The hotel is ideal for visitors who want to be near the theme parks, yet experience a resort vacation away from it all.

LOCATION: Marriott's Orlando World Center is located two miles from the Epcot entrance to Walt Disney World.

AVERAGE RATES: Standard rooms 💲💲💲. Rates vary with the season.

TELEPHONE: Hotel 407 239-4200. Hotel toll free 800 621-0638. Central reservations 800 228-9290. ◆

HOTELS

RESTAURANTS

Walt Disney World is one of the few places where guests can arrive at an elegant restaurant in a tee-shirt, shorts, and tennis shoes, and still feel right at home; most theme park restaurants do not expect guests to return to their hotels to change before dinner. The only exceptions to this casual dress code are at a few of the better resort restaurants, where guests tend to dress up (see "Resort Dining," page 197).

THEME PARK DINING

The full-service theme park restaurants provide unique dining atmospheres and are designed to be an extension of the Walt Disney World experience. The food may not be up to epicurean standards, and the prices tend to be high, but most visitors enjoy memorable dining adventures in the theme parks. Alcohol is served in all theme park restaurants except those in the Magic Kingdom, and smoking is prohibited at the Disney-owned restaurants. Most restaurants offer low-fat entrees, and most do a good job in accommodating vegetarians with special entrees. Kosher, vegan, and other special meals can be requested in advance through Disney Dining Reservations (407 939-3463). In the reviews that follow, the theme park restaurants were rated for FOOD, SERVICE, and ATMOSPHERE as shown:

★★★★	★★★	★★	★
THE VERY BEST	BETTER THAN MOST	SATISFACTORY	OF LIMITED APPEAL

PRICES: At most full-service restaurants, entrees range from $8 to $18 for lunch and $12 to $26 for dinner. Each restaurant review shows the AVERAGE PRICE RANGE for single entrees as follows:

> $ – UNDER $9
> $$ – $9 TO $14
> $$$ – $15 TO $19
> $$$$ – $20 TO $30
> $$$$$ – OVER $30
> $$$$$$ – OVER $40
> ♛ – OVER $50

SAVE

You can save time and money if you eat your large meal in the afternoon, while lunch prices are still in effect, then have a light dinner at a counter-service restaurant. You can also save up to 30 percent at selected restaurants in the World Showcase and elsewhere. Throughout the year, from 4:30 until 6 PM, Early Evening Value Meals are offered, which include an appetizer, entree, and beverage. You must ask which restaurants offer these when making reservations.

RESTAURANT RESERVATIONS: Experienced visitors plan where they will be each day and then make reservations at nearby restaurants well in advance of their trip. Restaurant seating usually fills early, especially during peak seasons. All Walt Disney World visitors can make reservations up to sixty days in advance by calling Disney Dining Reservations (407 939-3463). If the restaurant you want is already booked, make a backup reservation, then call back often to check for openings.

RESTAURANTS

MONEY $AVING PAGE

SAME-DAY RESERVATIONS: Visitors can make restaurant reservations on the day they are touring by calling Same Day Reservations after 10 AM (939-3463). Same-day reservations can also be made in person at each restaurant, or they may be made at the following theme park locations:

EPCOT: At the WorldKey Information Service at Innoventions East or at the WorldKey Information Service kiosk near the Germany pavilion.

DISNEY-MGM STUDIOS: At the Restaurant Desk, where Hollywood and Sunset Boulevards meet.

MAGIC KINGDOM: At City Hall, located near the park entrance on Main Street. ◆

SAVE

Readers receive a $50 Dining Certificate to use at the Dolphin or Swan Resorts! ⭐ (See page 272.)

FULL-SERVICE RESTAURANT LOCATIONS

WORLD SHOWCASE AT EPCOT

BIERGARTEN
BISTRO DE PARIS
CHEFS DE FRANCE
LE CELLIER STEAKHOUSE
L'ORIGINALE ALFREDO DI ROMA RISTORANTE
NINE DRAGONS RESTAURANT
RESTAURANT AKERSHUS
RESTAURANT MARRAKESH
ROSE & CROWN DINING ROOM
SAN ANGEL INN RESTAURANTE
TEMPURA KIKU
TEPPANYAKI DINING ROOM

FUTURE WORLD AT EPCOT

CORAL REEF RESTAURANT
THE GARDEN GRILL RESTAURANT

DISNEY-MGM STUDIOS

50'S PRIME TIME CAFE
THE HOLLYWOOD BROWN DERBY
HOLLYWOOD & VINE CAFETERIA
MAMA MELROSE'S RISTORANTE ITALIANO
SCI-FI DINE-IN THEATER RESTAURANT
SOUNDSTAGE RESTAURANT

MAGIC KINGDOM

CINDERELLA'S ROYAL TABLE
THE CRYSTAL PALACE
LIBERTY TREE TAVERN
THE PLAZA RESTAURANT
TONY'S TOWN SQUARE RESTAURANT

DISNEY'S BOARDWALK

BIG RIVER GRILLE & BREWING WORKS
ESPN CLUB
FLYING FISH CAFÉ
SPOODLES

DOWNTOWN DISNEY

BONGOS CUBAN CAFE
CAP'N JACK'S OYSTER BAR
FULTON'S CRAB HOUSE
HOUSE OF BLUES
PORTOBELLO YACHT CLUB
PLANET HOLLYWOOD
RAINFOREST CAFE
WILDHORSE SALOON
WOLFGANG PUCK CAFE

WDW RESORT RESTAURANTS

ARTIST POINT
ARTHUR'S 27
BASKERVILLES
BEACHES & CREAM
BOATWRIGHT'S DINING HALL
BONFAMILLE'S CAFE
CALIFORNIA GRILL
CAPE MAY CAFE
CHEF MICKEY'S
CONCOURSE STEAKHOUSE
CORAL CAFE ⭐
FINN'S GRILL
GARDEN GROVE CAFE ⭐
GRAND FLORIDIAN CAFE
GULLIVER'S GRILL ⭐
HARRY'S SAFARI BAR & GRILLE ⭐
JUAN & ONLY'S ⭐
NARCOOSSEE'S
1900 PARK FARE
OFFICIAL ALL STAR CAFE
'OHANA
OLIVIA'S CAFE
THE OUTBACK
PALIO ⭐
SEASONS
VICTORIA & ALBERT'S
WHISPERING CANYON CAFE
YACHT CLUB GALLEY
YACHTSMAN STEAKHOUSE

SAVE

RESTAURANTS

GUIDE TO RESTAURANT CUISINE

AMERICAN

Artist Point
Baskervilles
Big River Grille and Brewing Works
California Grill
Chef Mickey's
Cinderella's Royal Table
Coral Cafe ★
The Crystal Palace
ESPN Club
50's Prime Time Cafe
The Garden Grill Restaurant
Garden Grove Cafe ★
Grand Floridian Cafe
Gulliver's Grill
The Hollywood Brown Derby
Hollywood & Vine Cafeteria
Liberty Tree Tavern
Narcoossee's
1900 Park Fare
Official All Star Cafe
Planet Hollywood
The Plaza Restaurant
Rainforest Cafe
Sci-Fi Dine-In Theater Restaurant
Seasons
Soundstage Restaurant
Whispering Canyon Cafe
Wildhorse Saloon
Wolfgang Puck's Cafe
Yacht Club Galley

SEAFOOD

Cape May Cafe
Cap'n Jack's Oyster Bar
Coral Reef Restaurant
Finn's Grill
Flying Fish Café
Fulton's Crab House
Narcoossee's

STEAK & PRIME RIB

Baskervilles
Concourse Steakhouse
Harry's Safari Bar & Grille ★
Le Cellier Steakhouse
The Outback
Yachtsman Steakhouse

FRENCH

Bistro de Paris
Chefs de France

CONTINENTAL

Arthur's 27
Victoria & Albert's

ITALIAN

Flagler's
L'Originale Alfredo di Roma Ristorante
Mama Melrose's Ristorante Italiano
Palio ★
Portobello Yacht Club
Tony's Town Square Restaurant

ASIAN & POLYNESIAN

Nine Dragons Restaurant (Chinese)
'Ohana (Polynesian)
Tempura Kiku (Japanese)
Teppanyaki Dining (Japanese)

BARBECUE, CAJUN, CUBAN

Boatwright's Dining Hall
Bonfamille's Cafe
Bongos Cuban Cafe
House of Blues
Wildhorse Saloon

MEXICAN

Juan & Only's ★
San Angel Inn Restaurante

INTERNATIONAL

Biergarten (German)
Le Cellier (Canadian)
Restaurant Akershus (Norwegian)
Restaurant Marrakesh (Moroccan)
Rose & Crown Dining Room (British)
Spoodles (Mediterranean)

CAFETERIAS & BUFFETS

Baskervilles
Biergarten
Cape May Cafe
Chef Mickey's
The Crystal Palace
Garden Grove Cafe ★
Hollywood & Vine Cafeteria
1900 Park Fare
Restaurant Akershus
Soundstage Restaurant
◆

$AVE

RESTAURANTS BY PRICE RANGE

PRICE CATEGORIES & REVIEW LOCATER

Restaurants marked with this symbol 👑 indicate open buffets or all-you-care-to-eat meals.

$ $
Many Dinner Entrees Priced Under $14

PAGE	RESTAURANT	MEALS
198	Beaches & Cream	B L D
162	Big River Grille & Brewing Works	L D
198	Boatwright's Dining Hall	B D
198	Bonfamille's Cafe	B D
164	Cap'n Jack's Oyster Bar	L D
169	ESPN Club	L D
200	Garden Grove Cafe	B L
174	Hollywood & Vine	B L D
181	Official All-Star Cafe	L D
202	Olivia's Cafe	B L D
182	Planet Hollywood	L D
183	The Plaza Restaurant	B L D
185	Rainforest Cafe	L D

$ $ $
Dinner Entree Price Range: $15 to $19

PAGE	RESTAURANT	MEALS
197	Artist Point	B D
198	Baskervilles 👑	B L D
161	Biergarten 👑	L D
165	Chefs de France	L D
199	Chef Mickey's Restaurant 👑	B L D
166	Cinderella's Royal Table	B L D
200	Concourse Steakhouse	B L D
200	Coral Cafe 👑	B L D
168	The Crystal Palace 👑	B L D
170	50's Prime Time Cafe	L D
200	Finn's Grill	D
173	The Garden Grill Restaurant 👑	B L D
201	Grand Floridian Cafe	B L D
207	Gulliver's Grill (Character Meal)	D
175	The Hollywood Brown Derby	L D
209	House of Blues	B D
201	Juan & Only's	D
176	Le Cellier Steakhouse	L D
178	L'Originale Alfredo di Roma	L D
179	Mama Melrose's Ristorante Italiano	L D

180	Nine Dragons Restaurant	L D
184	Portobello Yacht Club	L D
186	Restaurant Akershus 👑	L D
187	Restaurant Marrakesh	L D
188	Rose & Crown Dining Room	L D
189	San Angel Inn Restaurante	L D
190	Sci-Fi Dine-In Theater Restaurant	L D
203	Seasons	B L D
191	Spoodles	B L D
207	Soundstage Restaurant 👑	B L D
195	Tony's Town Square Restaurant	B L D
194	Wildhorse Saloon	D
196	Wolfgang Puck Cafe	L D
204	Whispering Canyon Cafe 👑	B L D
204	Yacht Club Galley	B L D

$ $ $ $
Dinner Entree Price Range: $20 to $30

PAGE	RESTAURANT	MEALS
163	Bistro de Paris	D
199	California Grill	D
199	Cape May Cafe 👑	B D
167	Coral Reef	L D
171	Flying Fish Cafe	D
172	Fulton's Crab House	D
201	Harry's Safari Bar & Grille	D
177	Liberty Tree Tavern 👑	L D
201	Narcoossee's	L D
202	1900 Park Fare 👑	B L D
202	'Ohana 👑	D
203	The Outback	D
203	Palio	D
192	Tempura Kiku	L D
193	Teppanyaki Dining Room	L D
204	Yachtsman Steakhouse	D

$ $ $ $ $
Prix Fixe Dinner Priced Over $50

197	Authur's 27	D
203	Victoria & Albert's	D

For restaurant discounts, see page 272.

MONEY $AVING PAGE

$AVE $AVE $AVE $AVE $AVE

RESTAURANTS

BIERGARTEN

WORLD SHOWCASE AT EPCOT

★★ **FOOD**   ★★★ **SERVICE**   ★★★ **ATMOSPHERE**

REVIEWER'S COMMENTS: *Although the steam-table dishes can be heavy and the selection is meat oriented, many visitors really like the food. It's a beautifully designed place, but it can be noisy at mealtimes.*

FOOD: Biergarten features a traditional buffet of hearty German cuisine, including roasted meats and chicken, sauerbraten (a marinated beef dish), and a variety of German sausages (weisswurst, bratwurst, and knockwurst), along with red cabbage and potato salad.

LOCATION: The entrance to the restaurant is tucked in the back of the Germany pavilion in the World Showcase at Epcot. Guests can reach it by strolling through the *platz*, past St. George's statue and fountain.

DINING HOURS: Lunch from 11:30 AM, dinner from 4 PM until park closing.

AMBIENCE: Biergarten is a spacious dining room fashioned after the famous beer halls of Munich. Ornate street lamps, balconies overflowing with geraniums, and water cascading from an old mill create an instant vacation to Germany and lend an outdoor air to the restaurant. Communal seating and Bavarian-costumed servers carrying giant steins of beer add to the festivities. On the stage at the front of the hall, performances of German music, folk dancing, singing, and yodeling are featured throughout the day. The robust atmosphere of the Biergarten captures the essence of Oktoberfest, a traditional harvest celebration in Germany.

SAMPLE DINNER ENTREES: Selections from the Hot Buffet — *Sauerbraten* (marinated beef), *Bratwurst* (steamed pork sausage), *Knockwurst* and *Weisswurst* (sausages), *Kässeler* (smoked pork loin), *Wein Kraut* (sauerkraut), *Spätzle* (noodles).

Selections from the Cold Buffet — *Rotkohl* (red cabbage), *Heringsalat* (herring and apple salad), *Kartoffelsalat* (potato salad), and an array of cheeses and breads.

HEALTHY-CHOICE ENTREES: Selections from the Hot Buffet — *Huhn* (rotisserie chicken), *Kartoffel* (roasted potatoes).

Selections from the Cold Buffet — *Apfelmus* (applesauce), *Gurkensalat* (marinated cucumbers and onion), *Heringsalat* (herring salad).

LUNCH: Lunch and dinner menus are similar, although prices are lower at lunch.

BEVERAGES: A selection of fine German wines is offered, along with Beck's beer on tap, served in thirty-three-ounce steins. Spirits, including German liqueurs such as Jägermeister and Kirschwasser, are available, as are soft drinks, coffee, and tea.

AVERAGE PRICE RANGE: Lunch buffet 💲💲, dinner buffet 💲💲💲.

FEATURES: The restaurant is a favorite of many visitors, who rave about the food. Biergarten has recently added more options for vegetarians.

At various times throughout the day, diners can enjoy a lively stage show of German music and dance. Check the entertainment schedule for show times.

For those traveling solo, Biergarten can be a great place to meet fellow diners.

THE DOWN SIDE: The large dining hall can be noisy and crowded during peak dining hours.

The restaurant has an unmistakable cafeteria steam-table smell.

RESERVATIONS: All visitors to Walt Disney World can make reservations up to sixty days in advance by calling Disney Dining Reservations (407 939-3463). Same-day reservations can be made through WorldKey Information Service at Epcot, at the restaurant itself, or by calling Same Day Reservations after 10 AM (939-3463).

RESTAURANTS

BIG RIVER GRILLE & BREWING WORKS

DISNEY'S BOARDWALK

★★★　　★★★　　★★★
FOOD　　SERVICE　　ATMOSPHERE

REVIEWER'S COMMENTS: *The tasty food makes this a place we'll definitely visit again. If you like spicy foods, try the Spinach Con Queso appetizer. Service can be inattentive.*

FOOD: Big River Grille & Brewing Works offers traditional pub fare as well as familiar entrees updated with a new twist. Salads, sandwiches, burgers, and heartier dishes such as chicken, veal meatloaf, and lobster pot pie are designed to pair with the brews, and many entrees incorporate beer in their preparation.

LOCATION: Big River Grille & Brewing Works is located on Disney's BoardWalk Promenade, across from Midway Games.

DINING HOURS: Open all day for lunch and dinner, from 11 AM until 2 AM.

AMBIENCE: The smell of malt greets guests as they pass under bright green awnings to enter this sleek, modern restaurant with a fully operating microbrewery. The huge stainless-steel vats and other brewing equipment are visible behind glass walls, and guests walking through or sitting in the bar area can watch the brewmasters at work. An explanation of the brewing process is printed on the back of the menu.

SAMPLE DINNER ENTREES: *Tennessee Top Sirloin* (grilled sirloin topped with Jack Daniel's Gorgonzola sauce, served with white Cheddar mashed potatoes); *Bangers and Mash* (grilled sausages served over white Cheddar mashed potatoes with Tilt Pale Ale sauce); *Lobster Pot Pie* (lobster meat and root vegetables in a sourdough crust); *"Tilted" Veal Loaf* (grilled veal meatloaf served with white Cheddar mashed potatoes with Tilt Pale Ale sauce); *Smoked Turkey Breast Sandwich* (smoked turkey and dilled havarti cheese, served on sourdough bread). Entrees include a small salad.

HEALTHY-CHOICE ENTREES: *Catch of the Day* (seasonal fresh fish sautéed, blackened, or charbroiled and served with rice pilaf); *Rocket Red Ale Chicken* (chicken breast lightly sautéed with shiitake mushrooms in Rocket Red Ale sauce, served with rice pilaf); *Yellowfin Tuna Sandwich* (marinated and charbroiled tuna steak, served with lettuce, sesame mayonnaise, and topped with pineapple–green chile salsa).

LUNCH: The menu remains the same throughout the day.

BEVERAGES: The Big River Grille offers five microbrewed specialties on tap: *Tilt Pale Ale, Wowzer's Wheat, Rocket Red Ale*, and two seasonal brews which are made on the premises. Soft drinks, mineral water, tea, coffee, espresso, and cappuccino are also available, as are wine and spirits, including a selection of fine Scotches and Cognacs.

AVERAGE PRICE RANGE: Entrees 💲💲.

FEATURES: This microbrewery is an interesting addition to Walt Disney World's new line-up of unique restaurants. For one set price, guests can sample all five house microbrews, each served in a four-ounce glass.

The *Spinach con Queso* appetizer is a popular dish among guests who like spicy foods.

Big River Grille is one of the few Walt Disney World eateries that stay open late, and it is an ideal spot for a bite to eat after an evening touring the theme parks or visiting the clubs.

THE DOWN SIDE: Vegetarians may find the variety of hot selections quite limited.

Some guests may find the smell of the malt used in the brewing process unpleasant. To avoid it, request outdoor seating.

RESERVATIONS: No reservations are taken; diners are seated on a first-come, first-served basis. Smoking is permitted in the bar area.

BISTRO DE PARIS

WORLD SHOWCASE AT EPCOT

 ★★★★
FOOD

 ★★★★
SERVICE

 ★★★★
ATMOSPHERE

REVIEWER'S COMMENTS: *Very good food beautifully presented. The seafood dishes were wonderful. More relaxed and serene than Chefs de France, downstairs, and very French and romantic.*

FOOD: Bistro de Paris features classic French haute cuisine, including such appetizers as pâté de foie gras and smoked salmon. Entrees include seafood, meats, and vegetables served with a variety of unique light sauces. Despite its name, which suggests casual food, Bistro de Paris is the more upscale of the restaurants in the France pavilion, although in the future, it may align its menu more with Chefs de France, downstairs.

LOCATION: Bistro de Paris is located on the second floor at the France pavilion in the World Showcase at Epcot. Guests can find the restaurant by walking down the pavilion's cobblestone street. The entrance is at the rear of the Chefs de France building.

DINING HOURS: Dinner only, from 6 PM. The restaurant may open for lunch at peak-attendance times and during the summer.

AMBIENCE: Guests ascend a dramatic spiraling stairway to the restaurant. Hanging brass and milk glass chandeliers fill the dining room with soft, romantic light. The bistro motif is reflected in the seating arrangements, with long banquettes and red upholstered chairs. Mirrors and paintings in ornate gold frames adorn the walls, evoking a Parisian turn-of-the-century atmosphere.

SAMPLE DINNER ENTREES: *Le Filet de Boeuf Grillé avec Sa Fricassée de Champignons, Sauce au Poivre Vert* (grilled beef with mushrooms and a green peppercorn sauce, served with potato gratin); *Suprême de Canard aux Pêches* (roast duck with raspberry vinegar sauce, garnished with peaches and served with vegetables); *Carré d'Agneau Persillé à la Fleur de Thym sur Son Tian de Légumes* (rack of lamb roasted and flavored with herbs, served with mushroom tart and potato gratin).

HEALTHY-CHOICE ENTREES: *Filet de Bar sur Une Fondue de Tomate Confite au Fenouille* (grouper filet flavored with fresh herbs, served on a bed of minced tomato and braised fennel). A vegetable plate is available on request.

LUNCH: Lunch is served only during times of high attendance. Lunch entrees are lighter, and prices are lower than at dinner.

BEVERAGES: French wine and beer, as well as spirits, are served. Soft drinks, mineral water, tea, coffee, and café express are also available. The restaurant's most popular after-dinner drink, *Café Grand Marnier,* is made with café express, Grand Marnier liqueur, and whipped cream.

AVERAGE PRICE RANGE: Lunch entrees 💲💲💲, dinner entrees 💲💲💲💲.

FEATURES: Three of France's premier *cuisiniers*, Gaston Lenôtre, Paul Bocuse, and Roger Vergé, designed the menu for Bistro de Paris.

With its low lighting and intimate decor, and its secluded location overlooking the Parisian street scene below, the award-winning Bistro de Paris is an especially romantic setting.

THE DOWN SIDE: Because the entrees can be quite expensive, Bistro de Paris is not a good choice for the budget-minded.

Reservations at Bistro de Paris are difficult to secure since it is very popular and is usually open for just one meal.

RESERVATIONS: All visitors to Walt Disney World can make reservations up to fourteen days in advance by calling Disney Dining Reservations (407 939-3463). Same-day reservations can be made through WorldKey Information Service at Epcot, at the restaurant itself, or by calling Same Day Reservations after 10 AM (939-3463).

RESTAURANTS

CAP'N JACK'S OYSTER BAR

DISNEY VILLAGE MARKETPLACE AT DOWNTOWN DISNEY

★★ **FOOD**   ★★ **SERVICE**   ★★★ **ATMOSPHERE**

REVIEWER'S COMMENTS: *Cap'n Jack's is not as popular as it once was. The menu is very limited and the food quality has fallen off. The best bets are the raw seafood and the catch of the day. Servers can be brusque.*

FOOD: Cap'n Jack's features an array of fresh seafood, including shrimp, oysters, crab, clams, and scallops. The seafood is served in salads, cooked into crab cakes and other entrees, or can be ordered raw on the half shell. Chicken, beef, and pork ribs are also served.

LOCATION: The restaurant is located at the end of a pier in the center of Disney Village Marketplace. It sits on Buena Vista Lagoon, and guests can reach it by walking along the waterfront.

DINING HOURS: Open all day for lunch and dinner, from 11:30 AM until 10:30 PM.

AMBIENCE: The galley-style entrance at Cap'n Jack's has a glass-fronted display of the day's fresh seafood. The restaurant has two dining areas, one to the left of the galley and another surrounding the large hexagonal copper-topped bar in the middle of the restaurant. Both dining areas are small, but offer great views of Buena Vista Lagoon and the picturesque riverboat with Fulton's Crab House aboard. A boathouse atmosphere has been achieved at Cap'n Jack's with plank-wood flooring, thickly varnished wooden tables, and leather-slung chairs.

SAMPLE ENTREES: *Alaskan King Crab Legs* (steamed to order, served with coleslaw, a garlic bread stick, and melted butter); *Zesty Crab Cakes* (spicy crabmeat stuffing with onions and herbs, served with coleslaw and a garlic bread stick); *Steamed Oysters* (available by the half or full dozen); *Breast of Chicken* (marinated breast of chicken served with harvest rice, topped with herb butter); *Baked Garlic Oysters* (available by the half or full dozen); *Barbecue Pork Ribs* (rack of pork served with coleslaw and a garlic bread stick); and *Prime Rib of Beef* (10 ounce cut served au jus with baked potato).

HEALTHY-CHOICE ENTREES: *Catch of the Day* (fresh fish served with rice and a garlic bread stick); *Peel & Eat Shrimp* (prepared spicy, steamed, or chilled).

LUNCH: The same menu is offered both at lunch and dinner.

BEVERAGES: Cold beer is served in Mason jars with handles. Wine and spirits are also offered, as are coffee, tea, and soft drinks. Cap'n Jack's is known for its *Frozen Strawberry Margarita*, served in a large frosted glass.

AVERAGE PRICE RANGE: Entrees 💲💲.

FEATURES: Cap'n Jack's is a casual restaurant, with a relaxed atmosphere. The hexagonal bar is a great place to meet fellow vacationers while waiting for a table. Guests can order seafood appetizers at the bar.

Although the entrees provide a variety of choices, the *Steamed Oysters*, *Steamed Clams,* and *Peel & Eat Shrimp* are skillfully prepared and are the real draw here.

If it is in season and on the menu, try the stone crab from the Florida coast, which is wonderful and very hard to find.

Cap'n Jack's desserts, especially the *Key Lime Pie* and the *Chocolate Island* (chocolate cake layered with mousse and fudge), are popular with frequent diners here.

THE DOWN SIDE: During peak dining times, there can be long waits and signs at the entrance do not make it clear how guests are seated. Guests who would like a table must wait in line at the podium. If you just want to sit at the bar for a beverage or snack, simply bypass the line.

RESERVATIONS: No reservations; diners are seated on a first-come, first-served basis.

RESTAURANTS

CHEFS DE FRANCE

WORLD SHOWCASE AT EPCOT

★★★	★★★	★★★
FOOD	SERVICE	ATMOSPHERE

REVIEWER'S COMMENTS: *This very popular restaurant serves French nouvelle cuisine, incorporating fresh local ingredients. The service is professional and efficient, the setting light, bright, and busy .*

FOOD: Chefs de France features French nouvelle cuisine: seafood, meat, poultry, and vegetable dishes accompanied with distinctive sauces created by three of France's premier chefs. One or two of the beautifully prepared appetizers and a salad, ordered together, can serve as a meal.

LOCATION: Chefs de France restaurant is located in the mansard-roofed building that stands on the corner at the entrance to the France pavilion in the World Showcase at Epcot.

DINING HOURS: Lunch from 12 noon, dinner from 4:30 PM until park closing.

AMBIENCE: Chefs de France has undergone a total revamping and and has expanded into the area once occupied by Au Petit Café, the France Pavilion's former sidewalk restaurant. The overall look of the restaurant is still very French, with delicate, classical touches to the decor. The expansion gives diners a choice of the main dining area, where tables are dressed with crisp white linen and set with fresh flowers; or they may choose to dine in the large light-filled veranda area, which is hung with pots of flowers and has tall windows overlooking the World Showcase Promenade.

SAMPLE DINNER ENTREES: *Côte de Veau aux Champignons* (sautéed veal chop with a mushroom cream sauce, served with pasta); *Filet de Boeuf Mathurini* (tenderloin of beef sautéed with raisins in a brandy sauce, served with potato gratin); *Saumon à l'Oseille* (broiled fresh salmon with sorrel cream sauce, served with fresh vegetables); *Canard à l'Orange* (roast breast of duck with a sweet and sour orange sauce, served with polenta gratin and green beans); *Le Vol-au-Vent de Fruits de Mer, Sauce Homard* (snapper in a puff pastry with sautéed scallops and crab dumplings, served with lobster sauce); *Suprême de Volaille en Croûte, Sauce au Porto* (chicken breast marinated with herbs, baked in a puff pastry with vegetables and served with a port wine sauce).

HEALTHY-CHOICE ENTREES: *Brochette de Crevettes à la Provençale* (prawn skewers over rice, with basil butter); *Assiette Végétarienne* (vegetable plate).

LUNCH: Entree selections differ only slightly at lunch, and prices are lower than at dinner.

BEVERAGES: French wine and beer are served, as are spirits, soft drinks, and mineral water. Thick and strong café express, very similar to espresso, is also offered. The comprehensive wine list includes vintages specially selected by the chefs who created the menu.

AVERAGE PRICE RANGE: Lunch entrees 💲💲, dinner entrees 💲💲💲.

FEATURES: Chefs de France received the Ivy Award for restaurant excellence. The menu was created by three of France's premier chefs, Paul Bocuse, Roger Vergé, and Gaston Lenôtre.

A magnificent array of not-to-be-missed and reasonably priced desserts is offered.

The escargots with garlic and herb butter is a favorite appetizer among frequent diners here.

THE DOWN SIDE: It can be very difficult to get same-day reservations at this popular restaurant.

RESERVATIONS: All visitors to Walt Disney World can make reservations up to sixty days in advance by calling Disney Dining Reservations (407 939-3463). Same-day reservations can be made through WorldKey Information Service at Epcot, at the restaurant itself, or by calling Same Day Reservations after 10 AM (939-3463).

RESTAURANTS

CINDERELLA'S ROYAL TABLE

MAGIC KINGDOM

★★★
FOOD

★★★
SERVICE

★★★★
ATMOSPHERE

REVIEWER'S COMMENTS: *This restaurant has improved significantly in recent years, befitting its unique dining room and splendid setting. We had a quiet late lunch with an enchanting view.*

FOOD: Cinderella's Royal Table serves chicken, fish, and beef dishes creatively prepared in a style influenced by New American cuisine.

LOCATION: Formerly known as King Stefan's Banquet Hall, the restaurant is perched high atop Cinderella Castle in Fantasyland at the Magic Kingdom. The entrance can be found at the rear of the castle, facing Fantasyland.

DINING HOURS: Character Breakfast seatings (when offered) from 7:30 AM, lunch from 11:30 AM, dinner from 4 PM until park closing.

AMBIENCE: Cinderella's Royal Table recalls the fairy-tale splendor of once upon a time. Wall torches light the stone archways, and shields, swords, and suits of armor glint near the fireplace. Burgundy-carpeted stairs lead up to the large two-tiered dining room, where the tall cathedral ceiling, carved beams, patterned carpeting, and tapestry-covered chairs mimic a royal atmosphere. Tall, narrow arched windows inset with stained glass give guests an overview of Fantasyland. For twenty-five years, the restaurant inside Cinderella Castle was named King Stefan's Banquet Hall, after Sleeping Beauty's father (it *is* a small world, after all).

SAMPLE DINNER ENTREES: *Grand Duke* (barbecued braised lamb shank, served with Castle beans and blueberry corn bread); *Kingdom Feast* (beef tenderloin medallion and grilled shrimp, served with a rich Cabernet sauce); *The Loyal Knight* (spice-crusted salmon served with red pepper coulis and topped with aioli sauce). Dinner entrees include a choice of soup or salad.

HEALTHY-CHOICE ENTREES: *Earl's Poulet* (herbed chicken and sautéed vegetables, served over polenta); *Fairy Godmother's Vegetarian Plate* (sun-dried tomatoes, fresh mushrooms, pine nuts, broccoli, and raisins, tossed with extra-virgin olive oil, served on pasta).

LUNCH: Lunch and dinner menus are similar; however, the lunch menu also features large salads and smaller entrees, including *Bruno's Barbecue* (grilled chicken and pork loin basted with apricot barbecue sauce, served with vegetable slaw and blueberry corn bread). Lunch entrees include soup or salad, and prices are considerably lower at lunch.

CHARACTER BREAKFAST: Breakfast in the castle includes fruit, scrambled eggs, breakfast meats, potato casserole, and banana French toast.

BEVERAGES: Coffee, tea, orange juice, mineral water, and soft drinks are served.

AVERAGE PRICE RANGE: Character Breakfast 💲💲💲, lunch entrees 💲💲, dinner entrees 💲💲💲💲.

FEATURES: Throughout the day, Cinderella and other Disney Characters sometimes drop in to greet diners.

Cinderella's Royal Table is the only elevated restaurant with a view in the Magic Kingdom.

THE DOWN SIDE: Cinderella's Royal Table is very popular with visitors of all ages. Reservations for all meals, especially the Character Breakfasts, fill quickly, often a month or two ahead of time.

RESERVATIONS: All visitors to Walt Disney World can make reservations, including Character Breakfast reservations, up to sixty days in advance by calling Disney Dining Reservations (407 939-3463). Same-day reservations can be made at City Hall on Main Street, at the restaurant itself, or by calling Same Day Reservations after 10 AM (939-3463).

1015 2933

RESTAURANTS

CORAL REEF RESTAURANT

FUTURE WORLD AT EPCOT

★★★ ★★★ ★★★★
FOOD SERVICE ATMOSPHERE

REVIEWER'S COMMENTS: *Interesting preparations of fresh seafood. Quality and service vary from season to season. Subdued lighting with great fish-watching create the memorable dining experience here.*

FOOD: Coral Reef Restaurant serves a variety of fresh seafood that is prepared smoked, sautéed, or grilled. New American–style cuisine prepared with chicken, beef, or pasta is also available.

LOCATION: Coral Reef Restaurant is located in the Living Seas pavilion in Future World at Epcot. The restaurant has its own entrance at the side of the pavilion, where blue waves painted on the wall lead guests inside.

DINING HOURS: Lunch from 11:30 AM, dinner from 4:30 PM until park closing.

AMBIENCE: One wall of this softly lit multi-tiered restaurant is formed by one of the largest saltwater aquariums in the world, holding more than 5.7 million gallons of seawater and nearly eight thousand underwater inhabitants. Diners can watch the coral reef sea life through eight-foot-high acrylic windows, and use the brochure provided on arrival to help identify the fish. The undersea dining atmosphere is augmented by the room's dark blue walls and carpeting, its dim lighting, and its fascinating view.

SAMPLE DINNER ENTREES: *Vermont Maple-Glazed Salmon* (with corn pudding, roasted Brussels sprouts, and bacon); *Kansas City Pan-Seared Filet Mignon* (with au gratin potatoes, roasted peppers, watercress, and demi-glace barbecue sauce); *Lancaster Chicken and Egg Noodles* (with roasted vegetables, chicken herb jus, and thyme oil); *Penobscot Bay Clambake* (with lobster tail, shrimp, clams, smoked alligator sausage, and market vegetables in an herb clam broth). All entrees are served with soup or salad.

HEALTHY-CHOICE ENTREES: *Farmer's Market Vegetables* (wrapped in filo with lentil stew and spinach Boursin cream); *Monterey-Style Tuna* (with roasted vegetables, roasted red pepper coulis, and tepenade); *Santa Fe Barbecued Grouper* (with spicy black beans, jicama relish, and an empanada).

LUNCH: The lunch menu differs slightly from dinner, and features such items as *Southwestern Marinated Shrimp and Spinach Salad.* Neither soup nor salad is included with lunch, and prices are a bit lower.

BEVERAGES: Soft drinks, mineral water, tea, coffee, and espresso are served. International beers are offered, along with domestic and imported wines, spirits, and specialty drinks such as the *Sea Star,* a blend of Chablis wine, strawberries, lime juice, banana, and club soda.

AVERAGE PRICE RANGE: Lunch entrees 💲💲💲, dinner entrees 💲💲💲💲.

FEATURES: Diners sit at eye-to-eye level with an array of Caribbean reef fish, including sharks and barracuda. Keep an eye out for the grouper, weighing in at more than five hundred pounds. The best views are from tables in the middle of the third and fourth tiers.

THE DOWN SIDE: The Coral Reef's atmosphere and the fact that there are only two full service restaurants in Future World make reservations here hard to get. Lunch is often easier than dinner.

The entrees can be quite expensive — some visitors say "too expensive." Coral Reef is not a good choice for the budget-minded.

RESERVATIONS: All visitors to Walt Disney World can make reservations up to sixty days in advance by calling Disney Dining Reservations (407 939-3463). Same-day reservations can be made through WorldKey Information Service at Epcot, at the restaurant itself, or by calling Same Day Reservations after 10 AM (939-3463).

RESTAURANTS

THE CRYSTAL PALACE

MAGIC KINGDOM

★★ **FOOD**   ★★ **SERVICE**   ★★★ **ATMOSPHERE**

REVIEWER'S COMMENTS: *Despite the elegant Victorian-solarium look, this place is crawling with youngsters. If you're a Disney Character fan, you may be happier with a Character Meal at one of the resorts.*

FOOD: The Crystal Palace features all-you-care-to-eat buffet-style Character Meals for breakfast, lunch, and dinner. Hot entrees include beef, chicken, turkey, fish, and pasta.

LOCATION: The Crystal Palace, a Magic Kingdom landmark, is located at the end of Main Street on the left, facing Cinderella Castle. It can also be approached from the bridge that leads into Adventureland.

DINING HOURS: Breakfast from park opening, lunch from 11:30 AM, dinner from 4 PM until park closing.

AMBIENCE: This pretty, light-filled restaurant resembles the Victorian-era glass conservatory in San Francisco's Golden Gate Park, and gives guests the feeling that they're dining inside a giant greenhouse. A glass dome in the ceiling enhances the gazebo effect, as do the latticework ceilings and wrought-iron tables and chairs. Hot entrees are served cafeteria style at a long food counter in the center of the restaurant, and guests serve themselves from the nearby soup, salad, bread, and dessert bars. The tables along the window walls offer diners a view of beautifully landscaped gardens outside and the Cinderella Castle beyond. Disney Characters make frequent appearances to greet guests.

CHARACTER DINNER ENTREES: The all-you-care-to-eat menu includes *Soup Hot from the Kettle; Spit-Roasted Carved Meats; Chicken, Beef, and Fish Creations; Chef's Selection of Freshly Prepared Pastas*. Rice, potatoes au gratin, vegetables, salads, freshly baked breads, and desserts are included.

HEALTHY-CHOICE ENTREES: The long buffet includes a salad bar with a large variety of greens and vegetables, as well as fresh fruit.

CHARACTER BREAKFAST: The all-you-care-to-eat breakfast menu includes *Seasonal Fresh Fruit, Freshly Baked Pastries, Spit-Roasted Ham, Scrambled Eggs and Omelettes, Crystal Palace French Toast, Oven-Roasted Potatoes,* and *Breakfast Lasagna*. Hotcakes and a variety of cereals are also available.

CHARACTER LUNCH: The lunch buffet offers a *Creative Array of Salads, Chef's Choice of Soup, Variety of Freshly Prepared Pastas,* and the *Executive-Style Deli*. Freshly baked breads and muffins, as well as a variety of desserts such as cookies, brownies, and ice cream sundaes, are also available.

BEVERAGES: Coffee, tea, and soft drinks are served, with unlimited refills. All beverages are included with the meal.

AVERAGE PRICE RANGE: Character Breakfast 💲💲, Character Lunch 💲💲💲, Character Dinner 💲💲💲💲.

FEATURES: This restaurant has a wide selection of salad and dessert items. The Sundae Bar will appeal to ice-cream lovers.

Health-conscious diners may order breakfast dishes made with EggBeaters.

THE DOWN SIDE: The Crystal Palace is very popular with families, so there can be a long wait for tables during peak dining hours.

Visits by Disney Characters make meals here noisy, lively, and crowded.

RESERVATIONS: All visitors to Walt Disney World can make reservations up to sixty days in advance by calling Disney Dining Reservations (407 939-3463). Same-day reservations can be made at City Hall, at the restaurant, or by calling Same Day Reservations after 10 AM (939-3463).

RESTAURANTS

ESPN CLUB

DISNEY'S BOARDWALK

★★ **FOOD**   ★★ **SERVICE**   ★★★ **ATMOSPHERE**

REVIEWER'S COMMENTS: *Think tailgate party. The food, like the ambience, is casual, and service can be haphazard. You'll have to shout to be heard over the loud sportscasts.*

FOOD: ESPN Club offers American fare such as sandwiches, hamburgers, hot dogs, pasta, and salads. Appetizers are also served to guests who come to take in the ongoing sports events.

LOCATION: ESPN Club is located at the far end of Disney's BoardWalk, near the International Gateway to the World Showcase at Epcot, and below Disney's BoardWalk Inn.

DINING HOURS: Open all day for lunch and dinner, from 11 AM until 1 AM (open until 2 AM on weekends).

ATMOSPHERE: ESPN Club immerses guests in the atmosphere of a raucous sports bar and sports broadcast studio. Seventy-one television monitors showing sports events are scattered throughout the club: mounted overhead, inset in walls, and even in the rest rooms. The restaurant has hardwood floors, sports murals on the walls, and an eight-by-twelve-foot viewing screen at one end of the room. Tables are arranged around the large square central bar. Guests can also eat in Sports Central, which is actually an ESPN broadcast studio, complete with scaffolding for the studio lights and a glassed-in control booth. Patterned on a miniature basketball court, tiers of small tables surround the stage floor.

SAMPLE DINNER ENTREES: *The Fresh Fin Tuna Salad Sandwich* (served in pita bread with lettuce, tomato, and sprouts, served with chips); *Tailgate BBQ Pork* (slow-roasted pulled pork on a grilled roll, served with fries); *The Slider Burger* (a half-pound burger with choice of Cheddar or Swiss cheese on a freshly baked roll, served with fries).

HEALTHY CHOICE ENTREES: *Mighty Duck "Chick Trick"* (marinated grilled chicken breast on a freshly baked roll, served with fries); *Penne Pasta* (grilled vegetables and sun-dried tomatoes in a creamy Alfredo or tomato-basil sauce); *Traditional Caesar Salad* (romaine lettuce, your choice of shrimp or chicken, and garlic croutons with a Caesar dressing).

LUNCH: The menu is the same for both lunch and dinner.

BEVERAGES: Coffee, tea, and soft drinks are served, as well as a wide selection of beer and wine. A full bar is available in The Sidelines bar area, and features such specialty drinks as *The Adrenaline,* a concoction of fresh strawberries, banana, fruit punch, and choice of liquor.

AVERAGE PRICE RANGE: Entrees 💲💲.

FEATURES: ESPN Club has a good selection of domestic and imported beers, including Foster's Lager and Leinenkügel Red.

To one side of ESPN Club is Sports Central, with a working radio and television studio, where guests can dine while watching ESPN sports reviews and interview shows take place.

Guests who are more interested in sports than a large entree can order *Bloody Mary Chili* and other light appetizers to snack on as they watch the game, or they can try the restaurant's most popular dessert, *Mile-High Apple Pie*.

If you're a French-fry fan, this is the place to order them. They are crispy and cleverly served in a miniature basketball hoop.

THE DOWN SIDE: With TV monitors broadcasting multiple sports events at the same time and at full volume throughout the dining area, meals can be quite noisy.

RESERVATIONS: No reservations are taken; diners are seated on a first-come, first-served basis. Smoking is permitted in the bar area.

RESTAURANTS

50'S PRIME TIME CAFE

DISNEY-MGM STUDIOS

★★ **FOOD**   ★★★★ **SERVICE**   ★★★★ **ATMOSPHERE**

REVIEWER'S COMMENTS: *The hearty home-style dishes are nothing special, but the fifties atmosphere is great fun if you don't mind being singled out. This is not the place for low-profile dining.*

FOOD: The 50's Prime Time Cafe serves cuisine popular in that era, such as pot roast, meat loaf, chicken, and steak, prepared from family-style recipes and topped with lots of gravy. Seafood, hamburgers, and sandwiches are also available.

LOCATION: The restaurant is located on Vine Street across from Echo Lake at Disney-MGM Studios. Guests can find the restaurant by looking for the sign in the shape of a giant television above it.

DINING HOURS: Lunch from 11 AM, dinner from 4 PM until park closing.

AMBIENCE: Unique mini-kitchenettes are the setting for the home-style meals at the 50's Prime Time Cafe. There are ruffled curtains, vintage wallpaper, linoleum flooring, and plenty of vinyl and chrome. Servers known as "Brother" or "Sis" act as though they are bossy siblings, watching diners' manners and making sure they've cleaned their plates. During meals, clips from "The Honeymooners," "I Love Lucy," and other vintage sitcoms are broadcast on old-fashioned black and white TVs scattered throughout the restaurant's kitchenettes.

SAMPLE DINNER ENTREES: *Granny's Pot Roast* (country-style pot roast served with mashed potatoes and gravy); *Hot Turkey Platter* (fresh turkey over corn bread dressing, served with cranberry sauce, mashed potatoes, and gravy); *Magnificent Meatloaf* (traditional-style meat loaf, served with mashed potatoes, and mushroom gravy); *Charbroiled Ribeye Steak* (ribeye steak served with oven-roasted potatoes).

HEALTHY-CHOICE ENTREES: *Aunt Gen's Shrimp or Chicken Spectacular* (shrimp, fresh chicken breast, or a combination, seasoned with Southwest spices, grilled and served with rice pilaf); *Uncle Giovanni's Pasta* (penne pasta in a pesto sauce with shrimp and scallops); *Dad's Fishin' Trip* (seasonal fresh fish, served with garden vegetables).

LUNCH: Lunch features more sandwiches than dinner, and prices are slightly lower at lunch.

BEVERAGES: Coffee, tea, and soft drinks are served, and refills are complimentary. The soda fountain features such specialties as root beer floats, ice cream sodas, and milk shakes, including a peanut-butter-and-jelly-flavored shake. Beer, wine, and spirits are also available. Specialty drinks include *The Diner,* a blend of vodka, rum, cranberry, pineapple, and orange juice with a dash of grenadine and a squeeze of lime, and *The Poodle Skirt,* a frozen concoction of rum, banana mix, and fruit juices.

AVERAGE PRICE RANGE: Lunch entrees 💲💲, dinner entrees 💲💲💲.

FEATURES: Talented servers stay in character and provide memorable entertainment.
The Tune In Lounge, decorated with black and white TVs, offers comfortable seats and a unique setting for before-meals cocktails.

THE DOWN SIDE: The 50's Prime Time Cafe is very popular during peak seasons, and same-day reservations can be difficult to secure.

RESERVATIONS: All visitors to Walt Disney World can make reservations up to sixty days in advance by calling Disney Dining Reservations (407 939-3463). Same-day reservations can be made at Hollywood Junction (at the intersection of Hollywood and Sunset Boulevards) inside Disney-MGM Studios, at the restaurant itself, or by calling Same Day Reservations after 10 AM (939-3463).

RESTAURANTS

FLYING FISH CAFÉ

DISNEY'S BOARDWALK

★★★★ **FOOD**   ★★★★ **SERVICE**   ★★★★ **ATMOSPHERE**

REVIEWER'S COMMENTS: *This is a must-try restaurant, with the best food at Disney's BoardWalk. The seafood dishes are outstanding and the setting is lovely. A perfect after-Epcot dinner spot.*

FOOD: The Flying Fish Café serves distinctive cuisine with innovative flavor combinations. Entrees change frequently to reflect seasonal ingredients. Fresh seafood is featured, as well as chicken, steaks, and homemade pastas.

LOCATION: Flying Fish Café is located in the center of Disney's BoardWalk, overlooking the BoardWalk Green.

DINING HOURS: Dinner only from 6 PM until 11 PM.

AMBIENCE: The large murals and whimsical flying-fish motif at this relaxed, yet sophisticated restaurant pay tribute to the roller coaster and flying fish carousel of an earlier era at Atlantic City's Boardwalk. The main dining area is studded with large pillars surrounded by sleek tables inlaid with brushed steel. The look is both trendy and elegant. Copper tiles cover the restaurant's elegant bar and the counter fronting the kitchen's open grill. In a small, secluded dining area at the rear of the restaurant, comfortable booths surround a small fountain.

SAMPLE DINNER ENTREES: *Char-Crusted New York Strip Steak* (with roasted Yellow Finn potato, wild mushroom ragout, and sauce Foyot); *Crispy Fried Mixed Grill* (rock shrimp, calamari, and catch of the day, with cranberry bean stew and lemon-pepper aioli); *House-Made Ravioli* (with wild mushrooms, aged jack cheese, spinach, roasted artichokes, and sweet garlic broth) *Oak Grilled Double Cut Pork Chop* (with braised red cabbage, Cheddar potatoes and bourbon apple butter).

HEALTHY-CHOICE ENTREES: *Seared Ahi Tuna* (with spiced coriander crust, frisée, and gingered golden lentils); *Spicy Barbecue Glazed Atlantic Salmon* (with corn sticks and autumn corn salad); *Roasted Spring Chicken* (served with whipped potatoes, wild mushrooms, and natural juices); *Potato-Wrapped Yellow Tail Snapper* (with leek fondue and a Cabernet Sauvignon reduction).

BEVERAGES: Flying Fish Café offers a large selection of domestic and imported wines that includes over a dozen types of Champagne and a variety of sparkling wines. The restaurant features specialty drinks such as the *Flying Fish,* made with Crown Royale, peach schnapps, orange juice, and sparkling wine. Champagne-based cocktails are also available, as are soft drinks, mineral water, tea, coffee, cappuccino, and espresso.

AVERAGE PRICE RANGE: Dinner entrees 💲💲💲 to 💲💲💲💲.

FEATURES: Guests who enjoy watching the chefs at work can request seating at the counter along the front of the show kitchen. If you find the area too smoky from the grills, request a nearby table.

Chocolate-lovers will love the *Warm Chocolate Lava Cake* (with a liquid chocolate center and strawberry coulis). The dessert takes some time to prepare; if you know it's what you will want, order it early.

THE DOWN SIDE: Same-day reservations can be hard to get because this restaurant is developing a following. Visitors should plan ahead.

RESERVATIONS: All visitors to Walt Disney World can make reservations up to sixty days in advance by calling Disney Dining Reservations (407 939-3463). Same-day reservations can be made by calling the restaurant (939-2359), or by calling Same Day Reservations after 10 AM (939-3463). Smoking is permitted in the bar.

RESTAURANTS

FULTON'S CRAB HOUSE

PLEASURE ISLAND & DISNEY VILLAGE MARKETPLACE AT DOWNTOWN DISNEY

★★★★ **FOOD**   ★★★★ **SERVICE**   ★★★★ **ATMOSPHERE**

REVIEWER'S COMMENTS: *You can't beat the atmosphere at this busy, fun restaurant. This is an oasis for seafood-lovers, serving fresh fish flown in from around the world. If it's in season, order the stone crab!*

FOOD: The food focus at Fulton's is primarily on seafood, including lobster, crab, and fresh fish. Steak, chicken, and pasta are also served. The menu changes frequently to take advantage of seasonal fish from around the world.

LOCATION: This restaurant is inside a replica nineteenth-century riverboat docked at Buena Vista Lagoon, between Disney Village Marketplace and Pleasure Island at Downtown Disney. It is across from Portobello Yacht Club and the Wildhorse Saloon; all three fine restaurants are owned by Chicago-based Levy Restaurants.

DINING HOURS: Character Breakfasts at 8 AM and 10 AM, lounge open all day for light snacks until 2 AM, dinner from 5 PM until midnight.

AMBIENCE: With its dark mahogany paneling, Oriental rugs, and soft lighting, Fulton's Crab House has a warm, comfortable clubby atmosphere. The walls are hung with handsome prints depicting fish and a few mounted specimens, including a seven-hundred-pound marlin that hangs above the stairwell. The dining rooms on board the three-story riverboat include the Industry Room, which also features outdoor dining on the deck; and the Constellation Room, with its celestial-painted ceiling and lovely views of the sunset over Buena Vista Lagoon.

SAMPLE DINNER ENTREES: *Rock Shrimp Pasta* (Florida rock shrimp with fettuccine pasta, roasted peppers, onions, oyster mushrooms, and tasso ham); *Whole Maine Lobster* (steamed, served with red-skinned potatoes and drawn butter); *Fulton's Cioppino* (crab, shrimp, scallops, fresh fish, clams, and mussels in a tomato-herb broth); *Mustard-Crusted Trout* (sautéed trout filet coated with Dijon-scented herbed bread crumbs, served with corn whipped potatoes).

HEALTHY-CHOICE ENTREES: *Port Canaveral Black Grouper* (jerk spiced and charcoal grilled, with Scotch Bonnet cranberry glaze and lemon-almond rice); *Grilled Garlic Chicken* (boneless half chicken with garlic, rosemary, lemon, and thyme, served with corn whipped potatoes).

LUNCH: Although Fulton's is not technically open for lunch, the Stone Crab Lounge, which is open all day and overlooks Buena Vista Lagoon, features chilled seafood dishes and a number of special appetizers that are ideal for a light meal.

CHARACTER BREAKFAST: Popular Character Breakfasts are held here every morning. The all-you-care-to-eat menu includes smoked salmon, scrambled eggs, hash browns, apple pastry, fresh fruit, and mini muffins.

BEVERAGES: The restaurant's wine list features an excellent selection of Pacific Coast wines. Beers from around the world are served, as are spirits and specialty drinks, such as *The Sailor's Knot,* a blend of rum, orange and pineapple juices, and coconut milk. Soft drinks, coffee, espresso, and cappuccino are also served.

AVERAGE PRICE RANGE: Character Breakfast 💲💲, dinner entrees 💲💲💲 to 💲💲💲💲.

FEATURES: Guests waiting for a table can enjoy the view in the Stone Crab Lounge, which is located on the first deck.

THE DOWN SIDE: Without reservations, the wait can be up to an hour at this popular restaurant.

RESERVATIONS: All visitors to Walt Disney World can make reservations up to thirty days in advance for dinner, and up to sixty days in advance for Character Breakfasts by calling Fulton's Crab House directly (407 934-2628). The restaurant has a smoking area.

RESTAURANTS

THE GARDEN GRILL RESTAURANT

FUTURE WORLD AT EPCOT

★★ **FOOD**   ★★★ **SERVICE**   ★★★★ **ATMOSPHERE**

REVIEWER'S COMMENTS: *The hearty and filling American dishes served here are satisfying, if not spectacular. But the visually stimulating atmosphere is terrific, though, and servers are friendly and efficient.*

FOOD: The Garden Grill Restaurant serves all-you-care-to-eat traditional American cuisine, including meat, chicken, and seafood that may be smoked, grilled, or rotisserie-grilled. Some of the fish and vegetables served are actually grown in The Land pavilion gardens.

LOCATION: The restaurant is located inside The Land pavilion in Future World at Epcot. To reach it, guests walk to the back of the pavilion, along the balcony overlooking the attractions and the Sunshine Season Food Fair, below.

DINING HOURS: Breakfast from before park opening, lunch from 11:30 AM, dinner from 4 PM until park closing.

AMBIENCE: The Garden Grill Restaurant overlooks the Living with The Land attraction and revolves, giving guests an excellent view of its environmental exhibits. Diners pass through dioramas depicting a rainforest, a desert, and a prairie complete with buffalo. Roomy booths on two tiers make the excursion quite comfortable. Farmer Mickey and a cast of Disney Characters drop by from time to time to greet diners.

CHARACTER LUNCH AND DINNER: *Roasted Chicken with Rocky Top Seasoning, Hickory-Smoked Steak,* and *Farm Fresh Catfish* are served family style in sizzling skillets. The trio of all-you-care-to-eat entrees are accompanied with farm fresh salad, smashed potatoes, mushroom gravy, garden vegetables, smoked relish, squaw bread and biscuits, and apple butter. The same menu is served at lunch and dinner.

CHARACTER BREAKFAST: The family-style, all-you-care-to-eat Character Breakfast dishes include scrambled eggs, breakfast casserole, sausage, ham steak, fresh fruit, biscuits and gravy, French toast sticks, and cheese grits.

HEALTHY-CHOICE ENTREES: *Garden Pasta Primavera* (pasta tossed with fresh grilled vegetables and savory herbs) is available as a special order for guests who want a vegetarian meal.

BEVERAGES: Coffee, tea, and soft drinks are included in the price of the Character Meal. Also available but not included are regional American beers and California wines. The restaurant's full bar features such specialty drinks as the popular *Garden Grill Bloody Mary,* a house concoction that is garnished with celery from The Land's own greenhouses.

AVERAGE PRICE RANGE: Character Breakfast, lunch, or dinner $ $ $.

FEATURES: The slowly revolving restaurant provides an entertaining atmosphere at meals. For the best view, request a table on the lower tier. It takes about thirty-five minutes to make a complete revolution.

Guests with 7:30 AM reservations can enter Epcot early by showing their admission ticket and reservation number at the entrance gate.

THE DOWN SIDE: During periods of peak-attendance, it is very difficult to get same-day reservations for lunch. Dinner reservations are sometimes easier to secure.

Diners are seated in booths, so guests in wheelchairs or those with a child needing a high chair may find dining here awkward.

RESERVATIONS: All visitors to Walt Disney World can make reservations for Character Meals up to sixty days in advance by calling Disney Dining Reservations (407 939-3463). Same-day reservations can be made through WorldKey Information Service at Epcot, at the restaurant itself, or by calling Same Day Reservations after 10 AM (939-3463).

HOLLYWOOD & VINE CAFETERIA

DISNEY-MGM STUDIOS

★★★   ★★   ★★
FOOD   **SERVICE**   **ATMOSPHERE**

REVIEWER'S COMMENTS: *The Hollywood & Vine serves pretty good food at a very good price. If you drop by after peak lunch hours, there are no lines, making it a perfect place for a time- and money-saving meal.*

FOOD: The Hollywood & Vine Cafeteria serves American-style beef, chicken, veal, seafood, and pasta dishes, along with sandwiches, a variety of large salads, and desserts such as pastries and ice cream specialties.

LOCATION: The restaurant is located on Vine Street across from Echo Lake at Disney-MGM Studios, next door to the 50's Prime Time Cafe.

DINING HOURS: Open all day. Breakfast from park opening, lunch from 11 AM, dinner starting from 4 PM only during the summer and holidays, when the park stays open late.

AMBIENCE: Hollywood & Vine "Cafeteria of the Stars" is a replica of a Tinseltown diner from the late 1940s. In one room, a sprawling forty-foot mural features famous landmarks from Hollywood and the San Fernando Valley. Another very vivid mural features a detailed nighttime view of Hollywood Boulevard. Black and white photographs with scenes of early Hollywood hang on the walls. The large dining room, decorated with pink geometric carpeting and black Venetian blinds, is divided in half, with a long chrome cafeteria counter taking center stage. Guests select their food at the cafeteria, pay the cashier, and then hope to be "discovered" while dining at a Formica-topped dinette table or in one of the restaurant's pale pink Naugahyde booths.

SAMPLE ENTREES: *Rodeo Drive Ribs* (a half slab of hickory-smoked pork ribs with baked beans); *Hollywood Stir-Fry* (stir-fried chicken or beef with vegetables, served with spring rice); *Academy Special* (seasoned fried-chicken tenders, served with French fries). *Chicken Parmesan* (boneless chicken filet with cheese, served on spaghetti with marinara sauce).

HEALTHY-CHOICE ENTREES: *Catch of the Day* (fresh fish served with spring rice); *Hollywood Chef's Salad* (ham, turkey, and shredded cheese atop a bed of greens); *Cahuenga Chicken* (roasted half chicken, served with spring rice).

BREAKFAST AND LUNCH: The breakfast menu includes egg dishes, pancakes, French toast, and the restaurant's special *Rodeo Drive Steak* (country-fried steak with white gravy, served with scrambled eggs, biscuit, and choice of potatoes or grits).

Lunch and dinner entrees are almost identical, although a few specialty sandwiches are available in the afternoon, including the *Studio Combo,* a classic deli sandwich.

BEVERAGES: Wine and beer are available at the cafeteria, as are coffee, coffee drinks, tea, and soft drinks.

AVERAGE PRICE RANGE: Breakfast, lunch, or dinner entrees 💲.

FEATURES: Hollywood & Vine Cafeteria is a good choice for a quick meal or for light eaters. The line usually moves quickly, even during busy times.

A selection of pastries and ice cream specialties is available from a front counter all afternoon.

The Tune In Lounge is an entertaining and relaxing stop for a before- or after-dinner drink. It can be entered directly from inside the Hollywood & Vine Cafeteria.

THE DOWN SIDE: Hollywood & Vine Cafeteria attracts large crowds during busy mealtimes. There can be long lines and lots of noise. Mid-afternoon is the best time to go.

RESERVATIONS: Cafeteria-style self-service; no reservations are taken.

RESTAURANTS

THE HOLLYWOOD BROWN DERBY

DISNEY-MGM STUDIOS

★★★
FOOD

★★★
SERVICE

★★★
ATMOSPHERE

REVIEWER'S COMMENTS: *The atmosphere is very comfortable. It's our favorite place to unwind at Disney-MGM Studios. The food is not special, but the server can help you pick a few winners.*

FOOD: The Hollywood Brown Derby serves charbroiled beef, grilled lamb and pork, sautéed veal, roasted chicken, seafood, and pasta.

LOCATION: The Hollywood Brown Derby is housed in a Mediterranean-style building on the plaza at the end of Hollywood Boulevard in Disney-MGM Studios. It is across the plaza from the Chinese Theater.

DINING HOURS: Lunch from 11 AM, dinner from 4:30 PM until park closing.

AMBIENCE: Red carpet paves the way through the two-tiered Hollywood Brown Derby. The main dining area has white linen–covered tables favored by visiting celebrities. Booths line the walls of the surrounding upper tier, and there are shaded tables on the outdoor patio. The restaurant's mahogany wainscoting, chandeliers, airy lace curtains, and heavy velvet drapes impart the atmosphere of vintage Hollywood power dining. The restaurant's signature collection of caricatures adorns the walls, and Streetmosphere performers, impersonating such characters as Hedda Hopper, mingle with diners to search out good gossip or provide musical interludes on the piano in the main dining area.

SAMPLE DINNER ENTREES: *Pasta Brown Derby* (penne pasta, fresh basil, sun-dried tomatoes, and fresh sugar snap peas tossed with shrimp in a tomato-garlic broth); *Filet Mignon* (grilled filet with garlic mashed potatoes, baby green beans, and sun-dried cherries); *Tenderloin of Pork* (marinated with honey, thyme, tomato, and Cognac, accompanied with wild rice griddle cakes and tomato Napoleon).

HEALTHY-CHOICE ENTREES: *Tuna au Poivre* (peppercorn-crusted tuna, pan seared and served with vegetable slaw and balsamic vinegar);

Sautéed Grouper (lightly dusted in flour, served on fresh vegetable medley with sauce meunière); *Roast Chicken* (half chicken, marinated and slow-roasted, served with potato crisps and baby greens with house vinaigrette).

LUNCH: The lunch menu features more salads and sandwiches than the dinner menu. Prices are slightly lower at lunch.

BEVERAGES: The wine list offers a selection of vintage California wines. Beer and spirits are also available, as are mineral water, soft drinks, tea, coffee, espresso, and cappuccino. Several after-dinner drinks are featured, including vintage ports and the specialty drink *Cafe Henry III,* a blend of Kahlúa, brandy, Galliano, Grand Marnier, and coffee.

AVERAGE PRICE RANGE: Lunch entrees , dinner entrees .

FEATURES: Although the Hollywood Brown Derby does not have a lounge, The Catwalk Bar, upstairs, is a great place for before-dinner drinks. There is an elevator adjacent to the restaurant's waiting area.

THE DOWN SIDE: The Hollywood Brown Derby is extremely popular and usually fully booked, especially during peak seasons. It can be difficult to secure same-day reservations.

RESERVATIONS: All visitors to Walt Disney World can make reservations up to sixty days in advance by calling Disney Dining Reservations (407 939-3463). Same-day reservations can be made at Hollywood Junction (at the intersection of Hollywood and Sunset Boulevards) inside Disney-MGM Studios, at the restaurant itself, or by calling Same Day Reservations after 10 AM (939-3463).

RESTAURANTS

LE CELLIER STEAKHOUSE

WORLD SHOWCASE AT EPCOT

★★★   ★★★   ★★★
FOOD   **SERVICE**   **ATMOSPHERE**

REVIEWER'S COMMENTS: *Not your usual theme park fare, the steak and seafood dishes can hit the spot for hearty appetites. The cool cellar atmosphere of the dining room creates a delightful interlude on a hot day.*

FOOD: Le Cellier has long been a cafeteria-style restaurant that featured regional dishes from the various provinces of Canada. It was one of the well-kept secrets among frequent travelers who appreciated its uncrowded, out-of-the-way atmosphere. Returning visitors will discover, in its place, a full-service Canadian steakhouse, the only theme park restaurant that offers steaks, prime rib, and seafood as the featured cuisine.

LOCATION: The entrance to Le Cellier Steakhouse is at the side of the Canada pavilion in the World Showcase at Epcot. Guests can reach it by walking down the ramp along the river flowing through the flowering Victoria Gardens.

DINING HOURS: Lunch from 12 noon, dinner from 4 PM until park closing.

AMBIENCE: The warmth of Canadian hospitality along with the cool, comfortable feeling of dining inside a giant wine cellar is conveyed to guests at Le Cellier Steakhouse. Thick stone walls are adorned with wrought-iron lanterns, and dramatic archways divide the dining room into several smaller, more intimate areas. The dark wood panels that line the walls are topped here and there with ironwork fashioned into Canadian maple leaf patterns. Guests are seated tables surrounded by tapestry-upholstered high-back chairs.

SAMPLE DINNER ENTREES: *Filet Mignon, Top Sirloin Steak, Prime Rib, Penne Pasta Vancouver,* and *Fresh Catch of the Day*. All entrees are served with rice or potatoes and vegetables.

HEALTHY-CHOICE ENTREES: *Baked Maple Glazed Salmon* (entrees are served with rice or potatoes and vegetables). Vegetarian platters can be prepared on request.

LUNCH: Lunch and dinner menus are similar, and most entrees are available at both meals. However, lunch prices are somewhat lower and the menu also features hamburgers and meal-sized salads.

BEVERAGES: In keeping with the wine-cellar atmosphere, Le Cellier Steakhouse features an exclusive selection if Inniskillin Wines from the Niagara Pennisula. La Batt's and Molson's beer are served, along with a variety of Canadian wines. Coffee, tea, mineral water, and soft drinks are also offered.

AVERAGE PRICE RANGE: Lunch entrees 💲💲, dinner entrees 💲💲💲.

FEATURES: Le Cellier Steakhouse may have one of the best entrances in the World Showcase. To reach the restaurant, guests meander through gorgeous flowering gardens, often accompanied by the music of a bagpipe band.

On hot afternoons, this dimly lit restaurant is a great place to relax and cool off. The best time to go is about 2 PM, when the lunch crowd is gone. The restaurant's location at the center of Epcot makes it an excellent rendezvous spot for visitors who have been touring separately.

THE DOWN SIDE: At peak lunch hours during busy seasons, reservations can be hard to get. Dinner is usually less crowded than lunch.

Vegetarians may find the entree selection somewhat limited at Le Cellier.

RESERVATIONS: All visitors to Walt Disney World can make reservations up to sixty days in advance by calling Disney Dining Reservations (407 939-3463). Same-day reservations can be made through WorldKey Information Service at Epcot, at the restaurant itself, or by calling Same Day Reservations after 10 AM (939-3463).

RESTAURANTS

LIBERTY TREE TAVERN

MAGIC KINGDOM

★★ **FOOD**   ★★ **SERVICE**   ★★ **ATMOSPHERE**

REVIEWER'S COMMENTS: *The simple American food and decor offer a pleasant lunch break while touring the Magic Kingdom. The roast turkey is a good value. The Character Dinner can be very noisy.*

FOOD: Liberty Tree Tavern features a Character Dinner with an Early American menu including turkey, steak, and ham. Traditional roast turkey accompanied with all the trimmings is available on the lunch menu every day, as are several New England–style dishes.

LOCATION: The restaurant is located at Liberty Square in the Magic Kingdom. It is housed in a colonial-style building across from the Liberty Square Riverboat landing.

DINING HOURS: Lunch from 11:30 AM, Character Dinner from 4 PM until park closing.

AMBIENCE: The Liberty Tree Tavern immerses guests in the atmosphere of an eighteenth-century American dining hall, with pegged wood flooring and paned-glass windows. The restaurant is divided into six themed dining areas, each decorated with reproductions of items associated with a famous historical figure, such as Ben Franklin's printing press and Betsy Ross's eyeglasses. One wall is fashioned from rough-cut stone and features a massive fireplace with an oak mantel. Iron candelabra hang from the beamed ceilings, and pewter and copper artifacts decorate the walls and moldings.

CHARACTER DINNER ENTREES: The all-you-care-to-eat menu includes *Honey-Mustard Ham, Roasted Turkey Breast, Marinated Flank Steak, Mashed Potatoes, Garden Vegetables,* and *Apple Stuffing*. Beverages are included with the meal; dessert, however, is not.

LUNCH: The lunch menu offers special salads and sandwiches, as well as hot entrees such as *New England Pot Roast* (braised beef in a Burgundy wine sauce, served with mashed potatoes and sautéed garden vegetables); *Chesapeake Cheddar* (an array of seafood in white wine sauce, served in a pastry shell and topped with Cheddar cheese, accompanied with sautéed garden vegetables).

HEALTHY-CHOICE LUNCH ENTREES: *Fresh from the Harbor* (grilled fresh fish served over cucumber relish, accompanied with sautéed garden vegetables); *Cape Cod Pasta* (sautéed shrimp and garden vegetables tossed with spinach linguine); *Capitol Idea* (a medley of vegetables, beans with rice, and grilled potato).

BEVERAGES: Coffee, tea, soft drinks, juice, espresso, and cappuccino are served. The *Star-Spangled Sherbet Punch,* a special nonalcoholic thirst quencher, is served in a Liberty Tree Tavern souvenir glass.

AVERAGE PRICE RANGE: Lunch entrees 💲💲, Character Dinner 💲💲💲💲.

FEATURES: On hot days, Liberty Tree Tavern is a great place to relax and cool off. At about 2 PM, the lunch crowds have gone and seating is often available.

The familiar American dishes at this restaurant make it a Magic Kingdom favorite for guests of all ages. The *New England Clam Chowder* is a lunch favorite among frequent guests.

THE DOWN SIDE: Same-day reservations can be very difficult to get during peak seasons, and noise levels can be quite high.

RESERVATIONS: All visitors to Walt Disney World can make reservations up to sixty days in advance by calling Disney Dining Reservations (407 939-3463). Same-day reservations can be made at City Hall on Main Street, at the restaurant itself, or by calling Same Day Reservations after 10 AM (939-3463).

RESTAURANTS

L'ORIGINALE ALFREDO DI ROMA RISTORANTE

WORLD SHOWCASE AT EPCOT

★★ **FOOD**　　★★ **SERVICE**　　★★★ **ATMOSPHERE**

REVIEWER'S COMMENTS: *The beautiful decor and strolling musicians create a charming dining experience. The food is adequate but unexceptional, and servers can be indifferent.*

FOOD: L'Originale Alfredo di Roma Ristorante serves Italian cuisine and freshly made pasta with a selection of sauces. The featured pasta is Le Originali Fettuccine all'Alfredo, a creation of the namesake restaurant in Rome. Also on the menu are chicken, veal, and seafood dishes prepared in regional styles.

LOCATION: The restaurant is located across from the cascading Fontana di Nettuno, at the back of the Italy pavilion in the World Showcase at Epcot. Guests pass under a white-pillared portico, softly lit at night by hanging lanterns, to enter the palatial pink-stuccoed building.

DINING HOURS: Lunch from 12 noon, dinner from 4 PM until park closing.

AMBIENCE: Photographs of international celebrities cover the walls of the restaurant's spacious entry area, where waiting guests are seated beneath an elaborate crystal chandelier. The elegant dining area, with mauve velvet chairs and pink tablecloths, has large windows looking out onto the piazza. The walls are covered with masterful trompe l'oeil murals depicting scenes from Italian country estates. Strolling musicians create a festive dining experience as they wander the room singing and playing Italian ballads and operatic arias.

SAMPLE DINNER ENTREES: *Salmone Fresco al Limone e Capperi* (North Atlantic salmon sautéed in a lemon, white wine, and caper sauce, served with roasted potatoes and spinach); *Costoletta di Vitello Salsa al Chianti e Tartufo Nero* (grilled veal chop with Chianti and black truffle sauce, sautéed mushrooms, and fresh asparagus, served with roasted potatoes); *Ziti alla Mediterranea* (ziti pasta with fresh mozzarella, Sicilian olives, fresh tomatoes, and basil);

Le Originali Fettuccine all'Alfredo (house-made wide-noodle pasta tossed with butter and Parmesan cheese); .

HEALTHY-CHOICE ENTREES: *Spaghetti al Pomodoro e Basilico* (spaghetti with tomato sauce flavored with garlic and basil); *Polletto Ruspante di Campagna* (roasted free-range chicken with rosemary and sage, roasted potatoes and vegetables).

LUNCH: Lunch and dinner menus are similar, although there are many more veal dishes at dinner. Prices are only slightly lower at lunch than at dinner.

BEVERAGES: Wine, beer, soft drinks, tea, and coffee are served, along with espresso and cappuccino. The wine list includes selections from various regions of Italy.

AVERAGE PRICE RANGE: Lunch entrees 💲💲, dinner entrees 💲💲💲.

FEATURES: The restaurant's pasta is made fresh daily on the premises. Guests can watch the pasta-making process through the large kitchen windows.

THE DOWN SIDE: Since this is one of the most popular restaurants in the World Showcase, it can be extremely difficult to book same-day reservations for dinner.

The tables are set very close together, and this busy restaurant can be very noisy at mealtimes.

RESERVATIONS: All visitors to Walt Disney World can make reservations up to sixty days in advance by calling Disney Dining Reservations (407 939-3463). Same-day reservations can be made through WorldKey Information Service at Epcot, at the restaurant itself, or by calling Same Day Reservations after 10 AM (939-3463).

RESTAURANTS

MAMA MELROSE'S RISTORANTE ITALIANO

DISNEY-MGM STUDIOS

★★★	★★★	★★
FOOD	**SERVICE**	**ATMOSPHERE**

REVIEWER'S COMMENTS: *Some of the dishes served here are exceptionally good, and the pasta is a good value. The service, especially between peak meal times, can be very friendly and inviting.*

FOOD: Mama Melrose's serves Italian cuisine with a California flair, and thin-crust pizzas baked in an oak wood–burning oven. Beef, veal, fresh fish, and chicken are prepared with a variety of Italian sauces. An all-you-care-to-eat pasta special is featured, topped with a choice of traditional Italian sauces.

LOCATION: The restaurant is tucked away in the New York Street Backlot, "behind" New York Street and just around the corner from Muppet*Vision 3D at Disney-MGM Studios.

DINING HOURS: Lunch from 11 AM, dinner from 4 PM until park closing.

AMBIENCE: Mama Melrose's is permeated with delicious smells from the wood-burning ovens and open kitchen, where guests can catch a view of the chefs preparing meals. The rafters and walls are festooned with grapevines, hanging wine bottles, tiny lights, and other paraphernalia. The dim lighting evokes the feeling of twilight. Hardwood floors, red- and green-checked tablecloths, and loud good humor create an offbeat trattoria atmosphere.

SAMPLE DINNER ENTREES: *Aunt Maria's Oak-Grilled Chicken* (marinated chicken breast with a sun-dried tomato/balsamic glaze, served with pesto-grilled California vegetables and corn cake); *Little Tommie's Linguini with Clam Sauce* (linguini with choice of red or white clam sauce, served with fresh Manila clams); *Uncle Giovanni's "Sicilian Style" Risotto with Sausage, Pancetta, and Broccoli* (fresh Italian sausage, pancetta, and fresh broccoli, sautéed and served with a tomato-basil risotto). Dinner entrees include soup or salad.

HEALTHY-CHOICE ENTREES: *Sophia's Wood-Fired California Vegetables* (fresh vegetables marinated in a pesto dressing and cooked over a wood-fired grill); *Sun-Dried Tomato and Basil Crusted Salmon* (fresh salmon with a tomato and basil crust, accompanied with fresh vegetables and corn cake).

LUNCH: Lunch and dinner menus are similar, although prices are slightly lower at lunch and entrees do not include soup or salad.

BEVERAGES: Californian and Italian wines are featured at Mama Melrose's. Coffee, tea, soft drinks, espresso, and cappuccino are offered, as are beer and spirits. *Italian Root Beer*, a house favorite, is made with Galliano, Kahlúa, and a touch of soda.

AVERAGE PRICE RANGE: Lunch entrees $ $ $, dinner entrees $ $ $.

FEATURES: The oak wood–burning brick ovens and a hardwood charbroiler enable chefs to produce top-quality grilled meats and pizzas. The individual-sized pizzas are popular appetizers.

Mama Melrose's is a pleasant place to drop in for a beverage in the afternoon, once the mealtime crowds have gone. Guests are seated at dinner tables and given fresh-baked bread and olive oil to snack on.

THE DOWN SIDE: The restaurant is very large and can be quite noisy during peak dining hours.

RESERVATIONS: All visitors to Walt Disney World can make reservations up to sixty days in advance by calling Disney Dining Reservations (407 939-3463). Same-day reservations can be made at Hollywood Junction (at the intersection of Hollywood and Sunset Boulevards) inside Disney-MGM Studios, at the restaurant itself, or by calling Same Day Reservations after 10 AM (939-3463).

RESTAURANTS

NINE DRAGONS RESTAURANT

WORLD SHOWCASE AT EPCOT

★★	★★	★★★
FOOD	**SERVICE**	**ATMOSPHERE**

REVIEWER'S COMMENTS: *The dining area suggests elegance, but the average-quality entrees never rose to the occasion, though some of the appetizers were quite good. The prices seemed disproportionally high.*

FOOD: Nine Dragons Restaurant serves several different styles of Chinese cuisine: light and mild Mandarin, hot and spicy Szechuan and Hunan, subtly flavored Cantonese, and internationally inspired Kiangche from Shanghai. Meats, poultry, seafood, and vegetables are prepared with a variety of seasonings and sauces. The menu was created by the chefs at the Beijing Hotel in China.

LOCATION: The restaurant, a reproduction of the Summer Palace in Beijing, is located just past the Gate of the Golden Sun at the China pavilion in the World Showcase at Epcot. It is entered through an elaborately carved arched doorway.

DINING HOURS: Open all day. Lunch from 11 AM, dinner from 4:30 PM until park closing.

AMBIENCE: An elaborately carved rosewood partition dominates the entry to the large open dining room of the Nine Dragons Restaurant. Plush, dark cranberry-colored carpeting, black-lacquered chairs, intricately painted ceilings, and white linen tablecloths give the dining room a formal atmosphere. Ornate paper lanterns add to the light that pours in from octagonal windows. The tables in the front of the restaurant offer a good view of the World Showcase promenade.

SAMPLE DINNER ENTREES: *Beef in Spicy Sha Cha Sauce* (sliced beef stir-fried with bamboo shoots and snow peas); *Kang Bao Chicken* (stir-fried chicken with peanuts, celery, and dried hot peppers); *Treasure Duck* (boneless duckling braised and deep-fried, served with sweet and sour sauce); *Shrimp or Scallops Royale* (stir-fried shrimp or scallops, in a spicy black bean sauce with green peppers); *Buddha's Delight* (bean curd stir-fried with vegetables). All entrees are served with rice and tea.

HEALTHY-CHOICE ENTREES: *Saucy Chicken* (stir-fried chicken, onions, carrots, and green peas); *Imperial String Beans* (string beans cooked in a lightly oiled wok); *Stir-fried Scallops and Garden Vegetables* (scallops stir-fried with vegetables).

LUNCH: Lunch and dinner menus are similar, although prices of some dishes are quite a bit lower at lunch.

BEVERAGES: Wine, Tsing Tao beer, and spirits are served. Fresh melon juice is available, as are soft drinks, mineral water, coffee, and tea. The restaurant features several specialty drinks, including the *Shanghai Surprise*, made with ginseng brandy, rum, grapefruit, lemon, and orange juice; and the *Xian Quencher*, a mixture of fresh melon juice and rum or vodka.

AVERAGE PRICE RANGE: Lunch entrees 💲💲💲, dinner entrees 💲💲💲.

FEATURES: It is fairly easy to secure same-day or last-minute reservations for lunch and dinner at Nine Dragons.

Popular dishes among frequent diners are the *Kang Bao Chicken* and *Beef in Spicy Sha Cha Sauce.*

THE DOWN SIDE: Dishes are served as individual meals with rice, rather than family style as in most Chinese restaurants in the United States. Many visitors consider the restaurant overpriced.

RESERVATIONS: All visitors to Walt Disney World can make reservations up to sixty days in advance by calling Disney Dining Reservations (407 939-3463). Same-day reservations can be made through WorldKey Information Service at Epcot, at the restaurant itself, or by calling Same Day Reservations after 10 AM (939-3463).

RESTAURANTS

OFFICIAL ALL STAR CAFE

DISNEY'S WIDE WORLD OF SPORTS

 FOOD   **SERVICE**   **ATMOSPHERE**

REVIEWER'S COMMENTS: *The hamburgers, including the veggie ones, were terrific and the servers were fun and informative, but we had to yell to be heard over the extremely loud sound levels.*

FOOD: The Official All Star Cafe serves chicken, steaks, seafood, pasta, pizza, huge salads, and hamburgers with a beef, turkey, or veggie patty.

LOCATION: The Official All Star Cafe is located at Disney's Wide World of Sports, near the main entrance to Walt Disney World off Highway 192.

DINING HOURS: Open all day from 11 AM until 1 AM.

AMBIENCE: Giant photos of athletes and signs that spin with flashing lights mark the entrance to this restaurant. Inside, the walls are lined with an amazing array of sports memorabilia, and racing cars and other sports vehicles hang from the ceiling. A huge scoreboard sits above the central bar, and the dining room is hung with projection screens and video monitors. While dining, guests can watch televised sports events and sports-themed videos selected by a live VJ, who provides updates on breaking scores and other happenings. The Official All Star Cafe is part of the Planet Hollywood restaurant group.

SAMPLE DINNER ENTREES: *T-Bone Steak* (one pound of the finest USDA Choice T-bone steak grilled to order, served with baked potato and fresh grilled vegetables); *Mushroom, Onion & Swiss* (a half-pound of USDA Choice chuck, eight ounces of fresh ground turkey, or a Garden-burger, served on a toasted All Star roll with lettuce, tomato, sliced onion, steak fries, and pickle); *Gold Medalist* (sliced roasted chicken, broccoli florets, and diced tomato, on mozzarella cheese and garlic cream sauce, served on a thick herb-Parmesan cheese crust).

HEALTHY-CHOICE ENTREES: *Lemon Herb Chicken* (herb-marinated chicken breast grilled to order, served with ratatouille, baked mashed potatoes, and chilled ranch sauce); *Linguine Pomodoro* (chopped fresh tomatoes, garlic, and basil, topped with linguine and Parmesan cheese); *Chef's Catch* (the freshest seafood available).

LUNCH: The menu is the same for both lunch and dinner.

BEVERAGES: The Official All Star Cafe serves beer, wine, and spirits, including specialty drinks such as *The All Star* (Absolut vodka, Bacardi rum, Chambord, and Triple Sec with a splash of sour mix and cranberry juice, served in a take-home sports bottle) and *The Super Bowl* (a ring of salt, Cuervo Gold, Cointreau, shaken with sweet and sour mix). Milk shakes, malts, lemonade, soft drinks, tea, and coffee are also served, as are cappuccino, latte, mocha, and espresso.

AVERAGE PRICE RANGE: Entrees 💲💲.

FEATURES: The Official All Star Cafe features dreamy milk shakes and spectacular desserts. The two most popular desserts among regulars are the *Banana Split Cheesecake* (guaranteed to satisfy any sweet tooth) and the *Chocolate Chip Cookie Supreme* (a must for chocolate-lovers).

This is the closest full-service restaurant for guests staying at Disney's All-Star Resorts, and is a great place for late-night dining after a long day in the theme parks.

THE DOWN SIDE: During peak dining times, there can be a long wait for seating.

The restaurant's loud music levels can make conversation very difficult. This is a place to soak up the atmosphere and goings-on.

From time to time, bright lights play across the room. If strobe lights bother you, request a table in an unaffected area.

RESERVATIONS: No reservations taken; diners are seated on a first-come, first-served basis.

PLANET HOLLYWOOD

PLEASURE ISLAND & WEST SIDE AT DOWNTOWN DISNEY

★★★★	★★★★	★★★
FOOD	**SERVICE**	**ATMOSPHERE**

REVIEWER'S COMMENTS: *Consistently great dishes. We loved the Thaishrimp and the apple strudel. The atmosphere is so remarkable, you almost forget that the music is way too loud for conversation.*

FOOD: Most of the dishes at Planet Hollywood were developed by the restaurant chain's creative owners and highly skilled master chefs. Entrees include salads, hamburgers, pasta, pizza, ribs, chicken, steak, and the chef's special seasonal entrees, all served in generous portions.

LOCATION: Planet Hollywood is located at Pleasure Island, close to the AMC Theatres and Disney's West Side. Hovering dramatically over the lagoon inside a gigantic blue celestial sphere, the restaurant is impossible to miss.

DINING HOURS: Open all day for lunch and dinner daily, from 11 AM until 2 AM.

AMBIENCE: A long canopied stairway (perfect for that "Hollywood" entrance) leads up to the intricately designed tri-level restaurant. Each level reflects a different movie genre, such as science fiction or action-adventure, and props and memorabilia from famous films hang from the walls and ceilings. There are two bars, a gift shop is tucked behind the visiting stars' "hand-print" wall, and enormous monitors show music videos, film clips, and scenes from Planet Hollywood grand openings around the world. There's an air of excitement here — the sense that a celebrity could show up at any moment. Planet Hollywood is always busy, its staff is upbeat, and its razzle-dazzle ambience is memorable.

SAMPLE DINNER ENTREES: *Thai Shrimp* (butterflied shrimp tossed with julienned vegetables, peanuts, green onions, cilantro, spicy sweet chili sauce, and linguine); *St. Louis Ribs* (smoked spareribs, served with Planet Hollywood's own barbecue sauce, French fries, and black bean relish); *Fajitas* (choice of chicken, beef, or a combination, with a traditional presentation of whole-wheat tortillas, guacamole, pico de gallo, sour cream, and mixed cheeses, served with black beans and Mexican rice).

HEALTHY-CHOICE ENTREES: *Gardenburger* (a meatless patty made from fresh mushrooms, onions, low-fat cheese, seasonings and spices, served on a Hollywood roll with lettuce, tomato, red onions, and dill pickle); *Penne Primavera* (penne pasta tossed with herbs, olive oil, and an oven-roasted vegetable medley of eggplant, tomatoes, onions, sweet peppers, zucchini, yellow squash, and garlic).

LUNCH: The menu is the same for lunch and dinner.

BEVERAGES: Along with beer, champagne, and wine, Planet Hollywood features a large selection of specialty drinks in souvenir glasses, including *The Terminator* (a cyborg's mixture of vodka, rum, gin, Grand Marnier, Tia Maria, Kahlúa, and sweet and sour mix, splashed with cranberry, then topped with draught beer). Coffee, tea, and soft drinks are also served, as are espresso and cappuccino.

AVERAGE PRICE RANGE: Entrees 💲💲.

FEATURES: Planet Hollywood features several inspired desserts, including *Hollywood Mousse Pie* and an *Apple Strudel* made from an original recipe of Arnold Schwarzenegger's mother.

Parties of six who want to experience the fun atmosphere without the noise can request a table in one of the two sound-suppressed booths.

THE DOWN SIDE: The wait for seating can be over an hour. Arrive before 11 AM for lunch, or before 5 PM or after 9 PM for dinner.

RESERVATIONS: The restaurant does not take reservations; diners are seated on a first-come, first-served basis.

RESTAURANTS

THE PLAZA RESTAURANT

MAGIC KINGDOM

★★
FOOD

★★
SERVICE

★★
ATMOSPHERE

REVIEWER'S COMMENTS: *The menu has a limited selection of expensive lunchroom sandwiches. Come here for the ice cream. The dining area is very pretty, but service can be slow in this crowded restaurant.*

FOOD: The Plaza Restaurant offers a typical American lunchroom menu of grilled and cold sandwiches and hamburgers. Its biggest draw, however, is a whimsical selection of soda fountain treats, including the Magic Kingdom's best and largest ice cream sundae.

LOCATION: The Plaza is located at the end of Main Street to the right, facing Cinderella Castle in the Magic Kingdom. It can also be reached from the walkway leading into Tomorrowland.

DINING HOURS: Open all day for lunch and dinner, from 11 AM until park closing.

AMBIENCE: The Plaza Restaurant is housed in an ornate Victorian building with a light-filled atrium veranda off to the side. The interior has splendid Art Nouveau touches, with carved white wall panels and an array of gold-etched mirrors. Marble-topped tables are scattered throughout the cheerful dining room, which has an abundance of windows topped with gauzy white valances. The view from the round veranda takes in both Cinderella Castle and the sci-fi archway to Tomorrowland. As a tribute to the restaurant's turn-of-the-century atmosphere, waitresses wear long Victorian dresses.

SAMPLE ENTREES: *Hot Roast Beef* (smoked roast beef with sautéed mushrooms in a brown sauce, served on a submarine roll); *Grilled Turkey Sandwich* (smoked turkey, melted mozzarella cheese, bacon, tomato, and onion on wheat bread); *Reuben Sandwich* (corned beef, Swiss cheese, sauerkraut, and Thousand Island dressing grilled on marble rye bread); *Grilled Onion and Mushroom Burger* (ground hamburger served with lettuce, tomato, onion, and fries, with provolone cheese). All sandwiches are served with German-style potato salad.

HEALTHY-CHOICE ENTREES: *Fruit Plate* (seasonal fresh fruits served with strawberry cream cheese and specialty bread); *Chef's Salad* (garden greens and tomatoes tossed with ham, turkey, Swiss cheese, and choice of dressing); *Fresh Vegetable Sandwich* (sliced cucumber, squash, alfalfa sprouts, tomato, and Swiss cheese on multi-grain bread with dill spread). On request, sandwiches can be prepared on reduced-calorie bread.

LUNCH: The same menu is offered throughout the day.

BEVERAGES: Coffee, tea, soft drinks, and juice are served, and espresso, cappuccino, and café mocha are also featured. *Creamy Hand-Dipped Milk Shakes,* the Plaza's signature specialty, come in vanilla, chocolate, and strawberry. Ice cream floats and sodas are also available.

AVERAGE PRICE RANGE: Entrees $.

FEATURES: Ice cream–lovers will feel right at home in The Plaza Restaurant. In addition to the listed specialties, there is the *Bicycle Built for Two,* a create-your-own-fantasy ice cream treat.

The Plaza Restaurant is a great place to come in and cool off on hot afternoons, after the lunch crowd has thinned out. Ask to be seated at a table on the veranda.

For health-conscious diners, fountain specialties can be prepared with nonfat and sugar-free ice cream.

THE DOWN SIDE: The Plaza is very popular. Since no advance reservations are taken, there are sometimes long lines during peak dining times. Waits can be up to an hour.

RESERVATIONS: No reservations taken; diners are seated on a first-come, first-served basis.

RESTAURANTS

PORTOBELLO YACHT CLUB

PLEASURE ISLAND & DISNEY VILLAGE MARKETPLACE AT DOWNTOWN DISNEY

★★★	★★★★	★★★
FOOD	SERVICE	ATMOSPHERE

REVIEWER'S COMMENTS: *This is a wonderful, relaxing place to try creative regional Italian cuisine. The service is excellent, and the upscale atmosphere offers a sophisticated getaway.*

FOOD: Portobello Yacht Club has an extensive and varied menu of regional Italian cuisine, including individual thin-crust pizzas, original pasta creations, and seafood flown in fresh daily. Also served are charcoal-grilled steaks, chicken, and pork loin flavored with fresh herbs and roasted in the restaurant's wood-burning oven.

LOCATION: Portobello Yacht Club is located at Pleasure Island at Downtown Disney, and faces Disney Village Marketplace. The restaurant is entered from outside of Pleasure Island.

DINING HOURS: Open all day. Lunch from 11:30 AM, dinner from 4 PM until midnight.

AMBIENCE: Despite its Italian name, Portobello Yacht Club seems to capture the casual, breezy atmosphere of a New England yacht club. High-beamed ceilings shelter an array of nautical paraphernalia and an entire wall of yachting photos. The tables are covered in white and mint-green tablecloths, with a decorative Italian plate at each setting. The long, comfortable mahogany bar is accented with brass and surrounded with black leather stools. Portobello's has several nooks and crannies for intimate dining.

SAMPLE ENTREES: *Costoletta di Maiale* (marinated oak-roasted loin of pork with fennel, carrots, onions, served with roasted garlic whipped potatoes); *Spaghettini alla Portobello* (Alaskan crab legs, scallops, clams, shrimp, and mussels with tomatoes, garlic, olive oil, wine, and herbs, lightly tossed with spaghettini pasta); *Bistecca Alforno* (grilled ribeye steak topped with a Parmigiano cheese crust, served with roasted garlic mashed potatoes and seasonal vegetables); *Spiedini di Gamberi* (grilled shrimp served with capellini pasta, broccoli rapini, garlic, lemon, basil, and Roma tomatoes).

HEALTHY-CHOICE ENTREES: *Linguine con Vongole* (linguine pasta with fresh Manila clams, garlic, white wine, cherry tomatoes, and parsley); *Pollo alla Griglia* (grilled boneless half chicken marinated in olive oil, garlic, and fresh rosemary with natural reduction, served with roasted garlic mashed potatoes and seasonal vegetables); *Pollo Piatto* (boneless breast of chicken pounded thin and charcoal-grilled with spinach, Roma tomatoes, mushrooms, rosemary cream, and angel hair pasta).

LUNCH: Lunch and dinner menus are similar; prices are somewhat lower at lunch.

BEVERAGES: Coffee, cappuccino, and espresso are offered. *Caffè Portobello,* a specialty of the house, is concocted with Grand Marnier and Frangelico. Wine, beer, and spirits are served. The impressive wine list features several very good California and Italian wines.

AVERAGE PRICE RANGE: Lunch entrees 💲💲, dinner entrees 💲💲💲.

FEATURES: The restaurant features one of Walt Disney World's most extensive selections of grappa, single-malt Scotch, and Cognac.

Portobello is popular among frequent visitors, and along with Fulton's Crab House and the Whitehorse Saloon, it is one of the few late-night full-service restaurants at Walt Disney World.

THE DOWN SIDE: Tables for two are very hard to get when the restaurant is crowded, and there can be long waits.

RESERVATIONS: All visitors to Walt Disney World can make reservations up to sixty days in advance by calling the Portobello Yacht Club directly (407 934-8888). The restaurant has a smoking area.

RESTAURANTS

RAINFOREST CAFE

DISNEY VILLAGE MARKETPLACE AT DOWNTOWN DISNEY

★★ **FOOD** ★★★ **SERVICE** ★★★★ **ATMOSPHERE**

REVIEWER'S COMMENTS: *The crowd seems to like it, but the food combinations missed the mark for us. Go for the atmosphere. It's as good as the Jungle Cruise, although the line to eat here is much longer.*

FOOD: The Rainforest Cafe serves up American food infused with a multicultural influence. Steak, chicken, seafood, pasta, pizza, and salads are presented in unique flavor combinations.

LOCATION: Rainforest Cafe is distinguished by the sixty-five-foot "active" volcano situated above it. It is located at the far end of the Village Marketplace, within walking distance of the Townhouses at the Disney Institute.

DINING HOURS: Open all day, from 10 AM until 11 PM Sunday through Thursday. (Open until midnight on Friday and Saturday.)

AMBIENCE: The Rainforest Cafe has created a tropical jungle within its spacious dining rooms. Large trees and vines form a leafy canopy overhead. Among the cascading waterfalls and on overhanging cliffs, Audio-Animatronics animals inhabit the dining areas. Impressive aquariums filled with coral and tropical fish provide great views and softly glowing light. The environmental sounds of thunder, lightning, and rain are continuous, and the intermittent eruption of the volcano outside reverberates in the cafe.

SAMPLE DINNER ENTREES: *Rasta Pasta* (bow tie pasta, grilled chicken, walnut pesto, broccoli, red peppers, spinach, and fresh herbs tossed in a garlic cream sauce); *Rumble in the Jungle* (roasted turkey tossed with Caesar salad and stuffed into a warm grilled pita bread, served with tomatoes and cranberry relish, and topped with crispy fried onions); *Jamaica, Me Crazy!* (grilled pork chops, dusted with Jamaican and Cajun seasonings, nestled on a bed of red beans and rice); *China Island Chicken Salad* (shredded lettuce, grilled chicken breast, rice noodles, shredded carrots, and chopped scallions, tossed with sesame seed dressing).

HEALTHY CHOICE ENTREES: *The Southern Cross* (vegetable lasagna layered with spinach, mushrooms, zucchini, Bermuda onions, eggplant, and fresh peppers, topped with salsa marinara and Parmesan); *Chicken Monsoon* (grilled Cajun chicken breast piled on top of linguine and topped with shrimp and corn salsa); *Pelican's Catch* (catch of the day).

LUNCH: The menu is the same all day.

BEVERAGES: Soft drinks, fruit smoothies, and organic fruit and vegetable juices are served, as are coffee, espresso, cappuccino, and specialty coffee drinks. Wine, beer, and spirits are also available. The Rainforest Cafe features a variety of signature cocktails, including the *Margarilla,* a Margarita made with orange sherbet; and the *Rainbow Colada,* a combination of spiced rum, strawberries, banana, and pineapple.

AVERAGE PRICE RANGE: Entrees 💲💲.

FEATURES: The live parrot show out front is a fun diversion; the volcano you can't miss.

While waiting for their table, diners can browse the Rainforest Cafe's fun gift shop, featuring nature-themed items from all over the globe many highlighting endangered animals.

THE DOWN SIDE: The atmosphere is not for diners seeking a quiet interlude. The squawks and roars of the Audio-Animatronics creatures, along with the rumble of thunder and the erupting volcano, create a noisy dining experience.

Rainforest Cafe is very popular, so be prepared to sacrifice an hour or more of your vacation time waiting (in the gift shop) for a table.

RESERVATIONS: The restaurant does not take reservations, but be sure to check ahead, for the reservation policy may change.

RESTAURANTS

RESTAURANT AKERSHUS

WORLD SHOWCASE AT EPCOT

★★★	★★	★★★
FOOD	SERVICE	ATMOSPHERE

REVIEWER'S COMMENTS: *This spacious medieval-style restaurant presents a good-quality all-you-care-to-eat buffet, although some foods may be unappealing to some diners.*

FOOD: Restaurant Akershus features an all-you-care-to-eat Norwegian buffet known as a *koldtbord*. The cold selections include an array of Norwegian salads and smoked fish, and the hot dishes incorporate meat, poultry, seafood, and vegetables. Diners are encouraged to return to the buffet for separate courses, beginning with the appetizers, continuing with the cold buffet, and ending with hot entrees and cheeses.

LOCATION: The restaurant is tucked inside the Norway pavilion in the World Showcase at Epcot. The entrance is located across the traditional town square from Kringla Bakeri og Kafé.

DINING HOURS: Lunch from 11:30 AM, dinner from 4:30 PM until park closing.

AMBIENCE: Restaurant Akershus is fashioned after the medieval castle fortress that spans most of Oslo's harbor. Its four dining areas feature such period touches as beamed cathedral ceilings hung with iron chandeliers, tall clerestory-style leaded-glass windows with lace curtains, and walls of massive whitewashed bricks broken by dramatic stone archways. Tables are set with crisp white tablecloths, and diners serve themselves at the long buffet. Servers bring beverages and take orders for dessert.

SAMPLE DINNER ENTREES: Selections from the Cold Buffet — *Chicken Salad, Meat Salad, Potato Salad, Egg and Ham Salad, Herring, Smoked Salmon, Roast Beef, Cheese Platter,* and *Stuffed Pork Loin.* A variety of traditional breads is also available.

Selections from the Hot Buffet — *Smoked Pork*, *Venison Strips in Cream Sauce, Meatballs in Gravy*, *Macaroni and Cheese with Ham.* Side dishes include mashed rutabagas, fresh vegetables, and boiled red potatoes.

Vegetarian Selections — *Mixed Green Salad, Pasta Salad, Cucumber Salad, Cabbage Salad, Vegetable Salad,* and *Tomato Salad.*

HEALTHY-CHOICE ENTREES: *Fresh Baked Fish, Smoked Mackerel, Chilled Shrimp, Vegetable Salad, Tomato Salad, Cucumber Salad,* and *Cabbage Salad*.

LUNCH: The food selection available at lunch and dinner varies slightly, although the price is quite a bit lower at lunch.

BEVERAGES: Soft drinks, mineral water, tea, and coffee are available, as is Ringnes beer on tap. The wine list features a good selection from California vineyards, along with a more limited selection from France, Italy, and Portugal. Spirits are served, featuring Norway's Linie aquavit.

AVERAGE PRICE RANGE: Lunch buffet 💲💲, dinner buffet 💲💲💲.

FEATURES: Since Norwegian cuisine is not well known, guests may find it easy to get same-day reservations or walk in and be seated.

The lower lunch price makes this buffet ideal for visitors eating their main meal at midday.

THE DOWN SIDE: Some guests are disappointed with the food, although the restaurant is a favorite among many visitors. Before dining, walk in and look over the choices.

Vegetarian diners may find the variety of hot selections quite limited.

RESERVATIONS: All visitors to Walt Disney World can make reservations up to sixty days in advance by calling Disney Dining Reservations (407 939-3463). Same-day reservations can be made through WorldKey Information Service at Epcot, at the restaurant itself, or by calling Same Day Reservations after 10 AM (939-3463).

RESTAURANT MARRAKESH

WORLD SHOWCASE AT EPCOT

★★★	★★★	★★★
FOOD	SERVICE	ATMOSPHERE

REVIEWER'S COMMENTS: *Stop here if you want to enjoy an interesting meal. The surroundings are memorable and the food is quite tasty. Don't hesitate to ask questions of the friendly servers.*

FOOD: Restaurant Marrakesh serves the cuisine of North Africa, featuring meats and fish cooked with aromatic spices, as well as couscous, a light and flavorful steamed-grain dish that is generally regarded as the national dish of Morocco.

LOCATION: The restaurant is tucked away in the back of the Morocco pavilion in the World Showcase at Epcot. Guests can reach it by wandering past the courtyard fountain and following the passages through Morocco's exotic shopping bazaar.

DINING HOURS: Lunch from 11:30 AM, dinner from 4 PM until park closing.

AMBIENCE: The opulent multitiered Restaurant Marrakesh has slim carved pillars reaching up to a high ceiling that is hung with chandeliers and painted in the colorful geometric patterns of North Africa. The banquettes along the tiled walls provide seating in the upper-tier dining area, while the tables on the main floor below surround a small stage and dance floor where belly dancers and musicians perform. All the servers wear *djellabas,* the traditional long robes of Morocco.

SAMPLE DINNER ENTREES: *Shish Kebab* (grilled brochettes of lamb marinated in Moroccan herbs and spices, served with yellow rice and vegetables); *Couscous* (rolled semolina steamed and served with garden vegetables and a choice of chicken or lamb); *Tagine of Chicken* (braised half chicken seasoned with garlic, green olives, and lemon, served with yellow rice and garden vegetables); *Roast Lamb Meshoui* (lamb roasted in natural juices, served with yellow rice and vegetables); *Sultan's Sampler* (brochette of chicken, beef kefta, and beef shish kebab, served with yellow rice and vegetable couscous).

HEALTHY-CHOICE ENTREES: *Vegetable Couscous* (rolled semolina steamed and served with seasonal vegetables); *Tagine of Grouper* (fillet of grouper baked with tomatoes, green peppers, and garlic, served with yellow rice).

LUNCH: Lunch and dinner menus are similar, and prices are slightly lower at lunch.

BEVERAGES: Wine, beer, spirits, soft drinks, and mineral water are served. Along with coffee and espresso, *atai benna'na',* or fresh-brewed mint tea, is also offered. Restaurant Marrakesh features a special cocktail called *Marrakesh Express,* a mix of apricot brandy, orange juice, and cranberry juice, topped with peach schnapps. The wine list offers an interesting selection of French and Moroccan wines.

AVERAGE PRICE RANGE: Lunch entrees 💲💲💲, dinner entrees 💲💲💲.

FEATURES: Moroccan musicians and belly dancers entertain at both lunch and dinner. The unusual entertainment and the rich decor create an exotically romantic setting. Shows begin about twenty-five minutes after the hour.

Since many visitors are unfamiliar with Moroccan cuisine, it is often easy to secure same-day reservations at Restaurant Marrakesh or to dine without a reservation.

THE DOWN SIDE: Service is much too fast, and although tasty, the meats are sometimes dry.

RESERVATIONS: All visitors to Walt Disney World can make reservations up to sixty days in advance by calling Disney Dining Reservations (407 939-3463). Same-day reservations can be made through WorldKey Information Service at Epcot, at the restaurant itself, or by calling Same Day Reservations after 10 AM (939-3463).

RESTAURANTS

ROSE & CROWN DINING ROOM

WORLD SHOWCASE AT EPCOT

★★★   ★★★   ★★★
FOOD   **SERVICE**   **ATMOSPHERE**

REVIEWER'S COMMENTS: *Satisfying food and value for casual dining. The cozy decor and friendly servers make for a pleasant dining experience. This is a great place for a mid-afternoon break.*

FOOD: The Rose & Crown Dining Room serves traditional British fare, including cottage pie, prime rib, and London-style fish and chips wrapped traditionally in newspaper.

LOCATION: The Rose & Crown Dining Room is inside a pretty English countryside-style building and is the only full-service restaurant that sits on the edge of the World Showcase Lagoon. It is located directly across the promenade from the main pavilion at the United Kingdom.

DINING HOURS: Lunch from 11:30 AM, dinner from 4:30 PM until park closing.

AMBIENCE: The Rose & Crown Dining Room has a generous touch of cozy pub-style architecture, with wood-plank flooring, mahogany wainscoting, and shiny hardwood tables. Hanging milk glass chandeliers, white pressed-tin ceilings, and stained-glass room dividers provide atmospheric highlights. The Rose & Crown Pub, at the entrance to the restaurant, has a stand-up wraparound mahogany bar with etched-glass paneling. The restaurant and its adjoining terrace overlook the World Showcase Lagoon.

SAMPLE DINNER ENTREES: *London-Style Fish & Chips* (cod fried in beer batter, served with fried potatoes); *Cottage Pie* (sautéed ground beef with spices and brown sauce, topped with mashed potatoes and Cheddar cheese); *Prime Rib* (served with baked potato, Yorkshire pudding, and seasonal vegetables); *Chicken and Leek Pie with Cream Sauce* (chicken and vegetables baked in a pie crust, served with mashed potatoes). Traditional British pies are served with soup or salad at dinner.

HEALTHY-CHOICE ENTREES: *Vegetable Curry* (a mixture of seasonal vegetables sautéed with a spicy curry sauce, served with basmati rice).

LUNCH: The lunch menu differs slightly from dinner and includes a *Cold Chicken Curry Salad* (sliced grilled chicken over wild greens, mango, and grapes in a citrus-curry vinaigrette) and a *Traditional Ploughmans Lunch* (sliced turkey and ham served with English cheeses, a branson pickle, and fresh baked bread). At lunch, the British pies do not come with soup or salad, and prices are quite a bit lower than at dinner.

BEVERAGES: Bass ale, Guinness stout, and lager are served chilled or at room temperature. Wine and spirits are offered, including specialty drinks such as the *Shandy*, a concoction of Bass ale and ginger beer, and *Irish Coffee,* made with Irish whiskey, coffee, and whipped cream. Soft drinks, coffee, and tea are also available.

AVERAGE PRICE RANGE: Lunch entrees 💲💲, dinner entrees 💲💲💲.

FEATURES: The lively Rose & Crown Pub is a favorite spot among frequent visitors from around the world. It's a great place for cocktails and conversation in a convivial setting.

The Rose & Crown's unique location on the World Showcase Lagoon and its wide outdoor terrace provide excellent views. Diners who have reserved a late dinner and are seated at a terrace table can watch IllumiNations from here.

THE DOWN SIDE: The Rose & Crown fills its reservations quickly during peak seasons, so it can be difficult to secure same-day reservations.

RESERVATIONS: All visitors to Walt Disney World can make reservations up to sixty days in advance by calling Disney Dining Reservations (407 939-3463). Same-day reservations can be made through WorldKey Information Service at Epcot, at the restaurant itself, or by calling Same Day Reservations after 10 AM (939-3463).

RESTAURANTS

SAN ANGEL INN RESTAURANTE

WORLD SHOWCASE AT EPCOT

★★
FOOD

★★★
SERVICE

★★★★
ATMOSPHERE

REVIEWER'S COMMENTS: *This restaurant's enchanting setting creates a memorable dining experience. The seasonings are adjusted for American tastes, which can be disappointing. Go for the atmosphere.*

FOOD: San Angel Inn Restaurante features regional Mexican dishes. Seafood, beef, and chicken are prepared in savory sauces enhanced with chilies and a wealth of Mexican spices. *Plans are in the works to orient the menu toward Tex-Mex-style cooking. Look for a turnaround.*

LOCATION: San Angel Inn Restaurante can be found at the very back of the Mexico pavilion in the World Showcase at Epcot. The restaurant overlooks an indoor river.

DINING HOURS: Lunch from 11:30 AM, dinner from 4:30 PM until park closing.

AMBIENCE: After entering the Mexico pavilion, the only enclosed pavilion at the World Showcase, guests walk through a festive village setting at twilight to reach the restaurant at the edge of the river. A distant view of a smoking volcano and an exotic Mayan pyramid lend an aura of mystery to this romantic dining room. Red-sashed servers attend guests seated in rustic colonial-style tables and chairs. The restaurant is very dark and tables are lit with lanterns (bring a penlight to read the menus).

SAMPLE DINNER ENTREES: *Filete Ranchero* (grilled beef tenderloin served over corn tortillas, topped with ranchero sauce, poblano chili strips, Mexican cheese, and onions, and served with refried beans); *Enchiladas de Pollo* (corn tortillas filled with chicken, topped with tomato-chili sauce, cheese, sour cream, onions, and tomatillo sauce or mole sauce); *Mole Poblano* (chicken simmered with Mexican spices and a hint of chocolate, served with refried beans). Entrees are served with chips and salsa, Mexican rice, and a choice of soup or salad.

HEALTHY-CHOICE ENTREES: *Huachinango a la Veracruzana* (fillet of red snapper poached in wine with onions, tomatoes, and Mexican chilies); *Pescado Dorado* (fillet of mahi mahi marinated in chili sauce, grilled, and served with Mexican rice and vegetables).

LUNCH: Lunch and dinner menus are similar, although lunch does not include soup or salad, and prices are much lower than at dinner.

BEVERAGES: Mexican beers such as Bohemia, Dos Equis, and Tecate are served, as are wine and spirits. After-dinner drinks include *Mexican Coffee* (a mix of Kahlúa, tequila, and cream) and *Café de Olla* (coffee with cinnamon and brown sugar). Juice, soft drinks, mineral water, coffee, and tea are also available.

AVERAGE PRICE RANGE: Lunch entrees 💲💲, dinner entrees 💲💲💲.

FEATURES: San Angel Inn Restaurante has a small adjacent lounge where diners can unwind and enjoy a Margarita with chips and salsa as they wait for a table.

San Angel Inn Restaurante is regarded by many visitors as one of the most romantic dining spots at Walt Disney World.

THE DOWN SIDE: This restaurant is so dark inside that servers carry flashlights to help diners read the menu. Eventually, most eyes seem to adjust to the low light.

San Angel Inn's reservations fill quickly, so it is difficult to secure last-minute reservations.

RESERVATIONS: All visitors to Walt Disney World can make reservations up to sixty days in advance by calling Disney Dining Reservations (407 939-3463). Same-day reservations can be made through WorldKey Information Service at Epcot, at the restaurant itself, or by calling Same Day Reservations after 10 AM (939-3463).

RESTAURANTS

SCI-FI DINE-IN THEATER RESTAURANT

DISNEY-MGM STUDIOS

★★ **FOOD**   ★★★ **SERVICE**   ★★★ **ATMOSPHERE**

REVIEWER'S COMMENTS: *A one-of-a-kind drive-in-movie meal experience. The entrees are neither as unique nor as interesting as their descriptions. Service is quick and efficient.*

FOOD: The Sci-Fi Dine-In Theater Restaurant features hot entrees such as prime rib, oven-roasted turkey, barbecued chicken, broiled fresh fish, and pasta, along with a selection of hot and cold sandwiches and large salads.

LOCATION: The restaurant is located adjacent to the Chinese Theater at Disney-MGM Studios. Guests can find it by looking for the restaurant's sign, which looks like a movie theater marquee.

DINING HOURS: Lunch from 11 AM, dinner from 4 PM until park closing.

AMBIENCE: The waiting area for guests at the Sci-Fi Dine-In Theater Restaurant resembles the back of a typical movie set, with exposed wall studs and bolts. Guests enter the large dining area through what looks like a movie ticket booth and are seated at tables built into miniature fifties-style convertibles. It's always evening at the Sci-Fi Dine-In Theater Restaurant, with make-believe stars glistening in the sky against a moonlit Hollywood Hills mural. Cartoons and clips from campy science fiction films play continuously on the giant movie screen; sound is piped through drive-in speakers mounted on each car. All of the cars and most of the seats face forward. The restaurant's drive-in snack bar–style kitchen is located in the back of the fenced-in theater, where servers dressed as carhops pick up the food and deliver it to the cars.

SAMPLE DINNER ENTREES: *It Came From The Land* (penne pasta in basil sauce topped with sautéed chicken and house vegetables, served with a garlic bread stick); *Nothing But Beef* (chargrilled Porterhouse steak, served with seasonal vegetables and oven-roasted potatoes); *"No Wing" Chicken* (spaghetti tossed in tomato sauce topped with breaded chicken breasts and two cheese, served with a garlic bread stick). All dinner entrees come with choice of salad or soup.

HEALTHY-CHOICE ENTREES: *Fish Out Of Water* (catch of the day accompanied with seasonal vegetables); *Vegetables Again* (sautéed seasonal vegetables tossed in marinara or basil sauce over penne pasta, served with a garlic bread stick). Burgers made with vegetable patties are available on request.

LUNCH: The lunch menu has lower-priced sandwiches and salads, and fewer entrees.

BEVERAGES: Coffee, tea, juice, soft drinks, and milk shakes are served, as are beer, wine, and spirits. *Cosmic Coffee*, a popular house drink, is spiked with white crème de cacao and Malibu rum. The wine list includes California vintages.

AVERAGE PRICE RANGE: Lunch entrees 💲💲, dinner entrees 💲💲💲.

FEATURES: Dining here can be a memorable experience for those who enjoy unique dining environments.

THE DOWN SIDE: Watching science fiction and horror films while eating is literally out of this world, and the dining room is somewhat eerie and quiet because of the attention paid to the on-screen flicks. Not the place for conversation; except in a few cars, most guests face forward.

RESERVATIONS: All visitors to Walt Disney World can make reservations up to sixty days in advance by calling Disney Dining Reservations (407 939-3463). Same-day reservations can be made at Hollywood Junction (at the intersection of Hollywood and Sunset Boulevards) inside Disney-MGM Studios, at the restaurant itself, or by calling Same Day Reservations after 10 AM (939-3463).

RESTAURANTS

SPOODLES

DISNEY'S BOARDWALK

★★
FOOD

★★
SERVICE

★★
ATMOSPHERE

REVIEWER'S COMMENTS: *The food here sounds great, but doesn't really deliver, and service can be spotty. The pastas were quite good, and the breakfast dishes were just right.*

FOOD: Spoodles serves Mediterranean cuisine based on the Spanish tradition of tapas, an assortment of small mix-and-match dishes that arrive individually as soon as prepared, and are shared at the table. The menu draws from the foods of Greece, Spain, Italy, and North Africa, and includes salads, pasta, pizza, chicken, beef, lamb, and seafood. At lunch and dinner, guests can choose a full-sized entree accompanied with side dishes, or design their own epicurean feast by ordering an array of appetizer-sized tapas.

LOCATION: The restaurant is located on the Promenade at Disney's BoardWalk, and looks out over the midway and Crescent Lake.

DINING HOURS: Breakfast from 7 AM, lunch from 12 noon until 2 PM, dinner from 5 PM until 10 PM.

AMBIENCE: A large olive press, walls scattered with tapestries and mirrors, hanging Moorish light fixtures, and unmatched furniture and tableware combine to create a hodgepodge decor at this casual high-energy restaurant. The main dining area has an open kitchen and wood-fired brick ovens. Tapas (appetizers) are served family style for sharing, and each table has a stack of small colorful plates and a ceramic pot filled with utensils for diners to use.

SAMPLE DINNER ENTREES: *Seared Pepper Tuna* (served rare with shiitake mushrooms, green beans, watercress and shallot au jus); *Artichoke Ravioli* (with garlic, vino, chicken stock, cherry tomatoes, arugula, and Romano cheese); *Maltagliata* ("badly cut" pasta with scallops, green beans, potatoes, pesto, and fresh tomatoes); *Tagliata* (Tuscan beef chop with olive oil, lemon, arugula, rosemary, and cracked black pepper).

HEALTHY CHOICE ENTREES: *Oven-Roasted Organic Chicken Breast* (with carrots, turnips, spinach and yogurt raita); *Orecchiette Pasta* (with olive oil, garlic, hot peppers, cracked black pepper, broccoli rabe, and Romano cheese).

BREAKFAST AND LUNCH: The all-you-care-to-eat breakfast buffet includes scrambled eggs, bacon, sausage, ham, assorted baked goods, and house specials such as *Pizza del Sol* (pizza topped with fire-blasted egg, fresh asparagus, Italian sausage, and mozzarella) and *Oven-Roasted Vegetarian Rotolo* (fresh Moroccan flat bread wrap with roasted vegetables).

Lunch entrees are similar to those at dinner, although the lunch menu also features a selection of Mediterranean-style hot and cold sandwiches, such as the *Grilled Portobello Sandwich* (with roasted red peppers and goat cheese).

BEVERAGES: The Spoodles wine list features a large selection of Mediterranean wines. Coffee, tea, soft drinks, espresso, and cappuccino are offered, as are beer and spirits.

AVERAGE PRICE RANGE: Breakfast buffet 💲💲, lunch entrees 💲💲, dinner entrees 💲💲💲.

FEATURES: At the BoardWalk Pizza Window, visitors strolling on the Promenade can sample Spoodles' pizza-by-the-slice.

THE DOWN SIDE: Spoodles can get crowded, noisy, and confused during peak dining hours.

RESERVATIONS: All visitors to Walt Disney World can make reservations up to sixty days in advance by calling Disney Dining Reservations (407 939-3463). Same-day reservations can be made in person at the restaurant, by calling the restaurant (939-2380), or by calling Same Day Reservations after 10 AM (939-3463).

RESTAURANTS

TEMPURA KIKU

WORLD SHOWCASE AT EPCOT

★★★
FOOD

★★★★
SERVICE

★★★
ATMOSPHERE

REVIEWER'S COMMENTS: *Take a seat at the counter and dine on typical tempura-style cuisine. Chefs are happy to answer questions about the dishes, and the service is excellent and personal.*

FOOD: Tempura Kiku features seafood, chicken, beef, and vegetables dipped in a light batter, deep-fried, and served with a dipping sauce. While tempura is considered by many to be a traditional Japanese dish, it actually originated with the Portuguese, who opened Western trade with Japan. Sushi and sashimi are also available.

LOCATION: Tempura Kiku is located in the Japan pavilion in the World Showcase at Epcot. The restaurant is on the second floor, above the Mitsukoshi Department Store.

DINING HOURS: Lunch from 12 noon, dinner from 4:30 PM until park closing. The restaurant is closed between 3 and 4:30 PM.

AMBIENCE: This small dining room is just off the waiting room for Teppanyaki Dining, the larger restaurant next door. Warm gold-toned walls and traditional Japanese wood detailing contrast pleasantly with high-tech cookware in the center of this sushi bar–style restaurant. Guests are seated at the counter surrounding the cooking area, where they can enjoy the personal attention of their own white-hatted chef. Questions regarding ingredients and cooking styles are welcomed, and the chefs will gladly suggest meals for newcomers to Japanese cuisine.

SAMPLE DINNER ENTREES: *Tori* (deep-fried chicken strips with fresh vegetables); *Matsu* (deep-fried shrimp, scallop, lobster and fish with fresh vegetables); *Ume* (deep-fried shrimp and chicken strips with fresh vegetables); *Take* (deep-fried shrimp, skewered beef, and chicken strips with fresh vegetables); *Ebi* (deep-fried shrimp with fresh vegetables). Soup, salad, and steamed rice are included with the meal.

HEALTHY-CHOICE ENTREES: Most Japanese foods are low in fat, and several of the side dishes are excellent choices for light eaters. *Hiyayakko* (chilled tofu served with green onions and fresh ginger); *Sashimi* (assorted raw fish); *Nigiri-zushi* (assorted raw fish on seasoned rice; tuna rolled in rice and seaweed); *Gosho-maki* (crabmeat, avocado, cucumber, and smelt roe rolled in seasoned rice with sesame seeds and seaweed).

LUNCH: Lunch and dinner menus are similar, although lunch does not include a salad, and prices are much lower than at dinner.

BEVERAGES: Wine, plum wine, sake, and Kirin beer are available, as are soft drinks, coffee, and traditional Japanese green tea. The wine list offers a small but interesting selection of California wines. Specialty drinks offered from the full bar in the adjacent Matsu No Ma Lounge include the *Momonoki*, made with light rum, peach schnapps, and peaches; and the *Sakura*, made from light rum, white curaçao, strawberries, and lemon juice.

AVERAGE PRICE RANGE: Lunch entrees 💲💲, dinner entrees 💲💲💲💲.

FEATURES: Since no reservations are taken, Tempura Kiku is a good choice for visitors who do not have dining reservations, especially at off-peak hours. Guests waiting for seats can enjoy the view of the World Showcase Lagoon from the adjacent Matsu No Ma Lounge.

The counter service is fast and efficient, making Tempura Kiku an excellent choice for lunch. It's a particularly nice place for solo travelers.

THE DOWN SIDE: Groups of more than three will find it difficult to conduct conversations because of the counter seating.

RESERVATIONS: No reservations are taken at this restaurant. The counter seats twenty-five.

TEPPANYAKI DINING ROOM

THE WORLD SHOWCASE AT EPCOT

★★★
FOOD

★★★★
SERVICE

★★★
ATMOSPHERE

REVIEWER'S COMMENTS: *The preparation by skilled chefs wielding sharp knives is very entertaining. The Japanese dishes are Americanized, but the dipping sauces are tasty. Diners are seated communally.*

FOOD: Teppanyaki Dining Room offers meat, seafood, poultry, and vegetable dishes deftly prepared at the table by a white-hatted stir-fry chef. All the entrees are fresh, crisp, and sizzling.

LOCATION: Teppanyaki Dining Room is located in the Japan pavilion in the World Showcase at Epcot. Guests enter this second-floor restaurant from the wide staircase at the side of the Mitsukoshi Department Store.

DINING HOURS: Lunch from 12 noon, dinner from 4:30 PM until park closing.

AMBIENCE: Guests are seated in one of the five tatami-floored rooms that are separated by hand-painted shoji screens. Each dining room has four black-lacquered tables under gleaming copper venting hoods, and the sounds of traditional *koto* music can be heard in the background. The tables each accommodate eight guests around the *teppan* grill, where the stir-fry chef prepares the meals. Once the orders are placed, the entertainment begins. The chef dons a large white hat, pulls knives from a holster, and artfully slices, dices, seasons, and stir-fries each order. Those familiar with the Benihana of Tokyo restaurant chain will notice a similarity in the style of presentation.

SAMPLE DINNER ENTREES: *Ebi* (grilled shrimp); *Fujiyama* (grilled sirloin and shrimp); *Nihon-kai* (grilled shrimp, scallops, and lobster); *Beef Tenderloin* (grilled steak). All entrees are accompanied with a salad with ginger dressing, grilled fresh vegetables with udon noodles, and steamed rice.

HEALTHY-CHOICE ENTREES: *Tori* (grilled chicken), and *Kaibashira* (grilled scallops), both served with salad, vegetables, noodles, and rice. Chefs will prepare vegetarian meals on request.

LUNCH: Lunch and dinner menus are similar, although lunch does not include a salad, and prices are much lower, almost by half, than they are at dinner.

BEVERAGES: A fair selection of American wines is offered, as is plum wine from Japan. Kirin beer and hot sake are also available, as are cocktails from the full bar. A popular specialty drink, *Tachibana*, is concocted from light rum, orange curaçao, mandarin orange, and orange juice. Nonalcoholic blended drinks are also available, such as the *Momo*, which contains peaches, orange juice, and light cream. Soft drinks, green tea, and coffee are also served.

AVERAGE PRICE RANGE: Lunch entrees 💲💲, dinner entrees 💲💲💲.

FEATURES: With their speedy chopping and clever preparation and cooking techniques, the stir-fry chefs at Teppanyaki Dining Room provide memorable mealtime entertainment.

The nearby Matsu No Ma Lounge, overlooking the World Showcase Lagoon, makes waiting for tables a relaxing experience. After dinner guests can watch IllumiNations from the upper terrace in front of the lounge.

Solo travelers and parties of two can frequently get seating without reservations.

THE DOWN SIDE: The communal seating is not for visitors hoping for an intimate meal or private conversations.

RESERVATIONS: All visitors to Walt Disney World can make reservations up to sixty days in advance by calling Disney Dining Reservations (407 939-3463). Same-day reservations can be made through WorldKey Information Service at Epcot, at the restaurant itself, or by calling Same Day Reservations after 10 AM (939-3463).

RESTAURANTS

TONY'S TOWN SQUARE RESTAURANT

MAGIC KINGDOM

★★★	★★★	★★★
FOOD	SERVICE	ATMOSPHERE

REVIEWER'S COMMENTS: *The food is unexpectedly good, as is the service. In the late afternoon, Tony's is one of the more relaxing spots in the Magic Kingdom for a pleasant sit-down getaway.*

FOOD: Tony's Town Square Restaurant offers Italian-style hot entrees and pastas, as well as lighter dishes such as pizza, calzone, frittatas, pasta, and Italian sandwiches.

LOCATION: Tony's Town Square Restaurant is located at the beginning of Main Street on the right, across Town Square from City Hall, in the Magic Kingdom.

DINING HOURS: Open all day. Breakfast from one half hour before park opening, lunch from 12 noon, dinner from 4 PM until park closing.

AMBIENCE: The centerpiece at Tony's Town Square Restaurant is a large statue of the leading canine characters in *Lady and the Tramp*. Other reminders of the delightful Walt Disney film are placed throughout the restaurant. Guests may choose to dine in the main dining room, with its stained-glass windows, mahogany-beamed ceilings, and banquette seating, or in the sunny glassed-in patio, with its ceiling fans, terrazzo floors, and pleasant view of busy, bustling Town Square. Perky Italian music, playing in the background, enhances the setting.

SAMPLE DINNER ENTREES: *Country Penne* (penne pasta, Italian sausage, artichokes, broccoli, and cannellini beans tossed with Tony's house sauce and Asiago cheese); *Spaghetti "Speciale"* (traditional tomato sauce with meatballs served on a bed of spaghetti); *Chicken Florentine* (grilled whole chicken breast served with spinach cream sauce, polenta, and seasonal vegetables); *Steak Fiorentino* (sixteen-ounce T-bone steak rubbed with garlic and peppercorns and served with plum tomato, garlic, and penne pasta).

HEALTHY-CHOICE ENTREES: *Joe's Catch* (fresh catch of the day); *Turkey Piccata* (sliced turkey breast sautéed with mushrooms in a white wine butter sauce, served on a bed of linguine).

BREAKFAST AND LUNCH: The breakfast picks at Tony's include *Lady and the Tramp Waffles* and *Tony's Italian Toast*, as well as a selection of traditional egg dishes.

The lunch and dinner menu are similar. The lunch menu also offers pizza, salads, and Italian sandwiches. Prices are somewhat lower at lunch.

BEVERAGES: Coffee, tea, and soft drinks are served, along with espresso and cappuccino.

AVERAGE PRICE RANGE: Breakfast entrees $, lunch entrees $$, dinner entrees $$$.

FEATURES: On hot afternoons, Tony's is a great place to relax and cool off. After 2:30 PM, there are many empty tables and guests may order beverages or appetizers only, if they wish.

Tony's *Fried Calamari,* served with marinara and aioli sauces, is the most popular appetizer among frequent diners.

Patio diners facing Town Square can catch glimpses of afternoon parades from their table.

THE DOWN SIDE: Some readers thought that while the food and service at this restaurant were very good, the entrees seemed too expensive.

The restaurant is located in a very busy part of the Magic Kingdom and attracts many families, which can distract from a quiet lunch or dinner during busy hours.

RESERVATIONS: All visitors to Walt Disney World can make reservations up to sixty days in advance by calling Disney Dining Reservations (407 939-3463). Same-day reservations can be made at City Hall on Main Street, at the restaurant itself, or by calling Same Day Reservations after 10 AM (939-3463).

RESTAURANTS

WILDHORSE SALOON

PLEASURE ISLAND & DISNEY VILLAGE MARKETPLACE AT DOWNTOWN DISNEY

★★★   ★★★★   ★★★
FOOD   **SERVICE**   **ATMOSPHERE**

REVIEWER'S COMMENTS: *Generous portions of great barbecue dishes and a wide variety of grilled specialties. Servers are cheerful and efficient and the crowd is often lively and high-spirited.*

FOOD: The Wildhorse Saloon is known for its "unbridled barbecue," a tasty variety of smoked and grilled beef, chicken, and baby back pork ribs. Hamburgers, salads, and seafood entrees round out the menu.

LOCATION: The Wildhorse Saloon is located at Pleasure Island, across from the Fulton's Crab House riverboat. It faces Disney Village Marketplace, and can be entered from either side. It is under the same management as The Fireworks Factory restaurant that it replaced.

DINING HOURS: Dinner only from 5 PM until 12 AM, light menu served until 2 AM.

AMBIENCE: The Wildhorse Saloon's intriguing decor combines the country-western heritage of the Grand Ole Opry with modern highlights. Low lighting, neon accents, and a thirty-foot oil painting of stampeding horses set the tone. A whimsical upside-down sculpture of horses galloping across the ceiling embodies the eclectic spirit of the establishment. While waiting for tables, guests can browse the Wildhorse Saloon's western store for that Stetson they've been looking for. The latest country tunes and live performances can be heard from Wildhorse Saloon's dance hall, which boasts "It's as much fun as you can have with your boots on." The dance hall can be accessed from Pleasure Island, with separate admission.

SAMPLE DINNER ENTREES: *Grilled Pork Chops* (thick-cut pork chops grilled with maple syrup and Pommery mustard, served with warm red cabbage slaw and horseradish mashed potatoes); *Black Angus Ribeye Steak* (tender rib-eye steak seasoned and grilled, served with horseradish mashed potatoes and tomato-cucumber slaw); *Wildhorse Platter* (a half pound of Dungeness crab clusters, a one-third slab of baby back ribs, and a quarter mesquite-smoked chicken, served with sweet corn and baked potato); *Mesquite Smoked Chicken* (a fresh half chicken seasoned and slow roasted over mesquite wood, basted with barbecue sauce, and served with baked potato and seasonal vegetables).

HEALTHY-CHOICE ENTREES: *Oak-Roasted Salmon* (fresh seasonal salmon, oak plank–roasted and served with a roasted-tomato and corn relish and angel hair sweet potatoes); *Roasted Garlic Chicken* (fresh breast of chicken marinated and grilled, topped with fresh herbs and fire roasted, with a smoked-tomato reduction, mashed Gruyère sweet potatoes and seasonal vegetables). A vegetarian platter is available upon request.

BEVERAGES: Coffee, tea, and soft drinks are served, as well as domestic and imported beers and wine. The Wildhorse Saloon bar offers a number of unique specialty drinks.

AVERAGE PRICE RANGE: Dinner entrees 💲💲💲.

FEATURES: Along with neighboring Fulton's Crab House and Portobello Yacht Club, Wildhorse Saloon is one of the few late-night eating spots at Walt Disney World.

Desserts are home cooking at its best. Don't miss the *Tennessee Whiskey Bread Pudding*.

The Wildhorse Saloon's dance floor and bar at Walt Disney World is a replica of the one used for taping the line-dance show featured on The Nashville Network cable channel.

THE DOWN SIDE: Expect a lively but noisy meal in this rollicking dance-club setting.

RESERVATIONS: No reservations accepted. The restaurant has a smoking area.

RESTAURANTS

WOLFGANG PUCK CAFE

★★★★   ★★★   ★★★
FOOD   **SERVICE**   **ATMOSPHERE**

REVIEWER'S COMMENTS: *This is the place for delicious food in a trendy but tasteful setting. The food is consistently good, the servers knowledgable and interested. The salads sparkled and really hit the spot.*

FOOD: Wolfgang Puck, known for his uniquely innovative cuisine, brings a California flair to Disney's West Side with his eclectic and colorful cafe. Specialty pizzas, pastas, salads, chicken, beef, seafood, and sandwiches showcase his "no-boundaries" approach to cooking. Puck's daring cross-cultural style has strongly influenced many other talented young chefs.

LOCATION: The cafe is located in the heart of Disney's West Side, facing the waterfront of Buena Vista Lagoon.

DINING HOURS: Open all day from 11 AM.

AMBIENCE: The high-energy atmosphere was created by acclaimed designer/restaurateur (and Puck's wife and partner) Barbara Lazaroff. The Cafe's distinctive postmodern design features boldly colored mosaic tiles, dramatic custom lighting and furniture, handcrafted ceramics, and vintage serigraphs by Puck himself. The feeling is casual, bright, and fun — a whimsical setting in which to enjoy some truly creative cuisine.

SAMPLE DINNER ENTREES: *Chinois Chicken Salad* (with spicy honey mustard dressing); *Rotisserie Rosemary Chicken* (with choice of garlic mashed potatoes, French fries, or Caesar salad); *Spinach Papardelle* (with olive oil, sun-dried tomatoes, goat cheese, double-blanched garlic, and basil); *Wild Mushroom Tortellini* (freshly made pasta, with shiitake mushroom sauce, Parmesan, and herbs); signature wood-fired pizzas, such as *Vegetable Pizza* (prepared with basil pesto, mozzarella and fontina cheese, and organic tomatoes, and topped with roasted red peppers, mushrooms, fennel, eggplant, and caramelized onion); *Cafe Meat Loaf* (in port wine sauce, wrapped with bacon, with garlic mashed potatoes and an onion ring garnish).

HEALTHY-CHOICE ENTREES: *Seared Ahi Tuna* (with citrus ponzu sauce over Asian vegetables and crispy fried noodles); *Spaghettini with Tomato, Basil and Double-Blanched Garlic* (topped with Parmesan cheese); wood-fired *Cheeseless Pizza* (with marinated grilled vegetables, herbs, and garlic tomato sauce).

LUNCH: The menu is the same for lunch and dinner.

BEVERAGES: Coffee, peach ice tea, soft drinks, fresh-squeezed lemonade, espresso, and cappuccino are served. Wine, beer, and spirits are also available.

AVERAGE PRICE RANGE: 💲💲 to 💲💲💲.

FEATURES: For a romantic afternoon setting, ask for a window table or outdoor dining, offering lovely views of Buena Vista Lagoon.

The specialty house dessert, *Vanilla Crème Brûlée in a Chocolate Biscotti Cup,* by itself or coupled with a cappuccino, makes a tasty ending to a night out.

Between peak mealtimes, Wolfgang Puck Cafe is a good choice for a walk-in meal. There is also a take-out counter here, Wolfgang Puck Express, with sandwiches, rotisserie chicken, and pizzas and other snacks. It's great for an impromptu bite on the waterfront or for a flavorful meal to take back to your hotel room.

THE DOWN SIDE: During peak dining hours, waits for a table can be lengthy.

The fanciful tiling can make for a noisier-than-ideal environment. If you are seeking a quiet, conversational setting, come back another time when you can better enjoy the Cafe's pizzazz!

RESERVATIONS: No reservations; diners are seated on a first-come, first-served basis.

RESORT RESTAURANTS

The restaurants at the resorts offer some of the best dining experiences at Walt Disney World. Many resort coffee shops are also surprisingly good, and the prices are reasonable. The resort eating spots reviewed here were the most frequently mentioned in our Reader Survey, and the favorites among Walt Disney World regulars. The restaurants were rated for FOOD, SERVICE, and ATMOSPHERE as shown:

★★★★	★★★	★★	★
THE VERY BEST	BETTER THAN MOST	SATISFACTORY	OF LIMITED APPEAL

PRICES: Each restaurant review shows the AVERAGE PRICE RANGE for single entrees as follows:

$ – UNDER $8
$$ – $9 TO $14
$$$ – $15 TO $19
$$$$ – $20 TO $29
$$$$$ – OVER $30
$$$$$$ – OVER $40
♔ – OVER $50

All resort restaurants are open every day and serve beer, wine, and spirits. Some resort restaurants have smoking sections, which are noted in the reviews. Reservations should be made well in advance for busy holidays such as Thanksgiving and Easter. Kosher, vegan, and other special meals can be requested when reservations are made, or twenty-four hours in advance. ◆

ARTHUR'S 27

★★★★ FOOD   ★★★★ SERVICE   ★★★★ ATMOSPHERE

BUENA VISTA PALACE RESORT & SPA: The cuisine and service are elegant in this dramatically arranged dining room, and each spacious private booth has a breathtaking view. Entrees include Gulf shrimp, peppered tuna, and beef tenderloin. Four-, five-, and six-course prix-fixe meals paired with wines are also served. The extensive wine list features many excellent French vintages.

DINING HOURS: Dinner only from 6 until 10:30 PM. Evening dress is appropriate.

AVERAGE PRICE RANGE: Dinner entrees $$$$, prix-fixe dinners ♔.

RESERVATIONS: Reservations are required (407 827-3450). There is a smoking area.

ARTIST POINT

★★★★ FOOD   ★★★ SERVICE   ★★★★ ATMOSPHERE

DISNEY'S WILDERNESS LODGE: Artist Point serves a seasonal menu featuring Pacific Northwest specialties in a magnificent park lodge setting. Entrees include fresh salmon, crab, game, and meats, many of them smoked on the premises. The wines of Oregon and Washington are featured, along with a microbrewed house beer. A popular Character Breakfast buffet is served daily.

DINING HOURS: Character Breakfast from 7:30 until 11 AM, dinner from 5:30 until 10 PM.

AVERAGE PRICE RANGE: Character Breakfast buffet $$$, dinner entrees $$$.

RESERVATIONS: Reservations are recommended. Disney Dining Reservations (407 939-3463).

BASKERVILLES

★★★ FOOD   ★★ SERVICE   ★★★ ATMOSPHERE

GROSVENOR RESORT: Sherlock Holmes memorabilia is showcased in Baskervilles, where a popular all-you-care-to-eat prime rib dinner buffet is the draw for visitors. A traditional buffet-style breakfast is offered daily; lunch is a la carte and features salads, sandwiches, and light entrees.

DINING HOURS: Breakfast from 7 AM, lunch from 11:30 AM, dinner from 5 until 10 PM. (See also "MurderWatch Mystery Dinner Theatre," page 211, which appears here on weekends.)

AVERAGE PRICE RANGE: Breakfast buffet 💲💲, lunch entrees 💲, dinner buffet 💲💲💲.

RESERVATIONS: Dinner reservations accepted (407 827-6534). There is a smoking area.

BEACHES & CREAM

★★ FOOD   ★★ SERVICE   ★★ ATMOSPHERE

DISNEY'S BEACH CLUB RESORT: Facing the beach at Crescent Lake, this friendly and colorful restaurant serves up casual meals accompanied by ice cream sodas, shakes, and decadent desserts such as the Fudge Mud Slide. Breakfast is standard American fare, and the all-day menu offers Fenway Park hamburgers, hot dogs, and sandwiches. It's just a quick walk from the World Showcase.

DINING HOURS: Breakfast from 6:30 AM, all-day dining from 11 AM until 11 PM.

AVERAGE PRICE RANGE: Breakfast entrees 💲, lunch entrees 💲.

RESERVATIONS: No reservations. Diners are seated on a first-come, first-served basis.

BOATWRIGHT'S DINING HALL

★★ FOOD   ★★ SERVICE   ★★ ATMOSPHERE

DISNEY'S DIXIE LANDINGS RESORT: The hospitality and cooking of the Old South inspired the entrees at Boatwright's Dining Hall, including tin-pan breakfasts, seafood jambalaya, steaks, prime rib, and Cajun dishes. Also featured are family-style dinners of chicken, ribs, or catfish, and fresh-baked breads and pastries.

DINING HOURS: Breakfast from 7 until 11 AM, dinner from 5 until 10 PM.

AVERAGE PRICE RANGE: Breakfast entrees 💲, dinner entrees 💲💲 to 💲💲💲.

RESERVATIONS: Dinner reservations are recommended. Disney Dining Reservations (407 939-3463).

BONFAMILLE'S CAFÉ

★★★ FOOD   ★★★ SERVICE   ★★ ATMOSPHERE

DISNEY'S PORT ORLEANS RESORT: First conceived in the classic Disney movie *The Aristocats*, Bonfamille's Café is decorated to recall the atmosphere of New Orleans' French Quarter. Dinner entrees include steaks, seafood, and Creole specialties such as seafood jambalaya and spicy shrimp, crawfish, and oyster dishes. Breakfasts are lively and tend to be crowded.

DINING HOURS: Breakfast from 7 until 11:30 AM, dinner from 5 until 10 PM.

AVERAGE PRICE RANGE: Breakfast entrees 💲, dinner entrees 💲💲 to 💲💲💲.

RESERVATIONS: Dinner reservations are recommended. Disney Dining Reservations (407 939-3463).

RESTAURANTS

CALIFORNIA GRILL

★★ FOOD ★★★ SERVICE ★★★★ ATMOSPHERE

DISNEY'S CONTEMPORARY RESORT: Located on the resort's fifteenth floor, California Grill is a beautiful, modern dining room with a spectacular view and a theatrical open kitchen.

FOOD: Seafood, poultry, meat, pasta, pizza, and vegetable dishes are prepared in the busy open kitchen. Sushi is also available at a small sushi bar. The culinary focus is on fresh seasonal ingredients in inventive combinations. Portions are small, and guests often order several dishes to share.

SAMPLE DINNER ENTREES: *Peppered Yellowfin Tuna Seared Rare with Asian Black Bean Slaw and Red Chili Pepper Pesto; Mesquite Fired Veal T-Bone Steak with Chive-Ricotta Gnocchi.*

BEVERAGES: The wine list is extensive and features fine wines from California vineyards.

FEATURES: The restaurant has outdoor decks, and diners can view the Magic Kingdom fireworks. In the summer months when daylight lingers, there are panoramic views of Walt Disney World.

DINING HOURS: Dinner only from 5:30 until 10 PM.

REVIEWERS' COMMENTS: People either love this restaurant, or they don't. There were some standouts on the menu, like the ravioli, but overall, the dishes are often too fussy and overly complex. For a restaurant that features fresh ingredients, the beverage selection is very limited: no fresh juices or lemonade, just sodas and whatever comes out of a bar gun. Go for the view and the atmosphere. Order light, and stick to the simplest items on the menu.

AVERAGE PRICE RANGE: Dinner entrees 💲💲💲.

RESERVATIONS: Reservations are strongly recommended. Disney Dining Reservations (407 939-3463).

CAPE MAY CAFE

★★★ FOOD ★★ SERVICE ★★★ ATMOSPHERE

DISNEY'S BEACH CLUB RESORT: Beach scenes and striped umbrellas create a casual seashore atmosphere for Cape May Cafe's New England–style clambake. The buffet features fresh fish, mussels, oysters, and shrimp, as well as baby back ribs, chicken, soups, salads, and desserts. Lobster can be ordered separately. A popular Character Breakfast buffet is served here daily.

DINING HOURS: Character Breakfast from 7:30 until 11 AM, dinner from 5 until 9:30 PM.

AVERAGE PRICE RANGE: Character Breakfast buffet 💲💲💲, dinner buffet 💲💲💲💲.

RESERVATIONS: Reservations are recommended. Disney Dining Reservations (407 939-3463).

CHEF MICKEY'S

★★ FOOD ★★ SERVICE ★★★ ATMOSPHERE

DISNEY'S CONTEMPORARY RESORT: Clean lines and gleaming counters give Chef Mickey's an ultra-contemporary feel. The Character Breakfast buffet features traditional skillet dishes, breads, and fresh fruit. At the Character Dinner buffet, guests can choose from carved meats, chicken, seafood, pastas, and a salad bar. Mickey, Minnie, and their friends pop in to visit with diners.

DINING HOURS: Character Breakfast from 7:30 until 11:30 AM, Character Dinner from 5 until 9:30 PM.

AVERAGE PRICE RANGE: Character Breakfast buffet 💲💲, Character Dinner buffet 💲💲💲.

RESERVATIONS: Reservations are strongly recommended. Disney Dining Reservations (407 939-3463).

RESTAURANTS

MONEY $AVING PAGE

CONCOURSE STEAKHOUSE

★★★ FOOD   ★★ SERVICE   ★★ ATMOSPHERE

DISNEY'S CONTEMPORARY RESORT: Located in the hotel atrium, with the monorail passing overhead, the Concourse Steakhouse has a modern yet comfortable feel. Dinner features grilled steaks and prime rib along with poultry, seafood, and pasta dishes. The lunch menu includes California pizzas, salads, and sandwiches. Breakfast features Mickey waffles and traditional dishes.

DINING HOURS: Breakfast from 7 AM, lunch from 11:30 AM, dinner from 5:30 until 10 PM.

AVERAGE PRICE RANGE: Breakfast entrees 🍴, lunch entrees 🍴🍴, dinner entrees 🍴🍴🍴.

RESERVATIONS: Reservations are recommended. Disney Dining Reservations (407 939-3463).

CORAL CAFE

★★★ FOOD   ★★★ SERVICE   ★★ ATMOSPHERE

WALT DISNEY WORLD DOLPHIN: This family restaurant is a casual and colorful spot for breakfast and lunch. At dinner, it divides in two: On one side is a buffet of seafood, Italian, or American dishes; on the other side, a chic bistro serves seasonal Mediterranean cuisine with optional wine pairings. **SAVE** **Readers can use their $50 Dining Certificate here. (See "Vacation Discount Coupons!" page 272.)**

DINING HOURS: Breakfast from 6 AM, lunch from 11:30 AM, dinner from 5 until 11 PM.

AVERAGE PRICE RANGE: Breakfast buffet 🍴🍴, lunch entrees 🍴🍴, dinner buffet or entrees 🍴🍴🍴.

RESERVATIONS: Reservations are accepted (407 934-4000: hotel).

FINN'S GRILL

★★ FOOD   ★★ SERVICE   ★★ ATMOSPHERE

THE HILTON RESORT: Finn's Grill serves up seafood and steaks in a casual Key West atmosphere, with fanciful interpretations of fish fins adorning the walls. Fish entrees can be grilled, fried, blackened, steamed, sautéed, or broiled, and are served with a variety of sauces. Pasta, chicken, spareribs, and pizza are also served. The wine list has a good selection of California wines.

DINING HOURS: Dinner only from 5:30 until 11 PM.

AVERAGE PRICE RANGE: Dinner entrees 🍴🍴🍴.

RESERVATIONS: Reservations are accepted (407 827-3838). There is a smoking area.

GARDEN GROVE CAFE

★★★ FOOD   ★★★ SERVICE   ★★ ATMOSPHERE

WALT DISNEY WORLD SWAN: This restaurant resembles an airy garden atrium by day and transforms into Gulliver's Grill at night (see page 207). Breakfast is served a la carte or buffet. The lunch menu **SAVE** offers light entrees and sandwiches, including a Blackened Grouper Sandwich. **Readers can use their $50 Dining Certificate at Garden Grove Cafe. (See "Vacation Discount Coupons!" page 272.)**

DINING HOURS: Breakfast from 6:30 AM, lunch from 11:30 AM until 2 PM.

AVERAGE PRICE RANGE: Breakfast buffet 🍴🍴, entrees 🍴, lunch entrees 🍴🍴.

RESERVATIONS: Reservations are suggested (407 934-4000: hotel).

RESTAURANTS

GRAND FLORIDIAN CAFE

★★★ FOOD ★★★ SERVICE ★★ ATMOSPHERE

DISNEY'S GRAND FLORIDIAN BEACH RESORT: The Grand Floridian Cafe is a spacious light-filled family restaurant with tall arched windows that overlook the hotel's pool and courtyard. The menu offers seafood, meats, and poultry prepared with a Florida-style flair. Lunch features a selection of specialty sandwiches. Traditional breakfasts are also served.

DINING HOURS: Breakfast from 7 AM, all-day dining from noon until 11 PM.

AVERAGE PRICE RANGE: Breakfast entrees $, lunch entrees $$, dinner entrees $$ to $$$.

RESERVATIONS: Reservations are recommended. Disney Dining Reservations (407 939-3463).

HARRY'S SAFARI BAR & GRILLE

★★★ FOOD ★★★★ SERVICE ★★★ ATMOSPHERE

WALT DISNEY WORLD DOLPHIN: Tropical murals and tiger-stripe carpets impart an international jungle-explorer flavor to the civilized dining experience here. Entrees feature beef, chicken, and seafood grilled to order. A "yard of beer" is also available for the intrepid bon vivant. **Readers can use their $50 Dining Certificate at Harry's. (See "Vacation Discount Coupons!" page 272.)**

$AVE

DINING HOURS: Sunday Character Brunch from 8 AM until 1 PM, dinner from 6 until 11 PM.

AVERAGE PRICE RANGE: Sunday Character Brunch $$$, dinner entrees $$$$.

RESERVATIONS: Reservations are recommended (407 934-4000: hotel). There is a smoking area.

JUAN & ONLY'S

★★★★ FOOD ★★★ SERVICE ★★★★ ATMOSPHERE

WALT DISNEY WORLD DOLPHIN: Juan & Only's features traditional Mexican entrees such as enchiladas, burritos, and fajitas, as well as seafood, poultry, and meat dishes prepared in the regional cooking styles of Mexico. Entrees are served with rice and beans. **Readers can use their $50 Dining Certificate at Juan & Only's. (See "Vacation Discount Coupons!" page 272.)**

$AVE

DINING HOURS: Dinner only from 6 until 11 PM.

AVERAGE PRICE RANGE: Dinner entrees $$$.

RESERVATIONS: Reservations are recommended (407 934-4000: hotel). There is a smoking area.

NARCOOSSEE'S

★★★★ FOOD ★★★★ SERVICE ★★★ ATMOSPHERE

DISNEY'S GRAND FLORIDIAN BEACH RESORT: This restaurant overlooks Seven Seas Lagoon with a view of the Magic Kingdom. Narcoossee's chefs have recently introduced a creative menu featuring New Floridian cuisine, including Caicos baby conch, rare tuna filet, and roasted grouper with crabmeat crust. Entrees also incorporate chicken, pasta, and beef; lobster is a house specialty.

DINING HOURS: Lunch from 11:30 AM, dinner from 5 until 10 PM.

AVERAGE PRICE RANGE: Lunch entrees $$$, dinner entrees $$$$.

RESERVATIONS: Reservations are strongly recommended. Disney Dining Reservations (407 939-3463).

RESTAURANTS

1900 PARK FARE

★★ FOOD ★★ SERVICE ★★★ ATMOSPHERE

DISNEY'S GRAND FLORIDIAN BEACH RESORT: A turn-of-the-century band organ takes center stage in this buffet restaurant. At breakfast, guests can choose from traditional skillet dishes, pastries, and fruit, while the dinner buffet includes chicken, seafood, salads, and pizza. Disney Character appearances and periodic bursts from the organ can make for an eventful dining experience.

DINING HOURS: Breakfast buffet from 7:30 AM, dinner buffet from 5:30 until 9 PM.

AVERAGE PRICE RANGE: Breakfast buffet 💲💲💲, dinner buffet 💲💲💲💲.

RESERVATIONS: Reservations are recommended. Disney Dining Reservations (407 939-3463).

'OHANA

★★★ FOOD ★★★ SERVICE ★★★ ATMOSPHERE

DISNEY'S POLYNESIAN RESORT: Giant tikis, wood and stone floors, a thatched ceiling, and Polynesian artifacts enhance 'Ohana's South Pacific islands atmosphere. This is great spot for family or friends to gather for a sociable and entertaining island-style meal. The sixteen-foot open-pit grill flames dramatically as the dinner meats are barbecued on three-foot-long skewers.

SAMPLE DINNER MENU: Much of this all-you-care-to-eat dinner is served family style on large lazy susans filled with *Polynesian Beef Dim Sum, Napa Cabbage Slaw, Sticky Rice with Bok Choy Vegetables, Green Salad with Roasted Sesame Dressing, Marinated Cucumber Salad,* and *Toasted Flat Bread with Rosemary Seasoning.* The grilled meats include *Hawaiian Chicken, Cajun Jumbo Shrimp, Spiced Turkey, Mesquite Beef Tenderloin,* and *Fresh Seafood of the Day.*

BEVERAGES: Soft drinks, coffee, beer, wine, and spirits are available, including frozen tropical drinks from the adjacent Tambu Lounge. The wine list is very limited but includes 'Ohana's own Johannesburg Riesling, which is an excellent accompaniment to the flavors of the dishes.

DINING HOURS: Character Breakfast from 7:30 until 11 AM, dinner from 5 until 10 PM.

AVERAGE PRICE RANGE: Character Breakfast 💲💲, prix-fixe dinner 💲💲💲💲.

REVIEWERS' COMMENTS: Hearty, meat oriented dishes. The menu changes from time to time as the restaurant continues to evolve its cuisine. If you are dining about 9 PM, request a window table for views of the Electrical Water Pageant and the Magic Kingdom fireworks show.

RESERVATIONS: Reservations are strongly recommended. Disney Dining Reservations (407 939-3463).

OLIVIA'S CAFE

★★ FOOD ★★★ SERVICE ★★ ATMOSPHERE

DISNEY'S OLD KEY WEST RESORT: With its light and airy dining room and outdoor veranda, Olivia's evokes the laid-back ambience of Key West. Prime rib is featured at dinner, along with fresh fish, poultry, pasta, and meat dishes prepared in the culinary style of the Florida Keys. The lunch menu is similar to dinner, and also includes a number of hot and cold sandwiches.

DINING HOURS: Breakfast from 7:30 AM, lunch from noon, dinner from 5 until 10 PM.

AVERAGE PRICE RANGE: Breakfast entrees 💲, lunch entrees 💲, dinner entrees 💲💲 to 💲💲💲.

RESERVATIONS: Reservations are accepted. Disney Dining Reservations (407 939-3463).

THE OUTBACK

★★★ FOOD   ★★★ SERVICE   ★★★ ATMOSPHERE

BUENA VISTA PALACE RESORT & SPA: Guests dine at the base of a waterfall that cascades down three stories of rough-hewn rock into a pond sparkling with swimming koi. The Outback features the open-pit flame-grilled cooking style of Australia's bush country. Entrees include steaks, barbecued baby back ribs, poultry, seafood, fresh fish, and more exotic fare, such as kangaroo and alligator.

DINING HOURS: Dinner only from 5:30 until 11 PM.

AVERAGE PRICE RANGE: Dinner entrees 💲💲💲💲.

RESERVATIONS: Reservations are recommended (407 827-3430). There is a smoking area.

PALIO

★★★★ FOOD   ★★★★ SERVICE   ★★★ ATMOSPHERE

WALT DISNEY WORLD SWAN: Palio serves excellent Italian cuisine in its festive and romantic dining room. Entrees include seafood, chicken, pasta, and veal dishes, as well as pizzas baked in the wood-burning oven. Strolling musicians provide pleasant tableside entertainment. **Readers can use their $50 Dining Certificate at Palio. (See "Vacation Discount Coupons!" page 272.)**

DINING HOURS: Dinner only from 6 until 11 PM.

AVERAGE PRICE RANGE: Dinner entrees 💲💲💲💲.

RESERVATIONS: Reservations are recommended (407 934-3000: hotel). There is a smoking area.

SAVE

SEASONS

★★★ FOOD   ★★ SERVICE   ★★ ATMOSPHERE

DISNEY INSTITUTE: The large relaxing dining room at Seasons offers a lovely view of the Disney Village Waterways. The menu, which features a different food theme every night, is influenced by New American and international cuisines, and is sometimes created by the Disney Institute's visiting chefs. Dinner can also be reserved along with an evening performance at the Disney Institute.

DINING HOURS: Breakfast from 7 AM, lunch from 11:30 AM, dinner from 5:30 until 10 PM.

AVERAGE PRICE RANGE: Breakfast entrees 💲💲, lunch entrees 💲💲, dinner entrees 💲💲💲.

RESERVATIONS: Dinner reservations are recommended. Disney Dining Reservations (407 939-3463).

VICTORIA & ALBERT'S

★★★★ FOOD   ★★★ SERVICE   ★★★★ ATMOSPHERE

DISNEY'S GRAND FLORIDIAN BEACH RESORT: Victoria & Albert's preserves the grand dining tradition in a formal, elegant setting. The seven-course prix-fixe menu (with optional wine pairings) changes nightly and reflects seasonal foods. The exquisitely prepared main entrees are bracketed by appetizers, soup, salad, and dessert. An ideal choice for special occasions.

DINING HOURS: Victoria & Albert's has two dinner seatings, 6 PM and 9 PM. Evening dress required.

AVERAGE PRICE RANGE: Prix-fixe dinner 👑 (add about $30 additional for wine pairings).

RESERVATIONS: Advance reservations are required. Disney Dining Reservations (407 939-3463).

RESTAURANTS

WHISPERING CANYON CAFE

★★ FOOD ★★★ SERVICE ★★ ATMOSPHERE

DISNEY'S WILDERNESS LODGE: A boisterous atmosphere, rustic wooden tables, and comfortable chairs make guests feel welcome at this casual, friendly restaurant. Skillet breakfasts are all-you-care-to-eat. Lunches include skillets, as well as sandwiches and salads. A campfire cookout–themed dinner is featured, with all-you-care-to-eat barbecued beef, chicken, spareribs, sausage, and smoked turkey.

DINING HOURS: Breakfast from 7 AM, lunch from 11:30 AM, dinner from 5 until 10 PM.

AVERAGE PRICE RANGE: Breakfast skillets $, lunch entrees $$, dinner entrees $$$.

RESERVATIONS: Reservations are suggested. Disney Dining Reservations (407 939-3463).

YACHT CLUB GALLEY

★★★ FOOD ★★★ SERVICE ★★ ATMOSPHERE

DISNEY'S YACHT CLUB RESORT: Sailors' knots and models of yesteryear's racing boats accent this family restaurant with unexpectedly good food. Breakfasts are a la carte or buffet. Sandwiches, including a tasty grilled fish sandwiche, are offered at lunch. Dinner entrees include the Landlubber's T-Bone, as well as seafood, barbecued ribs, pasta, and poultry.

DINING HOURS: Breakfast from 7 AM, lunch from 11:30 AM, dinner from 5 until 10:30 PM.

AVERAGE PRICE RANGE: Breakfast $$, lunch $$, dinner entrees $$$.

RESERVATIONS: Reservations are suggested. Disney Dining Reservations (407 939-3463).

YACHTSMAN STEAKHOUSE

★★★★ FOOD ★★★ SERVICE ★★★ ATMOSPHERE

DISNEY'S YACHT CLUB RESORT: Polished wood-plank floors, private booths, and secluded dining areas provide a cozy, clubby atmosphere for steak-lovers. The entrees prepared in the glassed-in kitchen include prime cuts of beef, lamb, and pork. A limited selection of chicken and seafood dishes is also available. The restaurant offers an impressive list of wines and imported beers.

DINING HOURS: Dinner only from 5:30 until 10 PM.

AVERAGE PRICE RANGE: Dinner entrees $$$$.

RESERVATIONS: Reservations are required. Disney Dining Reservations (407 939-3463).

LATE-NIGHT DINING

Planet Hollywood • *Pleasure Island* • **2 AM**
ESPN Club • *Disney's BoardWalk* • **2 AM**
Official All Star Cafe • *Disney Sports Complex* • **1 AM**
Portobello Yacht Club • *Pleasure Island* • **Midnight**
Fulton's Crab House • *Pleasure Island* • **Midnight**
Big River Grille • *Disney's BoardWalk* • **Midnight**
Watercress Cafe • *Buena Vista Palace* • **Midnight**
Ristorante County Fair • *Hilton* • **Midnight**
Courtyard Cafe • *Courtyard by Marriott* • **Midnight**
Parakeet Cafe • *Travelodge* • **Midnight**

OPEN ALL NIGHT

Hunger isn't always predictable for travelers. Here are some eateries and food stores that are open 24 hours:

Cap'n Cook's • *Polynesian Resort*
Gasparilla Grill • *Grand Floridian Beach Resort*
Roaring Forks • *Wilderness Lodge*
Tubbi's Buffeteria • *Dolphin*
Crumpet's Cafe • *Grosvenor*

GROCERIES

Exxon Tiger Mart • *Pleasure Island*
Exxon Tiger Mart • *Disney's BoardWalk*
Gooding's Supermarket • *Crossroads Shopping Center*

RESTAURANTS

DINING EVENTS

Walt Disney World continues to expand its lineup of both sophisticated evening entertainment for adults and special entertainment events for the whole family. A recent addition, Disney's BoardWalk, is both an attraction and resort complex, complete with dance, music, and sports clubs, interesting restaurants, and even an on-site microbrewery. At Downtown Disney, the premier nightclubs can still be found on Pleasure Island, but Disney's West Side, next door, is becoming *the* place for entertainment dining and live concerts with the opening of celebrity-owned and -operated restaurants, supper clubs, and concert halls. Walt Disney World's classic dinner shows, such as the Polynesian Luau, are ever popular with both first-time visitors and regulars alike; and Character Dining, which takes place daily in restaurants throughout Walt Disney World, appeals to visitors of all ages. Starting on page 208, the premier dinner shows and dining events are rated for ENTERTAINMENT, FOOD, SERVICE, and ATMOSPHERE as follows:

★★★★ THE VERY BEST   ★★★ REALLY WORTHWHILE   ★★ SATISFACTORY   ★ DISAPPOINTING

CHARACTER MEALS

Over the past few years, dining with Disney Characters has become an increasing popular vacation "must." Character Meals are scheduled daily at restaurants in the theme parks and at the resorts, and are frequented both by young families and a large number of young-at-heart adults. During the meals, Disney Characters act as hosts and drop by tables to greet diners, sign autographs, and have their pictures taken with guests. Character Meals are usually all-you-care-to-eat events, and prices range between $12 and $24 for adults, and $8 and $15 for children, including beverages. Reservations can and should be made up to sixty days in advance through Disney Dining Reservations (407 939-3463). From time to time, new Character Meals are added and others disappear; those listed below are currently among the most popular:

FULTON'S CRAB HOUSE AT PLEASURE ISLAND

CHARACTER BREAKFAST: Mickey and his shipmates are on hand to welcome guests aboard Fulton's elegant Mississippi riverboat. Guests dine on cherrywood-smoked salmon, French toast, sausage, scrambled eggs, breakfast potatoes, and fresh fruit. (See also "Fulton's Crab House," page 172.)

SCHEDULE: Character Breakfasts are served daily. There are two seatings: 8 AM and 10 AM.

THE GARDEN GRILL RESTAURANT AT EPCOT

ALL DAY CHARACTER DINING: Every meal is a Character experience at this rotating restaurant. Hosted by Farmer Mickey, Minnie, and Chip 'N Dale, the familiar dishes are influenced by home cooking, and include smoked ham, eggs, and grits at breakfast, and steak, chicken, seafood, and mashed potatoes and gravy at dinner. (See also "The Garden Grill Restaurant," page 173.)

SCHEDULE: Character Meals are served all day from before park opening until park closing.

CINDERELLA'S ROYAL TABLE AT THE MAGIC KINGDOM

CHARACTER BREAKFAST: By far the most popular theme park Character Meal, the Once Upon a Time breakfast is highlighted with appearances from Cinderella, Fairy Godmother, Snow White, Belle, and Peter Pan. Guests feast on eggs, potato casserole, fruit, breakfast meats, and banana French toast. (See also "Cinderella's Royal Table," page 166.)

SCHEDULE: Character Breakfasts are served daily from before park opening until 10 AM.

LIBERTY TREE TAVERN AT THE MAGIC KINGDOM

CHARACTER DINNER: Housed within an eighteenth-century dining hall at Liberty Square, Minnie, Pluto, Goofy, and friends host a colonial-style buffet dinner with an Early American menu, including flank steak, honey-mustard ham, vegetables, salads, and roast turkey with all the trimmings. A special children's menu is available. (See also "Liberty Tree Tavern," page 177.)

SCHEDULE: Character Dinners are served daily from 4 PM until park closing.

ARTIST POINT AT DISNEY'S WILDERNESS LODGE

CHARACTER BREAKFAST: Pocohantas, John Smith, Meeko, Governor Radcliffe, and sometimes Goofy join guests in the rustic dining room at Artist Point. Guests are served stuffed French toast, all-grain pancakes, breakfast meats, eggs, and breakfast potatoes. (See also "Artist Point," page 197.)

SCHEDULE: Character Breakfasts are served daily from 7:30 until 11:30 AM.

CAPE MAY CAFE AT DISNEY'S BEACH CLUB RESORT

CHARACTER BREAKFAST: Admiral Goofy, Pluto, and Chip 'N Dale visit with guests as they serve themselves from the large buffet. Biscuits with sausage gravy, cheese blintzes, meats, fruit, and bread pudding are among the beach-party-inspired dishes offered. (See also "Cape May Cafe," page 199.)

SCHEDULE: Character Breakfasts are served daily from 7:30 until 11 AM.

CHEF MICKEY'S AT DISNEY'S CONTEMPORARY RESORT

CHARACTER BREAKFAST AND DINNER: The large selection of dishes at the 110-foot-long buffet and the appearance of Mickey and friends make this one of the two most popular Character Meals. Mickey Waffles are the specialty among familiar breakfast items, and dinner includes carved meats, peel-and-eat shrimp, and a make-your-own-sundae bar. (See also "Chef Mickey's," page 199.)

SCHEDULE: Character Breakfasts are served daily from 7:30 until 11:30 AM; Character Dinners are served daily from 5 until 9:30 PM.

1900 PARK FARE AT DISNEY'S GRAND FLORIDIAN BEACH RESORT

CHARACTER BREAKFAST AND DINNER: Mary Poppins and friends greet guests at this popular Character Breakfast, and Mickey and Minnie handle the late shift at dinner. Both meals feature a hearty, ample buffet, including French toast and omelettes at breakfast, and roasted meats, seafood, and vegetable dishes in the evening. Children can serve themselves from their own buffet. (See also "1900 Park Fare," page 202.)

SCHEDULE: Character Breakfasts are served daily from 7:30 until 11:30 AM; Character Dinners are served from 5 until 9 PM.

GULLIVER'S GRILL AT WALT DISNEY WORLD SWAN

CHARACTER DINNER AND MAGIC SHOW: Gulliver's Grill offers the upscale version of the typ[...] Character Meal in a tree-filled atrium with a trickling fountain and high, domed ceiling. The restaurant['s] theme is based on the story of Gulliver's Travels, which is carried out with odd-sized utensils and off-beat menu names. On Monday, Wednesday, Thursday, and Friday, Tigger, Rafiki, Goofy, Timon, and Winnie the Pooh mingle with guests, signing autographs and posing for pictures. (Who would have guessed these guys hung out together?) The entertainment turns intriguing on Tuesday and Saturday, with interactive tableside magic and awe-inspiring illusions performed by a gifted magician.

FOOD: Steak and seafood are the specialties here, but guests will also find a good selection of lamb, chicken, and pasta. A four-course Chef's Choice meal is offered daily, which includes appetizer or soup, Caesar salad, choice of selected entrees, and dessert from the open pastry kitchen.

SAMPLE DINNER ENTREES: *Crabbrkrammd Brobdingnag Fleek* (baked jumbo shrimp stuffed with crab in a garlic butter sauce, served with rice pilaf); *Splacknuck Noycentindir* (tender eight-ounce cut of filet mignon, served with grilled vegetables, salsa, and béarnaise sauce). All entrees are correctly spelled and come with Caesar salad, fresh Italian bread, and choice of baked potato or rice pilaf.

DINING HOURS: Character Dinner or Magic Show Dinner from 5:30 until 10 PM.

REVIEWERS' COMMENT: Great food and a lot of it, plus superb service. The skillfully prepared entrees are arguably the best of any Character Meals at Walt Disney World. The Caeser salad is a standout. Desserts are created on the spot in the glassed-in kitchen and should not be missed.

PRICE: Entrees range from $15 to $28; about $25 for the Chef's Choice meal. **Readers can use their $50 Dining Certificate at Gulliver's Grill. (See "Vacation Discount Coupons!" page 272.)**

TIPS: Gulliver's Grill is within walking distance of most Epcot resorts and a quick boatride from either Epcot or Disney-MGM Studios. Cruise in for dinner after a park tour and treat yourself to a cab home.

RESERVATIONS: Reserve seven days in advance by calling the Swan (407 934-4000).

SOUNDSTAGE RESTAURANT AT DISNEY-MGM STUDIOS

CHARACTER BREAKFAST AND LUNCH: This spacious restaurant, giving a credible impression of a studio soundstage, is the site of Disney-MGM's very popular Character Meal. Amidst sets from recent Disney animated features and soundstage production props, Disney' most talented and glamorous characters, including as Aladdin, Belle, Esmeralda, and Quasimodo, drop by to charm guests.

FOOD: The Soundstage Restaurant features all-you-care-to-eat buffets at both breakfast and lunch.

SAMPLE BREAKFAST ITEMS: Breakfast dishes include scrambled eggs, omelets, sausage, French toast, waffles, fruit crepes, home-fried potatoes, biscuits and gravy, hot and cold cereals, and fresh fruit.

SAMPLE LUNCH ITEMS: Lunch features baked herbed chicken, baked fish, beef stew, rice pilaf, pasta salads, potatoes, and vegetables. There's also a soup, salad, and fresh fruit bar, as well as a dessert bar.

DINING HOURS: Character Breakfast from park opening until 11 AM, Character Lunch until 4:30 PM.

REVIEWERS' COMMENTS: The very broad selection of high-quality dishes ensures that there will be something for everyone. The fantastic array of desserts is a real treat.

PRICE: Character Breakfast costs about $16 for adults, and about $7 for children; Character Lunch costs about $20 for adults, and about $10 for children. All meals include a refillable beverage.

RESERVATIONS: Reserve up to sixty days in advance through Disney Dining (407 939-3463). ◆

OOP-DEE-DOO MUSICAL REVUE

FORT WILDERNESS RESORT AND CAMPGROUND

ERTAINMENT   *(Very hokey material executed by very talented performers.)*

(Ample portions, but the quality frequently varies from adequate to disappointing.)

★   SERVICE   *(Polite, fast, friendly, and professional.)*

★ ★   ATMOSPHERE   *(Boisterous. Kids have a great time here, and many adults are great fans.)*

LOCATION: The Hoop-Dee-Doo Musical Revue is held nightly at Pioneer Hall, in the heart of 700-acre Fort Wilderness Resort and Campground. (See "Fort Wilderness & River Country," page 107.)

ENTERTAINMENT: This Wild West hoedown is performed nightly by the enthusiastic Pioneer Hall Players. The dinner show starts with a banjo and piano serenade, which is followed by a song-and-dance vaudeville performance that relies heavily on broad humor, sight gags, pratfalls, puns, and lots of audience participation. The colorfully costumed performers interact humorously with the audience, and guests with birthdays or anniversaries are singled out for special attention, as are newlyweds.

DINING ROOM: The large pine-log lodge has two levels: a ground floor with a stage at one end, and a balcony supported by large rock pillars. The room is lit with hanging wagon-wheel fixtures and decorated in a rustic wilderness motif with stuffed animal heads, snowshoes, and antlers.

SAMPLE MENU: The family-style all-you-care-to-eat dinner includes *Appetizer* (chips and salsa, and fresh-baked bread); *Salad* (lettuce, slices of cucumber, carrot, and cabbage) with *Vinaigrette Dressing; Pieces of Golden-Brown Country Fried Chicken; Barbecued Ribs* (tasty short ribs cooked in barbecue sauce); *Spicy Corn* or *Corn-Right-on-the-Cob; Beans;* and *Mom's Homemade Strawberry Shortcake*. The menu may vary. Kosher, vegetarian, or other special meals must be ordered at least twenty-four hours in advance through the Hoop-Dee-Doo Musical Revue Office (407 824-2803).

BEVERAGES: Soft drinks, milk, coffee, iced tea, beer, and wine are included with the meal. Cocktails are not included, but can be ordered by servers from Crockett's Tavern next door.

PRICE: The ticket price is about $42 ($22 for children). Taxes and gratuities are not included in the ticket price, and servers expect a 15 to 20 percent tip.

SHOW TIMES: Shows are at 5 PM, 7:15 PM, and 9:30 PM. Families frequent the 5 PM show.

MAKING RESERVATIONS: Reservations for the Hoop-Dee-Doo Musical Revue should be made as far in advance as possible. All Walt Disney World visitors may book dinner shows up to two years in advance by calling Disney Dining Reservations (407 939-3463). For same-day reservations, call the Hoop-Dee-Doo Musical Revue Office (407 824-2803). Tickets can be purchased in advance at Guest Services in any Walt Disney World resort or at Pioneer Hall at least one hour before show time. All visitors should arrive at least one half hour before show time, or their reservation may be cancelled.

TIPS: Pioneer Hall is not easy to find at night, and it takes a lot longer than you think it will to get there. Busing from another resort can be very difficult; you must change buses. There is no parking inside Fort Wilderness. If you are driving, you can park at the Fort Wilderness Guest Parking Lot and catch the shuttle from there to Pioneer Hall. Shuttle buses also run from Disney's Wilderness Lodge. There are ferries to Fort Wilderness from the Magic Kingdom and the Contemporary resort.

NOTE: There is no smoking permitted at the Hoop-Dee-Doo Musical Revue. Dress is casual. ◆

HOUSE OF BLUES

DISNEY'S WEST SIDE AT DOWNTOWN DISNEY

★★★★ **ENTERTAINMENT** *(For big-name acts, this state-of-the-art club is where you want to be.)*

★★★ **FOOD** *(Quality food, creatively prepared. The brunch has some especially delicious dishes.)*

★★★ **SERVICE** *(Fast and friendly. Servers are very knowledgeable about the various performers.)*

★★★ **ATMOSPHERE** *(Unique and interesting dining and a concert hall made for music-lovers.)*

LOCATION: House of Blues, with a separate restaurant and concert hall, is located at Disney's West Side, overlooking Buena Vista Lagoon.

MUSIC HALL: Live performances by top-rated musicians are the norm at this combination restaurant and concert hall resembling an old Mississippi juke joint. Blues is the inspiration for many American musical forms, and the evening performances in this acoustically advanced music hall showcase all styles, including rhythm and blues, reggae, country, gospel, pop, jazz, alternative, and of course, the blues. During the day, guests at the all-you-care-to-eat Gospel Brunches dine on soul food as they experience a rousing spiritual performed by the area's most talented gospel singers. Guests here can extend their House of Blues experience to several hours — first catching a bite to eat in the restaurant, and afterward taking in a live concert in the music hall.

RESTAURANT: The House of Blues restaurant, adjacent to the music hall, combines the warmth of an antiquated southern home with a modern twist — each booth has access to the World Wide Web. A medley of bold colors, textures, original African-American folk art (the "visual blues"), and scattered musical instruments create a unique atmosphere. Video and audio monitors situated throughout the dining room show clips of blues greats, and a talented blues band entertains diners during meals.

SAMPLE MENU: The House of Blues serves Mississippi Delta cuisine that incorporates fresh seasonal ingredients. Their signature dish is ***Jambalaya*** (shrimp, scallops, tender chicken, tasso, and andouille sausage tossed in a Creole sauce with Cajun rice). Also on the menu are pastas, barbecued meats, hamburgers, and wood-fired pizzas all prepared with a spicy bayou flair. Desserts include the house favorite, ***Warm Bread Pudding with Whiskey Sauce***.

BEVERAGES: Soft drinks, juices, coffee, cappuccino, and espresso are available. The full bar features domestic and imported beers, vintage wines, spirits, and specialty drinks.

DINING DETAILS: The House of Blues restaurant is open from 10:30 AM until 12 midnight. Lunch entrees range from $9 to $15. Dinner entrees range from $10 to $20. The restaurant does not take reservations for lunch or dinner; diners are seated on a first-come, first served basis.

PERFORMANCE DETAILS: Evening performances start between 8 or 9 PM. Tickets range from about $15 to $50, depending on the performer. Tickets for evening performances can be purchased for both future and same-day events and are available through Ticketmaster outlets and the House of Blues box office, located at the front of the music hall (407 934-2583).

GOSPEL BRUNCH DETAILS: The Gospel Brunch is served daily in the concert hall, beginning mid-morning. The brunch costs about $26, including tax and gratuity. Gospel Brunch reservations can be made up to seven days in advance at the House of Blues box office (407 934-2583).

NOTE: Both the club and restaurant have smoking sections. Dress is casual. ◆

JOLLY HOLIDAYS

DISNEY'S CONTEMPORARY RESORT

★★★★ ENTERTAINMENT   *(Great sound, lighting, and performances. A pleaser for all ages.)*
★★ FOOD   *(In recent years, the food quality has gone downhill — home cooking it's not!)*
★★★ SERVICE   *(The servers are skilled professional convention workers, but sometimes rushed.)*
★★★ ATMOSPHERE   *(It's remarkable that such a large ballroom can be made to feel so festive.)*

LOCATION: The Jolly Holidays Christmas dinner show is staged in the Fantasia Ballroom at Disney's Contemporary Resort, which is located on the monorail line in the Magic Kingdom Resorts Area.

ENTERTAINMENT: Guests are entertained before dinner (and periodically during the meal) by musical performers, but it is after dinner that the action really begins. The lights go down and all four stages in the ballroom are used, which keeps guests swiveling in their seats. The show is modified and new elements are added yearly, but the theme is generally centered around Santa's visit on Christmas Eve, with performances by a cast of more than one hundred elaborately costumed singers and dancers, and popular Disney Characters, including Mickey and Minnie. The show runs heavy on the sentimental, but what could be more appropriate for Christmas?

DINING ROOM: The Fantasia Ballroom is on the ground floor of the Contemporary's large convention center. Three of the four walls of this vast ballroom are turned into elaborate stages, and the room is filled with round tables that seat ten and are festively decorated with Christmas-themed tablecloths, napkins, and centerpieces. Most tables are near at least one stage, and the aisles between tables are also used by the performers, so everyone has a unique view. The ballroom's prismatic mirrored ceiling is used to create special lighting effects with spotlights, lasers, and strobes.

SAMPLE MENU: The all-you-care-to-eat holiday dinner, with all the trimmings, is served family style at each table. The menu includes a ***Relish Tray, Mixed Green Salad with Vinaigrette Dressing, Sliced Turkey Breast with Giblet Gravy, Walnut Dressing, Cranberry Sauce, Baked Ham with Cherry Sauce, Mashed Potatoes, Seasonal Vegetables,*** and a ***Surprise Christmas Dessert***. Food and beverages are replenished frequently by servers. The menu may vary.

BEVERAGES: Unlimited soft drinks, coffee, tea, and red and white wine are included with the meal.

PRICE: Tickets cost about $60 ($55 for juniors, $35 for children). Taxes and gratuities are included.

SHOW TIMES: Jolly Holidays plays five nights per week until just before Christmas. Shows are usually scheduled at either 5 or 8:30 PM. Families with young children frequent the early shows.

MAKING RESERVATIONS: This dinner show is produced in conjunction with Disney's Magical Holidays Package (see "Vacation Package Values," page 20). Beginning in late October, any visitor can make dinner-show-only reservations by calling Disney Dining Reservations (407 939-3463). The show may be paid for at the time it is booked. There is a forty-eight-hour cancellation policy. For same-day reservations, call the Guest Services desk at Disney's Contemporary Resort (824-1000).

TIPS: Seating begins about twenty minutes before show time. Several bars, usually set up in the large lobby outside the ballroom, dispense Christmas spirits.

Guests are seated communally at tables for ten; location is based on guests' reservation number.

NOTE: There is no smoking permitted at the Jolly Holidays dinner show. Dress tends to be festive. ◆

MURDERWATCH MYSTERY DINNER THEATRE

GROSVENOR RESORT

★★★★ **ENTERTAINMENT** *(An outstanding professional cast. One of the best shows at WDW.)*
★★★ **FOOD** *(Above-average buffet-style food, good prime rib, and a very good value.)*
★★★ **SERVICE** *(Self-service. Attentive, helpful servers bring beverages and clear plates.)*
★★★ **ATMOSPHERE** *(A pleasant, charming setting for music, humor, dinner, and — murder.)*

LOCATION: MurderWatch Mystery Dinner Theatre is staged at the Grosvenor Resort, located on Hotel Plaza in the Disney Village Resorts Area. The show is held in Baskervilles restaurant.

ENTERTAINMENT: Guests are asked to help solve a murder with a zany and animated group of players, some of whom are clandestinely planted in the audience before the show. A few subtle altercations occur while guests are dining, to attract attention to the large cast and to create suspicion. After witnessing a murder, compiling clues, guessing at motives, and listening to a number of hilarious, heartrending confessions, guests are asked to choose the most likely suspect. The winners receive their awards on stage. Show plots and endings vary, so there's always a new "whodunit" to enjoy.

DINING ROOM: Guests are seated at tables or banquettes in a spacious but intimately proportioned Edwardian-style dining room. The walls of this recently remodeled restaurant are decorated with framed etchings illustrating scenes from famous Sherlock Holmes detective stories.

MENU: The all-you-care-to-eat buffet includes ***Roast Prime Rib of Beef, Fresh Red Snapper, Coq au Vin, Baked Stuffed Pasta Shells, Fresh Mixed Vegetables,*** and a complete ***Salad Bar***. Side dishes include ***Wild-Blend Rice with Raisins and Almonds*** and ***Duchess Potatoes.*** Guests select from an array of desserts at the ***Dessert Buffet***. The menu may vary.

BEVERAGES: Coffee and tea are available at the buffet. Soft drinks, wine, and beer, as well as cocktails from Moriarty's Pub, next door, are brought to the table by servers.

PRICE: Tickets are about $35 (about $15 for children), including taxes and gratuities. Guests pay as they enter. **Readers receive a $5 discount per person. (See "Vacation Discount Coupons!" page 272.)**

SHOW TIMES: There is always one show at 6 PM on Saturday nights; during peak seasons, show times are at 6 and 9 PM. During summer months, there may be a special al fresco dinner show and buffet on the lawn. Shows may also be scheduled on additional nights during peak seasons.

MAKING RESERVATIONS: Reservations for the MurderWatch Mystery Dinner Theatre can be made up to three months in advance by calling the Grosvenor Resort (800 624-4109 or 407 827-6534). Same-day reservations are available as space permits.

TIPS: Don't miss the Grosvenor's Sherlock Holmes Museum, a replica of the famous detective's 221B Baker Street digs. The museum is tucked into the back of the restaurant and includes such props as Holmes's Meerschaum pipe and purple dressing gown, and the famous Stradivarius violin. Give yourself a little extra time after the show to view the collection and meet the performance's friendly cast.

    The atmosphere at these shows is more like that of a supper club than a regular restaurant, so there are usually very few little children present. The children who do attend are generally old enough to understand the premise of the show and are often drawn into the action as clue hunters by the hosts.

NOTE: Dress is casual dinner wear. The restaurant has a smoking area. ◆

POLYNESIAN LUAU

DISNEY'S POLYNESIAN RESORT

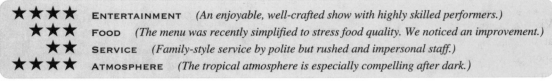

★★★★   **ENTERTAINMENT**   *(An enjoyable, well-crafted show with highly skilled performers.)*

★★★   **FOOD**   *(The menu was recently simplified to stress food quality. We noticed an improvement.)*

★★   **SERVICE**   *(Family-style service by polite but rushed and impersonal staff.)*

★★★★   **ATMOSPHERE**   *(The tropical atmosphere is especially compelling after dark.)*

LOCATION: The Polynesian Luau dinner show is staged nightly in Luau Cove, an open-air dinner theater near the beach at Seven Seas Lagoon, behind Disney's Polynesian Resort.

ENTERTAINMENT: The show begins after dinner, with a South Seas island fashion show and the musical interlude of a Hawaiian band. After a brief intermission, the talented performers appear on stage and the action quickly heats up: Women in ti-leaf skirts relate history through their fluid motions, men in traditional face paint pound out ritual dances from the Kingdom of Tonga, fast-moving Tahitian dances are driven by staccato drums, and dramatic Samoan fire-dancers spin burning torches for the finale.

DINING ROOM: A partial roof covers the large fan-shaped outdoor dining area, protecting guests from the occasional rains, but leaving the stage open to the sky. Guests are seated at long, candlelit quasi-communal tables that radiate out from the stage.

SAMPLE MENU: The family-style all-you-care-to-eat dinner includes *Fresh Tropical Fruit with Banana Rolls; Lanai Barbecue Roast Chicken with Polynesian Fried Rice; Oven-Roasted Pork; Fresh Sautéed Vegetables in Garlic Butter;* and *Pineapple Upside-Down Cake*. The menu may vary. Kosher, vegetarian, or other special meals must be ordered at least twenty-four hours in advance through the Polynesian Luau Office (407 824-1593).

BEVERAGES: Soft drinks, coffee, iced tea, hot chocolate, milk, beer, and wine are included with the meal. Guests may also select a *Mai Tai* (a blend of rum and fruit juices), which is not as potent as it sounds.

PRICE: The ticket price is about $40 (about $22 for juniors and children). Taxes and gratuities are not included in the ticket price, and servers expect a 15 to 20 percent tip.

SHOW TIMES: The early show seating is at 6:45 PM; the late show seating is at 9:30 PM.

MAKING RESERVATIONS: Reservations for the Polynesian Luau should be made well in advance. All Walt Disney World visitors may book dinner shows up to two years in advance by calling Disney Dining Reservations (407 939-3463). Same-day reservations may be made by calling 824-1593.

Reserved dinner-show tickets must be picked up before show time. Tickets can be purchased at Guest Services at the Polynesian or any Walt Disney World resort, or at the Guest Relations Desk in the major theme parks. Guests are assigned a table number at that time.

TIPS: The performance is most dramatic when it is dark, so try to book the late show during the summer. If your timing is right, you can see the Magic Kingdom fireworks show during dinner.

Visitors who would like a sneak preview of the Polynesian Luau should venture out to Luau Cove at about 8 or 10:45 PM. The stage can be glimpsed from the courtyard at the entrance.

NOTE: There is no smoking permitted at the Polynesian Luau. Dress casually for an outdoor setting. Arrive about one half hour before the scheduled show time. Shows are rarely cancelled, even in the rain, but if the weather is very cold, call the Luau Cove Podium (824-2189) to confirm. ◆

SPORTS

Visitors who like to combine sports activities and events with their vacations will find plenty of options at Walt Disney World, which prides itself on the quality and diversity of its recreational facilities and sports activities. The resorts offer a variety of sports and recreation activities, which are listed beginning on page 216. Disney's Wide World of Sports complex features facilities for professional and amateur competitions in more than thirty different sports (see "Disney's Wide World of Sports," page 214). Throughout the year, Walt Disney World hosts sports events that attract participants and spectators from around the world. To find out about sports events vacation packages, call Walt Disney Travel Company Sports Reservations (407 939-7810). Some of the most popular annual sports events at Walt Disney World are listed below.

WALT DISNEY WORLD MARATHON: In early January, thousands of runners gather to compete on a 26.2-mile course through the three major theme parks and several Disney resorts. On the two days preceding the race, a Sports and Fitness Expo at Disney's Contemporary Resort is open to all visitors. Participation in the marathon is open to anyone who signs up in advance. For information and registration forms, call the Walt Disney World Sports Line (407 363-6600).

THE INDY 200 AT WALT DISNEY WORLD: Indy Racing League members compete each January in this high-speed auto race at the Walt Disney World Speedway, a 1.1-mile tri-oval track located near the Magic Kingdom. Three Day Tickets, good for race day and all practice and qualifying trials, range in price from about $40 to $100. Single Race Day Tickets, if available, range from about $50 up to $120. Advance tickets can be purchased through the Indianapolis Motor Speedway Ticket Office (800 822-4639). Race Day tickets can be purchased at the Transportation and Ticket Center or at the WDW Speedway. The WDW Speedway is also home to an attraction that teams professional drivers with visitors who wish to ride in a NASCAR vehicle at speeds up to 145 m.p.h., or to learn the basics of driving one. For information, call Richard Petty's Driving Experience (800 237-3889).

U.S. MEN'S CLAY COURT CHAMPIONSHIPS: In late April, the United States Tennis Association (USTA) launches the men's clay-court season in the U.S. with the men's singles and doubles competition. The event, held at Disney's Wide World of Sports, features some of the world's top-ranked tennis competitors. Call the Walt Disney World Sports Line (407 363-6600) for information.

OLDSMOBILE SCRAMBLE CHAMPIONSHIP: This golf competition is held a few days before the Walt Disney World/Oldsmobile Golf Classic in October. The tournament pits teams made up of one professional and four amateur golfers against each other, with a prize of over $15,000 going to the winning pro. For information, call the Oldsmobile Scramble Headquarters (800 582-1908).

WALT DISNEY WORLD/OLDSMOBILE GOLF CLASSIC: Walt Disney World has hosted this major PGA Tour event every October since 1971. About 200,000 spectators attend the tournament to watch the top names in golf compete for a $1.5 million prize on Disney's Magnolia, Palm, and Lake Buena Vista courses. Call the Golf Classic Office (407 824-2250) for information.

CLASSIC CLUB PRO-AM: Held concurrently with the Walt Disney World/Oldsmobile Golf Classic, this event gives golfers willing to pay annual Golf Classic Club membership fees of about $5,000 the chance to play alongside the pros. For information, call the Golf Classic Office (407 824-2250). ◆

DISNEY'S WIDE WORLD OF SPORTS

Walt Disney World visitors who are also sports fans will find a number of activities to interest them at Disney's Wide World of Sports. The new athletic complex offers visitors the opportunity to be spectators at top-caliber amateur and professional sports competitions, to sign up for a variety of special sports clinics to fine-tune playing and coaching skills, and even to participate in selected competitive events scheduled at various times of the year. Disney's Wide World of Sports hosts events and programs that are ideal for families and groups who would like to share in an athletic experience. The Amateur Athletic Union (AAU) schedules numerous regional and national championship events here each year. Disney's Wide World of Sports is home to the Atlanta Braves during spring training season, and is the activity headquarters for the team's Gulf Coast Rookie League and Instructional League. The Harlem Globetrotters use the complex as their training and development site, and schedule games here each year to showcase their dazzling playing style. The Basketball Hall of Fame holds a number of tournaments at the complex, along with its Fantasy Camps for youngsters and adults who want to hone their hoop skills with a pro. Disney's Wide World of Sports is the site of the United States Tennis Association's Men's Clay Court Championships each spring; and in 1999, the complex will host many of the events for the Senior Sports Classic VII: The Senior Olympics, which is the largest competition in the nation for athletes age fifty and over.

LOCATION: Disney's Wide World of Sports is located in the southwestern quadrant of Walt Disney World, near Blizzard Beach water park and Disney's Animal Kingdom. Nearby resorts include Disney's All-Star Resorts and Disney's Coronado Springs Resort.

FACILITIES: Disney's Wide World of Sports covers more than 175 acres and features professional-level training and playing facilities for over thirty types of sports activities. A full-service restaurant, radio and television broadcast facilities, and a large "town commons" area for outdoor gatherings and awards ceremonies can also be found at the complex, and plans are in the works to add an Olympic-size swimming and diving pool, an ice hockey rink, and a number of other sports facilities.

EVENTS TICKETS AND RESERVATIONS: The sports events at Disney's Wide World of Sports are very popular and sell out quickly. Advance tickets are recommended and can be purchased through your local Ticketmaster outlet. To find out about upcoming events, including how to participate in selected ones, call the Walt Disney World Sports Line (407 363-6600). For information on sports events vacation packages, call Walt Disney Travel Company Sports Reservations (407 939-7810).

SPORTS EVENT AREAS

THE FIELDHOUSE: This huge building, with six hardwood-floor basketball courts, a large weight room, full shower and locker facilities, and four classrooms, can accommodate about five thousand spectators on its main floor when only one basketball court is in use. Indoor sports activities are held here, including sports clinics and competitions in basketball, badminton, boxing, fencing, gymnastics and tumbling, handball, martial arts, table tennis, weightlifting, and wrestling.

THE BALLPARK: This modern baseball stadium is patterned on an old-style baseball park, complete with a stylized scoreboard on the outfield's walls. The stadium has lights for night games, a press box with full broadcast capabilities, and two decks that can seat over eight thousand spectators.

⊙ **BASEBALL QUADRAPLEX:** This giant cloverleaf-shaped area has four baseball fields that meet Major League size regulations. Each field can accommodate about five hundred spectators, and one field has lights for night games.

⊙ **YOUTH BASEBALL FIELDS:** These two fields have viewing bleachers and meet the regulations for Little League size standards.

⊙ **SOFTBALL QUADRAPLEX:** This huge circle-shaped area has four regulation softball fields with "skin" infields, lights for night games, and bleachers for spectators.

⊙ **TENNIS COMPLEX:** This outdoor complex is made up of eleven lighted tennis courts and a full-featured tennis stadium. During championship events, the stadium's regular seating for eleven hundred spectators can be expanded to accommodate up to ten thousand.

⊙ **BEACH VOLLEYBALL COURTS:** This large area has five white sand courts for beach volleyball games and tournaments.

⊙ **MULTIPURPOSE FIELDS:** Four large, well-manicured fields, one with lights for night games, are designed to be flexible enough to handle practice sessions and games in a number of sports, including football, soccer, field hockey, rugby, and lacrosse.

⊙ **TRACK & FIELD COMPLEX:** This spectacular venue for track and field competitions features an all-weather, four-hundred-meter nine-lane polyurethane track, a runway for triple and long jump activities, and a separate runway for pole vaulting. The site also has areas marked for infield throwing and landing, and lights for nighttime events.

⊙ **VELODROME:** Billed as "the fastest bicycle track on earth," this velodrome was taken apart in Atlanta, Georgia, where it was used for the 1996 Olympic Games, and reassembled at Walt Disney World. The steel-framed structure features a seven-meter-wide waterproof 250-meter wood track with thirteen-degree straights and forty-two-degree turns.

OFFICIAL ALL STAR CAFE: This nationally known sports-themed restaurant features an extensive collection of authentic sports memorabilia and a sleek, contemporary look. Video monitors placed throughout the dining and bar areas show a dazzling array of live and taped sports events. The all-American menu features steaks, chicken, seafood, pasta, hot dogs, and specialty hamburgers with beef, turkey, or veggie patties. Beer, wine, and spirits are served, as are espresso and cappuccino. Open all day from 11 AM until 1 AM. (See "Restaurants," page 182.)

SPORTS CLINICS AND PROGRAMS: Visitors wishing to hone their playing, officiating, coaching, or groundskeeping skills can participate in a number of specialty clinics and programs at Disney's Wide World of Sports, including the Basketball Hall of Fame's Fantasy Camps. The clinics and programs are scheduled at various times of the year for adults, teens, youngsters, and even mixed age groups. The athletes, coaches, and others who participate as instructors are top professionals in their field. For descriptions of the sports clinics and programs, call the Sports Line (407 363-6600).

RESERVATION TIPS: Sports events, clinics, and programs vary with the season, and many sell out or fill quickly. If you would like to attend or participate in one of them during your visit to Walt Disney World, call the Walt Disney World Sports Line (407 363-6600) to check the schedule well ahead of time and *before* you book your travel reservations. ◆

BICYCLING

Bicycling is one of the more pleasant exercise diversions at Walt Disney World. Several resorts have bicycle paths ranging from beach promenades and wilderness areas to manicured fairways and flower-lined streets. Rental fees start at about $5 per hour or $13 per day, depending on the resort and type of bike. Surrey bikes that hold from four to eight peddlers range from $13 to $16 per half hour. Bikes are available year round, but in the summer, early-morning rides are the most pleasant, since afternoons tend to be hot, humid, and often rainy. Bicycle rentals end at sundown.

TROPICAL ISLAND BICYCLE CRUISE

DISNEY'S CARIBBEAN BEACH RESORT: The paved promenade encircling forty-acre Barefoot Bay lake lets bikers spin casually past white sand beaches and sample a range of exotic tropical landscaping and colorful Caribbean-style lodges. Bicyclists may cross the wooden bridges leading to Parrot Cay Island, where the path meanders along the shore, by clusters of waterlilies and reeds that ring the island. The island has the themed architecture of an old Caribbean fortress, complete with cannons pointing out over the lake. The path travels past aviaries filled with colorful birds before continuing across Barefoot Bay to the main promenade.

WHERE TO RENT: Bicycles can be rented at the Barefoot Bay Boat Yard, located in the center of the Caribbean Beach resort at Old Port Royale. Bicycles are available to both Walt Disney World resort guests and day visitors. Day visitors must stop at the Caribbean Beach resort entrance check-in to get a nonregistered-guest pass that will allow them to enter the resort.

BIKING AREAS: Bicycles may use the promenade that encircles Barefoot Bay and the sidewalks of the individual island villages. Bicycles are not permitted on the perimeter roads of the resort. The overall path length is about 1.5 miles. Joggers and pedestrians share the promenade with bikers. The best time for a bicycle ride here is mid-morning, after resort guests have departed for the theme parks.

EASY RIDER

DISNEY'S PORT ORLEANS & DIXIE LANDINGS RESORTS: Bikers riding either single or tandem bicycles can follow the paved areas and rustic paths of these two resorts on a town-and-country tour through the Old South. The path follows the Carriage Path encircling Port Orleans, a fanciful replica of the French Quarter in New Orleans. It continues along the winding riverfront path to Dixie Landings, passing by graceful plantation mansions set on wide lawns with weeping willows, and continuing past rustic bayou lodges sheltered by pines draped with Spanish moss.

WHERE TO RENT: Single and tandem bikes are available at both resorts. At Port Orleans, bicycles can be rented at Port Orleans Landing, near the marina. At Dixie Landings, bicycles can be rented at Dixie Levee, near the marina. Bicycles may be rented by registered guests only.

BIKING AREAS: Bikers may ride on any of the sidewalks and inner roadways of both resorts, as well as all along the Carriage Path. Bicycles are not permitted on the perimeter roads of the resorts. The overall path length is about 2.5 miles. Pedestrians, joggers, and luggage-conveyance vehicles share this path with bikers.

SPORTS

WILDERNESS RIDE

DISNEY'S WILDERNESS LODGE & FORT WILDERNESS: Nine miles of meandering roads and trails in Fort Wilderness serve as bike paths for visitors riding either single or tandem bicycles. The lightly traveled paved roads have occasional cars and buses, but the off-road trail system is a biker's dream. It meanders along waterways, past beaches, through shady forests, and across bridges and boardwalks. This is considered one of the best bicycle paths in Walt Disney World, and makes a great afternoon getaway for active families or groups who might enjoy a wilderness expedition and picnic.

WHERE TO RENT: Bicycles, including tandem bikes, can be rented at the Bike Barn in the Meadow Recreation Area at Fort Wilderness, and at the Teton Boat and Bike Rental at Wilderness Lodge. Bicycles are available to both Walt Disney World resort guests and day visitors.

BIKING AREAS: Bikers may use all roads, paths, and trails throughout Fort Wilderness. The overall path length is about nine miles. Maps showing the roads and trails of Fort Wilderness are available at the Bike Barn. (See also "Fort Wilderness & River Country," page 106.) Biking path areas are also used by pedestrians and electric carts, and sometimes cars and buses, so bikers should use caution.

FROM OLD KEY WEST TO DOWNTOWN DISNEY

DISNEY'S OLD KEY WEST RESORT & THE DISNEY INSTITUTE: Combining the features of two adjoining resorts, the path meanders through the winding streets of Old Key West, lined with charming vacation cottages and palm trees. It runs past the green fairways of the Buena Vista Golf Course and crosses footbridges over the waterways. It continues along shady forest lanes past the Treehouses at the Disney Institute, and continues all the way to Disney Village Marketplace at Downtown Disney.

WHERE TO RENT: Bicycles, including tandem bikes, may be rented at either Hank's Rent 'N Return at Old Key West or at the marina at Disney Institute. Only guests staying at a Walt Disney World resort may rent bicycles at these two resorts.

BIKING AREAS: At both resorts, bicyclists may use resort roadways and paths designated for joggers, but may not leave the paved areas or travel on the golf paths. The overall path length is about three miles. Bike paths are shared with pedestrians and electric carts, so bikers should use caution.

ON THE BOARDWALK

DISNEY'S BOARDWALK RESORT: The path travels over the wood-slatted BoardWalk Promenade, following the shoreline of Crescent Lake. It runs past the sandy beach and dock at the Yacht and Beach Club resorts, then loops back and continues to the International Gateway at Epcot before returning to the BoardWalk Promenade. Visitors can ride solo or as one of a group of pedalers on a large "surrey," a four-wheeled cart that pedals like a bike.

WHERE TO RENT: Bicycles and tandem bikes can be rented at Community Hall, and surreys can be rented at Surrey Rentals, located across from the BoardWalk marina and dock. Bicycles and surreys are available to both Walt Disney World resort guests and day visitors.

BIKING AREAS: Guests may ride on the wide pathways that circle Crescent Lake, including the BoardWalk Promenade and bridges. The overall path length is about one mile. The path is also used by pedestrians, joggers, and small service vehicles, so bikers should use caution. ◆

SPORTS

SPORTS

BOATING & MARINAS

Walt Disney World is home to the largest privately owned fleet of watercraft in the world — and much of it is available to visitors who would like to explore the extensive waterways and interconnected lakes that span the forty-seven square miles of Walt Disney World. A variety of rental boats is available at all of the Walt Disney World lakes. Boats may also be rented to explore Walt Disney World's canal and inland waterway systems. Disney's Fort Wilderness Resort and Campground and the marinas in the Disney Village Resorts Area provide access to these waterways.

LAKES, WATERWAYS, AND MARINAS

The Walt Disney World marinas are open every day from about 10 AM until sundown, and after hours by reservation at some resorts. Each lake and waterway has unique characteristics and recreation opportunities.

SEVEN SEAS LAGOON AND BAY LAKE: Together, these two lakes make up the largest body of water at Walt Disney World, covering 650 acres. The lakes are connected by a unique water bridge and are used for boating, waterskiing, and fishing excursions. Forests and wetlands surround the lakes, which are accented by miles of white sand beaches. The wetlands are home to a large population of native waterfowl, including great white egrets, herons, and pelicans. Discovery Island zoological park lies in the middle of Bay Lake, and although boaters cannot dock there, they can circle for a closer look. Watercraft can be rented at the following marinas:

- Marina Pavilion at Disney's Contemporary Resort
- Teton Bike & Boat at Disney's Wilderness Lodge
- The Marina at Disney's Fort Wilderness Resort and Campground
- Catamaran Corner at Disney's Polynesian Resort
- Captain's Shipyard at Disney's Grand Floridian Beach Resort.

BUENA VISTA LAGOON AND THE DISNEY VILLAGE WATERWAYS: Buena Vista Lagoon, thirty-five acres of man-made lake, is the showcase lake of the Disney Village Resorts Area. Along its shores is Downtown Disney, which includes Disney Village Marketplace, Pleasure Island, and Disney's West Side. A convincing replica of a Mississippi riverboat, the home of Fulton's Crab House, is docked at Buena Vista Lagoon, and the lagoon's waters are used by ferries, fishing excursions, and boaters. The narrow Disney Village Waterways lead off from the lagoon and wind through pine forests and shady, vine-covered bayous. The waterways pass under footbridges and flow by fairways populated with golfers, while snowy white long-necked egrets pose among the water reeds, hoping a boat wake will wash something edible their way. The waterways lead past Willow Lake at the Disney Institute, branch off into the Trumbo Canal at Old Key West, and become the Sassagoula River at Dixie Landings and Port Orleans. Boaters can rent their craft at the following marinas:

- Cap'n Jack's Marina at Disney Village Marketplace
- Hank's Rent 'N Return at Disney's Old Key West Resort
- The Landing at Disney's Port Orleans Resort
- Dixie Levee at Disney's Dixie Landings Resort
- The Sports and Fitness Center at the Disney Institute.

○ **CRESCENT LAKE:** This lake is surrounded by some of the most intriguing architecture at Walt Disney World, including the fanciful Dolphin and Swan resorts, the faithfully replicated New England seaside architecture of the Yacht Club and Beach Club resorts, and the lively Atlantic City–style waterfront at Disney's BoardWalk. In the distance, the tops of the replicas of the Eiffel Tower and the Campanile of St. Mark's Square in Venice in the World Showcase are visible. Along the shores are white sand beaches, arched bridges, and promenades filled with strolling pedestrians, multi-passenger surrey bikes, and visitors on their way to Epcot's International Gateway. Crescent Lake is also used by ferries taking passengers to Epcot or Disney-MGM Studios. Watercraft can be rented at:

- The Bayside Marina at Disney's Yacht Club and Beach Club Resorts.

○ **BAREFOOT BAY:** This forty-acre lake is actually three interconnected lakes, one of which has Parrot Cay island in its center, spanned on both sides by wooden footbridges. There are white sand beaches along the shoreline, and the lake is encircled by a promenade used by pedestrians and bicyclists. Clusters of brightly colored Caribbean cottages are nestled in the lush tropical landscaping beyond. Boaters can rent their craft at:

- Barefoot Bay Boat Yard at Disney's Caribbean Beach Resort.

○ **LAGO DORADO:** This shimmering fifteen-acre lake is surrounded by the rustic colonial cabanas of the sprawling Coronado Springs resort. The one-mile-long Esplanade encircles the lake and is used by bicyclists and strolling pedestrians. Boaters can rent craft at:

- La Marina at Disney's Coronado Springs Resort.

○ **FORT WILDERNESS WATERWAYS:** Friendly ducks and not-so-friendly swans share these shady waterways with native waterfowl and boaters. At times, the narrow waterways give way to grassy banks, where hopeful anglers patiently hold their poles. More often, the canals become bayoulike, closed in by pine forests hung with gray-green Spanish moss. Here and there, boaters will find picnic-perfect inlets or coves filled with water reeds and an occasional blue heron standing guard. Watercraft can be rented at:

- The Bike Barn at Disney's Fort Wilderness Resort and Campground.

○ **LAKE BUENA VISTA:** This is both a natural lake and an extension of the man-made Buena Vista Lagoon, nearby. Lake Buena Vista is bordered by the Buena Vista Palace Resort & Spa and the Grosvenor Resort at Hotel Plaza. The lake is edged by dark green water reeds, with a dense stand of pine forest beyond. Its dark, glassy surface is ideal for the Sunkats that float on it and, of course, ideal for the swans and ducks to whom it belongs. Boaters can rent their craft at the following marina:

- Recreation Island Marina at Buena Vista Palace Resort & Spa.

○

SELF-OPERATED WATERCRAFT

Visitors can select from a wide variety of watercraft at the Walt Disney World marinas, including speedboats, sailboats, canopy boats, pontoon boats, pedal boats, kayaks, canoes, and rowboats. Boats can be rented by the hour or half hour and are available to both Walt Disney World resort guests and day visitors with a valid driver's license (a few exceptions are noted below). Self-operated boats are rented on a first-come, first-served basis and cannot be reserved.

BOATING

WATER SPRITES: These tiny one- to two-passenger mini speedboats sit low in the water and zip along at about ten miles per hour. Water Sprites are used exclusively on the lakes and are not allowed in the canals or narrow waterways.

> **RENTAL FEE:** Water Sprite rentals start at about $37 per hour. Water Sprites are available to both Walt Disney World resort guests and day visitors.

> **MARINAS:** Water Sprites are available at the following marinas and resorts: Contemporary, Grand Floridian, Wilderness Lodge, Caribbean Beach, Polynesian, Yacht Club, Beach Club, Fort Wilderness Marina, and Cap'n Jack's Marina at the Disney Village Marketplace.

JET BOATS: These sleek three-passenger speedboats hydroplane across the water at speeds up to 30 miles per hour. There are a limited number of Jet Boats available, and visitors must be at least eighteen years old to command the boat. Jet Boats are used only on Bay Lake and Seven Seas Lagoon.

> **RENTAL FEE:** Jet Boat rentals are about $75 per hour, with a one-hour maximum. Jet Boats are available to both Walt Disney World resort guests and day visitors.

> **MARINAS:** Jet Boats are available at the Contemporary resort.

SAILBOATS: Sailboats and catamarans are available in a variety of sizes and styles. The Sunfish, Cray Cat, and Hobie Cat 14 each hold two passengers; the Hobie Cat 16 holds three passengers; the Com-Pac holds four passengers; and the Capri holds up to six passengers. Visitors who wish to rent catamarans must be experienced sailors.

> **RENTAL FEE:** Sailboat rentals start at about $13 per hour. Sailboats are available to both Walt Disney World resort guests and day visitors.

> **MARINAS:** Sailboats are available at the following marinas and resorts: Contemporary, Wilderness Lodge, Grand Floridian, Polynesian, Yacht Club, Beach Club, Caribbean Beach, Coronado Springs, and Fort Wilderness Marina.

PONTOON BOATS: These motor-powered watercraft are canopied and sit high in the water atop gleaming stainless-steel pontoons. The twenty-foot self-operated Pontoon Boats are ideal for groups of up to ten passengers, and may cruise either the lakes or the waterways. For larger pontoon boats, which require a driver, see "Excursion Cruises," page 222.

> **RENTAL FEE:** Pontoon boat rentals start at about $48 per hour for twenty-foot boats. Pontoon boats are available to both Walt Disney World resort guests and day visitors.

> **MARINAS:** Pontoon boats are available at the following marinas and resorts: Contemporary, Grand Floridian, Polynesian, Yacht Club, Beach Club, Old Key West, Port Orleans, Dixie Landings, Caribbean Beach, Fort Wilderness Marina, Wilderness Lodge, and Cap'n Jack's Marina at Disney Village Marketplace.

CANOPY BOATS: Motorized canopy boats may be used on both the lakes and waterways. Their striped canvas canopies provide shade, and they are ideal sightseeing craft for up to eight passengers.

> **RENTAL FEE:** Rental fees for canopy boats run about $20 per half hour. Canopy boats are available to both Walt Disney World resort guests and day visitors.

> **MARINAS:** Canopy boats are available at the following marinas and resorts: Contemporary, Grand Floridian, Polynesian, Yacht Club, Beach Club, Old Key West, Port Orleans, Dixie Landings, Caribbean Beach, Fort Wilderness Marina, Wilderness Lodge, and Cap'n Jack's Marina at Disney Village Marketplace.

SPORTS

PEDAL BOATS: These small, colorful human-powered watercraft, also called paddle boats, will cruise along as fast as you can pedal. Their light weight makes them ideal for lazy explorations of the shoreline and for sneaking up on waterfowl for a closer look. Pedal boats hold up to four passengers, but only the front seats have pedals, so passengers in the back get a free ride.

> **RENTAL FEE:** Pedal boat rentals start at about $11 per hour. Pedal boats are available to both Walt Disney World resort guests and day visitors.

> **MARINAS:** Pedal boats are available at the following marinas and resorts: Polynesian, Yacht Club, Beach Club, Port Orleans, Dixie Landings, Old Key West, Caribbean Beach, Coronado Springs, and the Bike Barn at Fort Wilderness.

CANOES AND KAYAKS: Three-passenger canoes and single or double kayaks are the official watercraft of the Fort Wilderness Waterways. These waterways wind through hundreds of acres of forest and wetlands, are home to numerous waterfowl, and are a favorite spot for fishing. Boaters can buy bait and rent fishing poles at the time they rent their boat. Canoes are also used on the Disney Village Waterways and at the smaller lakes.

> **RENTAL FEE:** Canoe and kayak rentals start at about $13 per full hour. Canoes and kayaks are available to both Walt Disney World resort guests and day visitors.

> **MARINAS:** Canoes are available at the following resorts: Caribbean Beach, Coronado Springs, and the Disney Institute. Both canoes and kayaks, as well as fishing gear, are available at the Bike Barn in Fort Wilderness.

OUTRIGGER CANOES: These canoes were fashioned by the Polynesians for steady travel through the pounding surf. Outrigger canoes are restricted to Seven Seas Lagoon. Outriggers hold up to eight passengers and require a minimum of five persons of substantial weight to row.

> **RENTAL FEE:** Outrigger canoes are free, and there is no time limit. They are available to both Walt Disney World resort guests and day visitors.

> **MARINAS:** Outrigger canoes are available at the Polynesian resort.

SUNKATS: These motorized lounge chairs for two are ideal for drifting along and soaking up the sun on a lazy afternoon. They float high above the water on rubber pontoons.

> **RENTAL FEE:** Sunkat rentals start at about $30 per hour. They are available only to Walt Disney World resort guests.

> **MARINAS:** Sunkats are available at the Buena Vista Palace Resort & Spa.

EXCURSION CRUISES

Excursion cruises take visitors onto Bay Lake, Seven Seas Lagoon, or Crescent Lake, or through the bayoulike Disney Village Waterways. In the evenings, the excursion cruises provide great views of the dramatic lighting at the resorts and theme parks, including the fireworks shows. A private dining cruise is a unique and romantic way to celebrate a special occasion. Any Walt Disney World visitor can book an excursion cruise. Evening cruises times vary according to the fireworks show schedules.

THE BREATHLESS: *Disney's Yacht and Beach Club Resorts* — This sleek mahogany Chris-Craft speedboat takes visitors onto Crescent Lake for speedy private cruises during the day and also at night for very special views of the fireworks shows at Epcot and Disney-MGM Studios.

CAPACITY AND COST: The *Breathless* carries up to seven passengers plus a driver. Fees are about $70 per half hour for a daytime cruise, and about $150 for the forty-five minute fireworks excursion.

RESERVATIONS: Reservations are required for this very popular excursion and can be made up to thirty days in advance at the Bayside Marina at the Yacht and Beach Club (407 934-8000: hotel).

BOARDWALK CRUISES: *Disney's BoardWalk Resort* — These pontoon boat cruises take guests on a trip around Crescent Bay and the connecting waterways to celebrate a birthday, see the fireworks at Epcot or at Disney-MGM Studios, or enjoy other special occasions.

CAPACITY AND COST: The boats hold up to twelve passengers, plus the driver and an optional server. Fees are about $90 for the forty-five-minute fireworks cruise, and about $200 for the birthday party cruise (including a decorated boat, cake, and party favors). Fees for other special occasion cruises vary according to arrangements.

RESERVATIONS: Reservations are required and can be made up to thirty days in advance at Board-Walk Services (407 939-5101).

FIREWORKS CRUISES: *Disney's Contemporary and Polynesian Resorts* — These pontoon boats carry passengers across Bay Lake and Seven Seas Lagoon for views of the Magic Kingdom fireworks show and the Electrical Water Pageant.

CAPACITY AND COST: The boats carry up to twelve passengers, plus the driver, and cost about $30 per person for a one-hour cruise. Snacks and beverages are served.

RESERVATIONS: Reservations are required and can be made up to thirty days ahead. For departures from the Contemporary, call 407 824-1000; for departures from the Polynesian, call 407 824-2000.

STARLIGHT CRUISE: *Disney's Grand Floridian Beach Resort* — This pontoon boat cruise on Seven Seas Lagoon and Bay Lake takes guests on a private excursion to enjoy the Electrical Water Pageant, Magic Kingdom fireworks, and a romantic evening under the stars. Guests can arrange to have their choice of beverage waiting on board, as well as snacks, desserts, or a catered meal from one of the Grand Floridian's restaurants.

CAPACITY AND COST: The boat carries up to twelve passengers, plus a driver and optional server. Fees are about $90 per hour with a one-hour minimum. Food and beverage prices will vary according to items requested. An additional $50 is charged if a waiter is requested to serve dinner on board.

RESERVATIONS: Starlight cruises are offered year-round and start after 5 PM. Reservations are required at least twenty-four hours in advance and can be made up to two weeks ahead at Captain's Shipyard at the Grand Floridian (407 824-2439). Food and beverages can be ordered at the same time from Private Dining (407 824-2474).

PONTOON BOAT CRUISES: Any private group can book an extra-large pontoon boat with a driver to tour the Disney Village Waterways or Bay Lake and Seven Seas Lagoon. Large pontoon boats are available at most resort marinas and at Cap'n Jack's Marina at Disney Village Marketplace.

CAPACITY AND COST: Twenty-four-foot pontoon boats hold up to twenty passengers plus a driver. They rent for about $75 per hour, including driver.

RESERVATIONS: Daytime cruises only. Reservations can be made up to two weeks in advance by calling a resort that has a marina located on the lake or waterway you wish to tour. ◆

FISHING

Fishing at Walt Disney World has become increasingly popular and excursions fill quickly. Professional anglers lead the tours, and they are knowledgeable about the waterways and the very best fishing spots. The two main fishing areas are Bay Lake and Buena Vista Lagoon. At the time that Disney began development, Bay Lake supported a number of native fish such as largemouth bass, bluegill, Seminole killfish, lake chubsuckers, and spotted gar. As new lakes, lagoons, and waterways were created, the waters were further stocked with brown bullhead catfish and at least eight species of sunfish. The fish now propagate well and provide a balanced ecosystem that supports a large population of native waterfowl.

Private fishing excursions are available at most marinas, and should be reserved well in advance. You can also join the open excursion that leaves daily from Dixie Landings resort, or try your luck pole fishing from the shore. No fishing license is required at Walt Disney World. You can use your own equipment, if you wish, although tackle is provided and bait is readily available. A catch-and-release policy is strongly encouraged, although resort guests with kitchen facilities may keep fish caught in some areas (be sure to ask the excursion guide).

FORT WILDERNESS FISHING EXCURSION: Bay Lake, the largest natural lake at Walt Disney World, is the fishing ground for this excursion. The lake is surrounded by wetlands that are home to a large population of native waterfowl, including great white egrets, herons, and pelicans. Bay Lake is large and well aerated, so the fish caught here are relatively free of pesticides and bacteria. Visitors with kitchen facilities may keep their catch if they plan to dine on it. Largemouth bass that have been caught here have weighed as much as thirteen pounds. Pontoon boats are used for the fishing excursions, which leave three times daily from the Fort Wilderness Marina.

EXCURSION FEES: About $170 for two hours, which includes boat, guide, all tackle, bait, and refreshments. Maximum of five persons. Participants may bring their own fishing equipment.

TIMES: 8 AM, 12 noon, and 3 PM. Times vary throughout the year.

RESERVATIONS: Space can be reserved up to two weeks in advance (407 824-2621). Reservations are recommended, and visitors will find them to be essential during the busy summer months. The excursion is available to both Walt Disney World resort guests and day visitors.

NOTE: Excursion boats will also pick up guests at the following resorts: Polynesian, Wilderness Lodge, Grand Floridian, and Contemporary.

BUENA VISTA LAGOON FISHING EXCURSION: This excursion travels both Buena Vista Lagoon and the Disney Village Waterways. Buena Vista Lagoon and the picturesque bayoulike waterways that feed it were excavated from swamp land, and as a result, this system is smaller and less aerated than Bay Lake, and the fish caught may not be kept to eat. However, a mounting service is available for visitors who catch fish weighing in at over eight pounds. Pontoon boats are used for the excursions, which leave twice daily from Cap'n Jack's Marina at Disney Village Marketplace.

EXCURSION FEES: About $150 for two hours, including boat, guide, bait, and all tackle. Maximum of six persons. Visitors who get caught up in the experience can keep right on fishing for about $60 for each additional hour. Participants can bring their own equipment.

SPORTS

TIMES: 6:30 AM, 8:30 AM, 10:30 AM, and 12:30 PM. Times vary throughout the year.

RESERVATIONS: Reservations are required at least twenty-four hours in advance and can be made up to three months ahead (407 828-2461). This fishing excursion is one of the most popular at Walt Disney World and fills quickly in summer months, so visitors planning a summer trip should book this excursion well in advance. The excursion is available to both Walt Disney World resort guests and day visitors.

NOTE: Excursion boats will also pick up guests at the following resorts: Dixie Landings, Port Orleans, Old Key West, and Disney Institute.

YACHT CLUB FISHING EXCURSION: Fishing the waters of Crescent Lake makes visitors feel they are in the midst of a New England coastal resort. The two-hour fishing excursion is limited to a maximum of five participants on each trip and leaves three times daily from the Bayside Marina at Disney's Yacht Club Resort. A policy of catch and release is strongly encouraged.

EXCURSION FEES: About $165 for two hours, which includes boat, guide, all tackle, bait, and snacks.

TIMES: 7 AM, 9 AM, and 1 PM. Times vary throughout the year.

RESERVATIONS: Reservations are required at least twenty-four hours in advance and can be made up to two weeks ahead (407 824-2621: Fort Wilderness Recreation). This excursion is available to both Walt Disney World resort guests and day visitors.

NOTE: The first fishing excursion of the day, departing at 7 AM, is the most enjoyable for both atmosphere and catch ratio.

BOARDWALK FISHING EXCURSION: This two-hour fishing excursion begins on the waters of Crescent Lake and continues to the World Showcase Lagoon at Epcot to fish along the waterfronts of the eleven international pavilions. The excursion is limited to a maximum of five participants on each trip and leaves three times daily from the boat dock at Disney's BoardWalk. A catch-and-release policy is strongly recommended.

EXCURSION FEES: About $170 for two hours, which includes boat, guide, all tackle, bait, and refreshments.

TIMES: 7 AM, 10 AM, and 1 PM. Times vary throughout the year.

RESERVATIONS: Reservations are required at least twenty-four hours in advance and can be made up to thirty days ahead (407 939-5101: BoardWalk Services). The excursion is available to both Walt Disney World resort guests and day visitors.

NOTE: Usually only the first trip of the day, departing at 7 AM, will enter the World Showcase Lagoon, where the catch ratio is higher than Crescent Lake's and the atmosphere is peaceful.

SASSAGOULA RIVER FISHING EXCURSION: This two-hour fishing excursion begins along the tree-lined Sassagoula River, which feeds into Buena Vista Lagoon, a primary fishing site on this excursion. The early-morning fishing trip departs once daily from the Dixie Levee at Disney's Dixie Landings Resort. The fish caught here may not be kept to eat, and must be released.

EXCURSION FEES: About $60 per person, which includes boat, guide, tackle, bait, and beverage. The excursion is booked on a party-boat basis, where anyone can join the group. It carries up to five participants at a time and is a great way for solo travelers to meet others in a relaxed setting.

TIMES: One excursion daily at 6:30 AM.

RESERVATIONS: Reservations are required at least twenty-four hours in advance and can be made up to two weeks ahead at the Fishing Hole (407 934-5409). The excursion is available to both Walt Disney World resort guests and day visitors.

NOTE: One of the best features of this fishing excursion is that it will sail even if only one participant is aboard, making this a real treat during the occasional times when bookings are slow.

FISHING THE FORT WILDERNESS WATERWAYS:

Fishing is permitted in the miles of picturesque waterways that traverse Fort Wilderness. Fish may be caught from the grassy banks of the canals, or visitors can rent pedal boats, kayaks, or canoes and seek out likely looking fishing holes in the heavily forested areas. Guests with kitchen facilities may keep and eat fish caught in these waterways, although a policy of catch and release is strongly encouraged.

EQUIPMENT: Fishers can use their own equipment, if they wish. Canoes, kayaks, pedal boats, and cane poles can be rented at the Bike Barn in the Meadow Recreation Area at Fort Wilderness. Bait is sold at the Meadow Trading Post, nearby.

RENTAL FEES: Canoes rent for about $12 per hour; pedal boats rent for about $10 per hour. Cane poles rent for about $2 per hour or $4 per day; rod-and-reel combinations rent for about $4 per hour or $8 per day.

TIMES: The Bike Barn is open from 8 AM until sundown.

RESERVATIONS: No reservations are taken for canoes or pedal boats. Fishing at Fort Wilderness is available to both Walt Disney World resort guests and day visitors.

NOTE: Canoes hold up to three persons; pedal boats hold up to four people.

DOCK FISHING AT CAP'N JACK'S MARINA:

All visitors at Walt Disney World can rent old-fashioned cane poles to fish for bluegill in the Buena Vista Lagoon from the dock at Cap'n Jack's Marina at Disney Village Marketplace. All fish caught here, however, must be released.

EQUIPMENT: Cane poles can be rented at Cap'n Jack's Marina.

RENTAL FEES: Cane poles rent for about $4 per half hour, including bait.

TIMES: Cap'n Jack's Marina is open from 10 AM until sundown.

RESERVATIONS: No reservations are taken. Fishing at Cap'n Jack's Marina is available to both Walt Disney World resort guests and day visitors.

THE FISHING HOLE AT DIXIE LANDINGS:

Disney's Dixie Landings Resort has its very own fishing hole on the Sassagoula River, a part of the Disney Village Waterways. Visitors fish from an old-fashioned roped-off dock at the fishing hole, which is stocked with bass, bluegill, and catfish. A catch-and-release policy is encouraged. So far, the biggest catfish pulled from this fishing hole weighed in at seven pounds.

EQUIPMENT: Cane poles can be rented at the Fishing Hole on Ol' Man Island. Bait is provided and worm-hooking instructions are offered, a rare treat for the squeamish.

RENTAL FEES: Cane poles rent for about $4 per hour, including bait.

TIMES: The Fishing Hole is open from 8 AM until 3 PM (varies seasonally).

RESERVATIONS: No reservations are taken. Fishing at Dixie Landings is available to both Walt Disney World resort guests and day visitors.

NOTE: For about $2, visitors can get a souvenir Polaroid of themselves and their catch. ◆

SPORTS

FITNESS CENTERS & SPAS

For visitors who want to continue their exercise program while on vacation, or even start a new one, many of the better Walt Disney World resorts have well-appointed fitness centers, some staffed with professional fitness trainers. A few resorts have expanded their fitness programs and created complete full-service spas for both men and women.

FULL-SERVICE SPAS

In recent years, several upscale full-service spas have opened at in the resorts at Walt Disney World. The spas are available to all visitors for massage or other spa treatments, which sounds pretty good after a hard day in the theme parks. The resorts with full-service spas are ideal destination resorts for visitors who would like to make a spa day part of their Walt Disney World vacation.

THE SPA AT BUENA VISTA PALACE: *Buena Vista Palace Resort & Spa* — This fully staffed twelve-thousand-square-foot facility is the ultimate European-style spa experience. The tranquil and luxurious spa is a world apart from the rest of the hotel. The modern interior is light filled and spacious. The Spa garden has a private current pool. The fourteen treatment rooms have one-way windows looking out onto patio gardens, which provide guests with a serene view and complete privacy. The Spa offers therapeutic services such as herbal wraps, body scrubs, aromatherapy, and a wide range of massages, and it has a full-service salon for hair care, manicures, and pedicures. Deliciously healthy spa cuisine can be ordered poolside or on the patio. An ultra-modern Fitness Center, upstairs, offers personal training services and high-quality workout equipment.

SERVICES: Massage, aromatherapy, reflexology, herbal wraps, body scrubs, body polish, waxing, facials, hair care, manicures, pedicures, water aerobics, personal training, and nutrition counseling.

FITNESS EQUIPMENT AND SPA FACILITIES: State-of-the-art Cybex cardiovascular and weight-resistance equipment, steam room, sauna, outdoor current pool, and whirlpools.

FEES: Buena Vista Palace resort guests are charged about $10 for day use of the spa and fitness center facilities. Spa services are a la carte, and spa facilities are included in full- or half-day spa packages. Half-day spa packages start at about $135 and include a choice of two treatments, and a spa-cuisine lunch. **Save at The Spa! Readers receive a 50 percent discount on a second spa treatment. (See "Vacation Discount Coupons!" page 272.)**

RESERVATIONS: The Spa at Buena Vista Palace is open from 6 AM until 9 PM. Reservations are recommended about two weeks in advance; for appointments call 800 327-2906 or 407 827-2727.

THE SPA AT THE DISNEY INSTITUTE: *The Villas at the Disney Institute* — As part of Disney's expanding focus on wellness, this facility offers cutting-edge exercise equipment along with a full-service spa with ten private rooms for body and skin care treatments. The fitness center offers weight circuit training and computer analysis of strength and agility. The Spa specialists use holistic products and techniques, including aromatherapy massage, seaweed therapy, and hydration treatments.

SERVICES: Massage, body wraps, hydromassage, aromatherapy, French body polish, facials, manicures, pedicures, after-workout body therapy, and personal training.

FITNESS EQUIPMENT & SPA FACILITIES: Jogging track, up-to-the-minute Cybex cardiovascular and strength training equipment, indoor current pool, sauna, steam room, and whirlpool.

FEES: Guests staying at the Villas are charged about $15 per day or about $35 per length of stay for the use of the spa and fitness center facilities. Spa services are a la carte, and spa facilities are included in full- or half-day spa packages. Half-day packages at The Spa start at about $125 and include three treatments. Complete spa vacation packages are also available. A three-day spa package, which includes selected spa services, Disney Institute programs, accommodations, meals, and events, starts at about $950 per person.

RESERVATIONS: The Spa at the Disney Institute is open from 8 AM until 8 PM. Advance reservations are required; for appointments call 407 827-4455. For information on spa vacation packages, call 407 827-4800.

SPA AND HEALTH CLUB: *Disney's Grand Floridian Beach Resort* — The Grand Floridian extends its first-rate service and attention to detail to include its new luxurious Spa and Health Club. The paned glass windows of the turn-of-the-century-era building fill the elegant interior with cheery brightness. The nine-thousand-square-foot spa has sixteen private treatment rooms, including a couples room, for massage, body wraps, hydrotherapy, manicures, and pedicures. The Health Club offers personal training consultants and top-of-the-line Cybex equipment.

SERVICES: Massage, hydromassage, body wraps, facials, manicures, pedicures, personal training, body composition analysis, fitness evaluation, and nutritional counseling.

FITNESS EQUIPMENT & SPA FACILITIES: Cybex cardiovascular and strength-training equipment, steam room, sauna, whirlpool, and hydrotherapy tub.

FEES: Grand Floridian resort guests are charged about $12 per day for the use of the spa and fitness center facilities. Spa services are a la carte, and spa facilities are included in full- or half-day spa packages. A half-day spa package starts at $180 and includes three treatments. Complete spa vacation packages are also available.

RESERVATIONS: The Spa and Health Club is open from 9 AM until 7 PM. Advance reservations are recommended; for appointments call 407 824-2332.

FITNESS CENTERS

Among the best-staffed fitness centers are Body By Jake Health Studio, Ship Shape Health Club, and Muscles and Bustles. Fitness centers at the Contemporary, Dolphin, and BoardWalk resorts are available to guests staying at other Walt Disney World resorts.

DISNEY'S OLD KEY WEST RESORT: *R.E.S.T. Fitness Center* — The fitness center at Old Key West is located in the resort's recreation complex. This modest-sized equipment-filled room is unstaffed. There is one television and a separate massage room off to the side. The sauna-steam room and whirlpool are outside the club, and are coed.

EQUIPMENT AND FACILITIES: Nautilus, Lifestep, Lifecycle, treadmill, free weights, combination sauna and steam room, whirlpool, and massage by appointment (407 827-7700: hotel).

NOTE: Open from 6 AM until midnight. Complimentary. Available to registered guests only.

SPORTS

➡ **DISNEY'S YACHT CLUB AND BEACH CLUB RESORTS:** *Ship Shape Health Club* — This fully staffed health club overlooks Stormalong Bay. The whirlpool, sauna, and steam rooms are coed. Televisions are interspersed throughout the main exercise area, which has the latest equipment.

EQUIPMENT AND FACILITIES: Lifecircuit, Nautilus, Lifestep, Lifecycle, Liferower, Gravitron, NordicTrack, StairMaster, treadmill, free weights, steam room, sauna, whirlpool, and massage by appointment (407 934-3256).

NOTE: Open from 6 AM until 9 PM. Guests are charged about $15 for their entire stay, and about $24 per family stay. Available to registered guests only.

➡ **DISNEY'S BOARDWALK INN AND VILLAS:** *Muscles and Bustles* — This light, bright, and cheery health club has mirrored walls, televisions throughout, and a coed sauna and steam room. Top-of-the-line Cybex equipment is featured.

EQUIPMENT AND FACILITIES: Cybex strength-training equipment, StairMaster, Abtrainer, free weights, treadmill, stationary bicycle, steam room, sauna, whirlpool (outside), sunbed, and massage by appointment (407 939-2370).

NOTE: Open from 6 AM until 9 PM. Guests are charged about $8 per person for the first day, about $14 for length of stay, and about $20 for family stay. Tanning booth costs about $8 for fifteen minutes. Available to guests staying at any Walt Disney World resort.

➡ **DISNEY'S CONTEMPORARY RESORT:** *Contemporary Health and Fitness Club* — This newly remodeled, fully staffed health club, located on the third floor of the resort, offers modern equipment, coed sauna, and adjacent tanning and massage rooms.

EQUIPMENT AND FACILITIES: Nautilus, StairMaster, Lifecycle, Aerobicycle, NordicTrack, rowing machine, treadmill, free weights, sauna, whirlpool (outside), tanning booth, personal training and massage by appointment (407 824-3410).

NOTE: Open from 6 AM until 9 PM. Guests are charged about $10 per visit, about $16 per entire stay, and about $20 per family stay. Tanning booth costs about $10 for twenty minutes. Available to guests staying at any Walt Disney World resort.

➡ **WALT DISNEY WORLD DOLPHIN:** *Body By Jake Health Studio* — This fully staffed health club, operated by fitness professional Jake Steinfeld, features top-of-the-line exercise equipment, as well as a coed whirlpool. There are televisions in the weight room, and a wide-screen TV-video setup in the exercise studio.

EQUIPMENT AND FACILITIES: Polaris, Lifestep, Lifecycle, treadmills, free weights, sauna, whirlpool, personal training, and massage by appointment (407 934-4264).

NOTE: Open from 6 AM until 9 PM. Complimentary to registered guests. Available to guests staying at any Walt Disney World resort for a fee.

➡ **WALT DISNEY WORLD SWAN:** *Swan Health Club* — This fully staffed health club overlooks the lap pool and is outfitted with Sprint Circuit machines. A massage room is attached, and saunas are located in the adjoining locker rooms.

EQUIPMENT AND FACILITIES: Sprint Circuit machines, treadmill, rowing machine, free weights, sauna, whirlpool (outside), and massage by appointment (407 934-1360).

NOTE: Open from 7 AM until 11 PM. Complimentary. Available to registered guests only. ◆

GOLF & MINIATURE GOLF

Walt Disney World sometimes calls itself "The Magic Linkdom," and with good reason: It boasts five outstanding championship golf courses (three are on the PGA Tour) and a par-36 practice course. With ninety-nine holes of golf and nearly twenty-five thousand guest rooms, Walt Disney World is the largest golf resort on the planet. Each year, more than 250,000 rounds of golf are played on the Walt Disney World golf courses and nearly four hundred golf tournaments are held, including the biggest on the PGA Tour, the Walt Disney World/Oldsmobile Golf Classic (see "Year-Round Sports Events," page 213).

The golf courses are available to all visitors. Advance reservations are necessary for all the courses, especially during peak seasons and holidays; greens fees average about $120. Clubs, shoes, and range balls can be rented at all golf courses. Walt Disney Travel Company offers an all-inclusive Golf Getaway vacation package for visitors who would like to play often during their stay (see page 232 for details).

Golf for half price at Walt Disney World by playing at the right times! During peak golf season (September through mid-May), play after 2 or 3 PM and get a 50 percent discount on greens fees. Be sure to ask for the Twilight Golf rate when making reservations. During the summer months (from mid-May through August), you can book a game any time after 9 AM at any course for about $50, more than half off the cost of a preferred tee time. Guests staying at a Walt Disney World resort receive a discount of about 10 percent on golf during peak seasons.

MAGNOLIA GOLF COURSE

Designed by Joe Lee, the Magnolia Golf Course is long and tight and requires a great deal of accuracy. It is planted with more than fifteen hundred magnolia trees and features the unique "mousetrap" on the sixth hole, a sand trap shaped like Mickey. In fact, the course has a preponderance of sand and water, with large greens on a rolling terrain. The layout covers 6,642 yards from the middle tees. The final round of the PGA Tour's Walt Disney World/Oldsmobile Golf Classic is played on this course, and the Disney pros rate the Magnolia the third toughest of the five courses at Walt Disney World.

GREENS FEES: Peak-season fees are about $110 for Walt Disney World resort guests, and about $125 for day visitors; fee includes an electric cart.

FACILITIES: The golf course has two driving ranges, a putting green, locker rooms, and a beverage cart on the course. The Pro Shop carries golf apparel, equipment, and accessories. The Garden Gallery restaurant, nearby, is open for breakfast, lunch, and dinner, and the adjoining Back Porch Lounge is open all day. Both private and group lessons with PGA and LPGA instructors are available. To arrange for lessons, call WDW Golf (407 939-4653).

RESERVATIONS: Guests staying at Walt Disney World resorts may reserve tee times up to sixty days in advance. Day visitors may reserve up to thirty days ahead. Call WDW Golf (407 939-4653).

HOW TO GET THERE: The Magnolia Golf Course is located in the Magic Kingdom Resorts Area. There is free parking near the Pro Shop for Walt Disney World resort guests (day visitors are charged about $5 to enter and park in this area). Complimentary taxi service to and from the golf course is available to guests staying at Walt Disney World.

NEARBY RESORTS: Shades of Green, Grand Floridian, Polynesian, Contemporary, and Wilderness Lodge.

PALM GOLF COURSE

Like the nearby Magnolia Golf Course, the graceful Palm Golf Course is lined with beautiful trees, and the greens are mature. It is a picturesque course where it is not unusual to see deer and other wildlife in the early mornings, not to mention a certain alligator with a habit of strolling along the outlying fairways. This Joe Lee–designed course is a challenging one, with narrow greens, plenty of water hazards and sand traps, and some difficult doglegs. The layout covers 6,461 yards from the middle tees. The eighteenth hole has been rated the fourth toughest on the PGA Tour, and the Disney pros rate the Palm the second toughest of the five courses at Walt Disney World.

GREENS FEES: Peak-season fees are about $110 for Walt Disney World resort guests, and about $125 for day visitors; fee includes an electric cart.

FACILITIES: The golf course has two driving ranges, putting green, locker rooms, and a beverage cart on the course. The Pro Shop carries golf apparel, equipment, and accessories. The Garden Gallery restaurant, nearby, is open for breakfast, lunch, and dinner, and the adjoining Back Porch Lounge is open all day. Both private and group lessons with PGA and LPGA instructors are available. To arrange for lessons, call WDW Golf (407 939-4653).

RESERVATIONS: Guests staying at Walt Disney World resorts may reserve tee times up to sixty days in advance. Day visitors may reserve up to thirty days ahead. Call WDW Golf (407 939-4653).

HOW TO GET THERE: The Magnolia Golf Course is located in the Magic Kingdom Resorts Area. There is free parking near the Pro Shop for Walt Disney World resort guests (day visitors are charged about $5 to enter and park in this area). Complimentary taxi service to and from the golf course is available to guests staying at Walt Disney World.

NEARBY RESORTS: Shades of Green, Grand Floridian, Polynesian, Contemporary, and Wilderness Lodge.

LAKE BUENA VISTA GOLF COURSE

The play on the Lake Buena Vista Golf Course is short and tight, but the views and fairways are wide and open. The greens are fully mature on this course, although they can be bumpy at times because many beginning golfers play here. The island green at the sixteenth hole is considered particularly challenging. The beautiful country club–like PGA course, designed by Joe Lee, is lined with pine forests, oaks, and magnolias. The layout covers 6,655 yards from the middle tees, and the Disney pros rate Lake Buena Vista the fifth toughest of the five courses at Walt Disney World.

GREENS FEES: Peak-season fees are about $110 for Walt Disney World resort guests, and about $125 for day visitors; fee includes an electric cart.

FACILITIES: The golf course has a driving range, putting green, locker rooms, and a beverage cart on the course. The Lake Buena Vista Pro Shop carries golf apparel, equipment, and accessories. Both private and group lessons with PGA and LPGA instructors are available. To arrange for lessons, call WDW Golf (407 939-4653).

RESERVATIONS: Guests staying at Walt Disney World resorts may reserve tee times up to sixty days in advance. Day visitors may reserve up to thirty days ahead. Call WDW Golf (407 939-4653).

HOW TO GET THERE: The Lake Buena Vista Golf Course is located at the Disney Institute, in the Disney Village Resorts Area. There is free parking near the Pro Shop. The golf course is within walking distance of most of the Hotel Plaza resorts. Complimentary taxi service to and from the golf course is available to guests staying at Walt Disney World.

NEARBY RESORTS: Disney Institute, Buena Vista Palace, Hilton, Grosvenor, Hotel Royal Plaza, Courtyard by Marriott, Old Key West, Port Orleans, Dixie Landings, Travelodge, and DoubleTree.

◎

OSPREY RIDGE GOLF COURSE

This extra-long links-style course was designed by Tom Fazio with plenty of berms and mounds, and some excellent par-3s. The lakes and creeks were excavated to create the elevated ridge that is the central feature of this course. Nesting platforms have attracted ospreys to the course, and red-tailed hawks can be seen perched in the tall pine trees or flying overhead as they patrol the area. The course features large greens interspersed with wilderness areas, and has become a favorite with experienced golfers. The layout covers 6,705 yards from the middle tees, and the Disney pros rate Osprey Ridge the toughest of the five courses at Walt Disney World.

GREENS FEES: Peak-season fees are about $120 for Walt Disney World resort guests, and about $135 for day visitors; fee includes an electric cart.

FACILITIES: The golf course has a driving range, putting green, locker rooms, and a beverage cart on the course. The Pro Shop carries golf apparel, equipment, and accessories. The Sand Trap Bar and Grill in the Bonnet Creek Golf Club serves breakfast and lunch, and the adjoining lounge is open all day. Both private and group lessons with PGA and LPGA instructors are available. Call WDW Golf (407 939-4653) to arrange for lessons. Golfers who would like to evaluate their swing and compare how different golf clubs perform can also make reservations to use the complimentary video/computer evaluation system at the Callaway Golf Performance Center at Bonnet Creek.

RESERVATIONS: Guests staying at Walt Disney World resorts may reserve tee times up to sixty days in advance. Day visitors may reserve up to thirty days ahead. Call WDW Golf (407 939-4653).

HOW TO GET THERE: The Osprey Ridge Golf Course is located at the Bonnet Creek Golf Club, which lies between Fort Wilderness and the Disney Village Resorts Area. There is free parking in the large lot at the club. Complimentary taxi service to and from the golf course is available to guests staying at Walt Disney World.

NEARBY RESORTS: Fort Wilderness, Dixie Landings, Port Orleans, Old Key West, and Disney Institute.

◎

EAGLE PINES GOLF COURSE

This challenging course, designed by Pete Dye, requires strategic play. Golfers must think their way from tee to green through the stark, low-profile terrain. It's a tricky course, and its inwardly sloping fairways and unusual landscaping can be visually intimidating. Water comes into play at sixteen holes, and instead of rough, the fairways are lined with pine needles and sand, giving the course a distinctive look and allowing for fast play. The layout covers 6,224 yards from the middle tees, and the Disney pros rate Eagle Pines the fourth toughest of the five courses at Walt Disney World.

SPORTS

SPORTS

GREENS FEES: Peak-season fees are about $120 for Walt Disney World resort guests, and about $135 for day visitors; fee includes an electric cart.

FACILITIES: The golf course has a driving range, a putting green, locker rooms, and a beverage cart on the course. The Pro Shop carries golf apparel, equipment, and accessories. The Sand Trap Bar and Grill in the Bonnet Creek Golf Club serves breakfast and lunch, and the adjoining lounge is open all day. Both private and group lessons with PGA and LPGA instructors are available. To arrange for lessons, call WDW Golf (407 939-4653). Golfers who would like to evaluate their swing and compare how different golf clubs perform can also make reservations to use the complimentary video/computer evaluation system at the Callaway Golf Performance Center at Bonnet Creek.

RESERVATIONS: Guests staying at Walt Disney World resorts may reserve tee times up to sixty days in advance. Day visitors may reserve up to thirty days ahead. Call WDW Golf (407 939-4653).

HOW TO GET THERE: The Eagle Pines Golf Course is located at the Bonnet Creek Golf Club, which lies between Fort Wilderness and the Disney Village Resorts Area. There is free parking in the club's lot. Complimentary taxi service to and from the golf course is available to guests staying at Walt Disney World.

NEARBY RESORTS: Fort Wilderness, Dixie Landings, Port Orleans, Old Key West, and Disney Institute.

OAK TRAIL COURSE

The Oak Trail Course, also called the Executive or Family Course, has some of the most challenging holes at Walt Disney World, according to the pros. The nine-hole, par-36 course features two par-5s, two par-3s, and five par-4s, and the local pros play here to work on their game. The layout covers 2,913 yards from the men's tees.

GREENS FEES: About $25 for one round; about $35 for two rounds. Includes pull-cart. Walking only.

FACILITIES: The Pro Shop carries golf apparel, equipment, and accessories. The Garden Gallery restaurant, nearby, is open for breakfast, lunch, and dinner, and the adjoining Back Porch Lounge is open all day.

RESERVATIONS: Guests staying at Walt Disney World resorts may reserve tee times up to sixty days in advance. Day visitors may reserve up to thirty days ahead. Call WDW Golf (407 939-4653).

HOW TO GET THERE: The Oak Trail Course is located in the Magic Kingdom Resorts Area. There is free parking near the Pro Shop (day visitors are charged about $5 to enter and park in the area). Ask about current transportation options when making reservations.

NEARBY RESORTS: Shades of Green, Grand Floridian, Polynesian, Contemporary, and Wilderness Lodge.

Discount Golf Vacation Packages!

If you'd love to sample the Walt Disney World golf courses and still stay within your budget, Disney's Golf Getaway vacation package may be the ticket. These two-night minimum packages run from May to August and include accommodations at any Walt Disney World resort, one round of golf each day (including golf cart rental), and taxis to and from the courses. A two-night Golf Getaway starts at about $180 per person including taxes, based on double occupancy. Theme park tickets are not included. Call Walt Disney World Travel Company (800 828-0228) for details. ◆

Miniature Golf

Disney's Fantasia Gardens offers visitors the chance to play the increasingly popular game of miniature, or mini, golf. Billed as "A Golfing Fantasy," the facility consists of two 18-hole mini courses: Fantasia Gardens, a quirky course that challenges visitors to overcome themed obstacles and distractions; and Fantasia Fairways, a more serious course that lets visitors test their putting skills.

WHEN TO GO: The courses are open daily from 10 AM until midnight. All Walt Disney World visitors may play these courses, and no advance reservations are taken. The least crowded times to play are when the courses first open at 10 AM, and after 10 PM. Operating hours may vary, so check ahead with Disney's Fantasia Gardens (560-8760). The courses have no shade, so sun block, a hat or visor, and sunglasses are a must during the day. The courses may close during thunderstorms or unusually cold weather. If the weather looks uncertain, call Disney Weather (824-4104) for details.

HOW TO GET THERE: Disney's Fantasia Gardens is located at the intersection of Buena Vista Drive and Epcot Resorts Boulevard, across the street from the Walt Disney World Swan, in the Epcot Resorts Area. There is free parking at the entrance. There is no direct Walt Disney World transportation to the courses, but they are within walking distance of the following resorts: Swan, Dolphin, Yacht Club, Beach Club, BoardWalk Villas, and BoardWalk Inn.

ADMISSIONS: Visitors pick the course they wish to play, choose from a selection of brightly colored putters and golf balls, and receive a score card that includes game rules and instructions. Cost for one round of 18 holes at one course, including equipment, is about $10 for adults and about $8 for children; a second game on the same day is half price. A walk-up counter at the entrance serves ice cream, snacks, and soft drinks. Rest rooms and a public telephone are also found here.

FANTASIA GARDENS

Fantasia Gardens, or "The Hippo-est Golf In Town," is whimsically designed around musical pieces from the Disney animated classic, *Fantasia*. Dancing ostriches, twirling hippos, and other characters from the film preside at each of the course's holes. Musical interludes, shadowy caves, waterfalls, fountains, pop-up mushrooms, and other special effects make for an interesting game. At the final hole, Mickey presides as the sorcerer's apprentice, surrounded by brooms and water pails that tip and "spill" their contents, surprising and occasionally splashing players and other passersby. Experienced mini golfers rate Fantasia Gardens as so-so by mini golf standards and disappointing as a Disney attraction.

FANTASIA FAIRWAYS

Fantasia Fairways, "A Miniature Golfing Adventure," is a scaled-down version of an actual golf course. Artful landscaping, small hills, and manicured greens create a pleasant outdoor environment where visitors can practice and hone their putting skills. Water hazards, sand traps, and some tricky doglegs enhance the "golf course" ambiance and offer special challenges to a golfer's concentration and skills. Experienced mini golfers rate Fantasia Fairways as "an interesting change" from typical mini golf themes. Golfers rate it as a "charming and easy putting exercise." ◆

HORSEBACK RIDING

Any Walt Disney World visitor can join a guided wilderness trail ride at either Fort Wilderness or at the nearby Hyatt Regency Grand Cypress Resort. Both facilities offer trail rides suited for inexperienced riders. The Grand Cypress Equestrian Center also offers riding adventures for intermediate and advanced riders. Shoes (not sandals or high heels) are required, and long pants are suggested. Spring and fall are the best seasons for trail rides. In the summer, morning rides are the most pleasant, the earlier the better. In winter, afternoon rides are the nicest. Check-in time for all rides is thirty minutes prior to the scheduled departure. Times vary with the season, and rides may be cancelled in poor weather.

FORT WILDERNESS TRAIL RIDE

Visitors led by cowboy guides ride along a packed-sand trail wending through shady forests and sunny glades. Novices will feel comfortable on this walk-paced ride (no trotting or galloping) astride well-behaved horses that are sometimes used in the Magic Kingdom parades.

  FEE: About $20 per person for a forty-five-minute ride. A maximum of twenty participants per ride.

  RESERVATIONS: Reservations are recommended and can be made up to two weeks ahead by calling the Fort Wilderness Recreation Line (407 824-2832). For same-day reservations, call 824-2832.

  SCHEDULE: Rides leave daily at 8:30 AM, 10 AM, 11:30 AM, 1 PM, 2:30 PM, and 4 PM from the Trail Blaze Corral at Tri-Circle-D Livery, adjacent to the Fort Wilderness Guest Parking Lot. Parking in the lot is free to guests staying at a WDW resort (others are charged about $5).

HYATT REGENCY GRAND CYPRESS TRAIL RIDES

Mounted on gentle horses, up to four riders are led along the shady trails of the resort's extensive nature area. Three different types of rides are offered, and are available to all visitors. Reservations are required at least twenty-four hours in advance, and may be made up to thirty days ahead (407 239-1938).

Western Trail Ride: This walk-paced ride is ideal for novices. The ride departs from the resort's Western Trail Barn. Visitors park free at the resort's main lot and travel by shuttle or trolley to the barn.

  FEE: About $30 per person for a forty-five-minute ride.

  SCHEDULE: Seasonally at 8 AM, 9 AM, 10 AM, and 11 AM; and in the winter at 1 PM and 2 PM.

Intermediate Walk-Trot Western Trail Ride: The intermediate ride is geared to more practiced riders who can sit a trot. The ride departs from the resort's Western Trail Barn. Visitors park free at the resort's main lot and travel by shuttle or trolley to the barn.

  FEE: About $30 per person for a forty-five-minute ride.

  SCHEDULE: Seasonally at 8 AM, 9 AM, 10 AM, and 11 AM; and in the winter at 1 PM and 2 PM.

Advanced Trail Ride: This trail ride is for riders with English-saddle and cantering experience, and follows the pathways surrounding the Grand Cypress Golf Course. It is headquartered at the Grand Cypress' exclusive Equestrian Center, where visitors park free.

  FEE: About $45 per person for a sixty-minute ride.

  SCHEDULE: The Advanced Trail Ride is scheduled by appointment only. ◆

JOGGING PATHS

Most Walt Disney World resorts have jogging courses on their grounds or on designated paths nearby. The trails at the Disney Institute and Fort Wilderness have exercise stations, and any visitor to Walt Disney World can use the jogging paths. Maps of the designated jogging paths are available at Guest Services in most resorts. Some of the better jogging paths at or between the resorts are listed below:

➡ **DISNEY'S POLYNESIAN RESORT & SHADES OF GREEN:** One end of the 1.5-mile-long trail starts at the Polynesian resort's Luau Cove and runs through the resort, emerging near the fairways of the Magnolia Golf Course and continuing to Shades of Green resort. The trail loops back, passes under the monorail tracks, and runs along the beach at Seven Seas Lagoon, returning to Luau Cove.

➡ **DISNEY INSTITUTE, DISNEY'S OLD KEY WEST RESORT, & HOTEL PLAZA AT DISNEY VILLAGE:** The 2.4- to 3.4-mile-long trail can be picked up at the Disney Institute's Village Green. It follows the winding resort lanes into the streets of Old Key West, then loops back into the forest, crosses bridges over waterways, and follows a path lined with exercise stations before returning to the starting point.

➡ **DISNEY'S CARIBBEAN BEACH RESORT:** The 1.4-mile-long path runs along the promenade encircling Barefoot Bay lake. Joggers may also cross the wooden footbridges and run the path winding through Parrot Cay, the Caribbean-themed island in the center of the lake.

➡ **DISNEY'S PORT ORLEANS & DIXIE LANDINGS RESORTS:** The path's 1.5-mile-long loop runs along the Port Orleans Carriage Path, passing through the resort streets, then follows the banks of the Sassagoula River. It enters Dixie Landings resort, where it winds through pine forests, crosses the river to Ol' Man Island, and runs along the opposite shore, returning to Port Orleans.

➡ **DISNEY'S GRAND FLORIDIAN BEACH RESORT:** The 1.3-mile-long path starts near Narcoossee's restaurant at Seven Seas Lagoon and heads inland, passing through the resort's gardens. It continues along the white sand beach and Wedding Pavilion and past the tennis courts before looping back under the monorail to return to the Grand Floridian dock.

➡ **DISNEY'S FORT WILDERNESS RESORT AND CAMPGROUND & DISNEY'S WILDERNESS LODGE:** The trailheads to the one-mile-long Wilderness Exercise Trail can be found across the road from the Tri-Circle-D Ranch in Fort Wilderness, and on the forested side of the Wilderness Lodge. The narrow asphalt-surfaced course winds through the forest and has exercise stations placed along the way.

➡ **DISNEY'S YACHT CLUB, BEACH CLUB, & BOARDWALK RESORTS:** The path's 2.5-mile-long loop runs along Disney's BoardWalk Promenade and crosses the bridge toward Stormalong Bay. It passes the Yacht Club and Beach Club resorts, and follows the walkways past the Dolphin and Swan hotels. The path curves around Crescent Lake, crosses a bridge, and returns to Disney's BoardWalk.

➡ **WALT DISNEY WORLD SWAN & DOLPHIN:** This path varies from one to three miles. It begins at the beach and runs past the Swan, over a bridge, and along the BoardWalk Promenade toward Epcot. It heads over the bridge and past the Beach Club and Yacht Club resorts. The long path circles around the parking areas of the Yacht Club, Dolphin, and Swan before returning. ◆

SPORTS

NATURE WALKS

Visitors who would like a change of pace from the intensity of the theme parks can enjoy leisurely strolls along one of Walt Disney World's many nature walks. The trails explore a variety of environments, including wooded wilderness areas, marshy wetlands, and lush tropical groves, which are populated with birds, rabbits, squirrels, deer, lizards, and numerous other creatures.

WILDERNESS SWAMP TRAIL
Fort Wilderness

The Wilderness Swamp Trail is one of the most serene and varied of the nature trails at Walt Disney World, and one of the least traveled. The 2.2-mile-long trail starts in an old-growth forest of tall moss-draped trees. Ferns, vines, and low shrubs grow untamed along the trail, which emerges on the shore of an estuary. Here, a secluded sitting area provides the perfect spot for a picnic. The trail plunges back into the dense forest before leading onto a boardwalk that crosses the wetlands of a wilderness swamp. Water reeds and cattails grow among the partially submerged cypress forest, where wild waterfowl live. The trail once again enters the tree-canopied forest. Wildflowers, berries, woodpeckers, fluttering butterflies, chirping birds, humming insects, and tiny yellow-striped lizards add splashes of color, sound, and movement. The trail crosses the grassy banks of Chickasaw Creek and returns through the forest.

MAPS: A map showing the trailhead is available at Guest Services in the Fort Wilderness Reception Outpost (located in the Fort Wilderness Guest Parking Lot) and at the Pioneer Hall Ticket and Information Window in the Settlement Recreation Area. (See also the map, "Fort Wilderness & River Country," page 106.)

NOTE: Snacks, beverages, and picnic supplies are available at the Settlement Trading Post, located between Pioneer Hall and the beginning of the Wilderness Swamp Trail. Also, the Trail's End Buffeteria at Pioneer Hall will prepare meals to go for those who wish to picnic. The Wilderness Swamp Trail is a wonderful walk at any time of the day, but the early mornings and dusky evenings are the most dramatic, with deep shadows and much animal activity.

PARROT CAY ISLAND AND AVIARY WALK
Disney's Caribbean Beach Resort

The walk through Parrot Cay, a Caribbean-themed garden island in the center of forty-acre Barefoot Bay lake, is a short, leisurely stroll that covers about a quarter mile and is sure to delight bird-lovers. The walk starts at either of the wooden footbridges that connect the island to the promenade encircling the lake, and twists and turns through a lush tropical garden of palms, banana trees, and bamboo. The walk continues past a rustic octagonal gazebo fashioned from lodgepole pines, and over to Parrot Cay's high-light, an aviary populated with a variety of exotic birds. Here, cherry-headed conures and gold-cap conures from South America preen and display their colorful feathers, while bright Amazon parrots from Central America keep an interested eye on visitors and passersby. Nearby is a pleasant shaded area with wooden tables, a great place for the impromptu picnic.

MAPS: There is no map available that focuses on Parrot Cay; however, a map of the resort is available at the Caribbean Beach resort's Guest Services.

NOTE: Snacks, beverages, and other picnic supplies are available at the food court in Old Port Royale, located just across the footbridge to Parrot Cay. The Parrot Cay Island and Aviary Walk is pleasant at any time of the day, but the island's playground attracts large groups of children in the afternoons, so early mornings and evenings are best for quiet strolls. Parrot Cay is wheelchair accessible.

ZOOLOGICAL GARDENS WALK

Discovery Island

Discovery Island was designed to be the quintessential nature walk at Walt Disney World. Ferries carry visitors to the island from the Magic Kingdom Dock, the Marina Pavilion at the Contemporary Resort, and the Fort Wilderness Marina. The island's tree-canopied path wanders through a jungle lush with palm trees, flowering plants, curling vines, and exotic shrubs from around the world. Tweets, chirps, squawks, honks, and caws can be heard as the path enters a vast walkthrough aviary suspended high above a sheltered lagoon. It exits at an inlet that is the home to Florida's native brown pelicans. The boardwalk to the right follows the beach to the wrecked *Hispaniola*; to the left it runs alongside a flamingo-filled lagoon and a section of beach favored by giant Galapagos tortoises. As the path returns to the dock, visitors can catch an up-close view of the island's resident alligators and bald eagle.

MAPS: A map of the trail is available at the Discovery Island dock where the ferries land. (See also the map, "Discovery Island," page 114.)

NOTE: Admission is charged at Discovery Island, but is included in Length of Stay Passes and some Multiday Passes. Snacks, beverages, and other picnic supplies are available at the Thirsty Perch. Bird and reptile shows are scheduled throughout the day. Discovery Island is wheelchair accessible.

CYPRESS POINT NATURE TRAIL

River Country at Fort Wilderness

This trail is actually a narrow, roped boardwalk leading visitors on a quarter-mile path that follows the shoreline of Bay Lake into the wetlands. Moss-hung bald cypresses grow up out of the water and shade the path. These trees are native to the wetlands and were here long before the land was developed. In the shallow water, among the roots of the trees, are colonies of freshwater mollusks, which are extremely important to the food chain in this ecosystem. Small fish dart through the water, and egrets and heron stand among the water reeds fishing. There are a few aviaries along the way, where visitors can get an unusual up-close look at birds normally seen only in the wild. The birds at Cypress Point have been injured in the wild and rehabilitated, but cannot survive unaided.

MAPS: Maps are available at River Country's Guest Relations window from time to time. (See also the map, "Fort Wilderness & River County," page 106.)

NOTE: Admission is charged at River Country, but is included in Length of Stay Passes and some Multiday Passes. Snacks, beverages, and other picnic supplies are available at Pop's Place or the Waterin' Hole. There is a shaded picnic area at the end of the trail on the white sand beach. ◆

SWIMMING & BEACHES

Most Walt Disney World resorts have more than one swimming pool for guests to either swim laps or simply to cool off from the hot Florida sun. The resort pools are generally restricted to guests registered at that particular resort (with the exception of Vacation Club Members). Visitors who want to engage in serious water play should visit the water parks at River Country (see "Fort Wilderness & River Country," page 107); Typhoon Lagoon (see "Typhoon Lagoon," page 95); or Blizzard Beach (see "Blizzard Beach," page 101). There are numerous beaches at the Walt Disney World resorts, and anyone bringing along a towel can venture out and stake a place in the sand. All beaches have snack bars, rest rooms, and lockers nearby. In late spring and autumn, the lakes and waterways at Walt Disney World undergo a "seasonal turnover," with an increase in bacteria and algae levels. During those periods, swimming is prohibited in any area except resort pools. Signs are posted.

LAP POOLS: Swimmers who would like to exercise during their vacation should consider staying at a resort that offers a lap pool. Lap pools are usually one of several pools available, and tend to be deserted in the mornings. Lap pools or Olympic-sized pools can be found at:

◆ Walt Disney World Swan (shared by guests at the Walt Disney World Dolphin)
◆ Buena Vista Palace Resort & Spa (at The Spa).

WALT DISNEY WORLD RESORTS WITH POOLS LARGE ENOUGH FOR LAP SWIMMING INCLUDE:

◆ Disney's Contemporary Resort (in the recreation area near the beach)
◆ Disney Institute (near the Lake Buena Vista Golf Course Pro Shop)
◆ Fort Wilderness Resort and Campground (in the Meadow Recreation Area)
◆ Buena Vista Palace Resort & Spa (on Recreation Island)
◆ Disney's Yacht Club Resort (the "quiet pool")
◆ Disney's Beach Club Resort (the "quiet pool")
◆ Disney's Yacht and Beach Club Resorts — Stormalong Bay (the oval "current" pool).

WHITE SAND BEACHES: Most of the Walt Disney World resorts offer stretches of pure white sand beach for the enjoyment of guests. Many of the beaches are equipped with comfortable lounge chairs to relax in, or rows of jaunty striped cabanas for shelter from the sun. Besides the resort beaches listed below, there is also a charming deserted beach on Discovery Island, although swimming is not permitted there. During certain months, when bacteria counts rise, swimming in Florida lakes is not allowed. Beaches can be found at the following resorts and parks:

◆ Fort Wilderness Marina and Beach (large beach on Bay Lake)
◆ Disney's Contemporary Resort (large beach on Bay Lake)
◆ Disney's Polynesian Resort (large beach on Seven Seas Lagoon)
◆ Disney's Grand Floridian Beach Club Resort (large beach on Seven Seas Lagoon)
◆ Disney's Beach Club Resort (large beach on Crescent Lake — no swimming)
◆ Walt Disney World Swan and Dolphin (cove on Crescent Lake — no swimming)
◆ Disney's Caribbean Beach Resort (large beach and several small beaches on Barefoot Bay)
◆ Disney's Coronado Springs Resort (beach on Lago Dorado)
◆ Disney's Old Key West Resort (small beach on the Trumbo Canal — no swimming)
◆ Disney's Wilderness Lodge (small beach on Bay Lake). ◆

TENNIS & VOLLEYBALL

Most Walt Disney World resorts have well-designed tennis courts tucked into the forest or overlooking beaches, lakes, golf courses, and pools. Serious tennis players may want to take advantage of the tennis programs available at Walt Disney World, where certified tennis pros offer private lessons and challenging tennis clinics.

TENNIS PROGRAMS

DISNEY'S RACQUET CLUB AT THE CONTEMPORARY RESORT: The tennis courts at Disney's Racquet Club are located next to the Contemporary resort's north garden wing, along the shore of Bay Lake. All six courts are surfaced in top-of-the-line Hydro-Grid clay. Several of the courts are set up for competition play, complete with bleacher areas.

COURTS: The Racquet Club has six lighted courts and is open from 8 AM until 8 PM.

FEES: About $15 per hour (about $40 per family for an entire stay). Private lessons are about $50 per hour. Play-by-play video analysis is available for about $60 per hour. A ball machine may be rented for about $25 per hour. To arrange for tennis instruction, call the Racquet Club (407 824-3578).

RESERVATIONS: Recommended. Courts can be reserved twenty-four hours in advance (824-3578).

NOTE: Courts are available to both Walt Disney World resort guests and day visitors. Rental equipment is available at the Racquet Club pro shop, which also has two practice courts. The pro shop offers a "Tennis Anyone?" program that matches players with tennis partners. Guests can also make reservations and arrange for lessons on the Grand Floridian resort's two courts through the Racquet Club. The Racquet Club pro shop is open from 8 AM until 8 PM and offers a restringing service.

TENNIS PROGRAMS AT DISNEY INSTITUTE: The Disney Institute's clay tennis courts have been specially built to ensure an even moisture content year-round. Visiting tennis players can sign up for one or more of the instructional courses offered in the Tennis Program at the Disney Institute. The two-hour-long courses were designed in conjunction with Peter Burwash International, a world-renowned professional tennis organization. The courses in the Tennis Program feature play-by-play video analysis and focus on fine-tuning fundamentals, developing playing strategies, and combining weight resistance training with game techniques. Customized private and group lessons with a tennis pro are also available.

FACILITIES: Four lighted clay courts, video analysis, private lessons, a pro shop, and a ball machine. Courses in the Tennis Program are scheduled throughout the day.

VISITOR FEES: About $50 per two-hour course. Private tennis instruction is about $50 per hour. All visitors enrolled in Tennis Program courses may use the Sports and Fitness Center facilities.

RESERVATIONS: Required. All Walt Disney World visitors can reserve Tennis Program courses up to fourteen days in advance by calling Disney Institute Day Visitor Programs (407 827-4800). To arrange for private tennis instruction, call the Sports and Fitness Center (407 827-4455).

NOTE: The Disney Institute Tennis Program courses are open to all visitors at Walt Disney World. Among the courses offered is High Tech Tennis, which incorporates a workout with top-of-the-line Cybex machines into the player's tennis game.

TENNIS COURTS

BUENA VISTA PALACE RESORT & SPA: Located on the resort's large Recreation Island, the tennis courts overlook Lake Buena Vista. A wide lawn leads from the pool area to the courts.

COURTS: Three lighted tennis courts, open from 6 AM until 10 PM; complimentary.

NOTE: No reservations. Courts are available to registered guests only. Complimentary tennis equipment is available at the concierge desk in the Palace Suites, adjacent to the pool.

DISNEY'S BOARDWALK INN AND BOARDWALK VILLAS: Located on the far side of the BoardWalk Villas, these hard-surfaced courts are bounded by trees and the nearby canal.

COURTS: Two lighted tennis courts, open from 8 AM until 10 PM; complimentary.

NOTE: No reservations. Those wishing to play a private tournament can reserve courts twenty-four hours in advance for about $10. Courts are available to registered guests only. Equipment is available for rent at Community Hall.

DISNEY'S GRAND FLORIDIAN BEACH RESORT: These clay-surfaced courts are in a secluded, tree-banked setting. Players can see and hear the monorail gliding by as they play.

COURTS: Two lighted tennis courts, open from 8 AM until 8 PM; about $15 per hour.

NOTE: Reservations are recommended, twenty-four hours in advance (824-2332 or 824-3578). Courts are available to guests staying at any Walt Disney World resort. Rental equipment is available at the Grand Floridian Spa and Health Club.

DISNEY'S OLD KEY WEST RESORT: The tennis courts are located on the edge of the Trumbo Canal, in the resort's recreation complex. There are benches nearby for those waiting to play.

COURTS: Two lighted tennis courts, open from 9 AM until 11 PM; complimentary.

NOTE: No reservations. Courts are available to registered guests only. Rental equipment is available at Hank's Rent 'N Return.

DISNEY'S YACHT CLUB AND BEACH CLUB RESORTS: These two resorts share a set of tennis courts located on the far side of the Beach Club. The courts are surrounded on three sides by forest.

COURTS: Two lighted tennis courts, open from 7 AM until 10 PM; complimentary.

NOTE: No reservations. Courts are available to guests staying at any Walt Disney World resort. Complimentary loaner equipment is available at the Ship Shape Health Club.

DOUBLETREE GUEST SUITES RESORT: These quiet tennis courts, located near the pool, are surrounded by tall palms and pines. There is a shaded waiting and viewing area nearby.

COURTS: Six lighted tennis courts, open from 7 AM until 11 PM; complimentary.

NOTE: No reservations. Courts are available to guests staying at any Walt Disney World resort. Complimentary racquets are available at the hotel bell desk.

FORT WILDERNESS: Players at Fort Wilderness can enjoy tennis games in a quiet wilderness setting. To reach the courts, visitors must take a Fort Wilderness bus to the Meadow Recreation Area.

COURTS: Two lighted tennis courts, open from 8 AM until 10 PM; complimentary.

NOTE: No reservations. Courts are available to both Walt Disney World resort guests and day visitors. Equipment is available for rent at the Bike Barn, nearby.

→ **GROSVENOR RESORT:** The tennis courts are located behind the pool area and adjacent to the resort's handball and volleyball courts. There is a small waiting area nearby with shaded tables.

COURTS: Four lighted tennis courts, open from 9 AM until 10 PM; complimentary.

NOTE: No reservations. Courts are available to guests staying at any Walt Disney World resort. Complimentary loaner equipment is available at the Recreation Office near the pool.

→ **HOTEL ROYAL PLAZA:** The tennis courts are located at the far end of the property. They are backed up against the freeway, with little landscaping to offer a buffer from the noise.

COURTS: Four lighted tennis courts, open 7 AM until 11 PM; complimentary.

NOTE: No reservations. Courts are available to guests staying at any Walt Disney World resort. No playing equipment is available.

→ **SHADES OF GREEN:** The tennis courts are located at the edge of the Palm Golf Course near the south wing of the resort. A small landscaped area, shaded by palm trees, provides guests with a very pleasant place to wait for a game.

COURTS: Two lighted tennis courts, open from dawn until 10 PM.

NOTE: No reservations. Courts are available to registered Shades of Green guests only. There is a two-hour-maximum playing time. Complimentary racquets are available at the Front Desk, but guests must buy balls from the hotel gift shop.

→ **WALT DISNEY WORLD DOLPHIN AND SWAN:** These hard-surfaced courts are shared by both resorts and are bounded on one side by Disney's Fantasia Gardens miniature golf course.

COURTS: Four lighted tennis courts, open from 6 AM until 10 PM; complimentary.

NOTE: No reservations. Courts are available to guests staying at any Walt Disney World resort. Rental equipment is available at Body By Jake Health Studio.

VOLLEYBALL

There are volleyball courts throughout Walt Disney World. Volleyball is a "pickup" sport, and visitors can join a game in progress if a position is open. The hotel courts are generally for registered guests, but the courts at Fort Wilderness, Typhoon Lagoon, and River Country are available to all visitors.

◆ **DISNEY'S YACHT AND BEACH CLUB RESORT** — In a courtyard facing the beach at Stormalong Bay

◆ **DISNEY'S CARIBBEAN BEACH RESORT** — On the beach at Barefoot Bay, near Old Port Royale

◆ **DISNEY'S CONTEMPORARY RESORT** — On the beach at Bay Lake, adjacent to the Marina Pavilion

◆ **DISNEY'S CORONADO SPRINGS** — On the common area leading to the beach

◆ **DISNEY'S GRAND FLORIDIAN BEACH RESORT** — On the white sand beach at Seven Seas Lagoon

◆ **DISNEY'S OLD KEY WEST RESORT** — At the resort's recreation complex, near the tennis courts

◆ **DISNEY'S POLYNESIAN RESORT** — On the white sand beach at Seven Seas Lagoon

◆ **FORT WILDERNESS** — In the Meadow Recreation Area and on the Fort Wilderness beach

◆ **GROSVENOR RESORT** — Behind the pool area, surrounded by lawn and pine forest

◆ **TYPHOON LAGOON** — In the Getaway Glen Picnic Area, with a grassy berm for spectators

◆ **RIVER COUNTRY** — On the beach near Pop's Picnic Area, overlooking Bay Lake

◆ **VILLAS AT THE DISNEY INSTITUTE** — Near the tennis courts and Disney Village Waterways. ◆

SPORTS

WATERSKIING & PARASAILING

Waterskiers fly across the surface of Bay Lake all year long, and if you look up, you may see someone parasailing in the sky, tethered by a rope to a speedboat below and suspended from a brightly colored parachute soaring above. Everyone from novices to experts can make use of Walt Disney World's fleet of speedboats and waterskiing and parasailing equipment. Speedboat drivers are professional instructors and are certified by the American Waterski Association. They offer instruction and helpful tips to both beginning and advanced skiers. Waterskiing and parasailing excursions are available to all visitors.

WATERSKIING: Ski boats reaching speeds of up to fifty miles an hour tow waterskiers close behind as they skim along the water. Groups of up to five people can waterski together, with a two-person minimum. The fee for waterskiing excursions is per hour rather than per person, so teaming up with other waterskiers can be economical. Along with standard waterskis, excursion boats carry Scurfers (mini surfboards), Hydraslides (knee boards), and slalom skis.

FEE: About $100 per hour, which includes ski boat, driver-instructor, and waterskiing equipment. Participants may bring their own waterskis, if they wish. There is a maximum of five persons per boat, with a two-person minimum. Excursion groups are not mixed, except by request.

RESERVATIONS: Reservations are required at least one day in advance and can be made up to two weeks ahead at Disney Resort Recreation (407 824-2621). Excursion boats pick up skiers at the Fort Wilderness, Wilderness Lodge, Contemporary, Polynesian, and Grand Floridian resort marinas — be sure to specify where you wish to board. Waterskiing excursions are extremely popular during peak-attendance seasons, on warm weekends, and during holidays, so make reservations well in advance if you will be traveling to Walt Disney World at any of these times.

EXCURSION SCHEDULE: At least two waterskiing boats are in operation at all times on Bay Lake, where all waterskiing is done at Walt Disney World. Waterskiing excursions depart daily at 8:45 AM, 10 AM, 11:15 AM, 1:30 PM, 2:45 PM, and 4 PM. Times may vary with the season, and excursions can sometimes be delayed or cancelled due to poor weather conditions.

PARASAILING: Parasailing may look very daring, but it requires no prior experience. Paired or solo parasailers only need to settle into the parasail seat, put on the harness, and away they go, soaring up to 250 feet in the air as they are towed around Bay Lake by a speedboat.

FEE: About $75 per person for about 4 to 6 minutes of soaring; about $50 per person to ride along on the boat without going aloft.

RESERVATIONS: Reservations are required at least one day in advance and can be made up to thirty days ahead at the Contemporary's Marina Pavilion (407 824-2464). Parasailers who weigh less than 200 pounds must ride double, and will be paired with another visitor in order to ride.

SCHEDULE: Parasailing excursions depart from the Contemporary's Marina Pavilion every morning at 6:45 AM, 7:30 AM, 8:15 AM, 9 AM, and 9:45 AM; and, during the summer, on Wednesday and Saturday evenings at 6:15 PM, 7 PM, and 7:45 PM. Times may vary with the season, and excursions can sometimes be delayed or cancelled due to poor weather conditions. ◆

SPORTS

FAMILY & FRIENDS

The wide variety of activities, attractions, and accommodations at Walt Disney World make it an ideal destination for family vacations, group getaways, holiday gatherings and reunions, and special family celebrations. Walt Disney World's unique guided tours and the learning programs at the Disney Institute are ideal activities for both groups and solo travelers who would like to meet others (see "Guided Tours," page 247; and "Disney Institute," page 248). The resort-wide public transportation system and extensive child care services also allow groups and families to enjoy a variety of vacation experiences.

HOTELS FOR LARGER FAMILIES AND SMALL GROUPS

Most guest rooms at Walt Disney World sleep four persons; however, standard rooms that sleep five can be found at the following resorts: Dixie Landings, Polynesian, Contemporary, BoardWalk, Yacht Club, and Beach Club. The Disney resorts also offer lodging options specifically designed for larger families or groups of friends traveling together. These range from campsites and budget resorts with adjoining rooms to efficiency suites that sleep up to six and spacious vacation homes that sleep from six to twelve.

VACATION HOMES: Walt Disney World offers one-, two-, and three-bedroom condominium-style lodgings and detached vacation homes with fully equipped kitchens, which gives groups the option to prepare their own meals and dine together. Vacation homes are available at Disney's Old Key West Resort, Disney's BoardWalk Villas, and at The Villas at the Disney Institute.

EFFICIENCY SUITES: Efficiency suites have fold-out beds plus separate bedrooms and wet bars with refrigerators, coffeemakers, and microwaves. They are available at DoubleTree Guest Suites Resort, Buena Vista Resort's Palace Suites, and The Villas at the Disney Institute. There are also many affordable suites hotels surrounding Walt Disney World (see "Off-Site Hotels & Suites," page 152).

BUDGET RESORTS: The limited-amenity resorts at Walt Disney World provide a good value for groups on a budget. Blocks of rooms that sleep four can be booked at the following resorts: Dixie Landings, Port Orleans, Caribbean Beach (mini bar), All-Star resorts, Coronado Springs Resort, Courtyard by Marriott, Travelodge (mini bar), and Grosvenor (refrigerator). **The Grosvenor Resort offers _Walt Disney World for Adults_ readers a 50 percent discount on hotel accommodations, which can add up to big savings for groups! (See "Vacation Discount Coupons!" page 272.)**

TRAILER HOMES AND CAMPSITES: Disney's Fort Wilderness Resort and Campground provides a rustic outdoors setting for groups. The one-bedroom Wilderness Home trailers sleep six and have fully equipped kitchens and outdoor grills. Fort Wilderness campsites for tents and RV hookups start under $50 per night, the most economical stay at Walt Disney World. Creekside Meadow, a secluded area in the forest, offers groups of twenty or more a unique back-to-nature setting, as well as all the necessary camping gear. (See "Camping at Fort Wilderness," page 113.)

GROUP DISCOUNTS: Several travel clubs offer substantial hotel discounts at Walt Disney World (see "Discount Travel Tips," page 17). Walt Disney World also offers seasonal vacation packages that are economical for groups (see "Vacation Package Values," page 20). For larger groups, Disney Leisure Group (800 327-2989) discounts blocks of ten or more rooms (not including the budget resorts). ◆

CELEBRATIONS & GATHERINGS

Walt Disney World is a popular spot for gatherings and special celebrations, including family reunions, birthday parties, weddings, and anniversaries. Private parties have been held at such unlikely places as the stage of the Indiana Jones Epic Stunt Spectacular and the beach of Discovery Island at sunrise. Event catering for large groups can be arranged by calling Resort Sales and Service (407 828-3074). Guests staying in vacation homes, such as those at Disney's Old Key West Resort, can arrange for private catered meals or cookouts through Walt Disney World's Black Tie to Barbecue (407 827-3549).

GROUP DINING AT FULL-SERVICE RESTAURANTS: Most restaurants in the resorts and theme parks can accommodate large and small groups. Among the most popular restaurants for groups are Fulton's Crab House, Artist Point, and 'Ohana. To reserve a seating for groups of up to twenty or to make special requests (a birthday cake, for example), call Disney Dining Reservations (407 939-3463).

PRIVATE PARTIES AT PLEASURE ISLAND: Private parties can be arranged in any of Pleasure Island's seven nightclubs, which offer a variety of interesting atmospheres. Pleasure Island caters parties in the clubs from 5 PM until 8:30 PM (the average cost is about $1,200). For information, call WDW Park and Event Sales (407 828-2048). At Planet Hollywood, private parties for thirty to five hundred guests can be arranged by calling Planet Hollywood Catering Sales (407 827-7836).

ROMANTIC SETTINGS & CELEBRATIONS FOR TWO: There are so many romantic spots at Walt Disney World that entire vacations can be planned around that theme. In fact, more newlyweds honeymoon at Walt Disney World than anywhere else in the world, and then return year after year. Among the most acclaimed dining experiences and romantic settings are Bistro de Paris and San Angel Inn Restaurante in the World Showcase, Victoria and Albert's at Disney's Grand Floridian Beach Resort, Arthur's 27 at Buena Vista Palace & Spa, the Polynesian Luau dinner show followed by a view of the Magic Kingdom fireworks from the beach, and the Starlight Cruise, a private dinner cruise on Seven Seas Lagoon. (See "Excursion Cruises," page 222).

ORGANIZING TIPS FOR GROUPS

Groups who are meeting at the Orlando International Airport should plan carefully to avoid confusion. If members are arriving at many different times or late in the day, it may be smart and economical to spend that first night at the airport's Hyatt Regency. (See "Orlando International Airport," pages 254 and 255.)

HOLIDAYS: Group trips are often arranged during holidays, when Walt Disney World can be very crowded. Fall is the best time for group vacations, especially the three weeks after Thanksgiving, which have very light crowds, while offering festive holiday entertainment. Other holiday choices for groups, considering the crowds and weather, are the weeks of Thanksgiving, Presidents' Day, and Easter. The most difficult holidays for groups are Memorial Day, Labor Day, the week between Christmas and New Year's, and the Fourth of July (see "Holiday Events," page 15).

STAYING IN TOUCH: There are Message Centers in the Magic Kingdom, Epcot, and Disney-MGM Studios where visitors touring separately can leave and retrieve messages on a network that connects the three parks. Messages can also be phoned into the Message Center (407 824-4321). Cellular phones and pagers are available through Guest Services at any Walt Disney World resort. ◆

BABYSITTING & DAY CAMPS

Visitors traveling with children have a wealth of child care options at Walt Disney World, which can free them to explore the many adult-oriented attractions and entertainments that are offered. At the same time, Walt Disney World's child care centers are unique environments where kids feel entertained, not "sat." Drop-off programs require that children be toilet trained; no diapers, including pull-ups, are allowed. In-room sitting and in-park child care are also available and widely used at Walt Disney World. (See also "Camp Disney at the Disney Institute," page 249, for additional kids-only adventures.)

BOARDWALK HARBOR CLUB: *Disney's BoardWalk Resort* — This facility offers guests a place to keep their children amused while the adults head to the BoardWalk for some grown-up entertainment. Facilities include a large-screen TV, free video games, arts and crafts, and the usual assortment of Disney plush toys. Open to guests staying at any Disney-owned resort. The BoardWalk Harbor Club is designed for children age four to twelve.

> **RESERVATIONS:** Open from 4 PM until 11:45 PM daily. About $5 per hour; meals are extra. Reservations suggested (407 939-6301).

CAMP DOLPHIN: *Walt Disney World Dolphin and Swan Resorts* — This busy child care and activity center is designed for children age three through twelve, and provides a Dinner Club and movies in the evening. Other activities include crafts and games, and daytime camps run seasonally. Available to all Walt Disney World visitors; priority is given to guests staying at the Dolphin and Swan hotels. Occupancy is limited to fifteen children.

> **RESERVATIONS:** Open from 6 until 11 PM. A full night of entertainment, including dinner, is about $45. Reservations suggested (407 934-4241).

CUB'S DEN: *Disney's Wilderness Lodge Resort* — The Cub's Den is a fully supervised Western-themed dining and entertainment club for children age four through twelve. Children are treated to a kid-friendly picnic meal and enjoy a live animal visitor from Discovery Island, computer games, and art activities. As children get tired, they can cuddle up with a pillow and blanket in front of a wide-screen TV to watch Disney movies. Available to guests staying at any Disney-owned resort. Occupancy is limited to twenty children.

> **RESERVATIONS:** Open from 5 PM until midnight. About $7 per hour, which includes the picnic meal. One-hour minimum. Reservations suggested (407 824-1083).

HILTON YOUTH HOTEL: *The Hilton Resort* — In addition to the usual array of games, movies, and activities, this child care facility offers small beds set off in a quiet area for children who wish to take a nap or go to sleep before their parents return. Available to children age four through twelve staying at any resort on Walt Disney World property.

> **RESERVATIONS:** Open from 5 PM until midnight. About $4 per hour. Reserve at least one day in advance (407 827-4000: hotel).

KIDS' STUFF PROGRAM: *Buena Vista Palace Resort & Spa* — This educational and recreational camp is designed for children age four to twelve. Enrollment is on a first-come, first-served basis, and is available to Buena Vista Palace Resort & Spa guests and those using the conference facilities.

> **RESERVATIONS:** Day camps run from 10 AM until 1 PM and from 2 until 5 PM. About $15 per child. Evening camps are available on selected nights from 6 until 9 PM. About $15 to $25 per child, which includes dinner. For additional information, call 407 827-3701.

MOUSEKETEER CLUB: *Disney's Grand Floridian Beach Resort* — This small, pleasantly decorated club accepts a maximum of twelve children at one time and provides an assortment of toys, board games, computer games, books, and Disney movies. Available to children age four to twelve who are staying at any Disney-owned resort. Cookies and a beverage are provided.

    RESERVATIONS: Open from 4:30 PM until midnight. About $4.50 per hour, with a four-hour maximum. Reservations recommended (407 824-2985).

MOUSEKETEER CLUBHOUSE: *Disney's Contemporary Resort* — The Mouseketeer Clubhouse is basically a short-term care center with limited facilities and amusements. Designed for children age four through twelve, it offers computer games and an assortment of toys. The Clubhouse accepts guests from any Disney-owned resort and is limited to ten children.

    RESERVATIONS: Open from 4:30 PM until midnight. About $4 per hour, with a four-hour maximum; meals are extra. Reserve at least two days in advance (407 824-1000: hotel).

NEVERLAND CLUB: *Disney's Polynesian Resort* — Based on the story of Peter Pan, this themed club is very popular. Guests enter the building and find themselves in Wendy's bedroom, where they watch as their child is sprinkled with pixie dust and climbs through the window into the wonderful world of Never-Never Land. The fun includes a visit from some of the feathered and scaly inhabitants of Discovery Island, unlimited arcade games, and a wealth of Disney toys. The children are supervised in both group and individual activities, and a kid-pleasing buffet dinner is included. Designed for children age four to twelve. Available to all Walt Disney World visitors.

    RESERVATIONS: Open from 5 PM until midnight. A buffet is served from 6 until 8 PM. About $8 per hour, with a three-hour minimum. Reservations suggested, especially during peak seasons. Call Disney Dining Reservations (407 939-3463) or Same-Day Reservations (824-2000, ext. 2184).

SANDCASTLE CLUB: *Disney's Beach Club Resort* — This child care and activity center is open to children age four to twelve and features computer games, arts and crafts projects, and a library of children's books and movies. Available to guests at the Yacht and Beach Club resorts; guests staying at other Disney-owned resorts can use the facility on a drop-in basis after 4 PM, if space is available.

    RESERVATIONS: Open from 4:30 PM until midnight. About $5 per hour. Provision for a meal must be made for any child left more than four hours. Reserve at least one day ahead (407 934-6290).

IN-ROOM AND IN-PARK BABYSITTING: *ABC Mothers, Teachers, and Grannies* — This service provides both in-room and within-park child care. As the name suggests, ABC has experienced moms, teachers, and grandmothers on staff. All caregivers have undergone extensive background checks. They are bonded and licensed, and are completely knowledgeable about Walt Disney World.

    RESERVATIONS: Four-hour minimum. About $7 per hour for the first child ($1 per hour for each additional child), plus a $5 transportation fee. Reservations required (407 296-8103).

IN-ROOM AND IN-PARK BABYSITTING: *KinderCare* — For seventeen years, KinderCare-trained sitters, who are bonded and licensed, have provided both in-room and in-park child care at Walt Disney World, as well as at other area hotels. Caregivers bring along age-appropriate activities. A meal must be provided for the caregiver if the sit time runs eight hours.

    RESERVATIONS: Office open every day from 7 AM to 9 PM. About $11 per hour for one to three children, with a four-hour minimum, plus 30 minutes' travel time. The cost of the caregiver's admission is added for in-park child care. Reserve at least one day in advance and up to thirty days ahead (407 827-5444; outside of Orlando, call 407 846-2027). ◆

GUIDED TOURS

Walt Disney World offers visitors of all ages a variety of behind-the-scenes, special-interest, and private theme park tours. Some tours are especially useful for orienting first-time visitors, and many delight experienced visitors who want to make new discoveries. The guided tours listed below are among the best at Walt Disney World. Most of them require advance reservations, which can be made up to 90 days in advance through WDW Tours (407 939-8687). **American Express card holders may receive a 20 percent discount on selected tours by using their card when making reservations. Be sure to ask!**

KEYS TO THE KINGDOM: *Magic Kingdom* — This four-hour walking tour offers visitors an informative overview of the Magic Kingdom, lets them experience several attractions, and takes them into backstage areas and lower-level "utilidors" under the park. Two tours depart daily from City Hall at about 10 AM. Advance reservations are recommended. If space is available, visitors can join the tour by signing up early at City Hall. Cost: About $45 (excluding food and theme park admission).

INSIDE ANIMATION: *Disney-MGM Studios* — This 2¹/₂-hour walking tour explores in detail how animated films are created. Visitors get a behind-the-scenes look inside one of Disney's working animation studios, where feature films are being produced, and learn how to create and paint a Mickey Mouse animation cel of their own. The tour departs at 9:30 AM on Tuesdays and Thursdays; tour days may change. Reservations should be made at least six weeks in advance. Cost: About $45.

BACKSTAGE MAGIC: This seven-hour excursion takes visitors on a behind-the-scenes tour of the Magic Kingdom, Disney-MGM Studios, Epcot, and some resort-wide sites to explore how the Walt Disney World experience is created and maintained. Mini-buses shuttle visitors to each site for a look at the backstage areas. The tour also visits a working animation studio where Disney feature films are in production. Tours depart at about 9 AM on weekdays, and should be booked at least six weeks in advance. Cost: About $160 (including lunch in a special setting).

DISNEY'S YULETIDE FANTASY: This three-hour tour explores holiday traditions at Walt Disney World, and gives visitors a behind-the-scenes look at how decorations are created and used to transform the Magic Kingdom, Disney-MGM Studios, Epcot, and selected resorts into Christmas wonderlands. This tour is offered only in December. Reservations are required. Cost: About $45.

VIP TOURS: These private, custom-tailored tours let visitors explore Walt Disney World in any way they wish: from the theme parks and resorts to backstage and production areas, and even maintenance and greenhouse facilities. Knowledgeable guides lead the tours, which can be from three to eight hours long (a meal in a full-service restaurant is required for tours longer than four hours). VIP Tours are booked through Disney Special Activities (407 560-6233) and must be reserved at least three days ahead. Cost: About $65 per hour per guide (not including food and theme park admission).

SPECIAL-INTEREST TOURS: There are regularly scheduled tours throughout Walt Disney World that are great for families and small groups who want to sightsee together. Future World at Epcot offers the **Behind the Seeds Tour** and **DiveQuest** (see "Future World," page 31). The World Showcase at Epcot presents **Hidden Treasures of the World Showcase** and **Gardens of the World** (see "World Showcase," page 41). Discovery Island has several nature tours (see "Discovery Island," page 118). The Disney Institute offers several special-focus tours for adults and a variety of expeditions designed for children and young adults (see "Disney Institute," page 248). ◆

THE DISNEY INSTITUTE
Website: www.disneyinstitute.com

The Disney Institute is both a luxury resort and a unique discovery destination for visitors who would like to add a new dimension to their vacation. At the Institute, visitors can explore their special interests, try their hand at new skills, and expand their creative talents in more than forty different areas, ranging from animation to gourmet cooking to rock climbing. Visitors can attend informative lectures by guest experts, work with a personal trainer in the Sports and Fitness Center, indulge in a treatment at The Spa, and enjoy film screenings or live performances in the evening. The learning programs at Disney Institute are ideal for individuals who would like to try a new adventure and for families and groups who would enjoy a shared experience. The guest-to-instructor ratio is about fifteen to one, and instructors (including a rotating roster of artists in residence) are all top professionals in their field. The Disney Institute offers multi-day vacation packages that include programs, meals, and accommodations. Disney Institute also offers Day Visitor programs and evening Dinner and Performance packages.

LOCATION AND ACCOMMODATIONS: Disney Institute is located in the Disney Village Resorts Area, near Downtown Disney. Learning facilities are clustered in a setting that combines the laid-back bustle of a college campus with the ambience of a small town. Disney Institute accommodations are scattered across 250 acres of woodlands, waterways, and golf greens. Guests have a choice of accommodations, including Bungalow suites with wet bars and one- or two-bedroom Townhouses with kitchenettes (see "The Villas at the Disney Institute," page 149).

PROGRAMS: Disney Institute programs are imaginatively structured to create meaningful learning experiences. Each program offers several two- to three-hour courses in the morning and afternoon, which can be mixed and matched to suit visitor's interests and vacation schedules. The programs are:

ANIMATION: Explore the history, development, and different methods of animation. Learn how to paint cels, animate clay, and use computer animation techniques as you work on a real animation project, such as a public service announcement. (You'll take home a copy of the film you worked on, complete with your name in the credits.)

CULINARY ARTS: Learn about gourmet cooking techniques, food and wine pairings, international cuisines, and festive recipes for celebrations as you prepare dishes under the guidance of a master chef, then sample them with your classmates in the class cafe. Ingredients are washed, chopped, and measured before you arrive, and you don't even have to clean up the mess.

DESIGN AND DECORATIVE ARTS: Make your personal environment more functional and enjoyable, pick up expert tips on recognizing and caring for antiques, learn trompe l'oeil and faux-finish techniques that let you create special illusions, and explore the architecture of Walt Disney World.

GARDENS AND THE GREAT OUTDOORS: Get an insider's look at how Walt Disney World's gardens are created and maintained. Turn containers into miniature gardens, create imaginative topiaries, and learn to create decorations and gifts from your own garden. Explore Walt Disney World's conservation area by canoe, for a look at the variety of indigenous birds and animals that reside there.

LIFESTYLES: Learn techniques for researching your genealogy and your family's past history. Find out how to use your personal computer for desktop publishing and exploring the Internet and World Wide Web. Join visiting experts for special classes in a variety of topics, including dance, personal style and image, and money management.

MONEY SAVING PAGE

➤ **PHOTOGRAPHY:** Work with a photojournalist to capture an image that tells a story. Find out how to create memorable portraits with your camera. Discover the secrets of outdoor photography. Explore digital imaging and techniques for creating special photographic effects.

➤ **RADIO:** Step into a sound studio to learn the ins and outs of radio production, including how to create sound effects and voices for radio dramas, and how to host and DJ a radio show. Then, put your new-found knowledge to work as you broadcast live from Disney Institute's in-house radio station.

➤ **SHOW BIZ:** Sign up for workshops in acting, improv comedy, and voice-over techniques. Learn how to do stage, screen, and special-effects make-up. Find out how movies are made by making one your-self, and get the inside story on feature productions from the visiting artists who made them.

➤ **SPORTS AND FITNESS:** Sign up for exercise and relaxation classes and work with a personal trainer to develop your own custom fitness program. Assess your skills in golf and tennis, then use the techniques of the pros to develop your game. Learn to climb a rock or advance your climbing skills on a unique structure with special surfaces for all climbing-skill levels.

➤ **STORY ARTS:** Learn how Walt Disney combined his words and illustrations to tell great stories in his animated classics. Explore the Magic Kingdom to learn what it takes to create and maintain the fantasy atmosphere there. Study how Imagineers "tell" stories in three dimensions, then apply their techniques to tell a tale of your own.

➤ **TELEVISION AND VIDEO:** Learn professional techniques for making high-quality home videos. Find out what it takes to produce your own television news story in the field, how to edit your shots in the studio to tell the story clearly, and how to step in front of the camera and introduce your story. Then, broadcast your work live from Disney Institute's own in-house television studio.

➤ **CAMP DISNEY:** A wide variety of programs and field trips are offered to younger visitors staying anywhere at Walt Disney World. Youngsters age seven to ten can enjoy nature treks and theme park expeditions with peeks into backstage areas. Visitors age eleven to fifteen can sign up for fun and informative activities, including a unique scavenger hunt at one of the major theme parks. Advance reservations are recommended through Walt Disney World Tours (407 939-8687).

PROGRAM FEES: Three-day vacation packages, which include programs, accommodations, one-day theme park admission, and all meals, facilities, and events, start at about $660 per person, based on double occupancy (about $520 without meals). Day Visitor Programs, including one learning program, use of the Fitness Center facilities, and the evening event, start at about $50 (about $80 with two learning programs). Dinner and Performance packages, including dinner at Seasons Dining Room and the scheduled evening event, cost about $35 per person and are available to all visitors.

RESERVATIONS AND INFORMATION: To request a brochure or book a multi-day vacation, call Disney Institute Programs and Packages (800 282-9282). To reserve a one-day visit, call Disney Institute Day Visitor Programs (407 827-4800). For a fax listing of class sessions up to ninety days ahead, call Disney Institute Fax on Demand (800 324-5243). To reserve the evening Dinner and Performance package, call Disney Dining (407 939-3463) up to fourteen days in advance.

Disney resort guests will find ongoing promotions that let them sample Disney Institute programs for a low price. Ask Guest Services at your resort. Entertainment's Orlando guide has valuable two-for-one Day Visitor Program coupons. The chef-taught culinary program, where you prepare your own three-course meal, is very popular choice. (See "Entertainment Publications," page 19.) ◆

SAVE

FAMILY & FRIENDS

WEDDINGS & HONEYMOONS

Top-notch entertainment and recreation, and exquisitely themed resorts make Walt Disney World ideal for destination weddings and romantic honeymoon adventures. Disney's Fairy Tale Weddings arranges over seventeen hundred weddings each year in the resorts and theme parks, and for years Walt Disney World has remained the number one honeymoon destination in the world.

WEDDINGS: Any wedding fantasy can become reality at Walt Disney World. Ceremonies can be held afterhours in the theme parks, in the fantasy atmosphere of a themed resort, or inside Disney's Wedding Pavilion, an ornate Victorian summerhouse that floats on the edge of Seven Seas Lagoon. Several privately-owned premier resorts at Walt Disney World also offer enchanting wedding sites.

DISNEY'S FAIRY TALE WEDDINGS: Fairy Tale Weddings can be tailored to fit each couple's budget and taste, whether simple or elaborate, traditional or entirely original, and can be held at any resort or in Disney's Wedding Pavilion. There are three wedding categories: **DESTINATION WEDDINGS** are small weddings for gatherings of up to twenty of the couple's family and friends. A wedding consultant works with the bride and groom to plan the ceremony and reception (starting at about $8,000). With a **CUSTOMIZED WEDDING,** the couple's wedding day fantasy is meticulously designed by a wedding consultant, and the ceremony locations also include the theme parks. All details of the ceremony and reception, which can accommodate any number of guests, are included in Customized Weddings (starting at about $13,000, and averaging about $25,000). The simplest Fairy Tale Wedding, which is also a vacation package for couples, is the **INTIMATE WEDDING** (in another era, it might have been called the "Elopement Wedding.") Intimate Weddings include a cozy ceremony for two, honeymoon accommodations, and theme park admissions (starting at about $3,000). Contact Disney's Fairy Tale Weddings (407 827-3400) for more information and to request a brochure.

RESORT WEDDINGS: The elegant Buena Vista Palace & Spa has two wedding gazebos situated on either side of Lake Buena Vista, each with a cascading fountain nearby, and hosts hundreds of weddings and receptions each year. Contact Buena Vista Palace Convention Services (407 827-3360). The majestic Hyatt Regency Grand Cypress also boasts a charming wedding pavilion in a garden setting on Lake Windsong. Contact Hyatt Regency Grand Cypress Catering (407 239-3933) for information.

HONEYMOONS: Walt Disney World is a one stop shop for fantasy vacations, which explains its honeymoon popularity. Here, newlyweds can pursue a different romantic adventure every day — or many each day. They can ride horses through the forest at dawn, tour the world that afternoon with a stop for lunch in Paris, and fly across the waters on a speedboat that night in pursuit of spectacular fireworks. It's hard to put that kind of day together anywhere else, or make such magical memories.

DISNEY'S FAIRY TALE HONEYMOONS: Fairy Tale Honeymoon packages include accommodations, theme park admissions, and a selection of details that bring magic to the moment: chilled Champagne, a private in-room breakfast, romantic floral arrangements. Contact Disney's Central Resort Reservations (407 827-7200)for information on Fairy Tale Honeymoons.

RESORT HONEYMOONS: A range of honeymoon packages, from informal to luxurious, are also offered by the following resorts at Walt Disney World (contact them directly for vacation package brochures): Buena Vista Palace & Spa, The Hilton Resort, Hotel Royal Plaza, Shades of Green, Walt Disney World Dolphin, Walt Disney World Swan, and the Grosvenor Resort. ◆

DISNEY CRUISES

Disney takes to the sea with three- and four-day cruises aboard the *Disney Magic*, a modern ship designed with the look and feel of a classic oceanliner. The cruises offer activities designed to appeal to families, groups and friends vacationing together, and to couples pursuing an adult adventure. A sister ship to the *Magic*, the *Disney Wonder*, joins the Disney Cruise Line fleet in late 1998.

THE VOYAGE: Cruises depart from Florida's Port Canaveral for Port Nassau, in the Bahamas, for sightseeing and shopping. Then it's on to Castaway Cay, Disney's private island paradise, for an all-day Caribbean beach party and barbecue, as well as swimming, boating, snorkeling, games, music, massage, and lounging on the white sand beaches — including a beach exclusively for adults.

ONBOARD ACTIVITIES: An array of special activities lets voyagers of all ages customize their cruise. Guests can also indulge in pampering treatments at the full-service spa, the largest aboard any cruise ship. There's plenty of shopping and onboard sports, and the ship offers three pools — one for adults who like casual dips, one for active water enthusiasts, and one for kids to splash and play in, which can be transformed into a dance floor for nighttime parties. Other entertainment areas include:

• **BEAT STREET:** This entertainment area for adults is like a mini Pleasure Island, complete with three clubs: Sessions, a comfortable piano lounge; Off Beat, a comedy club that showcases the audience's improv skills along with the comics'; and Rockin' Bar D, a high-energy dance club with live music.

• **WALT DISNEY THEATRE:** This formal 1,040-seat theater with advanced theatrical technology showcases a different original Disney musical on each cruise night.

• **BUENA VISTA CINEMA:** This plush 270-seat theater with an ultra-sophisticated sound system screens several films each day, including classic animated films and the latest Disney movies.

• **LOUNGES:** Studio Sea offers family entertainment, the Promenade Lounge features live music in a casual setting, and the ESPN Skybox, high atop the ship, treats sports fans to satellite-beamed games.

• **TEENS AND CHILDREN:** A special teens-only coffeehouse and lounge offers movies, games, film-making and performing arts mini classes, as well as other teen activities. Oceaneer's Adventure, a huge kids-oriented program, provides play areas and adventures for youngsters age three to twelve throughout the day and evening. A trained staff of forty supervises all activities.

DINING: Guests dine in a different restaurant every evening: Parrot Cay serves Caribbean dishes in a friendly tropical decor; at Animator's Palate, guests dine on California cuisine as giant black and white animation sketches magically turn to color; and Lumiere's offers French cuisine in an ambience of casual elegance. An adults-only alternative, Palo, serves up Italian fare and spectacular views in a sophisticated candlelight setting.

ACCOMMODATIONS: Larger-than-average standard staterooms have a nautical motif and feature a sitting area, TV, hair dryer, in-room safe, and mini bar. Most outside staterooms have private decks.

RESERVATIONS: Three-day cruises start at about $800 per person, excluding airfare; four-day cruises start at about $900. Seven-day cruise/vacation packages that include airfare and a stay at Walt Disney World start at about $1,400 per person. For information, call Disney Cruise Line Reservations (407 566-7000). **Be sure to look into special cruise discounts before booking your trip! Members of AAA may receive discounts of about 20 percent, saving hundreds of dollars on Disney Cruises. Magic Kingdom Club members can also purchase Disney Cruises at a slight discount.** ◆

DISNEY VACATION PLANNING DIRECTORY

The area code in Orlando and at Walt Disney World is 407. Unless otherwise noted, you must first dial 407 for all numbers listed below when calling from outside the Orlando area.

GENERAL DISNEY INFORMATION

Walt Disney World Information **824-4321**
  Foreign Language Center 824-7900
  Hearing-impaired Guests (TDD) 827-5141
Switchboard to All Walt Disney World Hotels 824-2222

RESERVATIONS

WDW Central Reservations (Hotel) **934-7639**
Disney Dining Reservations **939-3463**
Walt Disney Travel Co. (Vacation Packages) 800 828-0228

(Also see "Hotels," page 123; Off-Site Hotels," page 152; "Resort Dining," page 197; and "Dining Events," page 205.)

ATTRACTIONS INFORMATION

Walt Disney World Information **824-4321**
Weather, Disney **824-4104**
Blizzard Beach 560-3400
Discovery Island 824-2875
Disney-MGM Studios Production Information 560-4651
Disney's Wide World of Sports 363-6600
Pleasure Island 934-7781
Pleasure Island AMC Theatres, Show Times 827-1300
River Country 824-2760
Typhoon Lagoon 560-4141

GUIDED TOURS

Walt Disney World Tours **939-8687**
Discovery Island Tours 934-2651
VIP Tours 560-6233

SPORTS RESERVATIONS

Disney's Wide World of Sports (hotline) 363-6600
Boating Excursions:
  The Breathless, Yacht Club Marina 934-8000
  Fireworks Cruise, Contemporary Marina 824-1000
  Fireworks Cruise, Polynesian Marina 824-2000
  Starlight Cruise, Grand Floridian Marina 824-2439
Fishing Excursions:
  Buena Vista Lagoon 828-2461
  Crescent Lake 824-2621
  Fort Wilderness 824-2621
  Sassagoula River 934-5409

Fitness Centers
  Body By Jake Health Club, Dolphin 934-4264
  Muscles and Buscles, BoardWalk 939-2370
  Contemporary Health and Fitness Club 824-3410
  Ship Shape Health Club, Yacht & Beach Club...... 934-3256
  Sports and Fitness Center, Disney Institute 827-4455
  Swan Health Club, Swan 934-1360
Golf Reservations 824-2270
Parasailing, Contemporary 824-2464
Spas:
  The Grand Floridian Spa and Health Club 824-2332
  The Spa at Buena Vista Palace 827-2727
  The Spa at the Disney Institute 827-4455
Tennis Reservations:
  Disney Institute Tennis Programs 827-4800
  Grand Floridian 824-3578
  Racquet Club, Contemporary 824-3578
Waterskiing Excursions 824-2621

SERVICES

Centra Care Walk-In Medical Care 239-6463
Florist, Gooding's Supermarket 827-1206
Florist, Walt Disney World 827-3505
House+Med and Medi+Clinic 396-1195
Lost and Found at Walt Disney World 824-4245
Pharmacy, Gooding's Supermarket 827-1207
Sand Lake Hospital 351-8500
Turner's Drugs 828-8125

TRANSPORTATION SERVICES

AAA Emergency Road Service 800 222-4357
AAA Service Station, Walt Disney World 824-0976
Disney AAA/Ocala Travel Center 352 854-0770
Orlando Airport, Paging 825-2000
Rental Cars:

			At WDW	
Alamo	800 327-9633			827-3437
Avis	800 831-2847			827-2847
Budget.	800 527-0700			850-6700
Dollar	800 800-4000			827-3038
National	800 227-7368			934-4930
Thrifty	800 367-2277			934-8834

Taxi Service at Walt Disney World 824-3360

(Also see "Local Transportation & Parking," page 256.)

TOOLKIT

PACKING TIPS

Casual clothes are the norm throughout Walt Disney World. The only exceptions are in some of the more elegant restaurants or, if you want to make an impression, the nightclubs at Pleasure Island or Disney's BoardWalk. All resorts provide shampoo, at the very least, and the better resorts also supply hair dryers. In the winter, Orlando can experience cold snaps, so before leaving, check with Disney Weather (407 824-4104). The items listed below are absolute musts for touring Walt Disney World in comfort.

CLOTHING: Pack comfortable, well-broken-in walking shoes — not only will you be spending much of your time on your feet, but good shoes will protect feet and toes from being trampled. Sandals can cause problems when boarding and disembarking rides, and should be used poolside only. In winter, bring a sweater for layering, and pack a jacket that is lined for warmth. Don't forget gloves to keep off the chill when standing in line outdoors. Most hotels have coin-operated washers and dryers.

SUN & WEATHER PROTECTION: Pack a lightweight hat or visor that shades your eyes. Bring a pair of sunglasses that provide full protection from UV rays. Choose a sun block rated SPF 15 or higher; the Florida sun will burn you even in the winter. Reapply it every hour or so. Umbrellas also provide good protection against the sun. (Sunburn is the most frequently treated problem at first-aid stations and nearby clinics.) It rains daily in summer, so pack a rain hat and collapsible umbrella that fits in your tote bag (rain ponchos can make you uncomfortably hot if worn too long).

TOURING ESSENTIALS: Bring a fanny pack, backpack, or roomy, lightweight tote bag with a comfortable shoulder strap — you will find it invaluable for carrying around brochures, entertainment schedules, sun block, small purchases, and bottled water. Self-sealing plastic bags are good for stashing wet bathing suits or food in your tote bag while you're touring. Pack a lightweight flashlight such as a penlight, which is useful for reading maps and entertainment schedules after dark, consulting guidebooks while waiting in line at dark attractions, and reading menus in dimly lit restaurants. You might want to bring a book to read while waiting in lines, or a cassette player with headphones for audio books or music tapes. You might want to carry a bottle of soap bubbles — they provide instant soothing entertainment if you (or any young-at-heart companions) begin to get restless.

UPON ARRIVAL: Fill your pockets with quarters for the toll roads and dollar bills for tipping. On your drive to Walt Disney World, you may want to stop and pick up supplies for your room. The most convenient grocery store is Gooding's Supermarket at Crossroads Shopping Center. (See the "Walt Disney World" map, page 23.) Purchase bottled water, including some small bottles of water you can refill and carry with you as you tour. Don't forget juice, soft drinks, coffee (if your room has a coffeemaker), beer, or wine. You may also want to pick up light snacks and fresh fruit or breakfast items, which can save lots of time and money on those early-morning tours. Most resort rooms have mini bars where you can chill your beverages. All have small refrigerators you can rent. **You'll save money by purchasing snacks and beverages outside the park, since resort prices for these items are unusually high. They will make your hotel room welcoming and pleasant, and you will be thankful that you have them after a long day of touring or first thing in the morning.** ◆

Smart

TOOLKIT

ORLANDO INTERNATIONAL AIRPORT

WEBSITE: www.state.fl.us/goaa/

This large futuristic airport is the fastest growing in the world, and the first stop for most Walt Disney World visitors. The main terminal has a variety of restaurants and retail shops, including large gift shops for the area's major theme parks. The elegant Hyatt Regency hotel is inside the main terminal, and is particularly convenient for visitors who are arriving late or leaving early. Automated trains transport passengers from three distant gateways to the huge main terminal, where ticketing areas, baggage claim, and ground transportation are located. (See also "Local Transportation & Parking," page 256.)

AIRPORT LAYOUT: After landing in Orlando, all passengers board automated trains at their satellite terminals to reach the main terminal. The trains arrive at both ends of the long main terminal, either in the light-filled East Hall, where the atrium is surrounded by the Hyatt hotel on the upper floors, or in the West Hall, where most restaurants and the Disney Store and travel center is located. Moving walkways connect the two large Halls. Passengers arrive on Level Three, where all ticket counters, shops, restaurants, and the hotel are located.

The long main terminal is also divided north and south into two very long mirror-image areas: Landside A (north) and Landside B (south). Baggage claim and ground transportation services are on both sides of Level Two. Car rental counters are on both sides of Level One. Each Landside is used by specific airlines, and each has its own ticket counters, baggage claim areas, car rental agency counters, ground transportation services, and parking lots. The main terminal can be confusing when you have several things to accomplish, such as renting cars, storing baggage, or meeting others, so listen to the recorded announcement on your train and keep an eye on the airport signs.

- ◆ 407 825-2001 — Information about airline gate locations; open 8 AM until 5 PM
- ◆ 407 825-2000 — Paging number for callers outside the airport
- ◆ 407 825-2352 — General airport information and help with departure and arrival times

MEETING COMPANIONS AT THE AIRPORT: 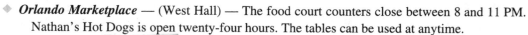 Travelers arriving on different airlines who want to rendezvous at the airport should plan carefully. To avoid mix-ups, it is always best to meet on Level Three of the Main Terminal, since Levels One and Two have duplicate services on both sides, and you must return to Level Three to cross over. For example, there are three Dollar Rental Car counters, so if you decide to meet at Dollar on Level One, you must specify the Dollar location nearest the airline of the passenger holding the car rental reservation (reservations are held at specific counters). If there is time between arrivals, you may want to meet on Level Three after retrieving your luggage. Among the most pleasant and reliable meeting spots on Level Three are:

- ◆ *Orlando Marketplace* — (West Hall) — The food court counters close between 8 and 11 PM. Nathan's Hot Dogs is open twenty-four hours. The tables can be used at anytime.
- ◆ *Chili's Too* — (West Hall, mezzanine level) — Southwest cuisine; open until 11 PM.
- ◆ *Stinger Ray's* — (West Hall) — Restaurant and bar; open until 11 PM.
- ◆ *The Atrium Rotunda* — (East Hall) — A pleasant hall with fountain and seating areas.
- ◆ *Shipyard Brewery Pub* — (East Hall) — Microbrewery and restaurant; open until 11 PM.
- ◆ *Hyatt Regency* — (East Hall, mezzanine level) — Meeting spots include the comfortable lobby area and McCoy's bistro-style restaurant, which is open until 11 PM. ◆

HYATT REGENCY
ORLANDO INTERNATIONAL AIRPORT

9300 AIRPORT BOULEVARD, ORLANDO, FL 32827
TELEPHONE (407) 825-1234 • FAX (407) 856-1672

If you're arriving at the Orlando International Airport at night, you may want to consider spending the night at the Hyatt Regency, inside the airport, instead of driving twenty miles in the dark to find Walt Disney World and your hotel. The next morning, you can drop your bags at your Disney-area hotel and tour the theme parks well rested. Your hotel will hold your luggage until your room is ready for check in, usually after 3 PM. **This travel strategy can also help save money on one day of car rental and on the cost of more expensive resort accommodations on that first night. The strategy works for early morning departures, as well. Be sure to ask about the Hyatt's weekend rates.**

LOCATION: The Hyatt Regency is located above the main terminal of the Orlando International Airport. It is accessible from within the airport and has its own entrance court outside.

AMBIENCE: Occupying the upper floors of the East Hall in the main terminal, the Hyatt Regency overlooks the airport's spacious indoor atrium and fountain. The mezzanine-level lobby has a quiet, elegant atmosphere with luxurious Oriental decor and large, comfortable seating areas. The spacious guest rooms are pleasantly decorated with a cool tropical motif and overhead fans. The hotel is frequented by business travelers.

AVERAGE RATES: Standard rooms about $190; about $120 on weekends.

AMENITIES: Twenty-four-hour room service, coffeemaker, in-room safe, hair dryer, newspaper delivery, turndown service, voice mail, and valet parking.

RESTAURANTS: *Hemispheres Restaurant* — Open for breakfast, lunch, and dinner featuring Italian cuisine. Daily until 10 PM; closed on Sunday.

McCoy's Bar and Grill — Lunch and dinner featuring seafood and steaks. Open every day until 11 PM.

RECREATION: Pool, fitness center, whirlpool.

FEATURES: Forget all about going to baggage claim. While guests check in, bellhops will retrieve luggage from the baggage claim area and deliver it to guest rooms. Bags are also transported from rooms to the ticket counter for departing guests. The tenth floor provides rooms that are specially equipped for business travelers.

DRAWBACKS: There are no mini bars in the room, which can be inconvenient for travelers arriving late who would like a beverage or snack.

HOT TIPS: Even-numbered guest rooms open onto the interior of the airport's glass-roofed atrium. Odd-numbered guest rooms face the runways and have large furnished balconies with soundproof glass doors.

Visitors who are flying out of Orlando early in the morning may want to spend their last night at the Hyatt Regency, which allows for a relaxed departure in the morning. The hotel's closed-circuit television system shows a listing of all flights, so guests can monitor departure times.

MAKING RESERVATIONS: First call the Hyatt Central Reservations Office (800 233-1234), then call the hotel directly (407 825-1234) to compare rates. Inquire about weekend or promotional rates and corporate rates. ◆

★★★
ATMOSPHERE

★★★★
SERVICE

★★★★
FRESHNESS

★★★
VACATION VALUE

REVIEWER'S COMMENTS: *This beautiful hotel made all the difference in the world. We stayed the night we flew in and hit WDW fresh the next morning. Bonus: The food at McCoy's was terrific.*

TOOLKIT

LOCAL TRANSPORTATION & PARKING

Nearly half of all visitors traveling to Walt Disney World will fly into the Orlando International Airport. There are number of transportation options to Walt Disney World, which is about thirty minutes south of the airport, including taxis, vans, limousines, and rental cars. Most services accept credit cards.

AIRPORT TRANSPORTATION SERVICES

TAXIS: Taxis are plentiful and carry up to six people for about $45 each way, plus gratuity. For parties of three or more, it can be less expensive and much faster to take a taxi than a shuttle. Taxi service is also available inside Walt Disney World, and can be very useful for travel between resorts if you don't have a car. Fares inside Walt Disney World range from $5 to $15.

SHUTTLE VANS: Mears Transportation (407 423-5566) provides twenty-four-hour mini-van transportation from the airport to the Walt Disney World resorts and area hotels. Vans leave every fifteen to twenty minutes from the baggage claim areas and cost about $17 per person one way, $25 round trip (children under four ride free). Passengers lift and stow their own luggage, and the van may stop to drop off passengers along the way. Reservations are taken for the return trip only.

LIMOUSINES: For groups of four or more, limousines are the most comfortable and often the most economical transportation. Limousine drivers are customarily tipped about 15 to 20 percent. Mears Transportation (407 423-5566) provides a Towncar that seats five for about $55 each way or $99 round trip. A stretch limousine that seats six costs about $99 each way, or $185 round trip. Florida TownCar (800 525-7246) provides prompt service for parties up to five for about $75 round trip, and they will stop on the way (for $5) so you can shop for room snacks and other essentials. For larger groups, Town Car Limousine (407 299-8696) has a fleet of fully equipped six- to ten-passenger stretch limousines starting at $95 each way or $185 round trip, which includes a 20 percent gratuity.

RENTAL CARS

DO YOU NEED A CAR? It all depends where you want to go each day and which hotel you're at. If you've come relax and visit only the theme parks, Disney transportation was designed for you. If you want to see and do a great deal more, and plan to dine at other resorts, you'll want a car. (Buses do not travel between resorts, and transfers can waste hours of your vacation.) If you want the convenience of a car without the parking hassle, taxis are a great alternative. If you're staying at a "hub" resort with many transportation options, you may not need a car as much. The hub resorts are the Beach Club, Yacht Club, Swan, Dolphin, BoardWalk, Grand Floridian, Contemporary, and Polynesian.

WHERE TO RENT: Car rental agencies located outside the airport may offer better prices, but the convenience of an airport location is considerable, especially on return. Off-site agencies are some distance from the airport and an additional 9 percent airport shuttle surcharge is added to off-site car rental charges, which evens the prices out. Car rental companies with drop-offs inside the airport are Avis, Budget, National, and Dollar. You can also can also rent a car anytime at Walt Disney World and return it there or drop it off at the airport at no extra charge. Car rental agencies located inside Walt Disney World include National (at the Exxon station near the Magic Kingdom, and at the

TOOLKIT

MONEY SAVING PAGE SAVE

Dolphin), Avis (Hilton), Budget (DoubleTree), Dollar (Courtyard by Marriott), Alamo (Buena Vista Palace), and Thrifty (Grosvenor). Most car rental agencies will pick you up at your hotel. **Readers receive both a free class upgrade from Dollar AND a handy prepaid Calling Card for fifteen minutes of free long distance calling. (See "Vacation Discount Coupons!" page 272.)**

DRIVING DIRECTIONS FROM THE AIRPORT: There are two main routes to Walt Disney World, which lies about twenty miles south of the airport (see the "Walt Disney World" map, page 23).

◆ **CENTRAL FLORIDA GREENEWAY (STATE ROUTE 417):** This is the simplest direct route. Take the South Exit from the airport (Disney World/Kissimmee), a long road that meets the Greeneway. Take 417 (south); there are two tollbooths along the way. The road exits at the intersection of State Road 536 (west), which takes you to the Epcot Resorts Area and the Magic Kingdom Resorts Area, and State Road 535 (north), which goes to the Disney Village Resorts Area, via Hotel Plaza Boulevard.

◆ **BEE LINE EXPRESSWAY (STATE ROAD 528):** This road passes other attraction areas such as Universal Studios. Take the North Exit from the Airport (Orlando) and follow the signs to 528 (west), the Bee Line Expressway. There are two tollbooths along the way. Exit onto Interstate Highway 4 (south) and take one of the numbered exits listed below:

   ◆ **EXIT 27:** Hotel Plaza, Disney Institute, and Crossroads Shopping Center (via 535)
   ◆ **EXIT 26B:** All Epcot Resorts and Dixie Landings, Port Orleans, and Old Key West (via 536)
   ◆ **EXIT 25B:** Magic Kingdom Resorts and Animal Kingdom Resorts (via 192)

CAR CARE & CAR PROBLEMS: Walt Disney World has three service stations: one near the Magic Kingdom, one near Pleasure Island (with a twenty-four-hour mini-mart), and one near Disney's Board-Walk (with a mini-mart and car wash.) The service station near the Magic Kingdom is an AAA-approved towing and repair center (407 824-0976). Complimentary shuttles are provided while your car is being serviced. For problems with rental cars, call the agency for assistance. If the agency has a rental counter at Walt Disney World, you can exchange your car quickly on property.

PARKING AT WALT DISNEY WORLD

THEME PARK PARKING: To survive the parking experience, jot down your car's location and license plate number, especially if you've rented a car. There are thousands of identical models in rental car fleets. Tying a bright plastic banner or scarf on your car is a good idea. It costs about $6 per day to park in the huge lots at the major theme parks; the lots are serviced by trams. That parking voucher is good all day at any theme park. Guests who are staying at a Walt Disney World resort park free.

RESORT PARKING: All resorts have free self-parking lots and many have valet parking services. At the Disney-owned resorts, valet parking is free, and guests tip the valet a dollar or two when they pick up their car. Valet parking fees (ranging from $5 to $10) are charged at most independently run resorts. Sometimes it can be more convenient to park at a resort near the theme park you are visiting than at the theme park, but Disney discourages this unless you have dining or recreational reservations at that resort. The best Walt Disney World transportation options are at the following resorts:

TO EPCOT AND DISNEY-MGM STUDIOS: Swan, Dolphin, BoardWalk, Yacht Club, and Beach Club resorts

TO THE MAGIC KINGDOM: Contemporary, Polynesian, and Grand Floridian Beach resorts

TO DISCOVERY ISLAND AND FORT WILDERNESS: Contemporary resort

TO HOOP DEE DOO MUSICAL REVUE, RIVER COUNTY, AND FORT WILDERNESS: Wilderness Lodge ◆

TOOLKIT

VISITORS WITH DISABILITIES

In keeping with the cutting-edge technologies used throughout Walt Disney World, the services and facilities for visitors with disabilities, although mostly invisible to the general traveler, are unparalleled in the travel industry. To accommodate visitors with hearing impairments, many attractions are in the process of being equipped with innovative captioning systems. Visitors with sight impairments are given Braille guidebooks, or cassette players that help them tour the parks. For visitors with mobility restrictions, Walt Disney World has assembled the largest wheelchair fleet in the world, including both standard wheelchairs and Electric Convenience Vehicles. First-aid offices in all the parks will let guests take a break from their wheelchair to rest on a cot. (They will also refrigerate insulin for visitors with diabetes.) And, of course, all hotels and public transportation are outfitted with devices for the convenience of visitors with disabilities.

VISITORS WITH MOBILITY RESTRICTIONS

Visitors with special needs should specify their requirements when making hotel reservations and request that Walt Disney World's Guidebook for Guests with Disabilities *be mailed to them or be waiting for them at check-in. Rental car companies or hotels can provide handicapped stickers for visitors who are driving.*

HOTELS: All Walt Disney World resorts have rooms equipped for guests with limited mobility. Resorts with some of the better facilities include Old Key West (lower beds, roll-in showers, handicapped parking near rooms), Dixie Landings (handicapped parking near rooms), Caribbean Beach (handicapped parking near rooms), Grand Floridian (door peepholes at wheelchair level, hand-held showers, elevator access to monorail), and Polynesian (automatic entrance doors, elevator access to monorail). The best off-site hotels include the Embassy Suites Resort Lake Buena Vista and the Caribe Royale Resort Suites. Both have bathrooms with roll-in showers, push-handle doorknobs, and low-height counters and control switches (see "Off-Site Hotels & Suites," page 152).

Resorts that may present physical challenges to visitors include the Contemporary (no elevator access to the monorail), Port Orleans (many curbs and sidewalks throughout the resort), Beach Club (inconvenient wheelchair ramps), Wilderness Lodge (steep inclines and inconvenient wheelchair access), BoardWalk (bumpy ride), and Fort Wilderness Campground (while some trailer homes are wheelchair accessible, the campsite grounds may be too soft for wheelchairs).

WHEELCHAIRS AND ELECTRIC CONVENIENCE VEHICLES: All Walt Disney World resorts have complimentary wheelchairs (with refundable deposit) for guests to use throughout their stay. Outside the resorts, wheelchairs and Electric Convenience Vehicles can be rented on a first-come, first-served basis at the Magic Kingdom, Epcot, Disney-MGM Studios, and Disney Village Marketplace (wheelchairs only). A limited number of complimentary wheelchairs (deposit required) are also available at Discovery Island, Typhoon Lagoon, Blizzard Beach, and Fort Wilderness (through Guest Services).

PARKING LOTS: All theme parks and resorts have handicapped parking areas near entrances. At the major theme parks, tollgate attendants will direct visitors with special needs to the handicapped parking areas (if visitors cannot leave their wheelchair), or to handicapped-designated end spots in the main lot with easy access to the trams (if visitors can take a few steps and their chair folds).

VALET PARKING: Valet parking is available and complimentary at the following resorts: Polynesian, Grand Floridian, Contemporary, Yacht Club, Beach Club, BoardWalk, Wilderness Lodge, and Hotel Royal Plaza. Valets expect a tip when cars are picked up. The following resorts charge valet parking fees ranging from $5 to $10: Swan, Dolphin, Hilton, Grosvenor, and Buena Vista Palace. Pleasure Island offers valet parking after 5 PM.

PUBLIC TRANSPORTATION: Many, but not all, Walt Disney World buses are wheelchair accessible. Visitors may have to wait for a specially equipped van. All monorail stations, except at the Contemporary resort, are wheelchair accessible. Most water launches are wheelchair accessible; however, for Discovery Island and Fort Wilderness trips, visitors may have to wait for a specially equipped ferry.

TELEPHONES: All public areas have wheelchair-accessible pay phones.

TOURING: Walt Disney World's *Guidebook for Guests with Disabilities* shows which attractions are wheelchair accessible and which require that visitors leave their chair in order to ride. Cast Members are not trained in transferring guests to and from wheelchairs, so visitors should bring companions to assist them. Visitors using Electric Convenience Vehicles must transfer to standard wheelchairs for many attractions. Special passes that allow visitors with specific problems to use auxiliary entrances to attractions are sometimes issued. Check at the Guest Relations window before entering parks.

VISITORS WITH HEARING IMPAIRMENTS

Walt Disney World recently began installing innovative new systems and devices at attractions to make them even more accessible to hearing-impaired guests. Visitors who would like their hotel room fitted with special equipment should specify their needs at the time they make their reservations.

HOTELS: All Walt Disney World resorts can supply guest rooms with strobe lights and a telecommunications device for the deaf (TDD). To make hotel reservations and special requests, call WDW Resorts Special Reservations (407 939-7807 voice; 407 939-7670 TDD). Closed-caption television is available in all guest rooms throughout Walt Disney World, except at some Hotel Plaza resorts.

TELEPHONES: All theme parks have amplified and hearing aid–compatible pay phones. Check with Guest Relations as you enter for a map showing telephone locations. TDDs for visitors with hearing impairments are available at City Hall in the Magic Kingdom, at Guest Relations in Disney-MGM Studios, and at The AT&T Global Neighborhood in Epcot.

TOURING: A written text of the narration for attractions and a special device that triggers captions to appear on preshow videos at attractions are available at Guest Relations in the Magic Kingdom, Epcot, and Disney-MGM Studios. Sign-language interpretation for the live shows in the theme parks is available and must be requested at least two weeks in advance through WDW Information for Guests with Disabilities (407 824-4500 voice; 407 827-5141 TDD). A new system called reflective captioning has been implemented at many of the attractions in the major theme parks. A list of attractions and their available technologies can be obtained through Guest Relations at the parks.

SIGNING TOURS: Visitors with hearing impairments can request to have a sign-language interpreter present, at no extra charge, on any tour they reserve at Walt Disney World by calling Walt Disney World Tours (407 939-8687) at least two weeks in advance.

TOOLKIT

MONEY $AVING PAGE

VISITORS WITH SIGHT IMPAIRMENTS

Visitors who travel with a guide dog should inform the hotel when making reservations. They may keep their animal with them, or they can arrange to board it at a Walt Disney World kennel. Visitors should also request that a copy of Walt Disney World's Guidebook for Guests with Disabilities *be mailed to them, which lists attractions that accommodate guide dogs.*

HOTELS: Most Walt Disney World resorts have Braille-marked elevators. The high-rise hotels are the easiest to get around in, with the exception of the Dolphin, where the floor plan is very confusing. The following resorts have sprawling layouts that may present a challenge to guests with sight impairments: Polynesian, Port Orleans, Dixie Landings, Caribbean Beach, Coronado Springs, and the All-Star Resort complex. The Grand Floridian resort also has rambling grounds, but offers trolley escort service from its outbuildings to the main lobby.

TOURING: All the major theme parks have Braille maps at their entrances. Braille guidebooks and complimentary tape players with touring cassettes (deposit required) are available at Guest Relations in the Magic Kingdom, Epcot, and Disney-MGM Studios. Visitors with a guide dog may want to bring a companion to take charge of the dog while they enjoy attractions that restrict guide animals. Cast Members are not permitted to take charge of guide animals. Special passes that allow visitors with limited sight impairments to ride an attraction twice in a row are sometimes issued. Check at the Guest Relations window before entering parks.

SPECIAL RESOURCES FOR VISITORS WITH DISABILITIES

Visitors with disabilities have a number of resources available locally to help them make the most of their Walt Disney World vacation. Those most often cited by frequent visitors are:

GUIDED TOURS: VIP Tours are private guided tours that let visitors explore Walt Disney World in any way that meets their special interests. Tours can be designed to meet special communication or interpretive needs as well, which makes them especially well suited to visitors with disabilities. For reservations, call Disney Special Activities (407 560-6233 voice; 407 827-5141 TDD) at least three days in advance, and describe any special needs at that time. (See "Guided Tours," page 247.)

HOLIDAY ASSISTANTS: This service provides trained helpers who accompany visitors with disabilities and push wheelchairs as needed at the theme parks, the airport, and at other recreational activities. Companion service fees are about $18 per hour, with a four-hour minimum. Meals and gratuity are additional. Multiday package rates are also available (407 397-4845).

CARE MED: This medical supply and referral service helps visitors secure medical resources such as wheelchair and electric wheelchair rentals, Electric Convenience Vehicle (ECV) rentals, portable oxygen machines, insulin, dialysis assistance, hospital beds, and additional aids. While Walt Disney World rents ECVs at the major theme parks, there are a limited number and they go fast. **Visitors who need the support and assurance of an ECV for touring the theme parks, and for touring recreation areas such as BoardWalk and Downtown Disney can rent ECVs for twenty-four hours, with free delivery to their hotel, for the same price as a theme park day rental, or about $30 (weekly rentals are $200).** Walt Disney World transportation and special vans are equipped to transport EVC users. Reserve in advance (800 741-2282). Website: www.caremed.org/ ◆

TOOLKIT

Smart

SHOPPING & SERVICES

If you forgot it, Walt Disney World probably has it. Some of the most sought-after items and services are listed below. (See the "Walt Disney World" map, page 23, for locations.)

- **BANKING & MONEY:** The Walt Disney World resorts will cash checks for guests (up to $50). Many resorts have automatic teller machines (ATMs) that are on the PLUS, Cirrus, and Honor networks.
  Theme Parks: Guest Relations at all theme parks will cash checks for visitors (up to $25). There are ATMs at all major theme parks, and at some smaller parks, such as Blizzard Beach. Epcot also has American Express Travel Services and Cash Machine.
  Disney Village Marketplace: There is an ATM located outside of Guest Services. A full-service branch of the Sun Bank is located across the street, on Buena Vista Drive.
  Crossroads: Gooding's Supermarket has an ATM and also provides foreign currency exchange.

- **EYEGLASSES & SUNGLASSES:** All Walt Disney World resorts carry sunglasses.
  Crossroads: Sunglass Hut International sells and repairs sunglasses. Gooding's Pharmacy carries both sunglasses and reading glasses.

- **FLORIST:** Floral arrangements and fruit baskets can be ordered from WDW Florist (407 827-3505).
  Crossroads: Gooding's Florist delivers to all area resorts (407 827-1206).

- **GROCERIES:** Most budget resorts offer a limited selection of groceries; all carry beverages and snacks. (See also "Late Night Dining" and "Open All Night," page 204.)
  Disney Village Marketplace: Gourmet Pantry has limited groceries, a bakery, and a deli.
  Crossroads: Gooding's Supermarket, the largest in the area, is open twenty-four hours a day.

- **LIQUOR:** Most Walt Disney World resorts sell wine, beer, and spirits.
  Disney Village Marketplace: Gourmet Pantry sells wine, beer, and spirits.
  Crossroads: Gooding's Supermarket sells wine and beer. Paesano's Ristorante and Liquors sells wine, beer, and spirits.
  Vista Centre: ABC Liquor sells wine, beer, and spirits.

- **MEDICAL CARE & MEDICATIONS:** House+Med Service provides twenty-four-hour physician house calls and dental referrals to all Walt Disney World area resorts (396-1195).
  Centra Care Walk-in Medical Care: This nearby clinic is open daily from 8 AM until midnight and until 8 PM on weekends (239-6463). It provides free shuttle service for resort guests. Turner Drugs (828-8125) will deliver prescriptions to the Walt Disney World resorts.
  Medi+Clinic: This walk-in clinic, open daily from 8 AM until 9 PM, is one-quarter mile east of Walt Disney World, off Highway 192 at Parkway Boulevard (396-1195). Transportation is available.
  Sand Lake Hospital: Emergency services are provided by Sand Lake Hospital, just north of Walt Disney World on Interstate 4 at Exit 27A (351-8500).
  Crossroads: Prescriptions can be filled at Gooding's Pharmacy (827-1207).

- **SHIPPING:** Most shops at Walt Disney World will ship purchases for guests.
  Shoppes at Buena Vista: A U.S. Post Office is located here.
  Vista Centre: Mail & Parcels Plus provides shipping materials and uses all major carriers.

- **TOBACCO:** Cigarettes are sold at resort gift shops and at selected merchandise shops in the theme parks. They are not on display, and must be requested. The premium resorts sell fine cigars. ◆

TOOLKIT

MONEY $AVING PAGE

CROSSROADS SHOPPING CENTER

Crossroads Shopping Center was built on a section of Walt Disney World property that is located on State Road 535, just across from the entrance to the Disney Village Resorts Area (see the "Walt Disney World" map, page 23). A large twenty-four-hour supermarket, several restaurants, and more than twenty-five different merchants are located here, including Sunglass Hut International, Mitzi's Hallmark, Crazy Shirts, Foot Locker, Beyond Electronics, and Pirate's Cove Adventure Miniature Golf Course.

$AVE ⭐ **Save money shopping at Crossroads! The stores listed below offer readers a 20 percent discount on selected merchandise (see "Vacation Discount Coupons!" page 272).**

⭐ **SUN WORKS:** This store is known for women's leisure fashions designed in comfortable fabrics and eye-catching colors. The styles available here work for both vacation and daily wear. Sun Works also carries a large selection of bathing suits.

⭐ **WHITE'S BOOKS & GIFTS:** This outstanding independent bookseller carries a wide selection of reading material, ranging from best sellers to local interest books. White's also stocks an array of wonderfully decorative, yet functional items such as picture frames, lamps, planters, bookends, unique timepieces, colorful glassware, pottery, and much more. Shipping service is available.

⭐ **CHICO'S:** Chico's features women's clothing and accessories in natural colors and materials. The clothing here is terrific for casual resort wear.

⭐ **PAESANO'S RISTORANTE AND LIQUORS:** This combination restaurant and liquor store features freshly prepared northern and southern Italian dishes with homemade flavor and presentation. There are separate lunch, dinner, and take-out menus. No reservations are accepted. The attached annex, Paesano's Liquors, is a fully stocked liquor store that also offers a wide array of miniature liquors and what may be the largest selection of wine in the Walt Disney World area.

⭐ **FISHTALE FREDDY'S:** Island-style clothing for men, women, and children is the look at FishTale Freddy's. The bright and bold collection of colors, styles, and attractive accessories, combined with a tropical rainforest motif, make this store a memorable place to shop.

GOODING'S SUPERMARKET

Gooding's Supermarket, which is open twenty-four hours a day, is the largest store at Crossroads, and while some area supermarkets may be less expensive, you can't beat Gooding's for convenience. It also has a pharmacy, full-service florist, and a large deli with prepared foods. It's an easy-to-find, no-hassle first stop on your way into Walt Disney World: the perfect place to pick up snacks and beverages for your room, which are a lot less expensive than a mini bar or room service.

CROSSROADS RESTAURANTS

Visitors will find many reasonably priced, nationally known restaurants to choose from at Crossroads, including Jungle Jim's (featuring barbecued ribs and more than one hundred hamburger combinations); Chevy's (fresh, tasty Mexican cuisine); Pebbles (American cuisine); Perkins Family Restaurant (above-average coffee-shop fare; breakfast served all day); Red Lobster (seafood and steak); Barnie's (coffee bar, light fare, and retail shop); Pizzeria Uno (pizza and pasta); McDonald's; and Taco Bell. ◆

TOOLKIT

INDEX

 USING THE INDEX

The organization of this book is self-indexing — that is, a single topic (a hotel, for example) appears on a single page wherever possible, and is arranged alphabetically within its section. Thus, the book is far easier to use in actual touring situations, since topics are literally at your fingertips. For deeper searches, the book's index functions like any other index, with a few distinctions. We list only the primary review pages for restaurants, hotels, and activities, so you won't waste time chasing down secondary references. This speeds access to the information that is most important to guidebook users. At the same time, this book has extensive page cross-referencing within the text, so you can pursue relevant information that interests you in context, which is generally more meaningful. We believe this editorial approach, although more difficult to execute, makes a better guidebook. The result is an index that works together with the book's organization, cross-referencing, and streamlined table of contents to give you as many pathways as possible to the information you are seeking.

ABC Sound Studio 50
Admission tickets 9, 93
Adventureland 60
Adventurers Club 80
Africa 122
African Aviary 116
Airport hotel 255
Airport shuttle service 256
Airport, Orlando International 254
Akershus, Restaurant 187
Alcoholic beverages (*see* Shopping)
Alfredo di Roma Ristorante 179
Alien Encounter 66
All-American Backyard Barbecue 111
All-In-One Hopper Pass 9
All-Star Resort, Disney's 128
Alligator Swamp 117
AMC Theatres 81, 85
America Gardens Theatre 41

American Adventure, The 40
American Automobile Association 19
American Express 19
AnaComical Players 27
Animal Hospital 116
Animal Kingdom Resorts Area 22
Animal Kingdom, Disney's 121-122
Anniversary celebrations 244
Annual events at WDW 12-14
Ariel's Grotto 64
Art of Disney, The 91
Arthur's 27 197
Artist Point 197
AstroOrbiter 66
Atlantic Dance 73
AT&T Global Neighborhood 26
Attractions: 21-122
    Blizzard Beach 100-105
    Discovery Island 114-120
    Disney Village Marketplace 88-93
    Disney's Animal Kingdom 121-122
    Disney's BoardWalk 73-77
    Disney's West Side 85-87
    Disney-MGM Studios 48-57
    Downtown Disney 78-93
    Epcot 25-47
    Fort Wilderness 106-113
    Future World at Epcot 24-36
    Magic Kingdom 58-72
    Pleasure Island 78-84
    River Country 109-110
    Typhoon Lagoon 94-99
    World Showcase at Epcot 37-47
Au Petit Café 165 (*see* Chefs de France)
Authentic All Star 91
Avalunch 103

Babysitting 245-246
Backlot Theater 51
Backstage Magic tour 247
Backstage Pass 52
Banking 261 (*see also* Services)
Barefoot Bay 219
Barnstormer 65
Baskervilles 198
Bay Cove 109
Bay Lake 218
Beach Club Resort, Disney's 129
Beaches, at the resorts 238

Beaches & Cream 198
Behind the Seeds Tour 31
Belle Vue Room, The 76
BET SoundStage Club 80
Bicycle paths 216-217
Bicycle rentals 109, 216-217
Biergarten 161
Big River Grille & Brewing Works 162
Big Thunder Mountain Railroad 61
Bike Barn 107, 108
Birthday celebrations 244
Bistro de Paris 163
Blizzard Beach 100 (*map*), 101-105
BoardWalk Bakery 76
BoardWalk, Disney's 74 (*map*), 73-77
BoardWalk Inn, Disney's 130
BoardWalk Villas, Disney's 131
Boat rentals 218-221
Boating 218-221
Boating, Excursion Cruises 221-222
Boatwright's Dining Hall 198
Body By Jake Health Studio 228
Body Wars 217
Boneyard 122
Bonfamille's Cafe 198
Bongos Cuban Cafe 87
Boulangerie Pâtisserie 44
Buena Vista Lagoon 218
Buena Vista Palace Resort & Spa 126
Buena Vista Suites 152
Butterfly Garden 117
Buzz Lightyear 65

California Grill 199
Camera rentals, film (*see* Services)
Campfire Program 111
Camping, Fort Wilderness 113
Canada pavilion 40
Canoeing 109, 221
Cantina de San Angel 32, 43
Cap'n Jack's Marina 91
Cap'n Jack's Oyster Bar 164
Cape May Cafe 199
Caribe Royale Resort 153
Car rental discount 272
Car rentals 256-257, 252
Car trouble 257
Caribbean Beach Resort, Disney's 132
Caribbean Coral Reef Ride 30

Carousel of Progress 65
Cascade Cove Picnic Area 97
Castaway Creek 96
Castle Forecourt Stage 67
Catering, private 244
Catwalk Bar, The 54
Celebrations, private 244
Cellular phones 244
Chair Lift 102
Character Meals 205-207
Character Christmas Shop 90
Chef Mickey's 199
Chefs de France 165
Child care 245-246
China pavilion 39
Christmas at WDW 15
Cinderella's Golden Carrousel 63
Cinderella's Royal Table 166
Circle of Life 29
Cirque du Soleil 87
City Hall Information Center 60
Cocktail lounges (*at the attractions*):
    Disney-MGM Studios 54
    Disney Village Marketplace 92-93
    Disney's BoardWalk 74-75
    Future World at Epcot 32
    Pleasure Island 83
    World Showcase at Epcot 43
Comedy Warehouse 80
Coming attractions 34, 70, 121-122
Concourse Steakhouse 200
Conservation Station 122
Contemporary Health and Fitness 227
Contemporary Resort, Disney's 133
Copperfield's Magic Underground 54
Coral Cafe 200
Coral Reef Restaurant 167
Coral Reef Ride 30
Coronado Springs Resort, Disney's 134
Cosmic Ray's Starlight Cafe 68
Countdown to Extinction 122
Country Bear Jamboree 61
Courtyard by Marriott 127
Cranium Command 27
Crescent Lake 219
Cretaceous Trail 122
Crockett's Tavern 112
Cross Country Creek 101
Crossroads Shopping Center 262
Crowds 11 (*chart*), 10
Cruises, Disney 250

Cruises, Excursion 221-222
Crystal Palace, The 168
Cypress Point Nature Trail 110

Dance clubs 73-74, 80-81
Day camps 245-246, 249
Dentist referral 261
Diamond Horseshoe Saloon Revue 66
Diabetic travelers 258
Diets, special 157
Dining Events:
    Character Meals 205-207
    Gulliver's Grill 207
    Hoop-Dee-Doo Musical Revue 208
    House of Blues 209
    Jolly Holidays 210
    MurderWatch Mystery Dinner Theatre 211
    SoundStage Restaurant 207
    Polynesian Luau 212
Dinner show discount 272
Dinner Shows 208-212
Dinoland U.S.A. 122
Directions to WDW 23 (*map*), 257
Disabled travelers 258-260 (*see also* Services)
Discount Travel Tips 17-19
Discount Coupons 272
Discover 89
Discovery Center 26
Discovery Island 114 (*map*), 115-120
Discovery Island Path 116
Discovery River 122
Disney-AAA Travel Center 19
Disney Cruise Line 251
Disney Institute 248-249
Disney Institute, Spa at the 226
Disney-MGM Studios 48 (*map*), 49-57
Disney Quest, arcade 87
Disney Village Marketplace 88 (*map*), 89-93
Disney Village Resorts Area 22
Disney Village Waterways 218
Disney's Animal Kingdom 121-122
Disney's BoardWalk 74 (*map*), 73-77
Disney's Wide World of Sports 214-215
DiveQuest 31
Dixie Landings Resort, Disney's 135
Dock Stage 91
Dolphin, Walt Disney World 150
Donald's Boat 65
DoubleTree Guest Suites Resort 143

Downhill Double Dipper 102
Downtown Disney: 78-93
    Disney Village Marketplace 88-93
    Pleasure Island 78-84
    West Side 85-87
Driving to WDW 23 (*map*), 257
Drug stores 261
Dumbo the Flying Elephant 63

Eagle Pines Golf Course 231
Eagles Watch 118
Easter at WDW 15
8TRAX 80
El Pirata y el Perico 68
El Rio del Tiempo 39
Electric cart rentals 112, 113
Electric Umbrella Restaurant 32
Electrical Water Pageant 111
Ellen's Energy Adventure 27
Embassy Grand Beach Vacation Resort 153
Embassy Suites Resort 153
Enchanted Tiki Lodge 61
Entertainment Publications 19
Epcot: 24-47
    Future World at Epcot 24-36
    World Showcase at Epcot 37-47
Epcot Discovery Center 26
Epcot Resorts Area 22
Equestrian Center, Grand Cypress 234
ESPN Club 74
Eurospain 90
Exercise (*see* Fitness Centers; *see* Sports)
ExtraTERRORestrial Alien Encounter 66
Events, annual at WDW 12-14
Eyeglasses 261

Fairy Tale Honeymoons, Disney's 250
Fairy Tale Weddings, Disney's 250
Fall Fantasy vacation package, Disney's 20
Family vacations 243-251
Fantasia Fairways 233
Fantasia Gardens 233
Fantasmic! 52
Fantasy in the Sky Fireworks 67
Fantasyland 63
Father's Day at WDW 15
Feathered Friends bird show 118
50's Prime Time Cafe 170

Film (*see* Services)
Finn's Grill 200
Fireworks Factory, The 195
   (*see* Wildhorse Saloon)
Fireworks shows:
   Disney-MGM Studios 52
   Epcot 30, 41
   Magic Kingdom 67
   Pleasure Island 82
First aid 261 (*see also* Services)
Fishing 223-225
Fitness Centers 227-228
Fitness Fairground 28
Flamingo Lagoon 117
Florists 261
Flying Fish Cafe 171
Food 'N Fun Plan, Disney's 17
Food Rocks 30
Foreign currency exchange 261
Foreign language assistance (*see* Services)
Fort Wilderness & River Country 106 (*map*),
   107-113
Fort Wilderness Marina 108
Fort Wilderness Resort and Campground,
   Disney's 136
Fort Wilderness Trail Ride 110
Fort Wilderness Waterways 219
Fountain View Espresso & Bakery 32
Four-Day Park-Hopper Pass 9
Four-Day Value Pass 9
Fourth of July at WDW 15
France pavilion 40
Friends, traveling with 243-251
Frontierland 61
Frontierland Shootin' Arcade 62
Frostbite Freddie's Frozen Freshments 103
Fulton's Crab House 172
Fulton's Stone Crab Lounge 83
Future World at Epcot 24 (*map*), 25-36

Galaxy Palace Theater 67
Gang Plank Falls 96
Garden Grill Restaurant, The 173
Garden Grove Cafe 200
Gardens of the World tour 42
Germany pavilion 39
Getaway Glen Picnic Area 97
Ghirardelli's Chocolate Shop 90
Global Neighborhood, The 26

Golf courses 229-232
Golf lessons 229-232
Golf tournaments 213
Golf vacation packages, Disney's 232
Gooding's Supermarket 253, 262
Goosebumps HorrorLand Fright Show 50
Gorilla Falls Exploration Trail 122
Gourmet Pantry 90
Grand Cypress Equestrian Center 234
Grand Floridian Beach Resort, Disney's 137
Grand Floridian Cafe 201
Grand Floridian Spa 227
Great Movie Ride, The 49
Groceries 90, 253, 261, 262
Grosvenor Resort 144
Group vacations 243-221
Guided Tours 247
Gulliver's Grill 207

Hall of Presidents, The 63
Halloween at WDW 15
Handicapped parking 258
Handicapped travelers 258-260
   (*see also* Services)
Harrington Bay Clothiers 90
Harry's Safari Bar & Grille 201
Harvest Theater 29
Haunted Mansion, The 63
Hayrides 111
Health clubs 227-228
Health spas 226-227
Hearing-impaired visitors 259
   (*see also* Services)
Hidden Treasures of the World Showcase 41
Hilton Resort, The 145
Holiday Events & Celebrations 15-16
Holiday Inn SunSpree Resort 154
Hollywood & Vine Cafeteria 174
Hollywood Brown Derby, The 175
Homewood Suites 154
Honey, I Shrunk the Audience 29
Honey, I Shrunk the Kids Adventure 50
Honeymoons 250
Hoop-Dee-Doo Musical Revue 208
Horizons 28
Horseback riding 234
Hospital 261
Hotel discounts 17-19, 124, 272
Hotel Plaza at Disney Village 22

Hotel value seasons 124
Hotel Royal Plaza 146
Hotels 125 (*map*), 123-156
Hotels, all suites 152-155
Hotels, guide to features 124
Hotels, Off-Site 152-156
House of Blues 209
Howard Johnson Park Square 154
Humunga Kowabunga 96
Hyatt Regency Grand Cypress 156
Hyatt Regency, Orlando Airport 255

IllumiNations 30, 41
Image Works, The 29
Impressions de France 40
Indiana Jones Epic Stunt Spectacular 51
Indy 200, The 213
Innoventions East 26
Innoventions Fountain 31
Innoventions West 26
Inside Animation 53, 247
It's A Small World 63
Italy pavilion 39

Japan pavilion 40
Jazz Company 81
Jellyrolls 74
Jet boats 220
Jim Henson's Muppet*Vision 3D 50
Jogging paths 235
Jolly Holidays 210
Journey Into Imagination 29
Juan & Only's 201
July Fourth at WDW 15
Jungle Cruise 60

Kayaks 109, 221
Keelhaul Falls 96
Kennels 113
Ketchakiddee Creek 97
Keys to the Kingdom tour 67, 247
Kilimanjaro Safari 122
King Stefan's Banquet Hall 166
   (*see* Cinderella's Royal Table)
Kosher dining 157
Kringla Bakeri og Kafé 43

L'Originale Alfredo di Roma Ristorante 179
La Maison du Vin 44
Lago Dorado 219
Lake Buena Vista 219
Lake Buena Vista Golf Course 230
Land, The 29
Le Cellier 176
Leaning Palm 97
Legend of the Lion King 64
LEGO Imagination Center 89
Length of Stay Pass 9
Let's Go Slurp'n 97
Liberty Square 62
Liberty Square Riverboat 62
Liberty Tree Tavern 177
Limousines 256
Liquor (see Cocktail Lounges; Shopping)
Living Seas, The 30
Living with The Land 29
Lockers (see Services)
L'Originale Alfredo di Roma Ristorante 178
Lost and found 252
Lottawatta Lodge 103
Low Tide Lou's 97

Mad Tea Party 63
Maelstrom 39
Magic Eye Theater 29
Magic Kingdom 58 (map), 59-72
Magic Kingdom Club 17
Magic Kingdom Resorts Area 22
Magic Mushroom Juice & Coffee Bar 93
Magic of Disney Animation, The 53
Magical Holidays package, Disney's 20
Magnolia Golf Course 229
Mail drops and stamps 261 (see also Services)
Main Street Bake Shop 68
Main Street Cinema 60
Main Street, U.S.A. 60
Making of Me, The 27
Mama Melrose's Ristorante Italiano 179
Mannequins Dance Palace 80
Maps:
    Blizzard Beach 100
    Discovery Island 114
    Disney-MGM Studios 48
    Disney Village Marketplace 88
    Disney's BoardWalk 74
    Fort Wilderness & River Country 106
    Future World at Epcot 24
    Hotels 125
    Magic Kingdom 58
    Pleasure Island 78
    Typhoon Lagoon 94
    Walt Disney World at-a-Glance 23
    World Showcase at Epcot 38
Marathon, Walt Disney World 213
Mardi Gras at WDW 12
Marinas 218-221
Marrakesh, Restaurant 187
Marriage at WDW 250
Marriott's Orlando World Center 156
Matsu No Ma Lounge 44
Mayday Falls 96
McDonald's 93, 262
Meadow Recreation Area 109
Medical help 261
Medications 261
Melt Away Bay 102
Message Center 33, 44, 55, 244
Mexico pavilion 37
Mickey D's 93
Mickey's Country Home 64
Mickey's Toontown Fair 64
Mike Fink Keel Boats 62
Miniature Golf 233
Minnie's Country Home 64
Mogul Mania 103
Money and banking 261 (see also Services)
Monster Sound Show 50
Month by Month at WDW 12-14
Morocco pavilion 40
Mother's Day at WDW 15
Movie theaters 81, 85
Mr. Toad's Wild Ride 64
Muppet*Vision 3D 50
MurderWatch Mystery Dinner Theatre 211
Muscles and Bustles 227

Narcoossee's 201
Native Neighbors animal show 118
Nature walks 236-237
Neon Armadillo Music Saloon (see BET
    SoundStage Club)
New Year's Eve at WDW 16
New Year's Eve Street Party 82

Newsletters, Disney 271
Nightclubs 73-75, 80-81, 85-87
Nine Dragons Restaurant 180
1900 Park Fare 202
North Creek Inlet 116
Norway pavilion 39

O Canada! 41
Oak Trail Golf Course 232
Oasis, The 221
Off-Site Hotels 152-156
Official All Star Cafe 181
'Ohana 202
Old Key West Resort, Disney's 138
Olivia's Cafe 202
Online information, Disney 271
Orlando International Airport 254
Orlando Magicard 18
Osprey Ridge Golf Course 231
Outback, The 203
Outback Snacks 119
Outrigger canoes 221

P

Package pickup 33, 45, 55, 70
Packing tips 253
Pagers, pocket 244
Palio 203
Palm Golf Course 230
Parades, afternoon:
    Disney-MGM Studios 52
    Magic Kingdom 66
Parades, evening:
    Electrical Water Pageant 111
    Magic Kingdom 67
Parasailing 242
Parking 257
Parking, handicapped 258
Parties, private 244
Pasta Piazza Ristorante 32
Pedal boats 221
Pelican Bay 117
Perri House Bed and Breakfast 155
Peter Pan's Flight 64
Pets at Walt Disney World 113
Petting farm 109
Pharmacies 261
Picnic areas: (see also Fort Wilderness &
    River Country; see also Nature Walks)

Blizzard Beach 103
Discovery Island 119
Typhoon Lagoon 97
Pinocchio Village Haus 68
Pirates of the Caribbean 61
Planet Hollywood 182
Planning Powertools 9-20
Plaza Restaurant, The 183
Pleasure Island 78 *(map)*, 79-84
Pleasure Island Jazz Company 81
Polynesian Luau 212
Polynesian Resort, Disney's 139
Pools 238
Pontoon boats 220
Port Orleans Resort, Disney's 140
Portobello Yacht Club 184
Portobello Yacht Club Bar 93
Post Office, U.S. 261
Powertools, vacation planning 9-20
Prescription drugs 261
Primate Point 116

Racquet Club, Disney's 239
Rainforest Cafe 185
R.E.S.T. Fitness Center 227
Reader Survey 269-270
Rental car discount 272
Rental cars 256-257, 252
Reptile Relations 118
Reservations:
    Dinner shows *(see* Dining Events)
    Hotels 123, 152
    Restaurants 157-158
    Sporting activities *(see* Sports)
    Sporting events 213, 214
Resortwear Unlimited 90
Resources for Teachers 26
Rest rooms *(see* Services)
Restaurant Akershus 186
Restaurant discounts 272
Restaurant Marrakesh 187
Restaurant, guide to cuisine 159
Restaurant, guide to location 158
Restaurant, guide to prices 160
Restaurant reservations 157-158
Restaurants at Crossroads 262
Restaurants, resort 197-204
Restaurants, theme park 157-196
River Country 106 *(map)*, 109-110

Rock & Roll Beach Club 81
Rose & Crown Dining Room 188
Rose & Crown Pub 32, 44
Royal Plaza Hotel 146
Runoff Rapids 102

Safari Village 122
Sailboats 220
San Angel Inn Restaurante 189
Sci-Fi Dine-In Theater Restaurant 190
Screen Door General Store 76
Seashore Sweets 76
Seasonal events at WDW 15-16
Seasons restaurant 203
Service stations 257
Services *(at the attractions)*:
    Blizzard Beach 103-104
    Discovery Island 119
    Disney-MGM Studios 54-56
    Disney Village Marketplace 93
    Disney's BoardWalk 77
    Epcot, Future World 33-34
    Epcot, World Showcase 44-45
    Fort Wilderness & River Country 112
    Magic Kingdom 69-70
    Pleasure Island 83
    Typhoon Lagoon 97-98
Settlement Recreation Area 108
Seven Seas Lagoon 218
Shades of Green 147
Shark Reef 96
Ship Shape Health Club 227
Shipping and mailing 261 *(see also* Services)
Shipwreck Beach 119
Shopping discounts 93, 262, 272
Shopping for necessities 261
Shopping, Crossroads 262
Shopping, Disney Village Marketplace 89-91
Shopping, Disney's BoardWalk 76
Sidelines, The 74
Sight-impaired visitors 260 *(see also* Services)
Ski Patrol Shelter 103
Ski Patrol Training Camp 103
Skyway to Fantasyland 66
Skyway to Tomorrowland 64
Sleepy Hollow 68
Slippery Slides 110
Slush Gusher 102
Smoking, in restaurants 157, 197

Smoking, tobacco 261
Snow Stormers 102
Snow White's Adventures 64
Sommerfest 43
Sorcery in the Sky Fireworks 52
SoundStage BET 80
Soundstage Restaurant 207
South American Aviary 117
Spa at Buena Vista Palace, The 226
Spa at the Disney Institute 226
Spa at the Grand Floridian 227
Space Mountain 66
Spaceship Earth 25
Spas 226-227
SpectroMagic 67
Splash Mountain 62
Spoodles 191
Sports 213-242
Sports, Disney's Wide World of 214-215
Sports & Fitness Center,
    Disney Institute 226, 228, 239
Sports events 74, 213, 214-215
Sports Central, ESPN 74
Spring Break 15
Star Tours 50
Stone Crab Lounge, Fulton's 83, 93
Storm Slides 96
Studio Backlot Tour 52
Studios Commissary 54
Summer Sands 91
Summerfield Suites Hotel 155
Summit Plummet 102
Sunglasses 261
Sunkats 221
Sunset Cove 92
Sunset Ranch Market 54
Sunshine Getaway package, Disney's 20
Sunshine Season Food Fair 32
Sunshine Tree Terrace 68
SuperStar Television 50
Surrey Rentals 76, 216
Swan Health Club 228
Swan, Walt Disney World 151
Swan's Neck Falls 116
Swimming 238
    Blizzard Beach 100-105
    River Country 109-110
    Typhoon Lagoon 94-99
Swiss Family Treehouse 61

T

TakeFlight 65
Taxis 256
Team Mickey's Athletic Club 91
Teamboat Springs 102
Telephone numbers at WDW 252
Telephone locations (*see* Services)
Temperatures, year-round 10 (*chart*), 11
Tempura Kiku 192
Tennis programs 239
Tennis courts 240-241
Tennis lessons 239
Teppanyaki Dining Room 193
Test Track 28
Thanksgiving at WDW 15
Theater in the Wild 122
Theater of the Stars 51
Theaters, movie 81, 85
Theme parks (*see* Attractions)
Thimbles and Threads 76
Thin Ice Training Course 103
Thirsty Perch Picnic Area 119
Thirsty Perch, The 119
Tickets, admission 9, 93
Tike's Peak 103
Tiki Room 61
Timekeeper, The 6
Tobacco 261
Toboggan Racer 102
Tom Sawyer Island 62
Tomorrowland 65
Tomorrowland Speedway 65
Tomorrowland Transit Authority 66
Tony's Town Square Restaurant 194
Toontown Hall of Fame 65
Tortoise Beach 117
Tours, guided: 247
   Backstage Magic 247
   Backstage Pass 52
   Behind the Seeds 31
   Disabled tours 259-260 (*see also* Services)
   Discovery Island Educational Tours 118
   DiveQuest 31
   Gardens of the World 42
   Hidden Treasures of the World Showcase 41
   Inside Animation 53, 247
   Keys to the Kingdom 67, 247
   Magic of Disney Animation 53
   Studios Backlot 52
   VIP Tours 247

Yuletide Fantasy 247
Tours, self-guided mini-tours:
   Pleasure Island 84
   Discovery Island 120
   Blizzard Beach 105
   Typhoon Lagoon 99
   Disney-MGM Studios 56-57
   Future World 35-36
   Magic Kingdom 71-72
   World Showcase 46-47
Toys Fantastic 90
Trail rides 234
Trail's End Buffeteria 112
Transportation 256-257
Travel clubs 17-20
Traveler's Toolkit 253-262
Travelodge Hotel 148
Tree of Life 122
Tri-Circle-D Ranch 108
Trumpeter Springs 116
Tune In Lounge 54
25th Anniversary Celebration 12
Twilight Zone Tower of Terror, The 51
2R's Reading and Riting 91
Typhoon Lagoon 94 (*map*), 95-99
Typhoon Tilly's Galley & Grog 97

U

U.S.A. pavilion 39
United Kingdom pavilion 40
Universe of Energy 27
Upstream Plunge Pool 110

V

Vacation Club, Disney's 138
Vacation Discount Coupons 272
Vacation package Values 20
Value Seasons 12-14 , 124
Vegetarian dining 157
Victoria & Albert's 203
Video camera rentals (*see* Services)
Village Marketplace, Disney 88 (*map*), 89-93
Village Tower, The 90
Villas at the Disney Institute, The 149
VIP Tours 247, 260
Virgin Records Megastore 87
Voices of Liberty 39
Volleyball courts 241
Voyage of The Little Mermaid 51

W

Walt Disney Theater, The 50
Walt Disney World at-a-Glance 23 (*map*), 22
Walt Disney World Dolphin 150
Walt Disney World Marathon 213
Walt Disney World Railroad 60, 62, 65
Walt Disney World Swan 151
Warming Hut, The 103
Water parks:
   Blizzard Beach 100-105
   River Country 109-110
   Typhoon Lagoon 94-99
Waterfront, The 82
Waterskiing excursions 242
Water sprites 200
Waves at Typhoon Lagoon, The 95
Weather at WDW 11 (*chart*), 10
Website, Disney 271
Weddings at WDW 250
Weinkeller 43
West End Stage 82
West Side, Disney's 86 (*map*), 85-87
Wheelchairs 258 (*see also* Services)
Whispering Canyon Cafe 204
White Water Rapids 110
Whoop-'n-Holler Hollow 110
Wide World of Sports, Disney's 214-215
Wildhorse Saloon 195
Wilderness Exercise Trail 108
Wilderness Lodge, Disney's 141
Wilderness Swamp Trail 108
Wildlife Express 122
Wildlife Walkway 117
Wolfgang Puck Cafe 196
Wolfgang Puck Express 87, 93
Wonders of China 39
Wonders of Life 27
World of Disney, The 89
World Showcase at Epcot 38 (*map*), 37-47
WorldKey Information Service 32, 44
Wyland Galleries 76
Wyndham Royal Safari Resort 155

Y

Yacht Club Resort, Disney's 142
Yacht Club Galley 204
Yachtsman Steakhouse 204
Yakitori House 44
Yard, The 74
Yuletide Fantasy Tour 247 ◆

READER SURVEY

Become part of the Walt Disney World for Adults Opinion Bank! Tell us about your vacation experience and what you thought of the attractions, hotels, restaurants, and more. Your opinions really do count! They affect the ratings in the book and help us provide exactly the kind of information you want and need.

Was this your first trip to Walt Disney World?　○ YES　☒ NO

If not, how often have you visited?　○ ONCE　○ 2 TO 4 TIMES　☒ 5 TO 9 TIMES　○ 10 TIMES OR MORE

What time of year was your most recent trip?　○ WINTER　○ SPRING　○ SUMMER　☒ FALL

Did you go during a holiday or school vacation?　☒ YES　☒ NO

How crowded did it seem to you?　○ OVERCROWDED　○ HEAVY　☒ MODERATE　○ LIGHT

How many were in your party?　○ 1 TO 2　○ 2 TO 4　☒ 5 TO 7　○ 8 OR MORE

Did you travel with children?　☒ YES　○ NO　What ages? _5 - 9_

Which hotel did you stay at? _Coranado Springs_

How would you rate it overall?　○ EXCELLENT　○ IDEAL FOR US　○ IT WAS OKAY　○ DISAPPOINTING

What did you like best about your hotel? _____

What did you like least? _____

Did you agree with our rating?　○ YES　○ NO　If not, why not? _____

How did you get to Orlando?　○ LIVE NEARBY　○ DROVE　☒ AIRPLANE　○ OTHER

Did you rent a car?　☒ YES　○ NO　If so, from which rental agency? _Alamo_

How would you rate the agency?　○ GREAT　○ ABOVE AVERAGE　○ TYPICAL　○ NOT GOOD

Which Disney transportation did you use **most**?　○ BUSES　○ MONORAILS　○ BOATS　○ ALL　○ NONE

Did Disney transportation work efficiently for you?　○ ALWAYS　○ USUALLY　○ SOMETIMES　○ NO

If not, what was the problem? _____

Did you use a discount travel card?　○ YES　☒ NO　Which one? _____

Did you buy a Disney Vacation Package?　○ YES　☒ NO　Which one? _____

In planning your trip, did you call Disney information?　☒ YES　○ NO

If so, how many times?　○ 1 TO 2　○ 3 TO 4　○ 5 TO 7　○ 8 OR MORE

Did you visit the book's website for Disney vacation information?　○ YES　☒ NO　○ I PLAN TO

Did you use any of the coupons in this book?　☒ YES　○ NO　Which ones? _$50 off at Swan_

How did they work for you? _____

Number these four theme park areas in the order that you enjoyed them most, with "1" being your favorite:

☐ MAGIC KINGDOM   ☐ DISNEY-MGM STUDIOS   ☐ EPCOT'S WORLD SHOWCASE   ☐ EPCOT'S FUTURE WORLD

How would you rate the recreation areas below?

TYPHOON LAGOON	⊗ DIDN'T GO	○ GREAT!	○ ENJOYABLE	○ DISAPPOINTING
BLIZZARD BEACH	⊗ DIDN'T GO	○ GREAT!	○ ENJOYABLE	○ DISAPPOINTING
PLEASURE ISLAND	⊗ DIDN'T GO	○ GREAT!	○ ENJOYABLE	○ DISAPPOINTING
DISNEY'S BOARDWALK	○ DIDN'T GO	○ GREAT!	○ ENJOYABLE	○ DISAPPOINTING
RIVER COUNTRY	○ DIDN'T GO	○ GREAT!	○ ENJOYABLE	○ DISAPPOINTING
DISCOVERY ISLAND	○ DIDN'T GO	○ GREAT!	○ ENJOYABLE	○ DISAPPOINTING
VILLAGE MARKETPLACE	○ DIDN'T GO	○ GREAT!	○ ENJOYABLE	○ DISAPPOINTING

▼

Please tell us about some of the restaurants you ate in and how you would rate them:

Restaurant: _Cinderella's Royal table_____ ○ GREAT! ○ ABOVE AVERAGE ○ OKAY ○ NOT GOOD

Comment? _____

Restaurant: _Gulliver's Grill - Swan___ ○ GREAT! ○ ABOVE AVERAGE ○ OKAY ○ NOT GOOD

Comment? _____

Restaurant: _____ ○ GREAT! ○ ABOVE AVERAGE ○ OKAY ○ NOT GOOD

Comment? _____

▼

What was the best part of your trip? _____

What was the most disappointing part? _____

Which parts of the book were most helpful to you? _____

_____

When will you return to Walt Disney World?   ○ THIS YEAR   ○ NEXT YEAR   ○ IN 2 YEARS   ⊗ NOT SURE   ○ NEVER

Other comments or tips you'd like to pass on: _____

_____

_____

Thank you for participating in the Walt Disney World for Adults Reader Survey!

Name: _____

Address: _____

_____

SEND A COPY OF THIS SURVEY TO:
Walt Disney World for Adults • 420 N. McKinley Street, Suite 111-328 • Corona, CA 91719

THE WALT DISNEY WORLD WIDE WEB

Walt Disney World — and all things Disney — have a huge presence on the Internet. In fact, the word *Disney* is one of the top fifty online search words people use when looking for websites to visit or when seeking information. The *Walt Disney World for Adults* website is one of the largest and most popular websites for planning a vacation at Walt Disney World. It does not have reviews and descriptions, which you can find only in this book, but it does have helpful information you cannot get from any book, such as the current operating hours at the theme parks (so you can plan a daily itinerary), the weather forecast for the week you are going, and tips from travelers who have just returned.

THE READERS CLUBHOUSE: This is a special area on the website designed exclusively for you. It has the latest insider touring tips, new travel discount offers, and comments and advice from other Club Members. You'll also find a list of updates that will keep the book you are holding up-to-the-minute fresh, and keep you one step ahead of the crowd. To get in, you need a password. The doorman will ask you to type in the first word on a particular page in this book. It's that easy! But keep this book handy, because the passwords change periodically. By limiting new touring strategies to an exclusive group, they are less likely to become ineffective through overuse. See you online!

Walt Disney World for Adults Online
http://www.wdw4adults.com

DISNEY NEWSGROUP — **rec.arts.disney.parks**: This newsgroup is one of the liveliest and brightest virtual communities on the Internet, frequented by a friendly core group of Disney fans and hobbyists who take time to answer the hundreds of questions that are posted here each week by people planning a Walt Disney World vacation. It makes fun reading and is a great source of first-hand information.

MAGAZINES AND NEWSLETTERS

For those who prefer to get their information on paper, and for Disney enthusiasts who just can't get enough, there are many independently published newsletters and magazines on topics ranging from Disney history to Disney collectibles. Those listed below focus on the theme parks, Walt Disney World in particular. You may wish to write and ask to purchase the current issue before subscribing.

DISNEY MAGAZINE: This official Disney magazine covers all Disney subjects including theme parks, and is a good source of news and events. Two-year subscription (8 issues), about $17.
 Disney Magazine, P.O. Box 37263, Boone, IA 50037-2263.

MOUSETALES: This quarterly newsletter, billed as the "Unofficial Newsletter of Walt Disney World," contains timely information and future projections. One year subscription (4 issues), about $14.
 Mousetales, P.O. Box 383, Columbus, OH 43216-0383.

NUT4DISNEY NEWSLETTER: A quarterly newsletter with helpful information about Walt Disney World current events; optional special updates and announcements are sent out monthly. One-year subscription (4 issues), about $20; subscription with ten updates, about $30.
 Harbor Landing Publications, 248 Route 25A, Suite 86, East Setauket, NY 11733-2945. ◆

VACATION DISCOUNT COUPONS!

Let us add some magic to your trip with discounts designed exclusively for *Walt Disney World for Adults* readers! These offers were carefully selected from among our favorite places at Walt Disney World, and many are not available anywhere else. They are our gift to early purchasers, who help us launch this new edition with strong initial bookstore sales. Be sure to use them before the end of 1998.

SAVE ON YOUR AIRLINE TICKET — UP TO $100 OFF PER PERSON!

Start saving money on your Walt Disney World vacation before you arrive!
This valuable offer applies to most major airlines and any type of fare.

FREE UPGRADE AT DOLLAR RENT A CAR, PLUS...

PREPAID CALLING CARD WITH 15 MINUTES OF FREE LONG DISTANCE CALLING

Best of all, Dollar Rent A Car is conveniently located inside Orlando International Airport. There is also a rental counter at Walt Disney World if you want to rent a car during your stay. (See page 256.)

CUT YOUR HOTEL BILL IN HALF AT THE GROSVENOR RESORT

Stay on Walt Disney World property at the Grosvenor Resort and get a 50 percent discount on your hotel bill. And, save 10 percent when you dine at Baskervilles. (See pages 149 and 198.)

50 PERCENT DISCOUNT AT THE SPA AT BUENA VISTA PALACE

Book one spa service (such as a relaxing massage after a tough day of touring) at this luxurious European-style spa at Walt Disney World, and receive a second pampering spa service at 50 percent off. Indulge in the beautiful spa facilities while you're there. (See page 226.)

$50 DINING CERTIFICATE AT THE WALT DISNEY WORLD SWAN OR DOLPHIN

You have a $50 dining credit at any of the terrific restaurants at the
Walt Disney World Swan or Walt Disney World Dolphin, including

Cabana Bar & Grill, Splash Grill & Terrace, Dolphin Fountain, Tubbi's Buffeteria, and:

Garden Grove Cafe and Gulliver's Grill — *Family cafe by day and Disney Character Meals and Magic Shows at night. (See pages 200 and 207.)*

Coral Cafe — *Family buffet and a la carte breakfast, lunch, and dinner. (See page 200.)*

Palio — *Romantic Italian bistro dinners and light entertainment. (See page 203.)*

Juan & Only's — *Mexican dinners served in a fanciful, festive dining room. (See page 201.)*

Harry's Safari Bar & Grille — *International-themed steak and seafood dinners. (See page 201.)*

ADMISSION DISCOUNT AT MURDERWATCH MYSTERY DINNER THEATRE

You will receive a $5 per person discount for our favorite dinner show at Walt Disney World, which takes place at the Grosvenor Resort. Enjoy an all-you-care-to-eat prime rib buffet while you help solve an intriguing murder that takes place during dinner. (See page 211.)

GET ESCORTED TO THE HEAD OF THE LINE AT PLANET HOLLYWOOD!

Long, long lines are the norm at this ultra-popular restaurant, but not for you! For movie- and music-lovers, Planet Hollywood is a must for a truly memorable dining event. (See page 183.)

20 PERCENT DISCOUNT AT CROSSROADS SHOPPING CENTER

Don't miss this shopping center at Walt Disney World, where you'll find a wide variety of reasonably priced restaurants and fascinating shops, many of which offer you a special discounts. (See page 262.)

Coupons Problems? Get Help and Updated Information!

WEBSITE: http://www.wdw4adults.com   EMAIL: coupons@wdw4adults.com
ADDRESS: Walt Disney World for Adults • 420 N. McKinley Street, Suite 111-328 • Corona, CA 91719